VISIONING ETERNITY

VISIONING ETERNITY

Aesthetics, Politics, and History
in the Early Modern Noh Theater

THOMAS D. LOOSER

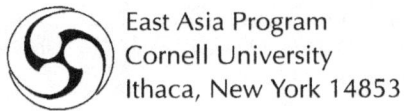

East Asia Program
Cornell University
Ithaca, New York 14853

The Cornell East Asia Series is published by the Cornell University East Asia Program (distinct from Cornell University Press). We publish affordably priced books on a variety of scholarly topics relating to East Asia as a service to the academic community and the general public. Standing orders, which provide for automatic notification and invoicing of each title in the series upon publication, are accepted.

If after review by internal and external readers a manuscript is accepted for publication, it is published on the basis of camera-ready copy provided by the volume author. Each author is thus responsible for any necessary copy-editing and for manuscript formatting. Address submission inquiries to CEAS Editorial Board, East Asia Program, Cornell University, Ithaca, New York 14853-7601.

Number 138 in the Cornell East Asia Series
Copyright © 2008 by Thomas D. Looser. All rights reserved
ISSN 1050-2955
ISBN: 978-1-933947-08-2 hc
ISBN: 978-1-933947-38-9 pb
Library of Congress Control Number: 2008926177

24 23 22 21 20 19 18 17 16 15 14 13 12 11 10 09 08   9 8 7 6 5 4 3 2 1

Map on 255: Permission for use graciously authorized by the artist, Hozumi Kazuo. Rendered by Ariel Looser.
Cover design by Vivian St. George. Book layout and design by Andrea Rosenberg.

∞ The paper in this book meets the requirements for permanence of ISO 9706:1994.

CAUTION: Except for brief quotations in a review, no part of this book may be reproduced or utilized in any form without permission in writing from the author. Please address inquiries to Thomas D. Looser in care of the East Asia Program, Cornell University, 140 Uris Hall, Ithaca, NY 14853-7601.

To Andrea and Ariel

Contents

Acknowledgments / ix

Introduction / 1

1. Locating Tokugawa Power / 19
Origins   23
The Space of Tokugawa Noh   29
Placing Edo   30
Locality   37
The Place of Religion   42
Nikkō   43
The Institutional Structure of Tokugawa Noh   48
Noh Time   54
Edo Castle and the Dream of Nikkō   61

2. The Value of the Stage / 75
The Boundaries of the Shogun's Economy   80
    The Space of Economy   80
    Production: Exchange Without Value   82
    Gifts and Governance   88
    Rice, Money, and the General Equivalent   96
    Noh: *The Reed Cutter*   101
Commerce, Capitalism, and Kabuki   103
    Kabuki, and the Prostitute as Ghost   109
    The Gift of Edo   113

3. **Longing for the Death of Time:
   The Poetics of Tokugawa Noh / 121**
   The Noh: Contours of Staging and Narrative Form   127
   Aesthetics of Deformation   152

4. **Times and Visions of the Instant / 171**
   (Double) Layers of Time   171
   Morphologies of Time: Change and Transformation   182
   Speed, or "Making a Clock in Slow Motion"   198
   Instants and Intensities   204
   Vision: Specularity, Spectacle, and the Eyes of Money   221
   Movement, Flows, and Capitals of Value   250

5. **In the Event: The Kōka *Kanjin* Noh
   Performance of 1848 / 265**
   Context: Changing Economics   266
   The Kōka Performance: Event of Repetition?   268
   Context: Spaces and States of Enclosure   276
   Negotiations   282

   References / 297

   Index / 307

Acknowledgments

This project has been with me for a very long time, and I have a world of people to thank. I have been uncommonly lucky in having exceptional people to work with throughout, and the names listed here are really indicators of whole communities of people who have been critically influential and supportive.

Nancy Munn helped give form to and lay out some of the most fundamental structuring of this project. Nancy has always had remarkable ability to see and understand the working of things even in areas entirely unfamiliar to her, and her advice was instrumental from the start; my great hope would be that some of her insight has somehow translated into my own scholarship, and into this book. Harry Harootunian's influence was as formative, not simply in connection with the specifics of early modern Japanese history, but more importantly in thinking through the critical questions to ask, in ways that would both open up the material and, ideally, the practice of social theory itself. Whether or not it is successfully reflected in this book, Harry has been a model of real scholarship for me. Norma Field, I think, knew far more about the material than she let on, but she imposed nothing on me; instead, she prodded me to think further about what I was doing, and the implications of what I was saying. She was a more than generous reader and advisor (once returning to me about 300 pages of manuscript, with comments on nearly every other page, just two days after receiving them). Tetsuo Najita gave me as hard a time as anybody, in the most effective and helpful ways. I remain truly grateful not only for his guidance but for his willingness to take me seriously from the start, and I still think about some of his comments—and still wish I had addressed some of them more adequately here. Marilyn Ivy has always seemed to understand what I was trying to say even when I was utterly inarticulate. She continues to be an ideal colleague to talk through ideas with, and she is one of those scholars whom I have in mind when writing, and is someone I would always hope to have read my work.

Susan Klein saw this through from beginning (we both attended some of the first noh plays I ever saw), until the end (providing one of the closest readings I was given of the final manuscript). She has been a most valued friend and colleague through all of it. Stefan Tanaka, too, provided an incisive and generous reading of the final manuscript. Mike Molasky kept me sane, encouraged, and clear-headed about everything, from directly practical concerns (how to write, how many chapters to have, how to look at housing mortgages), to knowing where to find the best sake and the best music. Everyone should have a friend like him. I will always miss the bar and coffee shop visits and periodic reading discussions I had with Bob Adams—along with being a very devoted student, he seemed to be able to create whole networks of friends in local communities wherever he was in Japan, and I was always glad to be included. Mike and Bob were part of a remarkable cohort from Chicago, which proved for me to be wonderfully productive. This included Noriko Aso, Mark Auslander, Alan Christy, Kevin Doak, Gerald Figal, Yoshikuni Igarashi, Tom LaMarre, Ellen Schattschneider, and Kentaro Tomio. It would be hard for me to imagine a better group.

At Waseda University, Professors Gotō Hajime and Torigoe Bunzō were both far more helpful and flexible than they needed to be. They allowed me freedom to work as I wished, while nonetheless offering advice, assistance, and structure. Yamaguchi Masao took me on even without formal affiliation, and provided me with work, travel companionship, and endless discussion about anthropology in Japan and in general.

Ochiai Noriko of the Edo Tokyo Museum in Tokyo, Hannah Seger at the University of Kansas Spencer Museum of Art, and Watanabe Yoriko of Hosei University's Nō Research Institute all were remarkably quick in helping me to secure rights for the use of images, and I am most grateful to these institutions for allowing me use of the images. At Cornell, I would like to thank Karen Brazell and her colleagues in Japanese studies, and Mai Shaikhanuar-Cota and everyone at CEAS for their help and patience, and their willingness to take this on.

Above all, I want to express my deep gratitude to all of my family. Because this is what I have chosen to do, they have helped me whenever I needed it, ignored me when I needed that, and supported and inspired me always. If there can be such a thing, for me, they are a true gift.

Research for this book has at different stages received very generous support from the Charlotte W. Newcombe Foundation, Fulbright-Hays, and the Social Sciences and Humanities Research Council of Canada.

Introduction

As elsewhere in the world, 1848 was a time of some significance in Japan. The years leading up to 1848 had been chaotic: inflation and contradictions in economic policy coupled with ruinous crop failure caused by bad weather had led to bankruptcies of hereditary officials and widespread famine among the peasantry. Economic breakdown was accompanied by political unrest at almost all levels of Japanese society. The 1830s had already seen the greatest outpouring during the 250 years of Tokugawa rule of *ikki* protests and rebellions, some of which aimed at specific reforms, while others were more abstractly protesting the general order of things. Incidents such as the Shonai affair in 1840, in which the government ultimately had to back down from a leadership appointment for a domain that was hereditarily related to the Tokugawa leaders, made clear that the shogunate was increasingly unable to manipulate and control the larger political geography of the state.

State horizons were challenged from without, as well. By the 1840s, shogunal rulers had heard of the decisive military victory of the British over the Chinese in the opium war, and of the trade treaty imposed on the Chinese. In 1844 the king of the Netherlands wrote a letter to the shogun, warning him that Japan, too, was threatened, and asking to expand trade. In 1846, U.S. Captain James Biddle arrived with a similar request, as a precursor to the infamous black ships of Commodore Perry that would reach Japan in 1853. Historians continue to cite Perry's arrival as the event that "opened" Japan, first of all to increased trade with the West, but also by extension—in an incipient way—to the political, social, and cultural conditions of modernity.

In the midst of the crises in the 1840s, the shogunate took the remarkable step of sponsoring a public noh performance. The noh was the official

2 / Visioning Eternity

ritual of state—the *shikigaku*[1] (式楽)—and so it is not altogether surprising that the shoguns would do this. But the scale of this performance was unprecedented. With planning begun in 1846 and the performance itself held in 1848, it was the largest and most spectacular noh performance ever held, official or otherwise. It was a "once in a generation" (*ichiyo ichidai*, 一世一代) performance, so called because only the head of the top-ranked noh family was allowed to hold such a performance, and at most only once within a given generation.[2]

The program consisted of fifteen days of performances spread out over a period of several months.[3] Representatives from every official school of noh, from most regions of the state, performed. During the performance days, the shogun ordered the closure of the kabuki theaters and the *misemono* market spectacles, and all sectors of the population were encouraged to attend the noh; approximately 5,000 people attended on each day, and in all, well over 50,000 people saw the performances.

Clearly this was meant to be a momentous occasion. The significance of the event was formalized when, upon its completion, the shogun commemorated its great success by declaring the start of a new era: Kaei (嘉永), or "the Celebration of Eternity."[4]

Although one might expect the shogun to benefit monetarily from a large noh program like this one, and almost certainly he did receive some earnings, generally the proceeds for these kinds of performances went directly to the head of the principal noh school.[5] Furthermore, as sponsor, the shogun would have to contribute resources that by 1848 had become

---

1. It is unclear precisely when the noh was officially decreed to be *shikigaku*—most likely it was in 1615—but its status as the ceremony of state had already been put into practice with the investiture of the first shogun, Tokugawa Ieyasu. This practice was maintained for every Tokugawa shogun through to the last, Tokugawa Yoshinobu, invested in 1866.
2. Ikeuchi lists only five other such performances that were permitted in the two and a half centuries of Tokugawa rule. Ikeuchi Nobuyoshi, *Nōgaku seisuiki*, vol. 1 (Tokyo: Nōgakkai, 1925), 200.
3. The first performance was on the sixth day of the second month of 1848, and the last was on the 13th day of the fifth month. The program was not originally planned to extend for such a long period. Performance dates were postponed in a number of cases for a variety of reasons, from shogunal convenience to rain.
4. Brief mention of this fact is made in Komiya, *Kaikoku hyakunen kinen bunka jigyōkai*, vol. 3 (Tokyo: Ōbunsha, 1956), and Keene, *Nō and Bunraku* (New York: Columbia University Press, 1990), 42.
5. The bulk of the earnings seem to have gone to the head of the Hōshō school, Hōshō Yagorō; including preparation fees and profits from the performances, he was given between twenty and twenty-five thousand *ryō*.

scarce and precious.[6] Why then, under near-cataclysmic conditions, would the shogun have invested heavily in, and attached so much to a noh performance? It may be logical enough that the shogun would have wished to signal the start of a new and hopefully more auspicious era. But why the noh? What value—money aside—did the noh hold for the shogunate? What value did it have in the concrete historical context of 1848?

This book focuses on these basic questions of value, especially as a means of understanding the importance of the 1848 noh performances (known as the Kōka kanjin noh). As background to this event, the following chapters range widely in the discussion of Edo-period noh, as it was reshaped and repositioned—including in relation to kabuki—by the early Tokugawa shoguns. The questions that frame this work derive from, and are therefore limited to, the 1848 noh event. At stake in the problem of value, though, are changing conditions of Tokugawa power, and more generally of social form.

The focus on value is, first of all, simply one way of historicizing the noh. Twentieth-century institutional divides have tended to encourage approaches to the noh that isolate it, as an autonomous realm of theatrical or sometimes ritual art with its own "cultural" (or art) history.[7]

More importantly, the categorical distinction between economic, political, and aesthetic value was not wholly present in Edo-period Japan. These

---

6. Despite the prospect of limited monetary return, the shogunate expended substantial funds on preparations for the performance and considerable energy in assuring strong attendance figures from all segments of the population. It is difficult to quantify the strictly financial outlay that came from the shogunate. For a performance of this magnitude the costs would have been high, for everything from salaries and construction costs for the performance grounds, to the seemingly endless series of gift-giving ceremonies prior to and during the performances, to the costs of entertaining visiting imperial and domain elites. There was substantial income to help offset these costs, including fees collected beforehand from the various wards of Edo, ticket sales, and fees paid by young "student" noh actors who appeared in some of the performances. Even these ticket sales and fees are difficult to calculate, however, especially insofar as in many cases they were effectively ceremonial payments, which were subsequently refunded by the shogun. The main point is that the shogunate not only had to make substantial financial commitments, but more generally clearly attached great value to this performance. For details on some of the fees and payments, see Ikeuchi, Nōgaku seisuiki, vol. 1, 205–215.
7. At the popular level, these divides have helped the noh to become a repository of a more transcendently essentialized Japanese identity. Raising the question of value necessarily returns the analysis to historically immediate and broad relations of social and political form. This would seem to be especially appropriate with the noh, given that so many of its characteristics that are now taken to be definitive of it, from the specifically classic poetic language and the slow pacing to the stage structure, were elements of a political ritual (the shikigaku) that was carefully legislated by the Tokugawa shogunate.

distinctions are themselves modern, with the notion of an independent realm of aesthetics emerging even later in Japan than in the West, and are tied to specific social and economic orders—capitalism in particular. These distinctions, therefore, and the social and economic orders in which they were embedded, were also part of what was at play in the noh in general and in 1848 more specifically; the question of value highlights this. Consideration of these distinctions, including the possibility for independently "economic" or "aesthetic" realms of value is thus critical to an understanding of the developments in 1848, and to the changing grounds of coherence of the early modern Japanese state.

It is important therefore to begin with an expanded concept of value. One way to think of this would be in terms of the critique of a "restricted economy." This is part of a critique that goes back at least to Marcel Mauss and Georges Bataille.[8] In the restricted form, economics is limited to the rational calculability of value in a secular realm of society; it is assumed that people are motivated by rational calculation in a world of scarcity—excess, and the impulse to squander and spend, are not determining factors. Underlying a restricted economics are a set of dualisms, including moral good versus practical utility, and the sacred versus the profane; capitalism is generally taken to be the principal catalyst of a restricted economy.[9] Even if these dualisms were emerging in Tokugawa-era Japan, the assumption that they were *not* fully present in the shogun's economy already means that the question of the shogun making money from the 1848 performance has less relevance, or

---

8. See Marcel Mauss, *The Gift: The Form and Reason for Exchange in Archaic Societies*, (New York: W.W. Norton, 1990) and Georges Bataille (Robert Hurley, trans.), *The Accursed Share* (New York: Zone Books, 1988).

9. See for example Bataille, for whom the idea of a "general" economy was based on a notion of expenditure, which could break the dualisms of a "restricted" economy. Capitalism, by this argument, restricts "nonproductive" expenditure by the delay and deferral of consumption through the reinvestment of surplus (*la part maudite*, or "the accursed share"). This creates false but systematic closures and totalizations. The general economy allows for an expenditure of pure loss that breaks with utility and the apparent identity of exchange value; in other words, it more easily and truly allows for difference. The potlatch is taken as a typical example of this kind of expenditure. Nonetheless it has long been known that there is on the one hand real waste in capitalist expenditure, and on the other hand the supposedly nonutilitarian expenditures of such examples as the potlatch nearly always are made with practical returns in mind. Any kind of freedom of the "general economy," including as a grounds for critique of modern capitalist divides, therefore strikes me as elusive. However, the idea that the mode of expenditure, especially of surplus, is important, and may have played an important role in determining social form in the Tokugawa era, will be addressed. Aesthetic form, too, embodies similar questions of "expenditure," identity, and closure.

at least should not be asked from the standpoint of practical, rational calculation alone. Similarly, more general debates as to whether official shogunal noh was a religious rite or a newly secularized social ritual make sense only to the limited extent that this opposition was already present for the shogun.

Furthermore, although it may now appear unnatural to think of economic value as being also in some sense "aesthetic," again—at least from the perspective of value orientations—a more generalized approach to economics allows for aesthetic form to be conceived of as existing on the same level as utilitarian economy. This is so especially given that aesthetics and economics were not at that time conceived of as autonomous; art was itself in a sense "economic," and not a secondary superstructural effect of a more material economic base. By these terms, aesthetic form is a material, embodied, and integral aspect of both value and social life.

Value, as employed here, thus involves a judgment that is at once moral, economic, and aesthetic. In the simplest of definitions, value is a privileged orientation of social and cultural form. Bakhtin's idea of the chronotope is still useful here. As the term itself indicates, a chronotope implies a structure of space and time, but a space and a time that are produced and oriented around a specific point of view within time and space.[10] The noh, for example, finds its privileged place of orientation in an eternal past, which because unchanging, founds a closed and unchanging cyclical time. Bakhtin's chronotope can be expanded to include monetary economic value—rice as a supposedly divine value form, for example, anchoring the shogun's economy—and ultimately the measure of moral worth, goodness, and the "truth" of things in general. Specific chronotopes hence ground and orient specific orders of time, space, and social relations between people. Value, then, has to do not only with the type of measure, but also with the cultural form produced—with the cultural form judged valuable.[11] Further, insofar as the chronotope orients general relations, and defines general parameters of what is good, then the "value" of an act or a thing also has to do with the capacity or potential to create that general order of relations of which that act or thing is a part. Accordingly, the value of money in a capitalist economy can be defined not just in terms of its ability to purchase a commodity, but in terms of its ability to embody the larger chronotopic order that capitalism defines.

---

10. See Mikhail Bakhtin, *The Dialogic Imagination* (Austin: University of Texas Press, 1981), 17, 29, passim.
11. For a somewhat similar point in a quite different context, see Nancy Munn, *The Fame of Gawa* (Cambridge: Cambridge University Press, 1986), 8–11, 20, passim.

Capital investment, for example, and its capacity for a future return that itself can then be reinvested, is premised on a specific point of value, that creates a specific future-oriented temporality, that also implies specific orders of social relations, and so on.

Nor do these value orientations consist of static relations. Value, as Marx and others have demonstrated, lies in transformation.[12] Specific forms and orientations of value imply specific modes of transformation. Thus, insofar as the geography of a state embodies a certain kind of value, then a particular mode of transformation and change is built into that body of the state. For example, capital value emerges and exists only in specific processes of transformation of money or products into investment returns or profits. A capitalist order is defined by these modes of transformation, as would be a state that is based on a capitalist economy and capitalist orientations of value.

In the same way, it can be said that social form consists of particular modes of transformation. The point can also be made in terms of historical change: social form is not merely found *in* history, but rather is itself always a mode *of* history. Social form is an order of relations which is not purely static, but which instead emerges within, and as, a process of change—just as any value form implies a certain mode of transformation out of which that "value" emerges. Tokugawa noh was hence a historical form, of course, but it also embodied a form of history.

In fact the noh was integral to the Tokugawa shoguns' monumental and strategic attempts to appropriate and organize a new kind of sociopolitical space, premised on an order of time that precluded essential change. Chapter 1 examines the position of the first Tokugawa shoguns, and the place of the noh in their efforts to build the foundation for a new kind of state. By carefully organizing ordered flows and exchanges of noh actors and performances, the shoguns and the provincial lords, or daimyo, at a lower level of the political hierarchy attempted to create a "ritually"[13]

---

12. As Taussig puts it, "[in Marx's] reasoning ... value lies not in a *source* nor in *exchange* per se, but instead in the *metamorphosis* of the object or service exchanged ... value lies in *transformation.*" Michael Taussig, *The Magic of the State* (New York: Routledge, 1997), 139.

13. The term "ritual" seems appropriate for several reasons. The shoguns themselves used the term ritual (*shikigaku* means either ritual or ceremony). Further, the shoguns were apparently trying to create an image of ritual structures of time and space that fit with qualities commonly ascribed to ritual structure, such as formalized behavior involving a resolution of the individual into the collective and a closure of time and space into repetitive cycles. This was a modern creation, however, and prior to the Tokugawa state the noh was considered a far more secular entertainment. For this reason and for others, Tokugawa noh was therefore a modern kind of ritual.

repetitive order.[14] In Chapter 1, the question of value orientation and social form is thus taken up in the context of the official practices of the noh. Each of the subsequent three chapters similarly takes up different grounds of value production as background to the 1848 event.

Chapter 2 looks at monetary economy, including the use of rice as the general equivalent governing the shogun's economic order, and its relation to the sometimes opposed and outlawed trajectories of capitalism. Brief examples for comparison are included, such as the status of the "dream portrait" of the founding Tokugawa shogun, which might otherwise be considered a problem of semiotics, or representation.

Chapter 3 turns to aesthetic form and the poetics of Edo-era noh. Given the emphasis on ritual, cyclical closure and permanence seen in the previous two chapters, there is a striking opposition of play types in official Tokugawa noh. Although one type is specifically ritualized and is founded on a neat unity of identities, the other type accentuates decomposition and failure of identity. This latter form would seem to be at odds with the kind of dependence on unified and bounded identities seen in the shogun's rice economy, and in the circulations of noh actors and performances. The tension between a more totalizing, "beautiful" play form and one of disintegration indicates features that are in some ways modernist. It also calls into question and complicates the grounds for closure seen in the previous two chapters.

Chapter 4 extends the inquiry into aesthetic form, but with a focus on temporality. As one sees elsewhere in the cultural conditions approximating modernity, time is tied to visuality and increasingly is experienced as taking on precedence as *the* principal basis for social form. As a result, all other grounds of existence are subordinated to time, as if time has an independent existence in and for itself. The tensions and contradictions of aesthetic form here work out as contradictions in different temporal orders; ultimately, these tensions in temporality are at play in the 1848 performances.

Each of these chapters should be understood as returning implicitly or explicitly to social form, but social form in a way that involves more than social organization, and includes the form of evaluation—an axiology— inherent in any social organization.

---

14. Chapter 1 considers these actions as constructing a utopic structure. Utopic projects were seen elsewhere in the Tokugawa era, and certainly not always with the same political implications: the obvious example would be Harootunian's analysis of nativist discourse. See Harry Harootunian, *Things Seen and Unseen* (Chicago: University of Chicago Press, 1988).

Value not only emerges in transformation, as noted above, but it furthermore is materialized only within the context of the concrete conditions of life. The desire one has for something, or the sense of goodness, worth, or beauty that is called "value" arises only when one comes into contact with the immediate world. Value, in other words, becomes realized in the material conditions of history. And in this engagement with history, the materiality of the world always exceeds any received order of value; value, and therefore ultimately social form, is never stable.

It is only in terms of the 1848 event that I claim to be showing this engagement with history—including the particular conditions then facing the early modern state, and the unique evaluation of those historical conditions that one can see happening in the 1848 noh performances. This is the subject of Chapter 5. This last chapter examines the status of the Kōka performances both as an "event" and as a ritual; the repetitive yet also singular character of the performances; and the ways this ritual event negotiated the determinate conditions of that moment in time.

Although I discuss practices from other times within the Edo period as background to the 1848 noh, these practices should be understood only in terms of the questions raised by 1848. Also, while I do not return to the event itself until the final chapter, this is not to suggest that stable structures of value persisted without change until the sudden eruption of 1848. This is not, in other words, an argument for an intermittent relation between stable cultural form and the disruptions of historical action (so that even if structure occasionally changes in action, there is still a fundamental distinction between structure and action).[15] Nor was the Edo period a time in which nothing really happened, an era without history, until 1848. The mid-nineteenth century was a particularly eventful time, however, and therefore interesting. In many ways it did point back to earlier shogunal practices, as I try to show, but these practices were nonetheless framed by the circumstances of 1848. Throughout, my own argument similarly refers back to that one historical moment.

One of the ironies of Japan's mid-nineteenth century is that although it was a time of great fragmentation and centripetal dissolution of power, one can yet also see elements of a new kind of coherence and unity—in some

---

15. In the field of anthropology, see Marshall Sahlins' *Culture and Practical Reason* (Chicago: University of Chicago Press, 1976)—a groundbreaking attempt to resolve the oppositions of structure versus action, and idealism versus material—and in sociology, Pierre Bourdieu's *Outline of a Theory of Practice* (Cambridge: Cambridge University Press, 1977). Though now classic works, both ended up to some extent reproducing a model in which structure is interrupted (and transformed) by action, which then returns to a new structure.

ways, conditions that are often associated with the modern nation. The Tokugawa state geography, for example, developed as a heterogenous space. Internally, the various domains not only held a great deal of political independence from the shogun, they also were differentially ranked and empowered according, in part, to the level of genealogical relation of the daimyo's family to the Tokugawa shoguns.

External borders were not all that clear, either. Especially in the north, the relationship of the Ainu people and their lands with the Japanese was continuously transforming: the Matsumae domain, the area now around the island of Hokkaido, was unlike any other, being partly under the rule of the Japanese and partly under the rule of a family that was not Ainu, but not entirely beholden to the Japanese either. The Ainu themselves traded at least as much with the Chinese and the Russians as with the Japanese, and at times wore Chinese or Russian clothing rather than Japanese; the Ainu people and their lands all made for a very uncertain border of northern Japan.[16] But by the nineteenth century, the genealogical relation of domain lord to shogun—and especially the status of being a *tozama* or "outside" daimyo (外様), versus a *fudai*, or "related" lord (譜代)—no longer made as much difference. Borders, too, increasingly were defined. In the north, the shogunate sent armies to "pacify" the Ainu, and, separating them from the increasingly hostile Russians, it brought them into a more strictly "Japanese" state identity. In this way, trade with countries that had become more truly external also was brought under more centralized Japanese control.

Although Tokugawa-era Japan is often portrayed as having been an eminently closed country throughout, the term for this closure (*sakoku*) did not appear until the nineteenth century, and in fact was a term derived from a Westerner.[17] With incidents such as the British defeat of the Chinese in the opium war, and the Dutch and American demands for similar treaties with the Japanese, Japan was increasingly being brought into an international order of war and trade, and itself treated as a nation among others. So both internally and from the outside, forces were pushing toward an increasingly nationalized order of state.

---

16. Information on these changes is clearly laid out in Brett Walker's *The Conquest of Ainu Lands* (Berkeley: University of California Press, 2001).
17. The description of Japan as a "closed country" was introduced by the Dutchman Engelbert Kaempfer. The translation of this work was not widely read in Japan until the mid-nineteenth century; Shitsuki Tadao published his "Sakoku-ron," based on Kaempfer's work, in 1801. There were terms indicating a policy of restricting flows of people and trade earlier however—a common one was *kaikin* ("maritime restrictions").

Shifts in the nature of power were visible as well. Earlier Tokugawa shoguns depended on an authoritarian sovereignty that (if also dispersed among the semiautonomous domains) emphasized rule by negative constraint. This was evidenced by the continuous issuance of decrees of prohibition. By the nineteenth century, however, there was less reliance on prohibition, or on geographic differentiation of power, and greater use of what Foucault has called biopower—power that works through a claim of beneficence rather than prohibition, and through a general and homogenized control of life. For example in the case of the Ainu, by the mid-nineteenth century the shogun was literally claiming to rule by beneficence—extending to the Ainu the goods and rights of all Japanese—and at the same time imposing new rules regarding hygiene and daily life.

The impetus toward something closer to a national form was in these ways part of the setting of the 1848 Kōka program. However, the motivation for at least some kind of centrality and even homogeneity can be seen in official Tokugawa noh more generally. This is taken up in Chapter 1.

But the question of modern forms of centrality and unity, especially as related to modern subjectivity, extends beyond the matter of the nation-state. A productive way to think about this, in relation to the concerns of this book, is in terms of the development of perspective and perspectival space. Perspectival space is mathematically homogenous, as seen for example in the case of single-point perspective painting. In order to unify and complete itself, this homogeneity at once requires and locates an external viewpoint (the *punto dell'occhio*)—the viewpoint of the observer that corresponds to the perspectival vanishing point. Although I am reducing what is in fact a very complicated set of variations, this is the position of the modern, renaissance subject, which is unified via this observational relation to rational, mathematical space.

Japan, however, did not have a moment, or epistemological break, equivalent to the Renaissance in Europe. Perspectival pictorial techniques were available in Edo-era Japan, but they were not used in the same way or with the same effect as in the West. If perspectival space and by extension the modern perspectival subject were not available as an organizing principle, the question then is what, if anything, *did* define the unity of Edo-period space and the subject of early modern Japan?[18]

---

18. The seminal work on mid-Tokugawa era Japanese subjectivity, looked at from the perspective of language, is Naoki Sakai's *Voices of the Past* (Ithaca: Cornell University Press, 1992).

The idea that there was no homogenously unified perspectival sense of space in the Edo period has been raised before, in varying ways. Late nineteenth century Western impressionists saw the "flatness" of Edo-era ukiyo-e woodblock prints as an indicator of an entirely nonmodern primitivism. More recently, in the late twentieth century, artists and critics connected to work such as "Superflat" art proposed a fundamental connection between Edo-period art and the compositional forms of digital media.[19] Although not all that clearly stated, in this case the claim is that both art forms and both eras stand outside the modern. For these critics and artists one of the critical issues is perspective: "flatness" or the lack of perspectival depth seen in a good deal of the early modern woodblock prints is correlated with the nonperspectival, multiplanar techniques that arise with digital art. Both types of art deny the perspectival unity and therefore the positioning of a modern observational subject. Superflat art is based on a rejection of the modernist opposition of rational economic utility and autonomous aesthetic beauty, and sees a similar lack of differentiation in the Edo era.

Nearly all the comparisons by these commentators, however, were made fairly strictly with early modern capitalism, and the culture associated with the period—and kabuki in particular. Edo life was far more complicated than that. Looked at more closely, the concept of a nonunified, or multiplanar mode of composition may be more apt than the commentators realize.[20] Although capitalism was present from the start of the Tokugawa period, over time its economic influence increased. Technically, capitalism was an illegal economy and the shoguns carefully and consciously attempted to establish an alternative economy based on rice. Clearly, these were two very different economies, with very different value orientations—and both had complicated relations with existing conditions that were in many ways feudal. The differing economic orientations also made up the environment of two very different cultural economies: the noh, for instance, was developed within the milieu of the shogun's rice economy, while kabuki, ukiyo-e woodblock prints, and other popular arts were very closely affiliated with the world of capitalism.

---

19. See, for example, Murakami Takashi, "The Super Flat Manifesto," and "A Theory of Super Flat Japanese Art," in Murakami, ed., *Superflat* (Tokyo: Madras, 2000).
20. For a fuller discussion of Superflat art and its relevance to Edo-era pictorial space, see Looser, "Superflat and the Layers of Image and History in the 21st Century," in *Mechademia* 1:1, Fall 2006.

Neither of these monetary or cultural economies could be used alone to describe the early modern era. Although in some ways they were directly opposed, they were not always dialectically opposed. To some extent the façade was maintained that social groups were divided by their participation in one or the other economy, with mercantile capitalists officially the lowest in a fixed-class hierarchy. Yet, in fact nearly everyone had to—and most wanted to—participate in both economies. Even the very first shogun, Tokugawa Ieyasu, while working to construct his rice-based economic system, was also using the merchant Shaya Shirōjirō as one of his principal advisors.

Consequently, to understand at any level the differing orientations of value that underlay Edo-era life requires an analysis that addresses the relationship between these different economies. Accordingly, an examination of capitalism is integrated into the analysis of the shogunal rice economy in Chapter 1 and into the discussion of the poetics of kabuki in Chapters 3 and 4.

Because the ground and space of everyday life during the Edo era were comprised of truly different worlds, it is not entirely accurate to say that in the Edo period there was no distinction at all between rational monetary calculations and aesthetic judgments. This was in some ways true of the rice-based economy promoted by the shogun, but not really true of the culture of capitalism. Again, to varying degrees, people participated in both.

This cross-participation of people in differing value systems also complicates the conceptualization of the possibilities of difference, opposition, and resistance, especially as based on center versus marginal periphery models, or the idea of contest emerging from class consciousness.[21] Kabuki is often portrayed as a site of marginalized opposition to the official center of Edo-period life. Although this view has some credibility, I will argue that resistance, and power, came to life more through a relation between the worlds of samurai-class noh and merchant-class kabuki than in an opposition of one to the other.

Given these differing worlds, each with distinctive horizons and orientations of value, it would be hard to think of anything like what Panofsky calls a

---

21. There were separate class affiliations for the two theaters, which were heavily enforced by the shogunate, but eventually these affiliations were as much a matter of ideology as they were of real practice. In fact, some of the most prominent and still revered authors of "commoner class" theater and literature, such as the great kabuki playwright Chikamatsu Monzaemon, were by birth of the samurai class; and in general, people from the samurai and the merchant classes were attempting to participate in both forms of theater and economy.

"formative will," coalescing a continuous, homogenous, systematic space like that indicated by perspectival pictorial composition.[22] Hence the problem here is: if one is to think of the everyday plane of experience in the Edo period as in any way unified, what, if anything, governs this unity? Despite the Tokugawa shoguns' occasional pretensions to divine kingship, the majority of people did not locate their relations to each other, and to the world, in terms of an overarching divine worldview—divinity was not *the* unifying force. But neither is there evidence for the modern observational subject serving as the organizing principle, integrating everything into a unified space. In fact, both these formations appear as possibilities within Tokugawa noh and especially in the more ritualized official presentations; the question of how they converged or were composed is critical to their overall form. This was certainly the case for the 1848 event.

In organizing the more important official noh programs, great care was taken in the placement of audiences to control who might see what, and how they might see it. Different subject positionings, of what appear to have been different visual regimes, were not only allowed for, but planned for, within the same performances. Disregarding the differences for the moment, one basic and important conclusion to be drawn from the attention given these visual regimes is that this is already *visual* space that is being ordered. By itself this might suggest something like a modern observational subject, but the substantive differences between the visual orders indicate other possibilities. The different orders of vision and their importance to the official public noh performances in general, as well as to the Kōka noh, are examined in Chapters 4 and 5.

In the 1848 Kōka noh, an organization of vision that was different from other official noh programs was evident. This reorganization of vision discloses the emergence of a new kind of integration, with a reconfiguration of the possibilities of unity and centrality and the subject positions that anchor this unity and centrality. Put in a different way, this book will argue that in the 1848 performance, the shogun (and everyone else) sat in a transformed position vis à vis history and the world.

Returning for a moment to Bakhtin's chronotopes, one of the difficulties in reading his outline of these is deciphering how he saw the different chronotopes relating to each other in history. On one hand, he seems to privilege certain chronotopes and their value orientations as the teleological endpoint

---

22. See Erwin Panofsky, *Perspective as Symbolic Form* (New York: Zone Books, 1991), 71.

of a progressive history; the value orientations of the "novel" in particular are newer, more open to difference, and tied somehow to the development of the nation as a sociopolitical form. In some ways, this could be read as an almost Hegelian history of the working out of an ideal, with the nation itself part of this ideal form. On the other hand, Bakhtin seems to say that a chronotope can appear at different times in history, and so would seem to be in a sense a transhistorical, perhaps even essentialist form. The chronotope of the novel, for example, is described as popping up in different forms and in different times and places at least since second-century Greece.[23]

There is perhaps some possibility in the way this book is structured that, similar to Bakhtin's outline of the chronotope of the novel, the Kōka performance of 1848 might be construed as a synthetic moment, subjected to the constraints of a Hegelian teleology. I am, as stated above, reading earlier practices and conditions through the context of 1848. But I am laying claim to history *only* in terms of the 1848 performance, and the specific questions that I have raised regarding the value of that performance. It is very much a history, but specifically of that particular moment. The value forms that I describe are primarily of that time and place—not transhistorical and certainly not in any way progressively ideal.

At least nominally, official Tokugawa noh was conceived of as a "ritual" form by the shogunate. The first shogun debated with his advisors about whether to use received forms of ritual such as *bugaku* or *kagura* for the rite of state, but he settled instead on the noh. Viewing the noh as a ritual, however, potentially puts it in an uncertain relation to modernity. Ritual often becomes a label for that which is traditional and is not or not yet modern. The construction of this kind of opposition was, in fact, part of Edo-era noh. But the Kōka event itself can be viewed as a form of ritual, even if in some ways it was less formal than other shogunal command performances. Ritual by this view lies neither wholly within nor outside of modern conditions. Instead, in what might be called the "ritual" negotiation and reevaluation of historical conditions that was visible in the 1848 Kōka event, the form and conditions of ritual itself are part of that negotiation. The new emphasis accorded the Kōka program, which, as a "once-in-a-generation" *kanjin* noh was organized quite differently from the performances otherwise held in the castle grounds, is thus in itself part of this reevaluation.

---

23. See *The Dialogic Imagination*, especially "Epic and Novel," and "From the Prehistory of Novelistic Discourse."

This study is also not the story of an invented tradition. It is not the story of the birth and production of a nation-state on the back of something "false," or empty in its claims. Doubtless much of the "classic" form of the noh was newly produced in the Edo era, and as with the concept of ritual, the distinction between the traditional and the contemporary was being developed in the noh—with the noh then located at the traditional pole of the opposition. However, these are real value orientations, with a real history, that in the mid-nineteenth century were integral to a changing state—and in being a site for the negotiation of these, the noh was also to some extent modern.

One final caveat regarding my discussion of the noh. Edo-era noh consisted of a wonderfully rich and varied set of practices. This book examines only official noh, and asks of it only a delimited set of questions that center on the value of the 1848 event. This is therefore not in any way a comprehensive picture or reconstruction of Edo-era noh. Furthermore, the questions that are being raised about the noh could be asked of other realms of social practice. Those realms of practice that are taken up here, including monetary economics and aesthetics, are examined for their relevance to the noh and are not comprehensive descriptions of Edo-era economic or aesthetic values.

Yet, while these different realms of practice have their own material integrity as domains of value production,[24] there is also no such thing as a specific domain of culture that exists as neatly bounded, whole and autonomous to other domains of practice. Rather than in such independent contents, culture in a sense exists only on the intersections of such practices. These intersections are not random, but bear a concrete responsibility and orientation to each other; it is in these concrete relations of intersection that value and meaning arise.

For this reason, extensive orientations of value come to be embodied in individual points of intersection that consequently take on something like the status of what Walter Benjamin called a fragment,[25] and Bakhtin an atom or monad: an element that embodies and reflects a larger world of which it is or was a part. In a limited way, I am approaching the noh and the Kōka performance as just such a fragment of the late Edo-era Japanese state. This book is therefore only about the noh, and a single perspective on the noh.

---

24. Value and culture are produced and reproduced differentially in the different arenas of social and cultural life.
25. The Benjaminian fragment is a remnant, or ruin, of a historical formation that, despite its fragmentary status, still contains within it the impress of a wider set of historical relations.

But in the juxtapositions that almost inevitably arise from examining the Kōka program, including between noh and kabuki, as well as between political practice, economic form, and aesthetic value, looking at the noh allows a reading of the landscape of late Edo-era social form.[26]

In this way, the Kōka event itself can be thought of as an "atom" within Japan's mid-nineteenth century. It was a point of intersection that bore connection and responsibility not only to other elements within the various political spaces of Japan at that time, but also to values and conditions impinging from the outside. The new order of things that the shogun commemorated in 1848 was not simply a result of dynamics entirely internal to Japan. But it was also certainly not just a result of the forced intrusion of an outside, as in the commonly held view of Perry's black ships opening Japan into modernity—implying that Japan up until that point had stood outside the conditions of modernity.[27] The Kōka event was one small, atomized fragment in which all of those relations were being reevaluated and performed. It at once points back to a set of conditions that can heuristically be called early modern, and it is a point of emergence of something new, beckoning forward to the modern nation-state.

• • •

Following is a brief historical overview of some of the practices and contexts in which the noh was used. Greater detail, where relevant, will be found in the remaining chapters.

The noh initially developed around the thirteenth century out of a variety of ritual and entertainment forms, including comic styles as well as practices of nontheatrical performers such as jugglers and acrobats. *Dengaku* (田楽), an agricultural rite, was probably most closely associated with the noh; the noh was nonetheless distinguished from all of these rites, including in name.[28] Not entirely a ritual, but still entailing elements of religious practice, the noh frequently was performed within the space of shrine and temple

---

26. On reconstruction (in this case, as a full picture of the early modern era) versus reading, see Harootunian, *Things Seen and Unseen*, 19–22.
27. This also means that to the limited degree that something like a "national" form of political space was arising at that time, at least in this case the development of the nation itself is not just a reaction to the forces of imperialism—although the imperialist activities of the British, Dutch, and Americans were already part of the context.
28. In the middle ages the noh was more commonly known as *sarugaku* (the art of imitation) than *noh* (the art of accomplishment). The term noh did not come into widespread usage until the Tokugawa period.

compounds, as was common practice for nonreligious and religious entertainments alike.

The noh was not originally aristocratic. The noh is characterized by a hegemonic incorporation of a great variety of styles, and many of them came from the countryside. Performers themselves were considered to be of the lowest classes. Nevertheless, patronage developed quickly during the fourteenth century. By this time the military leadership (the shogunate) had taken over the imperial nobility's role as political rulers, and it was these newly legitimate military rulers who patronized the noh as an art form. The noh was thus associated with the military rulership from the start. However, despite it being a source of cultural legitimation for the new rulers, it still was not the rigidly formal theater that it later became in the Tokugawa era. Attempts were made to create it in the image of a "stately" form, but it was also allowed to continue having novel, even avant-garde characteristics which may have been appropriate for a military form of power. For example, the shogun Ashikaga Yoshimitsu, who was most renown for having patronized the first real concretization of the noh as a theater of state, himself was widely known for attending performances in the most up-to-date, even "bizarre" styles of urban clothing—for example, "a narrow-sleeved, wide-hemmed costume of a pale blue lozenge pattern tied with a red sash, green leggings and red knee-length breeches."[29]

Yoshimitsu also was a patron of the noh actors and playwrights Kannami and his son Zeami—the two who have been canonized both in the Tokugawa era and in contemporary Japan as the true founders of the noh and the definers of the best and true noh styles. Yoshimitsu, furthermore, was revered as one of the great military leaders of Japanese history, and the shogun who, in 1392, was finally able to create some kind of statewide reunification. The shogunate collapsed in the fifteenth century, but the noh continued to be performed. It was widely popular among the general public, and developed into a dramatic form unlike that seen today, and in many cases closer to what kabuki has become with large casts of characters onstage, realistic props, etc.[30]

It thus seems likely that the Tokugawa shoguns were restaging the image of Yoshimitsu in their own early efforts to bring together a new state: an image of a military and political unifier, and patron of the originary figures

---

29. From Yoshimitsu's own Itsukushima diary, cited in Keene, *Nō and Bunraku* (New York: Columbia University Press, 1990), 31.
30. The plays of Kanze Nagatoshi (1488–1541) are a typical example of such styles.

of the noh. The Tokugawa shoguns also revived Yoshimitsu's office of the shogun, which some time after Yoshimitsu had fallen into disuse. Under the Tokugawa shoguns, the noh was controlled by the state, although it gained popularity as a practice, even if not always legal, among the merchants and other commoners. As a ceremony of state it was given an aura of ritual practice that it previously did not have. However, some nongovernmental public performances were permitted and generally were known as *kanjin* (勧進) or "subscription" noh. Although *kanjin* noh had in earlier times been done for more truly religious ends such as raising money for temples and shrines, or to build structures such as bridges—all of which would be "good works" that earned a kind of positive karma for all involved—they were now done more specifically for monetary gain. Thus, under the Tokugawas, the noh became at once more ritualized and yet also more commercial.[31]

With the fall of the Tokugawa shogunate and the start of the modern Japanese nation in 1868, governmental patronage of the noh was ended and it was widely assumed that the noh would quickly die out. But with the state visits of several foreign leaders such as U.S. President Grant and the appearance of Japan's own newly empowered emperor at a Japanese governmental officer's house, the noh was chosen as the most appropriately "Japanese" entertainment for such events. The basis of comparison was now with foreign nations, and the identity of the noh as "Japanese" at this point became a national one.[32] Although strongly subsidized by the government and considered largely a theater for older generations, the noh—and in recent years particularly the "bonfire" noh—remains relatively popular and an important site of Japanese identity.

---

31. A key concern of this book is this interrelation between the two apparently different kinds of economies of value, the different flows of desire, and the different modes of producing power.

32. Thus the noh was by the 1870s already given new patronage by the emperor, who himself had become ruler of the nation. The noh continued to develop not only these nationalist connections, but also relations to nationalist militarism. During World War II new noh plays were written, celebrating the might of the Japanese military and further developing the idea of a site of Japanese purity. This gradual movement of the noh's modern ideological implications could be traced, too, in the actual movements of one of the first noh stages built after 1868: first given to the Meiji emperor's (the first modern emperor) compound, it was then moved to Yasukuni shrine, the state shrine to Japan's military dead, which also can be seen as glorifying Japanese militarism.

1

Locating Tokugawa Power

> Our country over other peoples' countries
> Our people rather than others[1]
> —Yumiyawata

Nogami Toyoichirō sees in such early fifteenth century noh plays as *Yumiyawata* the precursory elements of a "Japaneseness" (*Nihonshugi*), an ideology centered around a divine country defined over and against others. In the fifteenth century, however, the idea of a "country" did not have any of the territorial breadth or the integrity of the early modern Japanese state, and the noh itself was a dispersed and widely varying set of practices. Nogami himself says that it was not until the Tokugawa period (1600–1868) that the noh became rigidly organized.[2] The noh may have had certain qualities which made it good to work with for the founding rulers of the Tokugawa state, but still, in its codified form as the official ceremonial (*shikigaku*) of the Tokugawa *bakufu* (military government), the noh was in many ways made into something very new. This chapter provides an overview of this codification, including the material practices of the noh in its position as *shikigaku*, and the particular kind of coherence these practices brought to the geography of the new state.

The Kōka noh performances of 1848, taken by the shogun as successful enough to be the foundation of a new historical era of ongoing Tokugawa rule, ironically was the last such set of performances ever to be held. But this use of the noh as foundational was to a large extent a replaying of customs which had in fact been part of the very beginning of the Tokugawa world, and which continued with remarkable consistency and stability through most of the Tokugawa period.

---

1. もとよりも人の国より我が国。他の人よりも我が人と。
2. Nogami Toyoichirō, *Nōgaku saisei* (Tokyo: Iwanami Shoten, 1935), 110, passim.

In the late sixteenth century, the social terrain of Japan remained heterogenous. Despite the large-scale military victories of Ieyasu (the first Tokugawa shogun), differing and competing spheres of power persisted. So too did regional cultural variation, with differences of linguistic dialect that in some cases made them mutually incomprehensible. Different groups lived according to their own calendars, and a number of different local currencies were still in use.

However, even before military domination was fully secured, the noh was one of many means being used to redefine the lines of power, and to create a new image of, and give a new consistency to, the contours of the state. The noh was transformed and systematized, both in its poetic form and in its everyday uses. The changes were dictated by the shogun, and were meant to encompass all noh schools, in all regions. At the same time, the noh itself was made an integral element of new political connections between leaders of the newly formed domains and the shogun; the noh, in other words, was one of the practices that helped in the appropriation of a new political space.

Part of what was at issue here was the political problem for the Tokugawa leaders not only of setting up relations of allegiance, but more generally of gaining control over everyday culture—the structures and rhythms giving form to everyday life as well as political power.

But the changes instituted by the first Tokugawa rulers were monumental. They were meant to embrace a vastly expanded social and geographic territory. Furthermore, like the 1848 Kōka noh event, these changes were meant to be the foundation of a new, eternal world image—and in this case, the changes implied a systematic refashioning of the world.

There was therefore a component to these transformations that should be considered as utopian. The noh can be seen as symbolically architecting,[3] through a varied set of cyclical ritualistic practices, an eternal order for and of the shogun. Like the 1848 Kōka performances, too, which ostensibly originated a new age of eternity, this new order apparently was meant to be a real break from the past. It was as if the shogunate was using the noh for what Louis Marin has called, in connection with utopic representation, the unfolding of an architecture of perfection through representation's freeing itself from historical ties.[4] By these terms, the noh can be thought to have involved a

---

3. This use of "architecting" includes the ideas of planning and constructing a figure and appropriating and giving form to a space—just as a building would.
4. Louis Marin, *Utopics: Spatial Play*, trans. Robert A. Vollrath (New Jersey: Humanities Press, 1984), xix.

utopic impulse insofar as it attempted to create an image of perfection, in which the image (representation), though actually practiced, was understood to be somehow disjoined from the contingencies of historical reality.

Therefore, although the shogunate built little of the type of monumental architecture or commemorative statuary that Marin sees in the West in comparable periods,[5] the shogunate's use of the noh can be viewed in a similar vein, as a utopically monumental gesture. This was not only a matter of the creation of an ideal image, or a static set of ostensibly perfected social relations. It was also a matter of social action, or praxis. That is to say, the ability to envision a social order that does not yet have a place of existence, the ability to recast existing relations, is itself a utopic praxis. As Mary Ann Doane puts it, "A utopia is the sighting (in terms of the gaze) and the siting (in terms of emplacement) of another possibility. The chance of escaping the same."[6] This utopic capacity to envision and put into effect a truly refashioned world is also part of the apparently foundational qualities of Tokugawa noh.

In this reworking of things, however, there are differing, even contradictory tendencies in what is being called utopic. There is the idea of a perfect world, an image separated from the contingencies of history, as opposed to the creative potential of "utopic" practice. Accordingly, there is the stasis or closure of perfection, versus critique and the virtual opening toward the new, toward difference, and toward a world which might not be altogether singular in perspective. Utopia would seem to indicate a totality, but, especially when thought of as a practice, it also implies the possibility of radical change and difference.

There are therefore very different possibilities for what it might mean to understand the Tokugawa shoguns' use of the noh as utopic. The question of in what way the Kōka event of 1848 might have somehow been a utopic gesture (and therefore, the relation between utopic practice and history) will be left to Chapter 5. Here I want to confine the discussion to the formal practices the early Tokugawa shoguns seem to have organized.

---

5. Louis Marin, "Classical, Baroque: Versailles, or the Architecture of the Prince," in Timothy Hampton, ed., *Baroque Topographies, Yale French Studies* 80 (1991), 167–182.
6. Mary Ann Doane, "Commentary: Post-Utopian Difference," in Elizabeth Weed, ed., *Coming to Terms: Feminism, Theory, Politics* (New York: Routledge, 1989), 78. On the notion of utopia as praxis, see Jean-Marc Blanchard, "The Pleasures of Description," in *Diacritics* 7 (1977), 22–34, and Marin, *Utopics*; and on utopic refashionings of community and aesthetic perspective, Alexander Gelley, "City Texts: Representation, Semiology, and Urbanism," in Mark Poster, ed., *Politics, Theory, and Contemporary Culture* (New York: Columbia University Press, 1993), and Miriam Hansen, "Of Mice and Ducks," *South Atlantic Quarterly* 92 (1993).

In general, the shogunate's use of the noh can be viewed as giving rise to new forms of imagination and collectivity. But in its official, ritualized structure, the noh was a closed, centered and legitimate form of representation.[7] The principal role of the noh under the Tokugawa bakufu was to give a fully realized image, a wholly institutionalized representation of an ideal order (*risōkyō*, 理想郷; "utopia" in the sense of "an ideal land," "an earthly paradise").[8] As a determined image of an ideal society, the noh was therefore contrary to the sort of utopic praxis that allows for the imagining of new possibilities.

Yet institutionalized ways of imagining the world are also dependent on fantasies; the ideal *risōkyō* order of the noh also had a *musōteki* aspect (夢想的; dreamlike and utopic in the sense of a vision or fantasy), with a complex relation to any kind of image of closure. The place of fantasy operative within the Tokugawa image of power is thus important. Within the new geography of Tokugawa power, and of Tokugawa noh, the shrine at Nikkō occupied a central position, and in the discussion below I will give some weight to that shrine as a place of utopic (by some terms heterotopic) fantasy.

What follows is thus an outline of the official image of early Tokugawa-era noh. Though only the official order of things, it is an image that is more than just a mere representation, distinct from what one might then look to as the real. It is a set of customs that, in its fully organized form, acted as a way of understanding the temporalities and spatial relations of social life, and was a prominent, empirical practice of these relations.[9]

I begin with Hideyoshi Toyotomi, the warlord whose attempts at military unification came just before Tokugawa Ieyasu. Although Hideyoshi's sometimes remarkable uses of the noh were in some ways unique, it is possible to see in these uses some of the basic conditions and contradictions of legitimacy that defined Tokugawa rule.

The chapter continues with a description of, first, the new geography, and second, the temporalities of early Tokugawa noh. I then return to Nikkō, and the utopic elements of this world.

---

7. As opposed to the neutral no-place that lies between and beyond historical situations, and which offers a place of vision beyond the limits of existing social and cultural forms. By other terms, a critique of existing ideology.

8. Koh Masuda, ed., *Kenkyusha's New Japanese-English Dictionary*, 4th edition (Tokyo: Kenkyusha, 1974), 1381.

9. This is thus an image which encompasses both the imaginary and practical relationship to the real. It is in effect a way of imagining one's relationship to the real, and by that limited definition, what is described in this chapter could also be called an ideology.

Locating Tokugawa Power / 23

Overall, this chapter is concerned with the formation of Tokugawa noh as part of a strategic effort to locate the grounds of a recasted social space—a legitimate space, the image of the center. My principal focus is on the places of overtly political usages of noh in Tokugawa life: the sites and moments, as well as the genres, of official noh. The effects, however, reveal a broader political culture that comprised a new mode of the social.

Origins

By the sixteenth century, the centrality of power in Japan of the middle ages had become fragmented. This splintering, made palpable in the local wars that dominated the terrain from the mid-1400s through the mid-1500s, is commonly referred to by the defining term of the era, *gekokujō* (下克上, "the lower conquers the upper"). The term suggests not only the constant overthrow and altering of governing authority, but also the appropriation and transformation of classic art forms by groups outside of the imperial center. In concrete ways, then, this might be thought of as a moment of openings: a time of newly emerging conditions, and new possibilities, for new sociocultural and political forms in general.

By the middle of the sixteenth century the wars were subsiding, but power was dispersed among the feudal domains, and allegiances were divided and crossed between military leaders, religious centers, and the imperial throne. A new form of centralization appeared with Hideyoshi. Largely achieved by violence, and often represented in the terms of imperial or religious affiliation, the field of this centralization was nevertheless increasingly one of secular politics.

Hideyoshi's own place of power, increasingly absolutist, depended on a dispersal of all contingencies of its founding into a pure representation of power. Yet it was precisely his status as the actual founder that gave his position legitimate authority. There was, therefore, a contradiction in the character of Hideyoshi's power. This is, furthermore, more complicated than what might typically be thought of as the conflict of achieved as opposed to ascribed power. Achieved power, in other words, would be that which Hideyoshi managed to accomplish militarily; legitimacy in this case would derive simply from military might. A common reading of this time period says, in summary, that early military rulers like Hideyoshi (and before him, Oda Nobunaga) first achieved power in battle, and then subsequently had to find a way to accrue to themselves an image of ascribed power—a legitimacy that would be based on more essential characteristics, that made them appear to be the best and true ruler. This would imply a more stable and ongoing rule. "Culture," and the ability to appreciate refined arts, is typically seen as one means of acquiring the qualities of essential, aristocratic right to rule.

However, it is important to remember, first of all, that Hideyoshi was in fact pursuing both military and more ascriptive modes of power at the same time; they were not necessarily in conflict. Rather, in Hideyoshi's time, contradictions lay as much within the ascriptive forms of power as between the achieved and the ascriptive. To explain, it is useful to consider some of the better known examples of Hideyoshi's noh before turning to the practices of noh under the founders of the Tokugawa state.

As later with Tokugawa Ieyasu, the noh for Hideyoshi was part of the founding and uniting of a new political space.[10] In the mid-sixteenth century, the affiliations of the various troupes and schools of noh were scattered among local lords, shrines, temples, and the emperor, and few of these ties had any quality of permanence. Hideyoshi's first serious effort to assume all these varied affiliations for himself was through the Komparu school of noh. The Komparu school was headquartered in the religious center of Nara, where it was tied to several shrines and temples. To a lesser extent, it was also associated with the imperial court in Kyoto. Hideyoshi paid the head of the Komparu school to relinquish his post in Nara and move to Hideyoshi's military base in Osaka. By 1593, Hideyoshi had assigned full stipends to all of the four principal noh troupes. In doing so, Hideyoshi was composing the noh's dispersed allegiances to religion, emperor, and military into an image of centralized and fixed obligation to his own political authority.

These consolidations were acted out literally within the noh as well: Hideyoshi's greatest potential enemies and allies, the regional lords Tokugawa Ieyasu, Maeda Toshiie, and Oda Nobukatsu at various times took to the noh stage with or in front of Hideyoshi, primarily to celebrate Hideyoshi's rule—and Hideyoshi paid them for doing so. In 1592, for instance, Hideyoshi had Tokugawa Ieyasu and Maeda Toshiie perform onstage along with him at the imperial palace to celebrate the birth of Hideyoshi's son and heir, Hidetada.

For the most part, in these uses of the noh Hideyoshi was simply creating an order in which he was the central object, or the effect of the structure—even though he was initially the producer of the structure. He was the

---

10. Hideyoshi's use of the noh is fairly well known. For a related, but somewhat different, discussion of the relation between the noh and power for Hideyoshi, see Steven T. Brown, *Theatricalities of Power* (Stanford: Stanford University Press, 2001).

legitimate center because the order of things made him so. Other leaders' attendance to his noh performances simply verified that.

This position, in which the locus of authority defined as legitimate was defined from within the broader order of relations, could only be achieved by a forgetting of the immediate contingent origins of Hideyoshi's power. For this Hideyoshi used the traditional means of genealogy. He tried to attach to himself the legitimacy of imperial power, first assuming the classical aristocratic name of Taira, and then maneuvering to be appointed *Dajō Daijin* (太政大臣, the highest post in the hierarchy of patrician offices).[11] In 1585, Hideyoshi became the first member of the military ever to accede to the ninth-century office of *kanpaku* (関白). This position as regent to the emperor originally included hegemony over the government and a hereditary preservation of this hegemony through the maintenance of hereditary ties to the emperor.

This is certainly ascribed power of a sort. Nonetheless, especially insofar as Hideyoshi wanted to be seen as the founder of an entirely new order, part of his power came precisely from being the only one and true figure of origination.

He clearly seems to have used the noh to enact for himself this position of legitimate creator or founder of new spaces. Before each of Hideyoshi's military efforts of conquest and appropriation, for example, Hideyoshi held noh performances. For instance, prior to departing for the first of his expansionist projects, the conquest of Kyushu, he had the heads of all four noh troupes come and perform before him in Osaka. During his 1593 invasion of Korea he went further, taking noh lessons during the campaign so that he could himself perform on stage. Before the invasion began, he had a portable noh stage built and brought it for performances on the battlefield.[12]

---

11. George Elison and Bardwell Smith, eds., *Warlords, Artists and Commoners* (Honolulu: University Press of Hawaii, 1981), 231.
12. The first play Hideyoshi performed himself was, appropriately, *Yumiyawata*. This play was itself associated with inaugurations (in particular of political communities, if not entire states), and was written for the investiture of the shogun Ashikaga Yoshimochi in 1395 (or Yoshinori, 1428—see Rimer and Yamazaki, *On the Art of the Noh Drama* (Princeton: Princeton University Press, 1984), 213) in celebration of a new, peaceful reign. The lines quoted in the epigraph to this paper are said to have derived from an eighth century oracle of the Usa shrine, whose pronouncements were invoked as godly will and therefore grounds for political advancement. See Ross Bender, "Metamorphosis of a Deity," in *Monumenta Nipponica* 33 (1975), 165–178. Hideyoshi had Yumiyawata performed first in the three-day program of noh celebrating his son's birth; this play also figures prominently in the formal cycle of Tokugawa official noh.

Similarly, while Hideyoshi went to extremes to place himself within the genealogical lines of the imperial inheritance, he manipulated the structure so that he would also retain for himself the role of initiator or creator. When he took the position of *kanpaku*, Hideyoshi did not follow the traditional tactic of entry by adoptive kinship into one of the five classical noble houses related to the imperial throne. He did not take on one of these houses' family names. Instead, he created an entirely new name for himself, essentially establishing his own house named after himself.

So too, in 1588, having "pacified" all of Japan (at least the area situated west of the Kantō), the emperor honored Hideyoshi with a visit. All important domain lords attended the celebratory banquet as well, and Hideyoshi had each of them sign an oath of allegiance to him. But the list of twenty-nine signatories[13] shows that all but five of them gave their family name as Toyotomi, Hideyoshi's own surname. Hideyoshi was thus again using genealogy to essentialize allegiance to his own position of power, and to locate himself within imperial-style legitimacy. Yet, the point for him was not to truly revive or resuscitate a world of imperial rule, which continued in a limited form anyway, in Kyoto. He may have wished to dispense with the contingencies of his own military accession to power, but he still wanted the legitimacy of being the founder of a new kind of state and a new world of power. Thus, he needed both the weight of ascribed or attributive power, and the authority of being the true founder of something new and therefore contingent.[14]

This was a political problem for Hideyoshi, as hegemon. The figure of Hideyoshi dancing in his noh plays also, though, reveals a semiotic question regarding the status of political representation in the late sixteenth century.

In part, this is merely a matter of content. Along with learning to play roles in a number of the older plays, Hideyoshi took the unique step of commissioning new noh plays that did not depict traditional themes, but rather

---

13. See Elison and Smith, *Warlords, Artists, and Commoners*, 237.

14. A similar point could be made about the way in which Hideyoshi used and needed the other lords as spectators. Their show of appreciation to him, and certainly their willingness to use his family name as part of complete genealogy, helped to provide closure for the image of Hideyoshi as rightful leader. But the "gratitude" they showed him was legislated by Hideyoshi himself. The oath he required all the lords to sign using his family name began with the written statement, "The measures ordained [by the *kanpaku*]...move us to tears of gratitude." So even their apparently emotional investment in authorizing Hideyoshi's power, and the tearful thanks which would seem to have created the conditions of an ahistorical, originless genealogy, was openly legislated by Hideyoshi himself. Citation quoted in Elison and Smith, *Warlords, Artists, and Commoners*, 236.

presented his own colonizing exploits. Such plays portrayed him as a great warrior who is nonetheless also a god, victor in Japan but over Korea and China as well; as a filial son and the source of his mother's attainment of bodhisattva-hood; and, posthumously, as the benevolent god Toyokuni, worshipped in China as well as Japan.[15] In this formulation, Hideyoshi managed to displace the origins of his military claim to power into an image of himself as godly, and his actions as of divine provenance. At the same time, by identifying that divine provenance with his own name rather than an identity from an earlier, perhaps more imperial mythical genealogy, Hideyoshi retained the impression that he himself *was*, somehow, the original inventor of this power structure.

More important, though, is what this says about the status of the sign. A key point to keep in mind is that Hideyoshi not only commissioned plays about himself, and that deified him, he in fact also often acted in those plays in the role of his deified self. If these were true rituals, then presumably he, in that role of his godly self, would be something like a natural or transparent sign: the appearance of an actual god. Yet it seems to have been a little more complicated than that.

By acting onstage in the role of himself, Hideyoshi literally became one with his represented self. In this discourse of Hideyoshi's representation of power, the discursive referent (Hideyoshi as the object and place of power) becomes—poses as—its own referent. Hideyoshi is defined as an object by, and entirely within, that discourse. His own bodily figure only helps to provide a kind of closure to his represented image. By this measure, Hideyoshi's representation of himself through the noh created the image of an authoritative form of rule for him, but one that also transcended him and his worldly body.[16]

Yet as has been made clear, as archiactor of a new structure of power, with the power to define it and be its subject or narrator, he had to transcend it, and place himself in the position of a clearly revealed origin. This is the other side of Hideyoshi's decision to get up on stage and act in his own roles.

---

15. In this as well as other respects there are some similarities to British Renaissance court masques, by which the ruler redefined himself from court hero to god of universal power. See Stephen Orgel, *The Illusion of Power* (Berkeley: University of California Press, 1975) 52, passim.
16. This is similar to Claude Lefort's description of ideological representation under bourgeois rule: "[bourgeois rule] must owe nothing to the movement which makes it appear. To be true to its image, the rule must be abstracted from any question concerning its origin." Claude Lefort, *The Political Forms of Modern Society* (Cambridge, MA: The MIT Press, 1986), 212.

He—the real, historical, physical Hideyoshi—was in effect revealing himself to be the creator of the discursive image of Hideyoshi.

The discursively constructed representation of Hideyoshi the powerful ruler—that is, Hideyoshi as simply an object of this discourse—was therefore dependent on a position outside that discourse. As creative subject of this discursive order, rather than just its object, Hideyoshi had to stand outside of it. That is what his physical presence in the plays about him brought. His bodily identity was a kind of supplement to the dramatic representations of him as a god. Hence, again, the dispersal of Hideyoshi's immediate historical origins as a powerful figure into the discursive order of representation was combined with a clear demonstration of where those representations came from. In this latter role, Hideyoshi's physical being is contingent—after all, who could play this role but Hideyoshi himself? The closure of Hideyoshi's representation as a god is consequently haunted, in a sense, by the contingency of his body.

In all of these ways, a contradiction can be seen in the figure of Hideyoshi the ruler. Asserting his discursive power—authority derived from his identification with the discursively defined place of power—Hideyoshi at the same time displayed himself as the condition, or source, of these relations of power, thus making visible the contingency of these discursively noncontingent relations of power.[17]

In this contradiction, Hideyoshi's power, as well as the power of the early modern Tokugawa state, originated. As suggested earlier, this was a contradiction of the historical moment, indicating general possibilities of that era. It was visible not only in the discrepancy between Hideyoshi's need for a noncontingent representation of himself as powerful, and the increasingly secular, political position of ruler which could never be equal with this representation, but also in the continuing references made to a divine, mythical Other World, as if this somehow would bring the two positions of rule together.

---

17. This same contradictory position is apparent in the way that Hideyoshi posed his own relation to history, and the events upon which he based his claim to power. Not only did he have noh plays written in celebration of his various actions and heroic exploits, in some cases he had the plays written *before* the event; the play would then first be presented at the actual time of the event being celebrated in the play. Hideyoshi's position as a powerful figure of history was thus both an effect of history, as celebrated in the noh play, and prior to (or author of) the history that made him powerful. The event in this kind of history, as signified by Hideyoshi's noh play, can hence be thought of as embodying these contradictory elements. Plays that Hideyoshi had written before the actual event include *Yoshino Mōde* and *Kōya Sankei*. For descriptions of these, see Brown, *Theatricalities of Power*, 121–128.

The Space of Tokugawa Noh

The first Tokugawa shogun, Ieyasu, came to power in a moment of new possibilities and openings similar to those of Hideyoshi's time. Hideyoshi died in 1598 while his heir was still a child, and the consolidation of power that he had achieved quickly began to disintegrate. Although the regional, particularized areas of earlier feudalistic sovereignty had been destabilized by Hideyoshi, no real centralizing power, either economic or governmental, had been installed under Hideyoshi. The imperial family did not have political hegemony, and the military office of shogun had been allowed to lapse prior to Hideyoshi's time. In 1600, Tokugawa Ieyasu emerged victorious from the battle of Sekigahara—a contest joined by nearly every domain lord. With this victory, he achieved a new and even greater unity than had been available to Hideyoshi.

Under these conditions, Ieyasu proceeded to architect and regiment wide-reaching social and political reforms. These reforms were utopian in the sense of Francoise Choay's utopist planner.[18] Referring to Le Corbusier and to Thomas More's *Utopia*, in Choay's view, the planner wants to impose a material institution upon a human collectivity—perhaps to augment its well-being, but according to a fully idealized plan. The plan is not designed to address the needs and desires of the existing life forms of the community, nor does it take its legitimacy from the structures of local customs and history (a role which Choay ascribes to the "builder" as opposed to the idealist planner). Rather, the plan is devised in the name of an aesthetic that is transcendent of historical forms. Ieyasu and the early Tokugawa shoguns worked to materialize their reforms as if according to this sort of a plan—not just of an edifice or a city, as with Choay's utopist, though I will discuss the construction of the city of Edo in these terms, but of the larger framework of the Japanese state. If this "plan" or ideal was a real source of social creativity, in its material institutionalization it was made to seem eternal and unchangeable. Furthermore, if the rule instituted by Ieyasu can in this way be considered utopian, it was also authoritarian; if this was a moment of openings, it was also an authoritarian era.[19]

---

18. I am following here the short analysis of Choay in Alexander Gelley, "City Texts," 243–244, although I am not directly following Gelley's argument, which on the pages cited seems to disregard the creative role of utopian theory.
19. I am implicitly raising the possibility that this point in history was utopic—not only for the reason of its authoritarian conditions of rule, but for the interplay between feudalistic and more central, precapitalist relations. For similar claims for a roughly comparable period in the West, see Marin, *Utopics*, xiv, passim, and Samuel Weber, "Taking Exception to Decision: Walter Benjamin and Carl Schmitt," in *Diacritics* 22 (1992), 8, n. 2.

In the strictly codified form instituted by the Tokugawa regime, the noh became a formalized political ritual practice, the effect of which was the production of social space and the attempted maintenance of control over it. This involved the staging of a mastery over a geography, and over change and time.

Accordingly social "space" here means both a temporal and a territorial orientation. Space (following de Certeau) is actualized through interaction with places, "places" being the order in which elements are positioned and configured. Space is the result of operations or practices which orient it, situate it, and materialize it,[20] but, rather than simply an effect, it exists in—it goes on in—these practices.[21] Space is therefore also a historical form, and a form of history. Space accordingly is associated with process, while place is linked more with the accomplishment of a process, with an indication of stability and, consequently, with the production of a law.[22] Finally, space, to quote Kristin Ross, "as a social fact, as a social factor and as an instance of society, is always political and strategic."[23] The noh was a spatializing practice; it was part of the political act of reimagining Japanese social space that was constituted by the founding of the city of Edo.[24]

Placing Edo

One of Ieyasu's first important acts was to create a new city as the base of his power—a move which, although not outside of previous practices of power-making, normalized the country into a new society. Ieyasu was attempting to lay out a new topography for what would be the early modern Japanese state; Edo became the place from which the Tokugawa shogunate could articulate and master the places that would make up this state. In this sense, borrowing loosely from de Certeau, the founding of Edo was a "strategic" move. It constituted an attempt to create an autonomous place from which the shogunate

---

20. See Michel de Certeau, *The Practice of Everyday Life* (Berkeley: University of California Press, 1984), 117; "In short, *space is a practiced place*. Thus the street geometrically defined by urban planning is transformed into a space by walkers . . . "
21. See also Nancy Munn, *The Fame of Gawa* (Cambridge: Cambridge University Press, 1986), 11, passim.
22. See Marin's study of Western baroque notions of space, place, and event, in "The Architecture of the Prince," especially 171–173.
23. Kristin Ross, *The Emergence of Social Space* (Minneapolis: University of Minnesota Press, 1988), 9.
24. The idea of social space used here does not imply a formalist semiotic code of the geography of the Japanese state. Part of the continuing interest in Lefebvre's notion of social space lies in its apparent promise of providing a position inclusive of both objective structural, institutional forms and subjective phenomenological experience, but defined by neither on its own.

could transform the uncertainties of geography and history into newly readable spaces.[25]

Ieyasu ordered the construction of Edo even before he took the office of shogun. At that point he was still using his authority and position as an imperial court official in the Kyoto castle of Fushimi, and was also still ostensibly faithful to the loose organization of daimyo (the *kōgi;* 公議)[26] originally set in place by Hideyoshi. Yet Ieyasu made it clear that he was planning a substantive change, not only in the pattern of vassalage, but in the overall structure of power, including the centrality of the court. Even the way he had the city built was a material sign of the relations he was forming: he ordered that the labor and the materials for the city come from all daimyo throughout the state. Once Ieyasu became shogun, he ordered all daimyo in the same way to build his castle. Ieyasu was erecting a place—and in doing so constituting the relations of subservience—from which he would stand out as a ruler with characteristics increasingly approximating that of a national hegemon. The noh contributed to this disposition of Edo and Ieyasu as the place of power.

Before Ieyasu, Hideyoshi had already begun to centralize noh's allegiances by assigning most of the country's actors to four "Yamato" schools of noh and then providing stipends to all four schools. However, Ieyasu went further by commanding that the heads of all four schools, including actors who had been living in Osaka, Hideyoshi's castle town, be brought together and made to live in Sunpu[27] where his headquarters were located. From there the actors were often brought to Edo. Under Hidetada, Ieyasu's heir, all principal actors were given land within the grounds of Edo castle for their permanent residence.[28] The stipends that had continued under Hideyoshi's heirs

---

25. See de Certeau, "On the Oppositional Practices of Everyday Life," *Social Text* No. 3 (1980); and *The Practice of Everyday Life*, 29 ff. For de Certeau, a strategic circumscription of place was a Cartesian gesture of modernism—the postulation of a totalizing, knowing self, distinguished from Otherness. Although in many ways it may be possible to conceive of the Tokugawa state as a modernist space along these lines, this would be only a partial understanding of more conflicting conditions.
26. The *kōgi* was an organization based on a pledge Hideyoshi had elicited from a large proportion of important daimyo to guarantee the lands not only of their fellow daimyo, but also of the imperial nobility.
27. During Hideyoshi's reign, Ieyasu had maintained a castle at Sunpu as his headquarters. Hideyoshi had relocated Ieyasu to the area that would become Edo as part of an overall redistribution of domain lands. To some extent, Ieyasu's decision to build a city there was consistent with Hideyoshi's territorial organization. However, with its focus on Edo, Ieyasu brought about a complete reorientation of that space.
28. See *Nō kyōgen*, I:91.

were terminated for actors who remained in Osaka. After land was provided in Edo, the actors were funded only if they agreed to relocate to Edo. The noh was declared the official *shikigaku* in 1615.

Thus from early on, the positioning and funding of noh actors displayed an image of unification and central allegiance, or minimally of control by the center. The enforced movements of noh actors also defined relations of extension out from, and control between, Edo and outlying domains. The noh school headmasters (*iemoto*), for example, were required to leave their hometown provinces only part of the time: the Tokugawas set up a cycle, whereby each of the four *iemoto* would live for one year in the castle, and then be allowed to return to their home province, the next time returning to Edo for six months and then going home for one year. Each was on a different cycle so that none were together at the castle for the same one-year period each time. The cycle alternated noh actors' allegiances to their own domains and to the castle, and privileged none of the domains in relation to the other—their ties went equally and solely from their own domains to the shogun in Edo.[29] This strategy was hence nearly identical to Ieyasu's *sankinkōtai* system, which required every daimyo to maintain a residence in Edo, and live there in alternate years. The physical presence in Edo of actors and daimyo, and their travels between domain and castle, thus inscribed a geography of allegiance and obeisance to the shogun.[30]

A similar structure of relations was staged both by the actor-audience relationship of the performances and the locations of performances. All major ceremonial performances in Edo required the attendance of the country's principal daimyo. For the first service in memoriam of Ieyasu, for exam-

---

29. For details on the calendar of service, see Ikeuchi Nobuyoshi, *Nōgaku seisuiki* (Tokyo: Noh Gakkai, 1925), I: 126–127. (*Nōgaku seisuiki* will hereafter be abbreviated as NS). In practice the shoguns always privileged one of the noh schools—for most of the era it was the Kanze family—and required that the *iemoto* of that school dance in most of the important ceremonies. For this reason, the Kanze *iemoto* often remained in the castle while the remaining three schools alternated. Also, the *iemoto* were allowed to remain in Edo during their "off duty" cycles, and often did.

30. The actual performance record of the noh in the Tokugawa era is complicated. Omote and Amano say that in terms of sheer number of performances (not necessarily official, or *shikigaku*-related noh), there may have been more noh plays held in the imperial palace in Kyoto than in the shogun's castle in Edo. They therefore say that Kyoto was a center for the noh. I am trying to show, though, that there was a more systematic and significant form of centrality than that deriving simply from numbers of performance. Omote and Amano do acknowledge that the spread and ongoing use of the noh in the Tokugawa era was due to the various regional leaders "following the will of the shogun." See *Nō kyōgen*, I:107, 109, 120.

ple, at the shrine dedicated to him at Nikkō, performances were given by the heads of all four schools of noh and the new Kita "style" (the Kita *ryū*, which was not yet allowed the full status of a school, or *ha*). Every daimyo of importance was called upon to attend. Even senior ministers within the central shogunate were at times ordered to see noh performances within the castle, such as those given by the child heirs of the shogun.

Furthermore, at times daimyo were ordered to present noh performances in their own domains, and on their own initiative would offer performances in honor of the shogun for occasions such as shogunal visits or as memorial services for Ieyasu. Similarly, whenever the shogun visited the daimyo at their mansions in Edo, a noh performance was expected. These performances were particularly important for relations with "outside" (*tozama*, 外様) daimyo.

The term *tozama*, along with *kamon* (家門; "one's family," "clan") and *fudai* (譜代; literally, "successive generations"), had been in common use by the sixteenth century. Each domainal ruler conceived of his own vassals in a permanent relation to himself, either as direct kin (*kamon*) or as hereditary vassals (*fudai*); *tozama* referred to lords entirely outside of the ruler's familial and political sphere of influence. With Tokugawa Ieyasu's accomplishment of control, these terms were extended statewide to define the position of each domainal lord vis à vis their relation to the Tokugawas: three ruling families (headed by Ieyasu's sons) were ranked and privileged as primary branches (*gosanke*, 御三家)[31] of the Tokugawa family and lesser cadet branches of "kin" (*kamon*) were later authorized; then lords who had been aligned with Ieyasu since the time of Hideyoshi's death were considered *fudai* "hereditary" vassals, while those lords who did not submit to Ieyasu until after the decisive battle of Sekigahara were regarded as "other" or "outer" *tozama* lords.

Thus *tozama* daimyo had no genealogical or hereditary allegiance to the Tokugawas—in some cases they had well-developed histories as loci of oppositional power—making relations with them particularly important to the shogun. As described above, allegiances with these daimyo and ties of submission and authority were in part shaped through the noh. The shogunate

---

31. Mito, Owari, and Kii. These were part of the six Tokugawa collateral houses, the other three being the "three lords" (*sankyō*—Tayasu, Hitotsubashi, and Shimizu). The *sanka* were established by Ieyasu, whereas the *sankyō* were founded by later shoguns; and unlike the *sanka*, the *sankyō* did not have fixed land holdings or castles, they did not have large fixed followings of vassals, and their retainers did not have titles and were not hereditary as these positions were bestowed by the current living lord.

went to great lengths to invite *tozama* daimyo for noh performances, to the extent that at times it risked angering *fudai* daimyo by its generosity and favoritism toward the *tozama* daimyo. The *tozama* in turn were reportedly "excessive" in their use of the noh as a form of flattery and homage toward the shogunate.[32]

The Maeda family of the Kaga domain (*han*) was the largest and strongest of the *tozama* daimyo, and had been one of Hideyoshi's most powerful allies. The relationship between the Maedas and the Tokugawas was therefore critical for the shogunate and provides an important example. Maeda family records are replete with records of noh performances. The family heads sponsored noh performances for the shoguns frequently in Edo and in Kanazawa, the principal town of Kaga domain, and they themselves performed occasionally. The Tokugawas returned these presentations with their own performances, and most were accompanied by exchanges of symbolic gifts such as horses and cranes, symbolic of longevity. These exchanges were fixed in other social registers, including marriages, which were themselves often accompanied by noh performances.[33]

For example, Tsunanori, the head of the Maeda clan, visited Edo castle in 1691. Upon arrival he was told that the shogun, Tokugawa Tsunayoshi, would be performing a noh play the following week, which he should attend. He was also told that the shogun wished him to perform at a later date. Tsunanori had never performed noh but because of the shogun's command, he immediately began to practice. At the shogun's performance, in addition to Maeda Tsunanori (*tozama*), the three Tokugawa *gosanke* branch houses were in attendance, along with the lord of Kōfu and other *fudai* daimyo. Some time afterward they were told that along with Tsunanori, they were all to perform for the shogun, and were given a little over a month's time to prepare.

The preparations were elaborate on the day of the daimyos' performance. Two priests were included among the dressing room attendants. The performers arrived several hours before the performance and were visited by one of the shogunal administration's junior councillors (若年寄, *wakadoshiyori*), who brought offerings of cakes from the shogun. Forty minutes after the shogun arrived, the performance began. The shogun's council of elders and the head priest of Ieyasu's shrine at Nikkō were also in the audience. The Tokugawa kin and *fudai* families left right after the performance, but Tsuna-

---

32. NS, I: 5.
33. Records of these performances run throughout the Kaga domain history. See Heki, Ken, *Kaga han shiryō* (Kanazawa: Meiji Insatsu, 1922–1958), vols. 1–10.

nori remained and was greeted personally by each member of the shogun's council of elders.³⁴

Thus by agreeing to perform in the program of noh plays, Maeda Tsunanori and the three Tokugawa house daimyo were equally enacting their fidelity to the Tokugawa order, and thereby becoming representatives of the shogun. But Tsunanori's privileged meeting with the council of elders underscored his status as a *tozama* daimyo even while the performance established ties that supplanted the lack of genealogical relationship or hereditary tie. The noh here both marked Tsunanori as an "outsider," reinforcing the Tokugawa genealogical organization of space, yet also overcame the lack of central allegiance that this implied. The Maeda family continued to support and attend performances throughout the Tokugawa era, and figured importantly in the final public noh performance of 1848.

As the noh became an accepted mode of representation of Tokugawa power, it also constituted a means of contesting the Tokugawas. This was the situation in 1641 when Tokugawa Iemitsu was born, the long-awaited male heir to the third shogun. As required by such an event, the heads of the major noh schools gathered to celebrate along with the daimyo of the important *tozama* domain of Kaga, Maeda Toshitsune, who offered his sincere congratulations to the assembled actors and the three Tokugawa house daimyo. Toshitsune then arranged for a congratulatory program of noh plays to be held a few days' later. Also included in the program, though, was a drummer from the Ishii school; at the time of Ieyasu's consolidation of power, when he had ordered all noh actors to leave Hideyoshi's castle in Osaka and report to his own castle in Sunpu, the Ishiis had refused and gone instead to the emperor in Kyoto. Accordingly, on the day of performance the drummer who was to play with Ishii, and who was affiliated with a different school located in Edo, claimed he was ill and refused to play. Maeda Toshitsune became furious and ordered that the Edo player be brought to him. The Edo player, however, experienced a quick and fortuitous recovery and did perform, but not before Maeda Toshitsune had strongly defended the Ishii school, exclaiming, "Who the hell is Tokugawa, anyway?" (*Tokugawa nani mono zo*).³⁵ At stake here were relations between the primary *tozama* domain, the imperial family, and the shogun. Yet as a contestation, it nonetheless

---

34. See Kajii Yukiyo and Mitsuda Ryōji, eds., *Kanazawa no nōgaku* (Kanazawa: Kitaguni Shoseki, 1973), 60–61, and *Nō kyōgen*, I: 111–112.
35. 『徳川なに者ぞ』. Quoted in *Kanazawa no nōgaku*, p. 45.

remained within a mode of representation that was created by, and definitive of, the Tokugawa regime.

The above incident reflects a more general division of geography, politics, and style integral to the Tokugawa reign. Geographically, the western area of Japan centering around Kyoto was opposed to the eastern area centering around Edo. As the site of the imperial capital, Kyoto traditionally had been referred to in terms of an "upward" direction (as in *kami*, 上, or *jōkyō*, 上京 —"going up to the capital"). The sociopolitical transformation accomplished by the Tokugawa shoguns, however, was such that "going up" now referred to travel to Edo. The same division and valorization of geographical and political "upper" and "lower" was applied to the division of noh schools: Prior to the Tokugawa era, the *kamigakari* (上掛かり) style of noh was associated with Kyoto (but also with the Kanze and Hōshō school). The *shimogakari* (下掛かり) style referred to Nara, and the Komparu, Kongō, and Kita schools. However, although the leaders of the four principal noh troupes were theoretically all affiliated with Edo, only the two schools with closest traditional ties to the Tokugawa family (the Kanze and Hōshō troupes) maintained their headquarters in Edo. The Komparu and Kongō troupes kept their headquarters in the western region. Accordingly, as the Kanze school came to be the most official troupe of the shogun's official noh, Edo too became definitive of central or "upper" style, as opposed to the lower and more local styles of Kyoto, Kaga *han* (domain), and elsewhere.

This hierarchy of geography and of style was also inevitably political. This was apparent in the Hōsai festival of the Toyokuni Shrine. This festival was held annually, and all four noh school headmasters were expected to gather and offer performances of noh that were considered "godly rites" (*shinji no gi*, 神事の議, which also refers to Shinto ceremonies), held for the country's "divine protection."[36] The shrine was located in Kyoto, and the festival had originally been meant to honor Hideyoshi. But in 1610, Kanze, the troupe with closest ties to Ieyasu, failed to attend. This was apparently an important step in breaking the appearance of a unity of the four noh schools as equals, and of Hideyoshi as the progenitor of that unity. Although the statewide unified order of noh was maintained, the Kanze school's absence from the Hōsai festival marked the ascendance of the Kanze school over the others, and a shift from the western region of Japan to Edo as the "upper" place of governance and principal metropole—as well as toward the

---

36. Quoted in NS, 4.

Tokugawa family as occupant of that place. After this incident the Hōsai festival quickly died out; it was revived after the Tokugawa era had ended.

Locality

Edo was not, however, a simple, absolute center within this political geography of the noh. By the latter years of the seventeenth century, nearly all of the country's daimyo had followed the Tokugawa lead and themselves become patrons of noh, including the sponsorship of actors and students. Some of these daimyo-sponsored noh actors were not affiliated with the four official noh families, and thus were not affiliated with the official Tokugawa *shikigaku* order. In some cases, daimyo used the noh to give form to their own local bases of power.

The Maeda family of the powerful *tozama* domain of Kaga is again an important example. In 1617 Tokugawa Hidetada (the third shogun) made the Maeda mansion in Edo the first stop on his visits to the various daimyo, presumably because of the recent birth of an heir to Maeda Toshitsune, the daimyo of Kaga. Toshitsune offered a program of noh plays that day in honor of the shogun's visit, and the following day presented a performance by all four noh troupes. From that time he sponsored his own noh family headmaster—his own representative, with his own style and expressing his position as a leader separate from and in many ways as powerful as the Tokugawa rulers.[37] Accordingly, in 1628 Toshitsune formally became a sponsor of an actor, who although a son of the Komparu family was not affiliated with any of the schools, and had danced with all four of the main schools. Thereafter the Maedas became the principal sponsors of first the Komparu troupe, and later the Hōshō, thereby assuming an important position within the Tokugawa order of noh, yet distinctly apart from the Tokugawa-sponsored Kanze family. Hence when Maeda Tsunanori switched Kaga *han*'s allegiance from the Komparu to the Hōshō school, he ordered the principal noh actors in his domain who had been dancing under the Kanze and Komparu names to switch and become "Hōshō" actors. In doing so he laid out a territory as well as an era, known as "the time of Kaga Hōshō."[38] The Maedas also continued to support non-*shikigaku* families, such as the Ishii troupe mentioned above, increasingly setting up a sphere of influence (地盤, *jiban*) distinct from the Kanze-oriented Tokugawa capital.

---

37. Omote and Amano, *Nōgaku no rekishi nō kyōgen*, 308.
38. *Kanazawa no nōgaku*, 53.

Maeda Toshitsune's actions after he retired, too, illustrate a model that nearly parallels Ieyasu's construction of the city of Edo. Toshitsune had shown an interest in urban reorganization throughout much of his reign as daimyo of Kaga han. In response to fires in 1631 and 1635, he had attempted to reconstruct most of the longstanding capital city of Kanazawa, imposing on it the social reforms he also sought. Separate residential quarters were established for each status group within the warrior hierarchy, and the position of these statuses was expressed by making the distance of each samurai's residence from the castle proportionate (in theory) to their status within the social hierarchy. Merchant and artisan groups were also each given their own proper, geographically separated locations. Along with materializing an ideal hierarchical organization of social categories, this also removed low ranking warriors from their masters' residences. One of the intended effects of this was to loosen personal ties and so to subject all samurai to a more direct daimyo rule.[39] As did the shogun's required circulation of noh actors and of daimyo in the *sankinkōtai* system, this resulted in a more absolute, and abstract, center of power.

Upon retirement, however, Toshitsune decided to construct a site that would be more completely his own. On empty marshland some distance from Kanazawa, he built a new castle (Komatsu), and with it an entire town, finishing them in 1651. He imported the entire population, and laid out places for vassals and commoners in a structure more fully planned than he had done in Kanazawa.[40] As with Edo, its completion was celebrated with a noh performance in the castle grounds to which all the townspeople were invited. Public performances within the castle were repeated annually, and, as at Edo, their success was considered an important means of ensuring peaceful rule over the population at large. So here too, at the local level of a *tozama* domain ruler, we find the utopic and authoritarian projection of an ideal order, including the location of a legitimate place of power, onto a physical territory.

That each domain in the Japanese state thus remained to some extent a realm separate from Tokugawa authority is also evident in the ceremonies of

---

39. Along with the fact that Toshitsune was also creating a new army corps, these changes worried the Tokugawa shogunate. The redirection of a canal, for example, spurred rumors that there might be military reasons for doing so, and that the head of construction had been put to death by the shogunate for keeping the exact course of the canal a secret. For an overview of urban planning under Toshitsune, see James L. McClain, *Kanazawa* (New Haven: Yale University Press, 1982), 74–84.

40. *Kanazawa no nōgaku*, 51–52.

investiture for provincial daimyo. From the time of the fourth daimyo of Kaga (1639), the investiture of a new daimyo was celebrated with a five-day performance of noh called "country-entering noh" (more literally, "congratulatory entering-the-country ritual noh—*nyūkoku shukuga no gishiki nō*, 入国祝賀の儀式能). The term "country-entering" (*nyūkoku* can also refer to immigration) may have been used in part because daimyo spent much of their time in Edo rather than in their own domains,[41] but it also served to indicate the strong sense of boundaries and of independent rule that defined their domains as apart from Edo's jurisdiction. Taking the office of daimyo still, in the seventeenth century, meant entering a relatively autonomous space.

Within these local domains, any person of social or political importance was given a special place at the celebratory investiture noh rites as well as the annual public noh presentations, and was expected to attend. So as with the equivalent performances at Edo, these programs authorized the place, and person, of (local) sovereignty.

Yet if these local celebrations were recognized at all by the Edo shogunate, it was usually at most only by a shogunal visit to the daimyo's mansion in Edo. Shogunal celebrations, on the other hand, were always recognized by full attendance at Edo by the country's major daimyo. The shogun and Edo thus occupy a position similar to the apex of a pyramid: each local domain daimyo is a center unto himself, yet each is ultimately defined in terms of his relation to, and each authorizes, the Edo shogunate as the center of legitimacy above all others. In a limited sense this is in accord with earlier studies of political economy in the Tokugawa state, which describe the seventeenth century local *han* as no longer being an entity for private governance. Though still acting as a military organ, these arguments contend that the *han* depended on the shogun as their source of ideological legitimacy; their success in showing deference to the shogun in turn provided the *han* with authorization.[42] Real political independence, however, did remain in varying degrees with each individual domain.

In general, it is therefore accurate to say that as a seat of power, Edo figured at the head of a hierarchy of domains that preserved for themselves a

---

41. Kajii and Mitsuda argue this. See *Kanazawa no nōgaku*, 46.
42. See, for example, Sasaki and Toby, "The Changing Rationale of Daimyo Control in the Emergence of the Bakuhan State." In John Whitney Hall et al., eds., *Japan Before Tokugawa* (Princeton: Princeton University Press, 1981), especially 271, 284, 290.

degree of independence. Nonetheless, even when powerful daimyo sought to further materialize their own separate realms of authority, as with the Maeda family of Kaga *han*, and even when these actions potentially contested the centrality of the shogun, the daimyo used the same ceremonial mode of self-representation that was created and put into effect by the Tokugawa shoguns. A similar argument could be made about the imperial enthronement ceremony, with noh occupying an important part of the emperor's enthronement during the Tokugawa era.[43] All actors related to the Edo shogunate were forbidden from performing in these ceremonial noh plays, while actors connected with *tozama* domains such as Kaga were encouraged to perform. Thus, at least superficially the imperial family was encouraging an expression of power that was contestatory to the shogun. But again, the mode of power was the shogun's rather than the classic imperial forms. By the late seventeenth century, the same conditions of allegiance and the same mode of organizing space and time came increasingly to define all of the Japanese state. To the extent that this held true, Japan had become a space of the same.

The sovereignty of Edo as center of a bounded state was given the coherence of genealogical and hereditary relationships. This suggests neither the universal homogeneity of a modern nation nor the loosely unified form of a state made up of independent feudatories. Local ties of kinship no longer demarcated wholly autonomous realms, and the shogun reserved the right to transfer daimyo from one domain to another at any time, discouraging the development of independent identities of difference. Furthermore, personal ties of allegiance were being discouraged even within the domains in favor of more abstract, universal ties to a central ruler—as, for example, in Maeda Toshitsune's reorientation of the city structure of Kanazawa. Yet as described above, the Tokugawas' set of vassal relations, predicated on conceptions of genealogy and heredity, were extended to the state as a whole and these remained through much of the Tokugawa era. Thus, rather than a relatively homogenous arrangement of equal provinces under a central ruler, the political space of the state was organized more into an organic unity of different elements, including domains of direct kin, hereditary *fudai* vassals, and "others" (the *tozama* daimyo). Land and political office continued to be redistributed, at least by the early Tokugawa rulers, according to those dis-

---

43. See NS I: 422–426.

tinctions.[44] The official Tokugawa order of noh, itself organized by fixed genealogical distinctions (the Tokugawa regime later mandated that noh actors maintain hereditarily fixed families), also imposed a set of genealogical allegiances of "lower" and "upper" noh onto the geography of the Japanese state. As the Kanze school became preeminent in conjunction with the Tokugawa shoguns as its sponsors, nearly all the six Tokugawa-related *fudai* families also chose to sponsor branches of the Kanze family as their representatives. *Tozama* daimyo such as the Maedas, on the other hand, sponsored other, often *shimogakari* families. Thus, even if the political was less and less tied into the kinship relations of local places, the place of Edo within the overall Japanese state was still given the grounding, continuity, and composition of fixed hereditary and genealogical relationships.

But only in part. The circulation of noh actors between their allotted residences in Edo and their home provinces brought all of them into a theoretically equal relationship with the shogun, defining lines of allegiance abstracted from the ties of kinship. So too, by the time of the third Tokugawa shogun Hidetada, red-seal certificates of investiture were issued by the shogun uniformly to all daimyo, and he thereby "asserted his authority over all daimyo without distinction between *fudai* and *tozama*."[45] On the one hand, the terms of genealogy continued to be applied at the level of representations of the state, lending an image of a fixed order of non-homogenous, hierarchical relations. On the other hand, though, the genealogy of the state became itself a more abstract idea. Thus as Asao and Jansen note, at the same time that the seals of investiture were being distributed to all daimyo equally, the relations between *tozama* and *fudai* continued but gradually were ritualized—taking the form of "a fictive battle in which the shogun, as military commander, rewarded and penalized his subordinates."[46] Edo was becoming

---

44. The three principal branch houses of the Tokugawas were allotted domains of large, productive landholdings, and were expected to guard the main entries into the Kanto region where the bakufu was located, but were given little political power of their own; *fudai* daimyo held smaller lands—though some were strategic militarily for protection of the shogunate—but were given the bulk of the responsibilities in the bakufu's administration; and *tozama* daimyo were allowed to retain what in several cases were large areas of land, although some had their lands reduced, but they were given no real positions of importance either military or governmental. See Tetsuo Najita, *Japan* (Englewood Cliffs, NJ: Prentice-Hall, 1974). In a number of cases in which *tozama* daimyo were entirely removed from their domains, the stated reason was disciplining for infractions of "the ancestor's regulations." See for example, "Shogun and Tennō," in John Whitney Hall et al., *Japan Before Tokugawa*, 267.
45. Hall, ibid., 266.
46. Ibid., 277.

The Place of Religion

The place of religion also was reorganized within the practices of the noh. Parallel to transformations in kin-oriented groups of power, many ties of sovereignty to local places of difference based on religion were broken, so that in terms of religion, too, there were fewer and fewer places of difference in the Tokugawa state.

Within the noh, religion was reinscribed as an underpinning of the state. Prior to the Tokugawa era, some provinces—in particular some ruled by sects of Buddhism—had been fairly powerful and relatively autonomous, some with comparatively independent economic systems and their own standing armies. There were as well a number of Shinto shrine and Buddhist temple centers without clearly defined ties either to the emperor alone, or to any one of the military leaders. The noh had been in the middle ages patronized to varying degrees by the Ashikaga shoguns, but until the Tokugawas came to power most troupes remained independent, and many were affiliated with local shrines and temples. By the sixteenth century, most shrines and temples had retained *dengaku* and *sarugaku* troupes (which can be glossed as early forms of noh) to perform their rites and memorial services; *gakuto* regulations not only gave these noh troupes the right to carry out the ceremonies of the shrine or temple, but in return for these services also gave the head of the troupe exclusive rights to tour his troupe throughout the area under the jurisdiction of the shrine or temple to which the troupe was attached.[47] The re-creation of noh as the official state ceremonial broke these ties of noh as representative of local religious realms. Because these noh troupes retained some affiliation with the shrines and temples, bringing them under the control of the shogun also brought the dominion of the shrines under control of the shogun. Accordingly, local sites of religious difference were reoriented to the center of a larger political space.

Nara, for example, as the capital of the eighth-century Yamato state, was one of the oldest extant imperial cities, and one of the most important centers of Buddhist temples and Shinto shrines. Two of the oldest forms of noh were connected with these: the Yamato *sarugaku* of the Kōfukuji temple, and the noh performed as part of the annual Wakamiya festival of the Kasuga

---

47. Nakamura Yasuo, *Noh* (New York: Walker/Weatherhill, 1971), 65–66.

shrine. The Tokugawa shogunate not only recognized both of these,[48] but in essence coopted them. As with most other official Tokugawa noh performances, licensed approval to hold them had to come from the shogunate. It was furthermore mandated that the representatives of each noh school who acted in these annual performances (all four schools were required to perform) must be head actors based in Edo—direct representatives, in other words, of the shogun. The ties and allegiances of the Kōfukuji and the Kasuga shrine to the Tokugawa shoguns were also demonstrated by the shogunate's sponsorship of these rites with annual allotments of rice.[49]

Local rites of religion, in particular those associated with the noh, were thus not suppressed in the Tokugawa shoguns' elaboration of political power. In fact many were encouraged by the shogunate. The Yamato *sarugaku* noh of the Kōfukuji itself became a fixed annual rite, performed "by rule of solemnity,"[50] only after the Tokugawa government made it so. But the reorientation of these rites carried out by their subjection to the Edo shogunate meant a loss of local, religious-based difference—here too, the construction of a geography of the Same—and, as part of this process, a reorientation of religion was brought into the service of a central, political seat of power.[51]

It is therefore not surprising that, as Tokugawa rule developed, even the local rites sponsored by the shogunate decreased in importance. This was the case with the Kōfukuji's *sarugaku* noh: while the shogunate had declared that all four troupes were to send their Edo actors to perform there, early on the Kanze school was exempted from this rule, and by a 1663 command, all Edo troupes were expected to have at least one actor remain in Edo during the annual Nara rites. The new place of religion in the Tokugawa order was exemplified by the construction of the Tokugawa shrine complex at Nikkō, just outside of Edo.

Nikkō

The divinity of Ieyasu as eternal founder, and Edo as foundation of the Tokugawa state took form with the shrine of Nikkō. Ieyasu stipulated on his

---

48. Initially the Kōfukuji's *sarugaku* was more popular and so was given greater attention. As it declined, the Wakamiya ritual noh had greater importance.
49. See NS I: 276–296, 429–430.
50. NS I: 70.
51. This pattern too, was duplicated at the level of local domain politics. The Maeda family, for example, sponsored the revival of temples in Kaga *han* which had been destroyed in the earlier warring years, and the noh rites performed in these temples, as a "politically astute measure" (see *Kanazawa no nōgaku*, 43–44).

deathbed that a shrine/temple be built at Nikkō to memorialize and deify him, and, according to some accounts, that his body should be moved there after one year. He was first buried in Sunpu, site of his first castle residence and the post of power to which he returned upon retirement from the Edo shogunate. One year later, in 1617, his body was transferred to the new Tōshōgū shrine in Nikkō. The shrine was then rebuilt and greatly enlarged by the third shogun, Tokugawa Iemitsu.

Although in Hideyoshi's case power-creating exchanges continued to involve the imperial court, the reconstruction of Nikkō as a Tokugawa shrine signified a move to recenter and redefine both imperial and religious power. The Tokugawa shogunate was certainly attempting to accrue something like an imperial form of power, as indicated by the shrine's blueprint. As Herman Ooms (largely following Asao Naohiro), Yūichiro Kōjiro, and others have pointed out, the shrine was in fact modeled directly after the relation between the imperial capital of Kyoto and the principal places of imperial religious affiliation: the Tendai Buddhist temple on Mount Hiei just outside of Kyoto, and the Shinto shrine at Ise. First, Ieyasu issued an edict which split the Enryakuji temple of Mt. Hiei into two, and located one in Edo. His son Hidetada then built the Kaneiji temple on the Edo site, to become the "Eastern Mount Hiei"—a Tokugawa family temple that would "protect the shogunal palace as Mount Hiei protected the imperial palace."[52] Tenkai, a Tendai monk in the service of the Tokugawa shogunate who helped initiate the new Tōshōgū shrine at Nikkō, justified its construction by the pattern of worship at Ise. Ise, he wrote, had been built to focus worship on the goddess Amaterasu to whom the imperial lineage traced its ancestry. And so, he argued, should the various places worshipping the deceased Ieyasu be concentrated in one place.[53] Nikkō was furthermore an appropriate site because it was located approximately the same distance from Edo as the imperial shrine of Ise was from Kyoto, and, perhaps to complete the parallel religious geography, the shrine was planted with the cypress trees, which were considered divine surroundings at Ise.

At the same time, the imperial family was taking on characteristics of the shogunal rule, even in its ritual. For instance, as mentioned above, early on in

---

52. Kōjiro Yūichiro, "Edo: The City on the Plain," in *Tokyo: Form and Spirit* (Minneapolis: Walker Art Center, 1986), 43; Herman Ooms, *Tokugawa Ideology* (Princeton: Princeton University Press, 1985), 175.

53. Asao Naohiro, *Nihon no rekishi*, *Sakoku* (Tokyo: Shōgakukan, 1975) 17: 276; Ooms, *Tokugawa Ideology*, 183.

the Tokugawa era the noh became an integral part of its enthronement ceremonies.[54] Still, the Tokugawa shrine at Nikkō (and the Kaneiji temple with which it was affiliated) was neither simply parallel to the imperial city nor a mere borrowing of imperial/religious elements. Instead it was a clear attempt to displace the ceremonial importance of Ise.

In 1645 the emperor granted Nikkō the highest shrine rank of *gu*, commanding that the shrine be worshipped, and reinstituted the practice of sending annual imperial envoys—now not only to Ise, but to Nikkō as well.[55] While the imperial envoys continued their annual visits to Nikkō throughout the Tokugawa era, the bakufu did not send emissaries to the imperial shrine at Ise. By 1647, the Tokugawa shogunate had the emperor's brother appointed *monseki* (priest prince) of Nikkō, in a joint abbotship over both Nikkō and the "Eastern Mount Hiei." In this way the emperor's brother was enlisted as the principal ritualist in the service of the shogun's new political regime,[56] and the religious powers of the imperial court were recentered, and redefined, as part of the political power of the shogun.

The shogunate expressed its hegemony over the imperial court in other ways as well. The shogunate's regulations for the court and nobles (*Kinchu narabini kugeshohatto*) issued in 1615, for example, removed the right of the court to make appointments of military men to court titles and require services of them. Samurai could still take court titles and ranks, but from the shogun, and with no obligations to the court. The same regulations gave the shogun the right to define the way era names would be given—formerly the sole dominion of the emperor. Furthermore, when Ieyasu ordered a statewide land survey, which included having all daimyo turn in their village registers and territorial maps to Ieyasu, he did so without using the imperial authority that had been previously required for such an undertaking. Definition of time and knowledge of space were taken into the purview of Ieyasu's sole authority.

As the edifice that memorialized and deified Ieyasu as the progenitor of this new authority, along with Edo castle, Nikkō was perhaps the most important political monument of the Tokugawa era. Nor was it merely a

---

54. One could in this sense draw some limited comparisons with the exchanges of sacerdotal and secular state insignia, titles, etc., in the formation of early modern absolutism in the West. See Ernst Kantorowicz, "Mysteries of State," in *Harvard Theological Review* 48 (1955), 65–91.
55. At the start of the Tokugawa era the imperial envoys were sent to all major temples, but quickly these visits were reduced to Ise and Nikkō, which suggests that these were the two most politically important centers of religion in the Tokugawa era. See Asao, *Nihon no rekishi*, 276.
56. Ooms, *Tokugawa Ideology*, 186.

means of expressing Ieyasu's already accomplished appropriation of power, or just an edifice expressing the legitimacy of his new state. With the construction of Nikkō, the Tokugawa shoguns were architecting themselves and creating the new space of power as in effect a new space of themselves—in a literal as well as a figurative sense. Again a comparison with a similar moment in the West is apt, as for example the case of Versailles: "one must analyze the palace of the King as the architectural device whereby the body of the King appropriates geographic-urban space. Through the palace, space is transubstantiated into a monarchic body, as original principle and unique or absolute power."[57] After Ieyasu's body was interred in the Tōshō shrine built for him, he was then referred to as *Tōshō daigongen* (東照大権現), the "Great Incarnation Shining over the East," a first step in transforming both Ieyasu and the space of power he had attempted to define. The shrine further enhanced Ieyasu with elements from the imperial court,[58] and both Shinto and Buddhist signs of divinity.[59] The divine cypresses planted in Ieyasu's name around the shrine complex physically marked off a boundary to the capital city, and the hundreds of cypresses lining the principal thoroughfare into the city appropriated this space as Ieyasu's own; a realm of, in a sense, Ieyasu.

If Nikkō thus located a representation of Ieyasu as the divine body of Edo, and in fact of all Japan and beyond, it also was meant to constitute the entire period of the Tokugawa reign as somehow defined by and as the identity of Tokugawa Ieyasu. Generations of shoguns visited the Tōshōgū or sent a proxy every month, on the anniversary date of Ieyasu's death. Tokugawa Yoshimune, according to one account, refused to sleep on the night before these visits, staying awake all night by telling his associates tales of Ieyasu, supposedly out of fear that if he did fall asleep and had a bad dream in connection with Ieyasu it would be polluting to their reign. The third shogun, Iemitsu, revered the "Tōshō Gongen" as his source of divine protection, and had portraits of Ieyasu painted which he kept either at Nikkō or on his own person, along with an amulet case containing a piece of paper describing himself as the "Second Gongen." Yoshimune, too, believed that simply con-

---

57. Marin, "The Architecture of the Prince," 178.
58. For example, the Yomeimon gate to his shrine was built with a special pillar taken from one of twelve at the imperial palace in Kyoto.
59. These included statues of Ieyasu as the avatar of the healing god Nyōrai; and even Ieyasu's divine name included clear reference both to Nyōrai and, through use of the same character for "shining" used in writing Amaterasu, to the Sun Goddess worshipped at the imperial shrine at Ise.

structing an atmosphere of recollection of Ieyasu would itself be enough to elicit the authority of the contemporary shogun's own person. As Tsuji Tatsuya notes, these anecdotes illustrate that along with the veneration of Ieyasu as a god was a certain "familiarity" with Ieyasu, "as if Ieyasu himself continued to be there."[60]

Nikkō, in other words, constructed a memory and a presence, and was monumental in this way as well. Ieyasu, as the Tōshō Daigongen, became at Nikkō a kind of mimetic presence that continued through the reign of successive Tokugawa shoguns. This mimetic presence was indicated, for instance, in Iemitsu's portraits of Ieyasu and his amulet papers identifying him with Ieyasu, and in Yoshimune's "atmosphere of recollection" of Ieyasu. It appeared throughout Japan, too, as in the "Tōshō Gongen" talismans affixed in castle towers, and the small shrines to Ieyasu that were worshiped by generations of heads of castles even in non-Tokugawa related domains.[61]

The form of this presence and memory was that of an eschaton. In the eschaton, experience is deferred in the direction of an origin and away from the present.[62] Because the origin is unshifting, it effects a closure over the space of power. The place of the origin and its fixity are therefore crucial; this may have been the reason that great care was exercised to maintain control over where and by whom these memorials to Ieyasu were erected. Numerous requests were made for permission to build local Tōshō shrines, but in the early Tokugawa period most were limited to the domains of the three Tokugawa branch houses. Asao lists an example of the bakufu initially refusing a request from the daimyo of Okayama, who was a brother-in-law of the shogun Iemitsu.[63] Therefore in this way too—by controlling the form and place of memory—care was exercised to secure Edo, and Ieyasu's identification with Edo, as the origin of Tokugawa rule, and as that which enacted closure over the structure of Tokugawa rule.

Nikkō, too, was integrated into the shogunal structure of the noh. Rather than the antique rites of *gagaku* and *bugaku* that continued to serve at the imperial shrine at Ise, the noh became the privileged form at Nikkō.[64]

---

60. Tsuji Tatsuya, *Kyōhō kaikaku no kenkyū* (Tokyo: Sōbunsha, 1963), 143–145.
61. See Asao, *Nihon no rekishi*, 278.
62. See Susan Stewart, *On Longing* (Baltimore: Johns Hopkins University Press, 1984), x. There is a specific historical form of desire implied here too, but that is outside the scope of the present argument.
63. Asao, *Nihon no rekishi*, 276, Ooms, *Tokugawa Ideology*, 184.
64. Well before the Tokugawas, the temples of the Nikkō complex were renowned for the collections of noh masks in their treasure houses.

Even the "God" (*waki*, ワキ or 脇) noh at the more traditional religious site of Nara was gradually demoted in favor of the God noh of the annual ceremonies at Nikkō. Furthermore, when the Tokugawa shoguns were inaugurated, they visited Nikkō, but only after a three-day public performance of noh. The employment of noh as a rite of investiture for all shoguns in this way approximated an enthronement ceremony (the term used—*tairei*, 大礼 —can mean "state ceremony" or "enthronement"), separate from and arguably supplanting the imperial rites and seat of power.[65]

The effect of this was the installation of a site which, if political, nevertheless was also divinely ordained and focused on a divine founder. The construction of the Kaneiji and the Tōshōgū at Nikkō attempted to define Ieyasu as the legitimate and true source, and therefore to identify Edo as the "proper" place, a point of absolute certainty for the shogunal representations of power. Located just outside the shogun's castle but connected to it with a cypress-lined thoroughfare, the shrine and its connecting thoroughfare helped to appropriate a new kind of space for the shogun. It formed an expansion of the space of the Tokugawas, connecting them and their castle to a more transcendent position. Further, by memorializing Ieyasu as a figure of absolute and ever-present origin, its apparent claim was to complete the Tokugawas' discourse of power. The building of Nikkō thus contributed to the totalization of the ideal Tokugawa plan of power. It also helped to reorder relations between preexisting places of power. It gave a new preeminence to the shogun and his rites over the imperial family and the imperial shrine at Ise. It was part of an increasingly systematized appropriation of varied local shrines and rites, now increasingly centered under the hegemony of the shogun. And, despite the importance of Nikkō, it was also part of an encompassment of religion into a largely civil government.

The Institutional Structure of Tokugawa Noh

The resulting image entailed a closed, controlled system of circulation focused on Edo, as for example with the regularized exchange between local provinces and the bakufu of noh actors and performances. I will return to the

---

65. Although it did not precisely construct a divine connection for the shogun in the way the enthronement ritual of a divine emperor or a king might, something like such a relation was constituted through the noh—including, for example, the association of the shoguns and the heads of noh schools with the God play *Okina*, which itself stood in a divine monarchical relation to the main categories of noh play types (it formed its own category of noh, transcendent to the others).

problem of limiting circulation in the discussion of economy (Chapter 2), but insofar as this image was also figured by the institutional structure of official noh, a brief description of the way it was reorganized by the Tokugawa shoguns is relevant here. Again, this seems especially important given the noh's position as one of the principal domains of custom through which essentially all leaders played out their expressions of power, and through which the Tokugawa shogunate was attempting to reimagine the state.

The noh as a performative genre was forced into a fixed and centered form at almost every level, with a convergence on the shogun and the city of Edo. The heads of the schools themselves were retained within the castle walls. Their social position was fixed: they were given samurai status, mansions in Edo for the principal actors, a rice stipend, and clothing. Their status was awarded by the shogun, and because they were technically not allowed to earn any other money or take gifts without approval from the bakufu, they were entirely dependent on the bakufu for both their place in society and their livelihood. Although their stipends were paid by the bakufu, all domains provided the bakufu a specific sum for this purpose, and so as with the building of Edo castle and Nikkō, the daimyo were made to contribute to the construction of the shogun's own representatives of power.

The positions of noh actors were made more rigid by laws stating that actors outside of the four official families were not considered legitimate noh actors. At the same time actors inside the four schools fell under the complete control of the shogunate. At the level of officially licensed noh, therefore, by recognizing only certain noh actors and families, including some sponsored by *tozama* daimyo (such as the Komparu family), one can again see the bakufu establishing a fixed geography of legitimacy. By making these positions hereditary, the bakufu created a structure of temporal permanence, or closed circulation in time.

These hereditary positions were themselves fixed and ranked in a hierarchy, according to role type: the families or houses which played the main roles (*shite*, シテ or 仕手) were ranked highest; then, in order, the houses which played "side" (*waki*, ワキ or 脇) roles; the accompanist (*tsure*, ツレ or 連れ) roles; the musicians, who were themselves ranked; followed by the comic actors (*kyōgen*, 狂言). Intricate hierarchies were further elaborated within each of these categories.[66] The headmasters (*iemoto*) of each of the four main families were all ostensibly of equal status, but one of the four was

---

66. See, for example, NS, I: 171–172.

always privileged by the shogun, and detained from their cyclical leave from the castle. Hence the principal figure of a countrywide hierarchy himself marked Edo and the shogun's castle as the source and center of the hierarchy.

Furthermore, outside of and above the official four-family organization of noh was a special status for an actor chosen by the shogun to be the shogun's own private performer, who would act only within the private spaces of the castle—never elsewhere, or for families other than the shogun's (the title was *rōkaban*, 廊下番, "corridor duty"). The chosen actor did not necessarily benefit from this position as it cut him off from peripheral sources of income, and from advancement within the noh hierarchies because he was no longer considered to be part of the official noh families. Yet because of its unique position, the *rōkaban* was also parallel to and representative of the Tokugawa shogun's own status as outside and transcendent of the country's five-class social structure.

Style, too, became a field for the construction of overarching control and permanence within the noh: with each of the four schools genealogically closed by governmental decree, play roles were then distributed only to noh actors who belonged to the four schools. Each school was further told that it must preserve its own tradition in an exact and unchanging form. According to a 1647 law, each of the noh families were required to "preserve" their own house trade style: "The passing on of the family traditions must not be neglected, the traditions of each school must be strictly adhered to, and no deviations should be allowed in performance. All matters concerning each troupe are the responsibility of the main actor of the troupe and should be under his strict control."[67] Each family's style was permanently concretized in newly printed librettos. By the second decade of the seventeenth century, a canonization of "traditional" noh plays had begun, and by the end of the century each family had provided the shogun with lists of the ritual noh plays that they could be expected to perform. Plays were classified into five fixed categories,[68] and a set scheme of play types for all performances was also defined. This crystallization of style, with minor differences defining each school, extended to every facet of the noh, including costuming, masks, the-

---

67. Omote Akira, and Amano Fumio, eds., *Nōgaku no rekishi nō kyōgen* (Tokyo: Iwanami Koza, 1988), II: 2; and quoted in Nakamura, *Noh*, 149.
68. God; warrior; woman or "wig"; monogurui "madness," "miscellaneous," or "contemporary"; and demon plays. A longstanding debate in the Japanese noh scholarship concerns whether these five categories existed before the Tokugawa period. There is little evidence of this classificatory scheme before the mention of the categories in the Tokugawa period *Nō hon sakusha chumon*, and in any event the categories were not fixed into law until the time of Tokugawa.

ater structure, etc. By assigning roles only to actors within the four schools, and by confining legitimate style to those schools, the shogunate organized control and closure over the circulation of noh practices.

The use of style to articulate Tokugawa hegemony has already been noted. The shogun's privileging of one *iemoto* over all others, and use of this school for all important ceremonial performances of state attended by all major daimyo meant that ultimately all were paying obeisance to the Tokugawa family's preferred noh style. Furthermore, whenever the daimyos hosted the shogun at their mansions, they entertained him with noh programs tailored to his tastes, thereby propagating standards set by Edo castle. By 1615, even the Komparu texts (used by actors in the *tozama* domain of Kaga, among other places) were being extensively edited to conform to the Tokugawas' preferred Kanze style. In this way, style helped to build a hierarchy into the landscape, and to amplify the Tokugawa identity within this landscape.

Finally, knowledge of the noh as institutionalized by the shogunate was a critical element in the formation and reproduction of this closed order. Just as noh actors and styles were bounded within the genealogies of the four schools, knowledge of each school's style was centralized, recorded, and delimited as a secret body to be revealed only to the actors within each school. *Iemoto* (heads of the noh schools) were commanded to be present at the written recording of all details of the art, including the repertoire of plays, the writers, history, and staging directions for each play, and an itemized list of all the masks, costumes, and other property owned by each troupe. This was done, in part, so that the actors could "perpetuate the art faithfully without deviation."[69]

This form of control over information also confirmed the *iemoto* as not only the absolute ruler of knowledge within his family, but also the source. Techniques were "revealed" to each actor only gradually over the course of their career, and the extent of this knowledge was limited according to the rank of the roles they would play. The *iemoto* held all of this knowledge and defined its authenticity or truth. Thus in Kita Hisayoshi's broad statement of noh theory, *Utaikyoku akumabarai* (1787), he wrote that the family head is himself the criterion of the "superb old knowledge;" and while a student may aspire to ultimately surpass his teacher in some way, this could only be a misapprehension of knowledge, which he would later regret.[70]

---

69. Nakamura, *Noh*, 136.
70. Quoted in *Nō kyōgen*, II: 103–106.

If the *iemoto* embodied knowledge in this way, control nevertheless ultimately rested with the shogun. Ieyasu's order for the documentation of all noh-related information gave control over that knowledge to the *iemoto*, but in the end to Ieyasu, allowing him to know each troupe "down to the smallest detail."[71] His command over the *iemoto*, who held the knowledge of each troupe, has already been described; this authority was formalized by his transfer of the management of noh actors from the comparatively unimportant actor's magistrate (*yakusha bugyō*) to the *wakadoshiyori* junior councillor, a position roughly equivalent to the current office for the prime minister.[72]

Secrecy can have similar effects of control, and secrecy was certainly part of the constitution of knowledge in the noh. Mandating that knowledge of the noh be kept secret, a closure of circulation was instituted (an essential characteristic of secrecy being the control of circulation). Because this knowledge was embodied first in the person of the *iemoto*, but finally in the shogun himself,[73] the shogun was constituted as the one who knows. All others were instituted in varying degrees of distance and difference from this apex of knowledge and truth, depending on their access to knowledge.[74]

The shogun theoretically knew everything down to the smallest detail; this was therefore a synoptic form of knowledge. This was equivalent to a more general construct of the Edo shogun as the embodiment of all knowledge of the state. The periodic investigations *(kakiage)* ordered by the shogunate into the minute details of each school of noh were in fact just one facet of a wider program of accumulating information on the occupations and family traditions of all the social classes.[75] In 1605, when Ieyasu relin-

---

71. Op cit, 136.
72. Kawatake Shigetoshi, *Nihon engeki zenshi* (Tokyo: Iwanami Shoten, 1960), 186.
73. It is significant that a copy of one of the most important and supposedly secret treatises on the noh, the *Kadenshō*, which had been in the keeping of the Kanze school since the middle ages, was handed over to be kept by Ieyasu. Recorded in NS, I: 3.
74. Secrecy can work only if others can in effect know what they do not know, or at very least know that they do not know. This does figure into the shogunal mode of power—see Chapter 3.
75. See NS, I: 362. The effort to accumulate information was not, however, limited to the bakufu. The emerging merchant class took it upon themselves to write, in the form of diaries, detailed accounts of the varied local customs, plans and projects, consumption habits, and so on. By the nineteenth century the desire for information had become strong enough that the writer of the *Fujiokaya nikki* paid informants for any kind of information whatsoever. See Moriya Katsuhisa, "Urban Networks and Information Networks," in *Tokugawa Japan* (Tokyo: University of Tokyo Press, 1990), 122. Literary diaries such as those left by Bashō, too, can be seen as part of this developing consciousness of a single knowable national space.

quished the office of shogun to his son, all daimyo were ordered to turn in all of their village registers and maps of their territories. While the emperor previously had the authority to request such maps and surveys, the shogun entirely assumed this authority.[76] Totalizing and homogenizing productions, surveys such as these also effect an image of mastery, of distanced observation—putting the observer in a position transcendent to the mapped order and in control of that order. Hence the shogun's hierarchically restrictive configuration of knowledge made him the ultimate embodiment and definition of knowledge, and helped to build the image of him as a transcendent master.[77]

The institutional order of noh formed roughly the same figure of representation as in the construction of Nikkō and the interchange of noh actors and performances: a totalizing system of controlled circulation.

The construction of a new metropole (Edo); the controlled circulation of noh actors and performances, involving both command by and flattery of the shogun; the "enthronement" and deification of the shogun by Nikkō; the establishment of controlled knowledge—all these helped to create the seat of the shogun (and the person of the shogun) as a proper place, from which Ieyasu could legitimately create and articulate his order of power. The result was a figure of space that included the transformation and extension of Ieyasu, and of all the Tokugawa shoguns, as bodies of power.

All of this constituted a performance of the conditions of power, in which the newly performed order substituted for the contingent conditions

---

76. The ability to compel a lord to prepare and present a map of his domain to the shogun was itself an expression of power. Thus, late in the Tokugawa era when the shogun's power began to weaken (at the time of the Tempo reforms, toward the mid-nineteenth century), the shogunate was unable to induce many lords to do this, and had to prepare revisions without their aid. Maps (*kuni ezu*) were prepared with great care, presented to the shogun with ceremony, and were kept in the shogunate's treasury and out of circulation.

The *kuni ezu* furthermore exemplified the growing homogeneity of space under the shogun's power. By the time of the Genroku revisions in the late seventeenth century, individual domain boundary lines were no longer included in the maps and a fixed scale of measure had been adopted and applied to maps of the entire country. On the *kuni ezu* see Kawamura Hirotada, *Edo bakufu sen kuni ezu no kenkyū* (Tokyo: Kokin Shoin, 1985).

77. This is an argument for at least the beginnings of a kind of panoramic cartographic knowledge that existed well before bird's-eye view maps of the nineteenth century. For a discussion of those maps, see Henry D. Smith, "World Without Walls: Kuwagata Keisai's Panoramic Vision of Japan," in Gail Bernstein and Haruhiro Fukui, eds., *Japan and the World—Essays on Japanese History and Politics in Honour of Ishida Takeshi* (London: The Macmillan Press, 1988). Synoptic knowledge, however, is not necessarily the same thing as panoramic knowledge (which among other things involves a separation from the object of knowledge).

of its production.[78] Thus at Nikkō, the memorializing of Ieyasu as divine, and therefore the legitimate author and authority of the Tokugawa space of power, also involved a forgetting of Ieyasu's earlier genealogies, including his previous position as head of only one of many warrior factions with equal claims to power, and beholden both to Hideyoshi and to imperial power.

The noh helped to make conventional a new political form and articulate it as part of the expanding geography of Japan. It instituted a single space of sameness, with the shogun as the place of authority and authorship. Thus the title Ōgosho (大御所), or, "Great Honorable Place" was given to the retired shogun, who despite being retired was still considered the most important political person. This political form created a closed hierarchy of relations, cut off from any appearance of transformative potential in society. These were therefore temporal as well as spatial relations.

Noh Time

"Utopia knows nothing of time, and the only time it knows is the rhythmic cycle of rituals, celebrations and accomplishments. These are immobile times and temporal images of eternity."[79]

From the start of his reign, Tokugawa Ieyasu acted to organize an absolutist state, one that would be "governed in perpetuity by the Tokugawas." Hence, from the start, the shogunate legislated against change. At least as indicated by the terms of an essential document known as the *Buke sho hatto* (Rules for Military Houses), which was reaffirmed on the accession of each new shogun, "change" meant "revolt."[80] The maintenance of political control over change and time, and over any change as a true revolt, was also the role of noh.

Nearly all shoguns held private, unofficial performances for entertainment, often at impromptu moments, and sometimes with great frequency. The ninth shogun Ieshige, for instance, would go from one banquet to another in different sections of the castle and have a noh performance at each; in some months he held forty-five or more performances.[81] These were considered informal, generally were held on the stage located in the "inner"

---

78. In this sense it is fictional—see de Certeau, *The Practice of Everyday Life*, Part II (and especially Chapter 5).
79. Louis Marin, *Utopics*, xxiv.
80. Quoted in George Sansom, *A History of Japan 1615–1867* (Stanford: Stanford University Press, 1963), 7–8. See Chapter 3 for a discussion of the terms for change or transformation—*henshin* and *henge*—used in noh and kabuki.
81. NS, I: 176.

castle (中奥, *nakaoku*), and only for private audiences. Some Tokugawa shoguns attempted to restrict or stop these private performances, but all insisted on the importance of maintaining formal, official noh.

First, a brief description of the principal genres of official noh—*machi-iri*; *shogun senge iwai*; *utaizome*; *matsubayashi*; *kanjin*; and *takigi* noh—keeping in mind that these categories were relatively unfixed with considerable overlap among them.

Machi-iri (町入り) noh, or "town-entering noh" was held within the precincts of the shogun's or daimyo's castle, and was the single occasion when townspeople were allowed into the castle grounds to see performances. Such performances were largely connected with the life cycle events of upper officials: a promotion; the birth or coming of age ceremony of a son; and at the highest level, the investiture of a new shogun or the death or birth of a new emperor. These performances typically lasted one to five days. For the longer performances marking more important occasions, the first day was considered the most formal, and the most important persons—members of the imperial court, high level *fudai* daimyo—attended on this day. It was also, however, the day on which commoners were always invited in.

Shogun senge iwai noh (将軍宣下祝い, "shogunal proclamation noh") was in effect a specific form of the machi-iri. It was a congratulatory/celebratory performance given at the start of the reign of a new shogun, and so marked a larger time segment than most of the others. Such performances almost always lasted five days.

Prior to the Tokugawa period, *kanjin* (subscription) noh was a means of raising funds for building or rebuilding temples, shrines, and bridges. Patronizing such performances had religious undertones of accumulating good karma for the afterlife. By the Tokugawa era, however, *kanjin* were either rather insignificant, single-day performances held by a noh school in need of cash, or, of far greater importance, to mark the pinnacle of the career of the principal noh family's *iemoto*. The latter were called "once-in-a-generation" noh. Including the Kōka noh, only six were allowed during the 250 years of Tokugawa rule.[82] These *kanjin* noh were public performances, held just outside the grounds of Edo castle. The last three of the Tokugawa era were given fifteen clear-weather days of noh, spread over weeks or even months.

---

82. There are debates as to whether all of these can be classified as true once-in-a-generation performances. See Ikeuchi, NS I, 200.

Utaizome (謡初, first singing) and *matsubayashi* (松囃, pine singing)[83] referred to the annual New Year's ceremonial noh, held on the third day of the first month. This was one of the most important of all the annual rites, and was attended by all important daimyos as well as representatives of the imperial court. It began with the shogun entering and commanding a view of the Grand Hall of the main castle, and then greeting the noh school heads (*iemoto*) of the three Tokugawa branch families. After commanding the principal noh *iemoto* to begin the performance, which centered on the "auspicious God" play *Takasago,* gifts were distributed first to the actors and later to the daimyos—an exchange which confirmed both the shogun's right to mark the new year and the daimyos' accession to this calendar.[84]

Takigi (薪, bonfire) noh was the name reserved for an annual outdoor ritual associated with the Kofuku temple and the Kasuga shrine in Nara. The continuation of this ritual indicates that the shogunate gave some latitude to Nara, which remained an important religious center. Yet noh actors needed permission to leave Edo to perform in it, and actors "on duty" in Edo were not given leave.

It is already visible from this outline that, in the Tokugawa regime, the noh served to identify a calendar, mapping the coordinates or events of a stable order of time within which social action would take place—a "time of social representing."[85] Defining events as moments of change or potential change, the noh marked nearly all such moments of transition and change that were significant to the shogunal order. For example, noh performances were held for the construction of new buildings, such as a mansion or castle (including in the various domains, as in the case of Maeda Toshitsune's castle); the birth of a shogun's heir, as in the birth of Iemitsu's son; the death of a shogun or an emperor; the embarkation of a shogun on a trip—when the shogun was traveling to Nikkō, for example, his palanquin was first blessed with a "longevity" or *hoide* noh; or the promotion of a bakufu administrator. Furthermore, this delineation of official moments was hierarchical, with the least significant generally being accorded the least number of noh plays. Thus the promotion of a bakufu official might be given a fairly short performance,

---

83. Or "pine dancing," 松拍子. The pine tree is a symbol of longevity.
84. With this power to define time, the relationship with *tozama* daimyo was important. Accordingly at these ceremonies, gifts to the Maeda family from Kaga were said to have piled up especially high. NS I:177.
85. Cornelius Castoriadis, *The Imaginary Institution of Society,* trans. by Kathleen Blamey (Cambridge, Massachusetts: MIT Press, 1987); see especially pp. 209–215.

Locating Tokugawa Power / 57

while the program of plays celebrating the investiture of a shogun, or the death of an emperor, would last for four or five days. In this way, the noh delineated a hierarchical organization of acts, moments, and events, in which the most significant was generally the most official (that is, closest to the shogun), and the least significant was not indicated by the noh at all (that is, did not figure into the time of representation at all).

This order of time was also increasingly national and homogenizing. Prior to Ieyasu and the Tokugawa state, the *utaizome* and the *matsubayashi* rites marking the official start of the new year were not yet unified. The *matsubayashi* consisted of noh troupes traveling from villa to villa to perform, but only for a select group of daimyo within the Ashikaga realm of power and on dates varying from region to region.[86] By integrating the *matsubayashi* into the annual New Year's *utaizome* first singing rites in Edo, which was attended by important figures from throughout the country, Tokugawa Ieyasu brought that local calendar under the compass of his time. The entire country now celebrated one official calendar, the defining moment of which was situated in the shogun's castle. In this way as in others, the noh was an extension through time of Tokugawa Ieyasu's political sphere.[87]

Along with the emplotment of significant moments of change, official noh also involved the surmounting of any real change—at critical moments of change, the noh enacted a transcendence of change. This is connected to a problem of political rule. For a regime that claimed to be eternal, "governed in perpetuity" by the Tokugawas, a paradox arises at transitional moments such as the transfer of rule from one shogun to the next. There is a clear need for a change of identities (otherwise rule would end with the existing leader's death), yet this rule must be represented as a regime of one unchanging identity. This contradiction is solved by a temporality of repetition, in which change becomes a reiteration of that which was. That is what the official noh performances accomplished. Just as the noh contributed to the expansion of Ieyasu's own identity across the physical geography of Japan, so too it thereby configured a temporal order through which a unitary Tokugawa identity extended.

---

86. See NS, I: 178–179.
87. Here, too, remained some expressions of local independence. Many lords continued to hold their own *utaizome* celebrations in addition to attending the shogun's, and in the case of the domain of Kaga, they did not rename their own *matsubayashi* rite an *"utaizome"* until 1830, nearly the end of the Tokugawa period. Nevertheless, even those daimyo who did hold their own *utaizome* often held them at their mansions in Edo. See for example *Kanazawa no nōgaku*, 42–43, 167, 338.

This is essentially a mimetic, or specular, order of rule. There were historical precedents for this, as in the use of mirrors by fourth-century monarchs for distribution to leaders within their sphere of influence. The mirror in that case was a concrete expression that the political authority being extended outward by the monarch was identical to, although separate from, himself. This also fit the image of the transfer of authority and of temporal change suggested by the reconstructions of the shrine at Ise. Every twenty years, the shrine housing the sacred mirror, which was said to embody the sun goddess Amaterasu, or her power, is rebuilt, but in a precise mirror image on a plot directly facing that of the shrine which is taken down. Change and the transfer of rule were indicated by an inversion, yet still constituted an invocation of, and an exact continuance of, the same. As an order of history, it implies a time without any real alteration.

The Tokugawas drew on these precedents, as in the construction of Nikkō, which was as renowned for its collection of early Japanese mirrors as for its noh masks.[88] Also, when the third shogun Iemitsu in 1636 ordered the reconstruction of Ieyasu's shrine, part of the rationale was that twenty years had passed since Ieyasu's first shrine had been built, and so a new shrine should be built following the same cycle as at Ise.[89] Iemitsu himself not only revered Ieyasu's image, but also carried a sheet of paper describing himself as the "second Gongen," a mimetic incarnation of his grandfather.

As a memorial, Nikkō took the form of a monument which can be understood as what Marin calls "a transcendental permanence founding all presence."[90] Ieyasu's entombed and deified body legitimated the presence of the present; the present was defined by an eternal origin, which was the deified Ieyasu. Thus Yoshimune's belief that the simple presence of memory of Ieyasu was enough to confirm each shogun's own authority.

In the noh itself this overcoming of difference and change by the renewal and re-presenting of the same is perhaps easiest to see in the annual New Year's "ritual" noh (*shiki noh*, 式能) of the *utaizome*. The auspicious *shūgen* plays typically performed at this time were believed to ritually reinitiate a world of eternal good. The simple utterance of these plays' lines was said to reinstitute an unchanging "wise rule," and give it divine sanction. Each per-

---

88. Okuda Yuzuru et al., eds., *Nikkō sono bijutsu* (Kyoto: Tanko-shinsha, 1962), 143–144.
89. Ooms, *Tokugawa Ideology*, p. 183. The new Tōshōgū, however, was not a mirror image of its predecessor at all, but was rather a much more opulent construct.
90. Marin, "The Architecture of the Prince," 178.

formance, therefore, denoted the year's change with a reinstatement of the same order of the good.

With the *utaizome*, as with the presence of Ieyasu's body at Nikkō, the shogun or domain lord always legitimated the time being ritually enacted. A true *utaizome* was limited to the occasion of the New Year, and to celebrations during which the lord himself was at very least within the borders of his province.[91] The ruler, in other words, was the initiator or source of this time;[92] the identity of time throughout the realm was that of the ruler. The expanding jurisdiction of the *utaizome*, covering all of the new Japanese state, was therefore part of the expanding legitimacy of Tokugawa identity.

Finally, the progression of time organized by the *utaizome*, and by the noh in general, was nonlinear. All aspects of the noh were believed to follow the principle of *jo-ha-kyū* (序 破 急 , "introduction/preface," "break," and "speed"), an aesthetic which describes an endless series of cycles moving from the first to the last and then back to the first. This was considered to apply to the New Year's rites as well; in fact it applied to everything since it was "a universal organizational principle for all things existing in time."[93] Hence the ritual calendar of the shogunate's noh was based on the cyclical renewal of a closed order of time, the origins of which were located in a noncontingent, transcendent past—one utopically free of history, and eternal.[94] With every renewal, the originary past was rendered immanent in the present, and the present order rendered incontestably correct. It allowed for a temporal progression, but only in terms of a cycle which, at the start of each new year, would return to the same place. Consequently, if performances of the noh were used to recognize moments that would be "events," the noh constituted such moments as part of an unchanging and repetitive cycle. "Event" here took the paradoxical form of the eruption of the same.

The temporal cycles of noh thus created an official statewide order of time. Yet this order also was given the integrity of being a mode of the cosmic or of cosmic change. The calendar that the Tokugawa shogun instituted with each year's *utaizome* therefore governed not merely the state, but the entire universe. According to Zeami, heaven established the world according to the rhythms of five "modes of cosmic change." These modes of cosmic change

---

91. *Kanazawa no nōgaku*, 92.
92. Thus it was always the lord's own actor who performed first in the *utaizome*.
93. Thomas Hare, *Zeami's Style* (Stanford: Stanford University Press, 1986), 294.
94. Thus the ritual objects used were given names such as the "Isle of Eternal Youth," a dipper for the ritual *sake*.

define all life, Zeami wrote, including the four seasons. They are of heavenly provenance—brought to earth through the dance of angels—and as principles extend to the bodies of all sentient beings. The five modes correspond to "five storages" in all sentient beings: the heart, lungs, spleen, liver and kidneys, which were said to be activated as the body moves in the dance of the noh.[95] Perhaps because the noh in this way realized proper cosmic order, practicing the noh was thought to both keep one physically healthy and be a cure for one's illnesses. Here too, cosmic "change" seems to imply the transcendence of any real alteration, in part by marking off any moments of possible change in the good and proper order of things. For instance when the shogun Iemitsu fell ill, noh was offered both at the moment of his illness and at the time of his recovery. Similarly, a noh play was held when the shogun had an inauspicious dream.

The noh was nonetheless an order of the state. The eighteenth-century geographer Hayashi Shihei wrote in *Fukeikun* that to detest the noh was "like rebelling against the entire order of Japan." Moreover, as a cosmic order both natural and divine, the musical instruments of noh, Hayashi said, form "the brilliant sounds of Japanese nature," and in noh music, "divine will and human will are together fulfilled."[96] The resulting image is a comprehensive law of similarity, a law of natural correspondences ruling both state and nature.[97] Thus in this image the acting out of noh, and the recitation of felicitous words, physically resuscitated the good, natural order, including good health and a good reign. It may be for this reason that the only words spoken by the lord of Kaga at his *utaizome* were that the weather is good, and thus the course of events throughout his reign would be good.[98]

The noh created an image of Ieyasu and Edo as autochthonous. Edo was a place of Ieyasu's own, not located by ties to earlier or other structures of power, and a place from which, as the only legitimate source, he appeared to exercise absolute closure. Similarly with the time of noh: the present or "now" is found in Ieyasu himself or in his ever-present memory, and in each of the Tokugawa shoguns. This place of the now does not shift or unfold in a

---

95. See Rimer and Yamazaki, *On the Art of the Noh Drama*, 77–78.
96. Hayashi referred also to the tea ceremony, giving it nearly as much importance as the noh. 『日本に生まれてこの二つを一円に忌み嫌ふは、日本の制に背くに似たり。』『大胴・小胴・太鼓・笛のはげしき大音は、日本自然の英音にして、神慮にも人慮にもよく相叶ふ。。。』Reproduced in *Nō kyōgen* II:394.
97. On the idea of a comprehensive law of similarity, see Benjamin, "On the Mimetic Faculty," in *Reflections*, 333–336.
98. Quoted in *Kanazawa no nōgaku*, 107.

linear representation of time, but rather is cyclically reestablished, in and by the place of the shogun, as in the examples of the shogun's annual *utaizome*, or his deified presence in Nikkō. In this sense, borrowing from de Certeau, the shogunate used the noh to create an absolute mastery over time through the founding of an autonomous place.[99]

Edo Castle and the Dream of Nikkō

In the broadest of terms, in the descriptions above the problem of Tokugawa power has largely been framed as a matter of locating relations among sites. As defined thus far, the mastery of these relations would seem to be complete. There was certainly a level of independence left for individual domain leaders, but overall, at least as seen in the institutionalized world of official noh, the position of Tokugawa hegemony appears firm. With relatively closed circulations between positions in space and events in time, the picture is one of a world coming to itself, or a world fully at one with itself. It is in this way an absolute image, if not a utopic one, without the tensions and contradictions that remained at the heart of Hideyoshi's image of power. This would be a world of reproduction without change.[100]

Yet this was not so straightforwardly a closed mimetic order. In fact the primary sites of Tokugawa rule show a much more complex relation to each other and to the certainty and unity of the Tokugawa image as a whole.

The embodiment of authority in the shogun's capital was in effect divided into two locations: Edo castle in the center of the city, and the Nikkō shrine complex at its boundaries. This can partly be read as emblematic of the opposition between and combination of the shogun's military-political and religious-spiritual forms of power. Beyond this distinction, though, which is in any event reductive, the castle and Nikkō raise important questions regarding the status of representation—including the place and operation of fantasy within Tokugawa representations of power.

Both the castle and Nikkō do have utopic qualities, as elements of a new and as-yet unknown world. This was not the first such gesture. The construction of Azuchi castle by Oda Nobunaga, Hideyoshi's predecessor who is generally thought of as the first to attempt a reunification of the Japanese state, was a similar act.

---

99. de Certeau, *The Practice of Everyday Life*, 36.
100. By Marin's description of utopic space-time, this might also be considered utopic: "utopia's a-temporality signifies constant space, a perpetual now, a permanence of the identical." See Marin, *Utopics*, xxvi.

Azuchi castle was evidently meant to be the base and centerpiece of Nobunaga's regime. No longer a castle built with strictly military purposes in mind, it was by all accounts a structure of true grandeur. At the highest level of the castle and just above a floor devoted entirely to Buddhist themes, Nobunaga commissioned a room without any precedent. The room was perfectly square, apparently a construct of moral rectitude. Entirely lacquered in black, the room's walls were covered with paintings that, to quote Carolyn Wheelwright's description, "following a chronological progression from the sage-kings of the mythical past through historical paragons of virtue to Confucius, [were] the codifier of a political system based on the integrity of a wise ruler." The room accomplished "a spatial transformation. The theme of a Utopia decreed by a prince sublimely confident of his mission to reunite and revivify the Japanese realm—that is to say establish his own new order, the Tenka [empire, state]."[101]

According to Wheelwright, this room and the castle as a whole heralded the start of a new age of (monumental) architecture. Nikkō might seem to fit the architecture of this new age, but there was a fundamental difference. It is possible to view Nikkō as the same kind of utopic or fantastic place relative to Edo castle that the top floor room was to Azuchi castle, but unlike the Azuchi room, Nikkō is separate from Edo castle.[102] This is part of a newly distinguished spectacular form of power, a "spectacle" both in the sense of an extraordinary display and something which initiates a division, as between viewer and viewed.

The temples and shrines at Nikkō are replete with utopian symbols and metaphors of a harmonious realm and uncharted, fantastic alterity. The gates to Ieyasu's Tōshō shrine are carved with images of some of the same Chinese sage rulers seen in Nobunaga's castle, as well as Chinese "otherworldly" persons (*sennin*, 仙人). They also contain a "phantasmagoric profusion" of lion- and elephant-like creatures, peonies, and so on.[103] Nikkō's bright colors are baroque: "intensified, heightened, deployed to the full, 'monumentalized,'

---

101. In Elison and Smith, *Warlords, Artists, and Commoners*, 110. Some of the best research on the architecture of Azuchi castle remains that of Naitō Akira. See Naitō, "Azuchi-jō no kenkyū," in *Kokka*, nos. 987 and 988 (February and March, 1976).
102. The castle at Azuchi had its own divides, too, however, including distinctions between public and private, official and nonofficial, and religious versus secular spaces. It is also worth noting that an atrium extended up though much of the castle, and a noh stage was built so that it alone extended out into the open atrium. It was therefore the one point visible from all the main lower floors, and thus was a point of mediation for all of them.
103. Okawa Naomi, *Edo Architecture* (New York: Weatherhill, 1975), 79.

simply because, if imagination is something which goes beyond reality, the embodiment of its images must go beyond the norms of visual experience."[104] Now often dismissed by art historians as mere gaudiness, perhaps the point of Nikkō's ostentatious color scheme was that it was truly novel.

Architecturally, some of the buildings were designed in a "Chinese"-like style (*karayō*, 唐様), but a "*karayō*" that was considered unlike any previously seen or known Chinese style. Despite being patterned in some ways after other shrines and temples, these structures were a new, "altogether different" mode of religious architecture.[105] Nikkō drew on received images of otherworldliness—the worlds of China, mythology, and religion—but even these were cast in a new, unprecedented vision.

As a site of fantasy, Nikkō bears comparison to a Foucauldian heterotopia and its relation to utopias.[106] Foucault describes utopias in much the same terms that have been raised in this paper: utopias present society in a perfected if sometimes inverted form, but they are fundamentally unreal places, sites without any real place. Nikkō did present images of a perfectly harmonious rule, as in the motifs of eternally good and wise governance represented by the Chinese sages, and in its very explicitly unique constructions of otherworldly themes, Nikkō did envision a placeless place. For these reasons, it might be considered utopic. Yet, Nikkō was also a real place, and in this sense fits Foucault's idea of a heterotopia: an "effectively enacted utopia," a "counter-site" which is somehow other to the sets of social relations it designates. While outside of all other places, the heterotopia is nonetheless linked to them and has a specific location in reality.

The experience that unites the utopia and the heterotopia, for Foucault, is that of a mirror. The mirror opens up a placeless place (in a mirror, one is able to see oneself in a place where one is not), and so is utopic. However, the mirror exists in reality, which is where one's image is seen. One therefore only begins to reconstitute oneself—there where one actually stands—through the redirection of one's gaze back toward oneself from this virtual image on the other side of the glass.

In these terms Nikkō was both utopic and a heterotopic place. Outside the capital and separated from the shogun's seat of power at the castle, it was the place of fantasy visualizing the image of perfect rule. Thus after the public

---

104. Argan, 1964, p. 55, speaking of the baroque era in Europe. Guilio Carlo Argan, *The Baroque Age* (Geneva: Skira, 1989), 55.
105. Yajima Kiyofumi, *Nikkō tōshōgū* (Tokyo: Shakai shisō kenkyūkai, 1962), 18.
106. Michel Foucault, "Of Other Spaces," in *Diacritics* 16 (1986), 22–27.

machi-iri noh ceremonies in the castle to celebrate a shogun's official investiture, the country's rulers proceeded to Nikkō to worship the perfect, deified form of the first shogun, and by extension, all Tokugawa shoguns.

This again raises the prospect that official Tokugawa rule might be understood as a closed, specular order of power. Nikkō, with its images of the Tōshō Daigongen, might be thought of as reflecting back to the shogun in Edo castle a pure image of divinity. Transcendent spiritual divinity and everyday military authority, Nikkō and Edo castle, thus would be conflated in a utopic unity.

The specular qualities of authority associated with Nikkō itself have been described earlier in this chapter. Not only were mirrors used as the icons of divinity, but the godly essence of Ieyasu as founder of the Tokugawa realm was at least in some ways felt to be mirrored in Iemitsu and the succeeding shoguns. The deified portrait of Ieyasu was, furthermore, placed in shrines throughout the state, and revered there by a large number of domain lords. Judging by these conditions, Nikkō's relation to Edo castle would seem to indicate a neat, directly mimetic closure of modes of authority (military and divine), as well as the spatial and temporal relations of authority that governed the state as a whole.

At question here, both in the relation between the shrines at Nikkō and the castle at Edo and in the godly portrait of Ieyasu, is the status not only of Tokugawa rule, but also of the governing mode of representation—the status of the ruling image. The picture thus far would seem to be that of an order that is utopic in its concordance between transcendent and practical positions of power, and striving toward absolutism as a mode of rule. But as in the example of Hideyoshi that began this chapter, the unity was not so complete.

The shogun's castle at Edo was clearly a central site of power, that—as in the countywide circulations of domain lords and noh actors that focused on Edo—claimed for primacy even over the imperial household in Kyoto. Edo castle may have retained some connotation of the military means by which the Tokugawa family came into rule, but for the most part it was an administrative and ceremonial capital. There, the Tokugawa shoguns' authority rested less on the exercise of military might, and more on the appearance of a given structural legitimacy. The cycles of noh actors and performances between outlying domains and Edo castle, and the *sankinkōtai* system of revolving all lords between their domains and the city of Edo—these practices made Edo, and the shogun, the focal point of centrality and the governing position of rule. The shogun's authority thus appeared to derive from these formal practices. As a ruler, he was produced as a construct of the given system. The castle itself can be seen in the same way: with the massive stones and labor for the castle supplied by lords from throughout the state, the shogunal place of power was literally a product of discursive order of the new state. As an effect of, or an object of, the given order, the legitimacy of the shogun was thus secure. Furthermore, given that the spatial and temporal relations formed by the noh were described as natural and cosmological, so too the shogun's position was naturalized as part of the constitutive essence of the world.

At the same time, however, this was a newly imagined world, a realm of the Tokugawas. Practices such as official noh, the *sankinkōtai* system, or the building of the castle may have helped to put out of view the more contingent conditions of Ieyasu's military accession to power, giving him a naturalized legitimacy, but Ieyasu's authority nonetheless also consisted of his role as the creator and origin of this world. It is well known that Ieyasu and the first Tokugawa shoguns set out an entirely new, fixed social hierarchy (with samurai meant to be the highest class, and merchants the lowest) at the same time that they were reformulating political relations. For these relations to have the force of the real—for these relations to seem not only legitimate, but in a more basic way true and real and even just thinkable—some creative force behind these new relations had to be identifiable. Ieyasu had to show himself as this creative element. The dilemma is therefore roughly the same as it was for Hideyoshi. The legitimacy of Ieyasu and the Tokugawas in general depended in part on being objects of the discursive order; the order constructed them, and gave them the legitimate place from which to act and to rule. Tokugawa power in that sense owed nothing to contingency, to the conditions that gave rise to their power. Yet as a new and specifically Tokugawa world, the guarantee of its legitimacy and authenticity rested on Tokugawa Ieyasu as its founder. Ieyasu thus had to be exhibited as creator of, and therefore external to, the same structure that discursively gave him the position of power and the ability to act.

It is the latter image of Ieyasu that was embodied in Nikkō. In contrast to Edo castle, which by its centrality within the Edo-era circulation of things placed the shoguns in the position of rulership, the shrines at Nikkō were a site of transcendence. Nikkō was physically located well outside the shogun's capital city and apart from the flow of everyday activity; one could argue that that was already a position of externality and transcendence. More importantly, Tokugawa Ieyasu was entombed at Nikkō and exhibited there as a god and, more specifically, as the divine origin of the Tokugawa realm. The inherent contradictions of Tokugawa power were thus expressed in the principal sites of Tokugawa power. The castle was part of an ongoing statewide system that showed no connection to any finite historical moment of fabrication. It was the focal point of an order that was simply there, and should always be there. The shogun himself was an objective construct of this order. At Nikkō, on the other hand, Ieyasu's power was shown to be transcendent of the given order of things, and there, as the subject or instigator of the Tokugawa realm, he had to be revealed precisely as its ground of possibility.[107]

Nor could these contradictions completely be reconciled in the figure of Ieyasu himself. As described above, Tokugawa power did still need an element of transcendence, and transcendence in the form of the divine. There remained a place of sacrality in the Tokugawa era that, like Hideyoshi's self-deifications, promised to effect a closure of the larger order of power. That would seem to be the role of Nikkō, and the identity of Ieyasu as the *Tōshō Daigongen*, revered at Nikkō's Tōshōgū shrine. Had the unqualified deification of Ieyasu really been possible, and true belief in him as a divinity still been possible—or, in other words, had it really still been possible to conceive of Ieyasu as the divine representative of Tokugawa authority—then this reconciliation would have been possible. Within the order of Tokugawa rule, Nikkō would have reflected a vision of the Tokugawas as not only political, but also as divine, perfect rulers. The utopic closure of this world, by and around the Tokugawas, would have appeared complete.

However, that was not the case, either at the castle or at Nikkō itself. In fact the images of Ieyasu enshrined at the Tōshōgū were not true portraits of Ieyasu as a god, nor were they depictions of Ieyasu drawn after his living person. Instead, they were "dream portraits"—godly depictions of Ieyasu *as dreamt by* his grandson Iemitsu, the third Tokugawa shogun. This is not to say that Ieyasu's divinity was "just" a dream for the Tokugawas, in the sense of a false belief. By most accounts, Iemitsu truly felt that Ieyasu had come to him, as a divine presence, in his dreams. Nonetheless, the images were not direct portraits of Ieyasu as an actual god. A genre of such paintings did exist, but

---

107. This opposition of the shogun's castle and Nikkō is a reduction of complex relations. There were times at the castle, for instance, when the shogun did want to appear as the manifest source of all order, and there were aspects of the imagery at Nikkō which made the shoguns out to be mere objects of representation. However, this simply means that the contradictory need for the Tokugawas to be both subject and object of their world, visible in the relation between the castle and Nikkō, was also visible within the practices at each location.

that was not what Iemitsu asked to have painted, and that is not what was worshipped at the Tōshōgū.[108] Accordingly, the figure enshrined at the Tōshōgū is neither the worldly Ieyasu, nor his deified being (the *Tōshō Daigongen*), but rather what the headings on each of the portraits explicitly define as the "*Musō*" (夢想; "dream," but also "fantastic," "utopic") *Tōshō Daigongen*.[109]

This was not, therefore, an image that could wholly resolve the political character of Ieyasu into a god. Nor was Ieyasu a divinity in such a way that succeeding shoguns might have been thought to be actual reinstantiations of him. Later shoguns did continue to worship him though, and Iemitsu did at times believe Ieyasu was "with" him. As a dream image of a god rather than a god, Ieyasu thus did not effect a utopic—or absolute—closure over the Tokugawa realm. The efficacy consisted instead of this "dream" (*musō*) of absolute closure.

The image of Ieyasu venerated as the founder of the Tokugawa order required an element of transcendence, yet could not be fully a divinity. The overall image of Ieyasu—the ruling form of representation of Ieyasu, and by extension, of the Tokugawa regime in general—was hence riven by conflict and contradiction in the same way that was visible in the contrast between Edo castle and Nikkō.

The composition of Tokugawa power, and the status of Ieyasu as a figure of unity, can also be understood in terms of the kinds of spectatorship that came to be associated with the castle and with Nikkō. This returns the discussion to practical social form.

Although originally commoners were allowed into Edo castle for the machi-iri noh performances, they were ostensibly excluded from entering "to offer and pray" at Nikkō's new Tōshōgū. Only the country's rulers and highest officials were to be permitted in to worship at Nikkō—both after the public noh rites at the castle and at all other times. Yet less than twenty years after its reconstruction, the bakufu was actively encouraging common people to

---

108. Photos of these are reproduced in *Tokugawa Iemitsu kōden* (Tokyo: Akiyoshi Insatsu, 1962), starting on p. 168. Another common motif is the *baku*, a beast apparently modeled after a tapir and said to consume bad dreams. For a survey of some of these portraits in English, see Karen M. Gerhart, "Visions of the Dead."

109. The complicated connection between dream images and the eternity of a perfect reign was also seen elsewhere as in the "dream-*renga*" poems. Although *renga* were traditionally an open-ended form of poetry, this genre was less so, and apparently included the use of metaphors from nature (such as everlasting "pine flowers" and generations of bamboo) to invoke images of eternity. These were composed by the shoguns and/or daimyo during the night in front of the gate at the Tōshōgū in Nikkō, and at the inner Tōshōgū shrine within the castle. See *Tokugawa Iemitsu kōden*, 448, for examples from 1629 and 1642. This is discussed further in Chapter 3.

come, in order to "display [Nikkō's] magnificent splendor" to the commoners.[110] There was, however, a basic difference: visits by upper class persons were still known as "*Nikkō mairi*" (日光参り; the verb *mairu* indicates a visit to a shrine or temple for worship or other religious purposes), and visits by commoners were officially called "*kenbutsu*" (見物, sightseeing, or spectating; it can also be used when referring to attending the theater).

Although apparently incompatible, at Nikkō both experiences were, logically, going on simultaneously, on the same stage. As the ruling class worshipped, the commoners were sightseeing, so that they were spectators of the rulers' worship. While the upper class veneration of Ieyasu may have produced an image of the Tokugawas as godly, the commoners' lack of belief presumably would have the opposite effect. But by their very curiosity and willingness to be spectators, the commoners were in effect acknowledging those rulers as the rightful occupants of the place of power—godly or not. It is in the nature of the spectacle and of spectating that the spectator is separated from the object of the spectacle, and this distance from the object of spectacle only enhances the spectators' respect and desire for that distanced object. Thus, within the commoners' spectatorial mode of experience of the Tōshōgū, they were constituting themselves as separated from and yet beholden to the rulers' communion with power. Their entry into Nikkō, in this early species of tourism, in fact excluded them from the divine world of the shogun even while they were beguiled by this world.

The same contradictions can be seen within the context of the machi-iri noh performances in Edo castle, which in most cases was held for the investiture of a shogun. As at Nikkō, commoners were only allowed in at select moments. The castle too, therefore, was a heterotopia vis à vis the commoners. While the shogun and other officials watched the machi-iri performance from a raised platform opposite the stage, commoners were made to sit in a gravel enclosure, in between and below the shogun and the stage. Despite apparently knowing little about the performance—another, intentional form of exclusion maintained by the shogunate—they enjoyed the spectacle, and reports say they appreciated the chance to see the shogun as much as the noh.[111] In this case the scene is at once a rite for the shogun and a spectacle for the commoners. The appreciation of the spectacle by the commoners, rather than providing them an opportunity to partake of power, excludes and disem-

---

110. *Nikkō tōshōgū*, p. 32.
111. See NS, I: 196–199, passim.

powers them, rendering them "illegitimate people" (a literal translation of one term used for the masses—*shomin;* 庶民). In their moment of entry, commoners realize and thereby constitute their position as excluded from knowledge; as excluded from communion with shogunal ritual origins (and therefore from official history); and hence as excluded subjects of power.

These spectacles and the boundaries of social form they produced were dependent on the divine and on ritual, which had to be not only present, but also in part given as theater. While offering what were in some ways the rites of a divine monarchy, the shoguns also were making a spectacle or theater of their own divinity. The social form for which this served as foundation was therefore premised on the juxtaposition of these apparently incompatible modes of experience—not in the simple representation of the shogun as a deity. The term *shikigaku,* with *shiki* meaning ritual and *gaku* typically reserved for nonreligious entertainments, itself thus embodies the contradictory types of experience inherent to the Tokugawa order.

Spectacle and ritual were co-present at both Edo castle and the shrines at Nikkō. The castle cannot therefore be reduced to a place of secularized spectacle as opposed to Nikkō as a place of divine rite. The shogun as a figure of rulership, accordingly, also cannot be reduced to simply a figure of divine power in opposition to the secularized world of the commoners.

At the same time, to borrow one further characteristic from Foucault's definition of the heterotopia, in Edo castle and at Nikkō one can thus see the juxtaposition of differing, incompatible spaces within a single real place. The divine rites of the shogun and the spectacle of the shogun worked collusively in some ways, and were contradictory in others, but they nonetheless also retained the status of different world orders, with different value systems. Ritual and spectacle together may have helped to create a single social hierarchy, with the shogun as its legitimate leader and the commoners as lower subjects, alienated from the exercise of power. But within this social hierarchy, too, the worlds of ritual and spectacle were worlds of difference.

There is the element of collusion between the shogun's use of ritual and spectacle, that did effect some degree of closure in the shogun's image of power. It is essentially a circular logic, whereby the shogun's invitation to the commoners to come and see the shogun's ritual machi-iri noh in the castle, or to see the shogun's shrine at Nikkō, grants these commoners the right to validate the shogun as their transcendent ruler. In doing so, the commoners validate the social hierarchy, at the same time that they bring together the worlds of spectacle and divine rite. This also would seem to resolve the structural problem in the shogun's relation to legitimacy—it allows the shogun to be both transcendent subject of power (it is the shogun who grants the commoners the right to legitimize him in the first place), and to be the given, immanent object of power (as legitimized by the commoners and other audience members of the official machi-iri noh performances).

The Tokugawas did remain in power for a remarkably long period, and the noh continued to be used as their official ceremony of investiture—and in other ways described in this chapter—throughout this time. In ways both practical and symbolic, clearly the noh helped to create a closure and completion of the Tokugawa image of legitimacy.

Nonetheless, whatever stability or coherence the noh might have given to the Tokugawa order, it did not dissolve the contradictions of that time. Shogunal power was neither resolved into pure divinity, nor into the secularized world of theatrical spectacle. Like Foucault's heterotopes, in Nikkō and Edo castle—and in the official noh performances that were at once rituals and spectacles—one can see the simultaneity of different, even incommensurable value systems. These different orders were brought together and into a kind of cooperation, a negotiation of differences upon which the shogun's power rested, but Nikkō and the machi-iri ceremonies at Edo castle remained spaces of heterogeneity. They rendered visible the world of Tokugawa power as a world consisting of different worlds.

Nikkō and the castle can be thought of as heterotopes, beyond the ordinary, but as Foucault said, the heterotope is the most real of spaces. It is a place in which the order of things finds its fullest, if ideal, articulation. In the case of the Nikkō and Edo castle, they were also the central places of rule. The Tokugawa image of rule was thus itself predicated on a world of contradictory and incompatible positions, and the ability to work across these differences.

The Tokugawa heterotope apparently claimed to disclose the totality of this heterogenous world. At very least, there does seem to be a desire to see the world as a totality, or in simpler terms there does seem to be a desire for totality. If this was utopic, though, it was not an image of utopia as homogenous. Or rather, if the Tokugawa heterotope was in any way utopic, utopia was set up only in the form of a dream, or a fantasy.

• • •

The noh was a figuring process of a new space of political culture, and more generally, of a new social and historical form. Space, that is to say, is itself a form of the social, so that the reconfiguration of space is a reconfiguration of the social. Moreover, as Castoriadis has explained, the social does not exist "in" time, but instead *is* a mode of time, or history: "The social *is* this very thing—self-alteration, and it is nothing if it is not this. The social makes itself and can make itself only as history; the social makes itself as temporality; and it makes itself in every instance as a specific mode of actual temporality, it is instituted implicitly as a singular quality of temporality." The reverse is also the case—history does not occur in or to a society, it *is* a form of society: "It is not that history 'presupposes' a society.... The historical *is* this very thing—the self-alteration of this specific mode of 'coexistence' that is the social as such; outside of this, it is nothing."[112] Space is thus a mode of the social, and the social also comprises a form of time and of history.

The official practices of the noh organized by the shoguns helped to articulate a new kind of capital, around which a new set of social positions and relations could be defined. This was a new geography, organized around the shogun in Edo as its center, its hierarchical apex, and its eternal, unchanging source. The circulations of noh actors and performances between the provinces and Edo, as well as the emergence of the noh as a preferred medium for representing power in differing sectors throughout the Japanese state, served to bring previous sites of political and religious difference into the single sphere of the Tokugawa realm. Similarly, rites such as the *utaizome*, which performed a calendar of time defined as the Tokugawa's own across the various domains, and the consistent repetition of rites such as the machi-iri and the *utaizome* throughout the reign of the Tokugawas—these practices extended a temporal "permanence of the identical" across the boundaries of the state.[113]

The temporality configured by the noh thus composed a form of society based on the shutting down of history. Insofar as the historical is the "self-alteration of the specific mode of coexistence that is the social," as Castoriadis put it, the amplification of the geography of Tokugawa identity was a denial not only of historical change, but also of places of sociopolitical difference. This denial of places of social and political alterity was thus a denial of places for the emergence of temporal difference, and therefore of places for the

---

112. *The Imaginary Institution of Society*, 215.
113. The fixed cycles of the noh, as described earlier in this chapter, served to reenact and reaccomplish an order which always remains the same, always is fully "accomplished." This is the sense in which I would interpret the translation of "noh" as "accomplishment"—the reenactment of completion, or a completed order.

emergence of history in this society. The political effect was an order that foreclosed the productive potential of society to transform itself.

Within this geography, there is an impetus toward a panoptic position of rule, or a kind of bird's-eye view that is able to take in, know, and govern, the fixed cycles of space and time as a totality. As an indicator of this position one could point, for example, to the shogun's role as the only locus of the complete knowledge of all practices of the noh. Not only did the shogun, at least in theory, know all the secrets of all the noh families across the state, but because these practices by shogunal statute were to remain unchanged through time, this shogunal knowledge too stretched both into the past and into the future.[114]

This geography also therefore has traits of the modern, particularly in the sense of a world coming into itself, and completing itself, as a homogeneity. To the extent that, in contexts such as the official ceremonial noh, the conflicting positions of the shogun as at once transcendent subject and immanent object of this geography were somehow reconciled, the structure of rule over this order was sealed as absolutist.

As explained in the previous section, however, this absolutist closure of geography and legitimacy is not by itself an adequate description of the Tokugawa image of power. The central places of rule, such as the Tōshōgū shrine at Nikkō and the machi-iri noh performances at Edo castle were, first of all, also predicated on fantasy and dreams—and fantasy, in its basic nature, is never fully closed.[115] Furthermore, perhaps more importantly, these places of rule were also heterotopic sites of contradiction and incommensurability. In the way that the shogun actively encouraged the view of these as worlds simply of spectacle for some people, and at the same time, for other people, worlds simply of ritual, one can already see these spaces as differentiated worlds of value.

Whatever negotiations of difference might have been present in these heterotopic places and moments, they therefore could not reflect an image of

---

114. The panoptic gaze of the shogun, stretching out over the people and into the future, is also apparent in the machi-iri performances. There, at a critical moment, the shogun was said to be able to look out over the people and ascertain their well-being, including as it extended into the future.

115. Within theories of utopic praxis, fantasy and dreams in particular are often thought of as elements of irrationality and negation. As such, these are elements that might allow for the imagining of new possibilities within the everyday order of things and therefore for bringing about social change.

unity in the form of homogeneity.[116] The order I have described thus is *not* entirely a modern one, at least in the sense of a homogenous unity. Certainly it did not form the kind of unity typically associated with the sociopolitical space of a nation. Nor was it truly utopic, if utopia is defined by a perfect uniformity, or a world of undifferentiated value. There was hence a kind of unrest, and a transience, built into the Tokugawa structure of power.

But there is still an element of utopic practice, in all its meanings, visible in the broad social gestures of the Tokugawa reorganization of the noh. In the ceremonies at Edo castle and the shrines at Nikkō, in combination with the systematized practices of official noh throughout the state, one can see a quest to make real an impossible unity—a unity that nonetheless therefore becomes its dream.

---

116. This is another way of saying that power in the Tokugawa order was not based on a pure specular, mirror-like mimetic image of rulership.

2

The Value of the Stage

> There is nothing in this world so interesting as money.
> —*Nippon eitaigura*[1]

The Tokugawa bakufu invested much in the noh throughout their two and a half or so centuries in power, but perhaps never more than in the Kōka performance of 1848. By this time the bakufu was in dire circumstances, faced with near total loss of political, social and economic control.[2] Yet they expended great resources in sponsoring the fifteen-day performance, which involved every noh school in the country and was attended by over five thousand people each day. Nonetheless, most of the cash profits went directly to the head of the principal noh school, Hōshō Yagorō Yūkan—not to the bakufu.[3]

The apparent disparity between the bakufu's troubled economic and political situation and their investment in this performance raises the issue of value, and monetary economic value in particular. This, then, is the motivating question of this chapter: what was the value of the Kōka performance for

---

1. 世に銭ほど面白き物はなき *Teihon Saikaku zenshū VII* (Tokyo: Chuo Koronsha, 1951), 108; see also page 81. In further citations of Saikaku's work below I rely on G. W. Sargent's translation. Here, however, my translation is different from his, "A zeni is a delightful thing" (*The Japanese Family Storehouse* (Cambridge: Cambridge University Press, 1959), 90. Also see Ivan Morris, trans., *The Life of an Amorous Woman* (New York: New Directions Publishing, 1963), 278.
2. In 1798, the shogunate had an emergency reserve of gold and silver that amounted to over one million *ryō*, but by 1830 this had declined to 650,000 *ryō*. By the 1830s, the economic distress was exacerbated by successions of peasant uprisings, urban "smashings," famine, disease, and a series of natural disasters.
3. See, for example, *Kōka kanjin nō to Hōshō Shikiyo*, 23. The complexities of calculating the overall monetary contributions of the shogun have been discussed in the introduction (see in particular footnote 6).

the bakufu, conceived of through monetary economics? Or more broadly, what was the value of the noh for the shogun?

In this chapter, my use of value encompasses practical calculation, monetary and otherwise. But it is assumed that the monetary economic considerations remain part of the more encompassing concept of value outlined in the introductory chapter: value in the sense of the privileged set of relations that decides political and social form, and in the sense of the esteemed source, the definition, of the good.

I am therefore approaching the problem of the Kōka performance along the lines of a more generalized economics. Part of such a generalized economics hinges on modes of exchange, or of substitution. One model for this derives from the work of Jean-Joseph Goux. For Goux, modes of exchange describe both a signifying process and an economic process; both semiotic and economic, they define the basic social and psychological formations of a given time and place.[4]

This implies a type of congruence between the various domains of social action, or a mode of equivalence.[5] Most typically conceived of as the money form of economic value, the equivalent is the standard measure that allows diverse things to be equated. Gold, for example, in a gold standard economy occupies a transcendent position that allows it to give monetary value to all other commodities. By these terms, an analysis of social value therefore involves an analysis of the hierarchy of the form of equivalence.

Accordingly, without relying solely on either the system of exchange or the transcendent money form, it is in part through an exploration of these that one can open up something of the "value" of the Tokugawa stages.

The economy of kabuki was deeply implicated in the economy of the noh. The shogunate consciously and deliberately legislated a separation into two economies from what had been a less divided and less feudal form—just

---

4. See *Symbolic Economies*, Jennifer Curtiss Gage, transl. (Ithaca: Cornell University Press, 1990).
5. One of the possible critiques of Goux's work is that he shows *only* an analogical congruence. For similar types of critiques, see Elizabeth J. Bellamy, "Discourses of Impossibility: Can Psychoanalysis Be Political?," in *Diacritics* 23 (Spring 1993), 24–38; and Gayatri Chakravorty Spivak, "Scattered Speculations on the Question of Value," in *In Other Worlds: Essays in Cultural Politics* (New York: Methuen, 1987), 154–175. However, on one or two occasions Goux does allow for a greater independence between what he calls "spheres of 'symbolic' practices"; "My thesis," he states, "is that *all* practices involving exchange or substitution tend to be geared to a single phase, a single form, of the logical dialectic of the symbolization process, but at the same time, *the logic of this process is specific to each sphere of exchange*" (*Symbolic Economies*, 93; final emphases added). Nonetheless, his analyses are otherwise framed almost exclusively in terms of analogy, homology, and metaphor.

as it had developed the aesthetic form of the noh by pushing it and the kabuki theater apart, from out of what had become a more amorphously homogenous set of dramatic practices. By the start of the seventeenth century, rice by no means occupied the position of a universal equivalent, and the use of cash was widespread among all classes. The Tokugawa shoguns' "return" to a rice-based economy was only part of a larger gesture, that attempted to separate from common practice what would ultimately become the two economies. This chapter focuses primarily on the economy of rice in its status as distinct from the economics emerging with the merchant commoners. But it should be understood that both systems partook of a larger social form, even if this form was multiple.

What follows, therefore, includes a discussion of how the two economies, or two orientations, were separate but dynamically interrelated. This includes an examination of the modes of substitution and exchange, as well as the transcendent equivalents, in which these orientations are embedded—but also of the figures used to represent each.

In particular, the economies of *both* the noh and kabuki were premised on an aspiration for some form of eternity. As was shown in the previous chapter, the figure of an eternal order, founded on a divine past, was central to the noh. Although more present-oriented, the economy of commerce that kabuki was so much a part of similarly pointed toward an eternity. This is evident in the very title of Ihara Saikaku's work, *Nippon eitaigura (The Eternal Storehouse of Japan)*,[6] one of the best-known expressions of the world of Tokugawa commerce. Written at the height of the newly emergent mercantile economy, the title intimates that there is some kind of eternal goodness, or wealth, to be sought in capitalist conduct. Yet the "eternity" (*eitai*, 永代) of the commercial world was not that of the noh. In contrast to the noh's eternity, based on the ever-renewing cycles of nature, *eitai* (literally "eternity," "permanence") is a term applied in reference to the ownership and value of commodities—typically, when referring to the amortization of an object's value, or to mortmain.[7] Thus, in the merchant economy eternity no longer is defined in terms of the perpetual cycles of nature, but rather in terms of the

---

6. This title has been given a variety of English translations—for example, *The Japanese Family Storehouse* for Sargent's full length translation (ibid.), or Najita's "Storehouse of Wealth" (*Visions of Virtue*, 21). But Ivan Morris's (ibid.) more literal version seems most appropriate to me here, and is what I have followed.

7. See Kenkyusha's *New Japanese-English Dictionary* (Tokyo: Kenkyusha, 1954), 226.

temporality of the value of a commodity; temporality, and value in general, is gauged by and as the apportionment of commodity value.

Interrogating these two value orientations becomes a means of understanding forms of experience basic to the early modern state of Japan. Noh and kabuki are then seen to be part of the two differing, interrelated economies, in the struggle of what Goux calls a universal process: "the accession to power of a representative and the institutionalization of its role."[8]

The analysis in this chapter is not yet a history, and certainly not a linear history. It is not about the emergence in the Edo period of capitalist values out of feudal ones. In fact, the shogunate's agrarian-based economy was in some ways a newer construct than was the developing commercial economy. And despite a dialectical relation between the feudal world of the noh and the commercial world of the kabuki, this relation had neither the teleology nor the resolution of a Hegelian dialectic. This perspective complicates any univocal dominant-versus-marginal framework of resistance. Kabuki and noh each contained the potential to critique the value forms of the other, while at the same time they were implicated in different hegemonic regimes.

Finally, this is neither an argument for economic determinism nor a defense of the cultural in opposition to the economic. To write of the wider values of modes of exchange is not necessarily to assert a theory of history based on the primacy of the economic in all social formations, reducing everything to economic imperatives. Nor does it necessarily assert the analogical equivalence of the economic in all social formations.[9] The autonomy and deterministic opposition of an independent realm of economics can be seen as itself a product of the modes of exchange of the early modern Japanese state.

Concurrent with the figuration of the new realm of political power, the shogunate attempted to enforce a new economy—a fixed, closed order based on the unchanging cycles of agrarian seasons that matches and was part of the largely closed geography described in Chapter 1. This entailed the reassertion of the image of a self-sufficient village unit as the valorized base of production, but

---

8. Goux, ibid., 12.
9. Certainly the money forms of the Tokugawa era cannot, for example, be simply equated as a pure analogy to the poetic or ritual structure of the noh, nor could either of these be viewed as direct homologies of (or, for that matter, epiphenomena of) class structure. A simple analogy between these social spheres would ignore the separate dynamics of each, as well as the ways in which they might be mutually attributive and supportive of each other instead of simply being comparable to each other.

also the careful separation and demarcation of commercial activity. Mercantile commerce was regarded as selfish profiteering that led to wasteful excess.

This judgment was not necessarily inaccurate: the merchant culture of the pleasure quarters is legendary. Its visual extravagance was displayed in the parades of Yoshiwara; the spectacles of *misemono*;[10] the array of theaters, legal and illegal; and the exorbitant clothing fashions, in many ways indistinguishable from theatrical costumes—with patrons not only copying styles seen on the kabuki stages, but repeatedly rushing to change their own clothes at intermissions during a day's performance. The merchant culture in particular was known for the great monetary expenditures that typified spending time in the pleasure quarters. Especially from the time of the Genroku era in the late seventeenth century, this kind of excess was increasingly associated with the pleasure quarters of Edo; Edo was the city of consumption/expenditure (消費都市) of the Tokugawa order.

Yet Edo was also the seat of the shogun, as well as the periodic residence of daimyo from throughout the country. For them, too, it seems, Edo became a place of spectacle and excess. In Donald Shively's words, "One of the most striking peculiarities of the life of the city ... was the manner in which Edo functioned as a stage on which the daimyo were displayed."[11] There, daimyo and their retinues of hundreds or thousands sought their own prestige in extravagance. Clearly there were politically pragmatic reasons for the encouragement of daimyo spending. A common argument is that consumption among the daimyo class was fostered by the shogunate precisely in order to drain off excess funds from these potential challengers to power.[12] Regardless, the main point here is that for the samurai class, prestige comes to be indicated by lavish expressions of wealth, and this lavishness is specifically linked with the city of Edo. Of the shoguns, even the first (Ieyasu), who perhaps more than any other called for a lifestyle of simplicity, was renowned for his wealth; and the posthumous construction of Ieyasu's opulent shrine at Nikkō created for him a permanent image of conspicuous expenditure, more than compensating for his supposed reluctance to spend his wealth while still alive.[13]

---

10. Andrew Markus gives a descriptive overview of these spectacles in "The Carnival of Edo: Misemono Spectacles from Contemporary Accounts," in *Harvard Journal of Asiatic Studies* 45, no. 2 (1985), 499–541.
11. Donald Shively, "Sumptuary Regulation and Status in Early Tokugawa Japan," in *Harvard Journal of Asiatic Studies* 25 (1964–1965), 149.
12. See for example Shively, ibid., 150.
13. On the extravagance of early modern military leaders, including with regard to architecture, see Shively, ibid. (especially 137–138).

Accordingly, despite the images of a closed economy cultivated by the bakufu, the issue of surplus, or excess, is relevant in the consideration of the samurai class and their economic orientations as much as it is for the merchants and their "economy." There were actually two different forms of consumption and excess, and as with the two notions of eternity, each had their own orientation. But both were associated with the capital city;[14] these in fact defined the governing center of the early modern state. So in addition to the larger orders of exchange of the Tokugawa era, it is worth looking more closely at surplus and the expenditure of surplus in these orders, and the orientations embodied by these forms of surplus expenditure.

I turn now to briefly lay out the modes of exchange, and the general equivalents, first of the order of things espoused by the shogunate, and then of the world of merchant commerce.

The Boundaries of the Shogun's Economy

The Space of Economy

The modern term for economy (*keizai*, 経済) has roots in organization through the delineation of space. *Keizai*, as others have noted,[15] derives from an abbreviation commonly made in the Tokugawa era of a longer compound, *keisei saimin* (経世済民) (or *keikoku saimin*, 経国済民), meaning

---

14. Kyoto was still the location of the emperor's throne. The case could be made that Edo effectively became the capital. It maintained political control over all the major cities, including Kyoto (through the Kyoto deputy, or *shoshidai*). What Moriya Katsuhisa calls a "national" consciousness of Edo as the capital grew to the extent that the city, once known as the Kōfu ("government by the bay") came to be known by the unofficial title of Tōto, or "Eastern Capital" (see "Urban Networks and Information Networks," in *Tokugawa Japan* (Tokyo: University of Tokyo Press, 1990), 103. Or one could point to the "pragmatic" answer to the question of whether Kyoto or Edo was the true capital given in a work by Miura Jōshin in the early seventeenth century: "'shouldn't the place where the king of the country, the shogun who protects the realm, resides be called the capital?'" (cited in Ooms, *Tokugawa Ideology*, 184). I refer to Edo as the capital here in the same general way that I did in Chapter 1: as the center of the Tokugawa realm of power, which formed the basis of the Japanese state. This includes Edo as the capital city, but also Edo as a center insofar as, by the middle Tokugawa era when Edo had become probably the largest city in the world, desire seems to have been captured by the city in general and Edo in particular.

15. See especially Najita, *Visions of Virtue in Tokugawa Japan* (Chicago: University of Chicago Press, 1987), and Harootunian, "Late Tokugawa Culture and Thought," in *The Cambridge History of Japan*, vol. 5 (Cambridge: Cambridge University Press, 1989); also Tessa Morris-Suzuki, *A History of Japanese Economic Thought* (London: Routledge, 1989).

"ordering the world" and "saving the people."[16] Thus in one of the most important and influential of Tokugawa-era treatises on political economy, the *Keizai Roku (Economic Annals)*, Dazai Shundai begins by stating that the first ideograph, *kei*, refers to "wise statesmanship." This same ideograph for *kei* (経) has linear spatial connotations: it can mean "longitude," or "length, height" *(tate)*, as well as the warp of woven cloth. Thus Dazai comments on the spatial, architectonic aspect of *kei*: "*Kei* literally means 'to control a thread'... When a weaving woman makes silk cloth, she first prepares the warp... *Kei* is also 'management' [or construction] (*keiei*, 経営)... When you construct a royal palace, you must first make a plan of the whole, and then you carry out the plan. This is *kei*."[17] The problem of economics was thus a problem of governance—truly a political economy, in other words—and governance was in part a problem of the constructive ordering of space.[18]

This kind of a statewide political economy, and thinking of the disposition of space as an economic-political problem, was not really possible until the Tokugawa era. Here too one might point to the *sankinkōtai* system, as well as to related social constructs such as the exchange of noh actors between Edo and the provinces. The annual processions of daimyo to Edo, and the flows of money that they necessitated, encouraged the emergence of a more unified state space, and unified in part by the new currents of goods and money.

It is widely known that the *sankinkōtai* system accordingly also set up the need for money and commerce. The requirement that all provincial lords spend part of each year in Edo in particular, and the Tokugawa stipulation that all provincial lords live in newly centralized castle towns, apart from their agrarian bases of production, in general meant that daimyo had to have access to money in order to acquire goods, which themselves became more mobile, and were in need of new avenues of transport to these castle towns. Political economy, space as a concern of political economy (and space *as* economic-political) and the flows of commerce thus arose in a conjoined state.

---

16. Najita, *Visions of Virtue*, 8. Morris-Suzuki translates it as "administering the nation and relieving the sufferings of the people," *A History of Japanese Economic Thought*, 4.
17. Cited in Morris-Suzuki, ibid., 13. (Because the ideograph for *kei* can also mean to pass, elapse, or expire—*heru, tatsu*—one could also argue that there is a temporal organization implied, but Dazai, at least, does not seem to have associated this with the meaning of *keisei*.)
18. Of course it was much more than this; I am, for the moment, ignoring the latter half of the compound of *keizai*.

Mercantile commerce was therefore integral to the Tokugawa state. Merchant capitalism was by no means new in the Tokugawa era, but it had developed in largely exclusive and excluded realms. One of the largest areas of capitalist activity, the port city of Sakai, retained a status almost equivalent to a unique and independent state until the early Tokugawa period. Market towns, though fairly prevalent even in the middle ages, were perceived as places of separation (*muenjo,* 無縁所; *engiri basho,* 縁切り場所), outside of the hierarchies of everyday politics and society.[19] But what were in the past detached spaces, in the Tokugawa era became part of the larger question of political economy. Hence when the bakufu tried to reassert a retrograde agrarianism, it was within conditions and according to qualities of space that had already vastly changed. The new unity of social and political space, sought for by the great military leaders of the late sixteenth century, was now achieved as much through the expanded movements and relations of the merchant capitalists as it was on the controlled distribution of an economy based on rice.

Production: Exchange Without Value

Just as the bakufu sought a fixity of social place, they also attempted to impose a fixity of economic value. In ways homologous to (and reinforced by) their use of the noh, they did this through the creation of the rice taxation and allotment system. This was theoretically a closed economy of simple exchange between the bakufu and the outer domains, between upper and lower classes, and, in a sense, between the past and the present. The countryside family-based agricultural unit was, in principle, the re-created source of production.

Commerce, to the extent possible, was confined and disjoined from both these agricultural units, and from the samurai classes. This attempted disjunction was, again, approached spatially. Commerce was to be limited to central cities, where merchants were allowed to act as the points of wholesale accumulation of provincial goods, and links to the developing statewide market.[20] Villages were to produce only agricultural and handicraft goods; merchants were not allowed to live in villages, and roads leading to some villages

---

19. See Amino Yoshihiko's *Muen, kugai, raku* (Tokyo: Heibonsha, 1978), and, on this work, Najita, *Visions of Virtue,* 19–20.
20. John Whitney Hall, "The Castle Town and Japan's Modern Urbanization," in *Studies in the Institutional History of Early Modern Japan,* Hall and Jansen, eds. (Princeton, N.J.: Princeton University Press, 1968), 180.

had notices prohibiting merchants from entering.²¹ Commercial goods, too, were prohibited from many villages.²² Within the space of the city, merchants were separated from the samurai. Merchants and samurai were confined to separate districts, and samurai were prohibited not only from engaging in commercial activity themselves, but also from renting out their residences for merchant activity. When the third shogun (Iemitsu) on a city inspection tour came across a samurai who had done just that, the punishment was exile.²³

Money, too, was restricted from the agricultural/samurai system of reproductive exchange. Money had in fact already been in fairly widespread use. T. C. Smith relates the account of a Korean ambassador in the fifteenth century marveling at the use of money everywhere—"everyone would accept it, beggars and prostitutes would take nothing else, and the wayfarer need carry nothing more than a full purse."²⁴ Yet although even a system of collecting taxes in copper coins (the *kandaka*) had been adopted by the mid-sixteenth century, the Tokugawa shogunate reinstituted the *kokudaka* system of collecting taxes, and assessing value, in rice.²⁵

The privileged separation of agricultural production from commerce, and the natural value of rice apart from money forms, in effect created the image of a closed economic circle, free of the difference that either commercial profit or monetary signs might interject.²⁶ The limiting of the country's exchange with the wider world can be understood as part of this process. But before considering the money form in detail, I will look first at the agricultural form advocated by the shogunate.

The self-sufficient farm unit structured by the genealogical relations of an extended family and valorized by the bakufu is best typified by the large farm holdings known as *tezukuri* (手作り). The *tezukuri* holding can be thought of

---

21. Shively, "Sumptuary Regulation and Status," 155.
22. Examples from one rural notice cited in Shively includes bleached cotton kimono, wooden geta, mirrors, chopsticks, etc.—items that are not particularly luxurious (Shively, ibid., 155). The intent seems to have been more geared toward simply stopping the flow and wider exchange of commodities.
23. Miura Hiroyuki, *Hōseishi no kenkyū* (Tokyo: Iwanami, 1919), 272–273.
24. Thomas C. Smith, *The Agrarian Origins of Modern Japan* (Stanford: Stanford University Press, 1959), 72.
25. See Emiko Ohnuki-Tierney, *Rice as Self* (Princeton, N.J.: Princeton University Press, 1993), 69.
26. I am setting aside for the moment the fact that the samurai class was separated not only from commerce, but also, having been shifted to the castle towns, from the agricultural realm of production. This complicates the image of a closed economic circle of production.

in terms of three concentric circles.²⁷ The center consisted of the holder's nuclear family; the next larger circle was composed of affinal and cognate relatives not in the direct line of descent; and the third, largest circle consisted of servants and small landholders called *nago* (名子). The servants of this outer circle were of two general types: the *fudai*, hereditary servants passed down in a family from generation to generation, and servants indentured for long periods. But all of the people in the third circle, though technically not within the circle of relation to the center by blood or marriage, were generally treated as part of the family. Servants lived with the master, and the master was responsible for their upbringing and general welfare; in the village population registers they were assimilated to the family members, albeit with notations that they were servants.²⁸ The unit overall thus maintained the composition of a closed and enduring family.

To understand the modes of exchange that characterized the larger *tezukuri* family circle, it is instructive to look at the exchanges between the master (*oyakata*, 親方) and those most distant from him—the small landholding *nago*. In principle, this relation largely mirrors that of the village landholder to the provincial lord. With their own land to cultivate, the *nago* were to an extent independent. They also worked a certain number of days for the *oyakata*, and were paid for their labor—what on the surface might appear to constitute a simple relation of wage labor. But the relation went well beyond the simple economic. *Oyakata* would provide food and seed to *nago* during the frequent times of crop failure; they provided *nago* furniture, cooking utensils, and appropriate clothing for dress occasions; paid for doctors, and so on. As Smith writes, "The continuous exchange between *oyakata* and *nago* of labor, capital, food, and protection for labor was unlike the exchange familiar to modern economies;" it was an economic exchange in the form of a social relationship, "not a direct exchange of economic values defined by an impersonal market." Labor services provided by the *nago* were based on the *oyakata*'s need, and the *nago*'s sense of obligation to fulfill the master's (and by extension the collectivity's) need. *Nago* were not necessarily paid more for more labor; rather than a means of payment for land, labor services were part of a "far-reaching system of personal obligation."²⁹

There were also "no individual transactions to which prices might apply" and "no market to price diverse commodities in a common unit, so

---

27. Thomas C. Smith, *The Agrarian Origins of Modern Japan*, 5–11.
28. Ibid., 8–9.
29. Ibid., 26–27, 29.

precise comparisons of value could not be made...even had this been thought desirable."[30] This was, then, a system of closed (if hierarchical) reciprocity. Self-sufficient, based on the simple production, reproduction, and exchange of natural use-value ("need" again being hierarchically determined between the *oyakata* and the *nago*), and therefore free of a money form, it was a closed circle of economy (in formal terms, it was free of economic value).[31]

Finally, in addition to farm labor, the *nago* owed their *oyakata* certain services that now would be regarded as ceremonial.[32] But these services were apparently not distinguished from everyday farm labor (both were called *suke*, 助け —"assistance"—in the document cited by Smith). Work and ceremony were part of the same economy of social life, and were thought of as essentially the same thing.

The desire for a closed natural economy, itself utopic, is evident in utopic visions of the state—including those implicitly critical of the way the shogunate was actually running things. That is the case with Andō Shōeki's *Shizen no yo (On the Natural World)*, to give an example, which describes the lack of difference, or pure equivalence, between natural and human labor value: "In the world of Nature, human beings work in accordance with the operation of Heaven and Earth; there is not the least divergence between man and Nature."[33] This identity of human and natural value is maintained through the enduring temporality of natural agrarian cycles: "This cycle of seasons and human labour has neither beginning nor end. This truly indicates the very concord of man and Nature in which Heaven's way of giving growth to everything conforms to the human way of direct

---

30. Ibid., 27.
31. I mean this in two senses. Because there was theoretically no difference in the system of goods—difference, for instance, that would be introduced by the relation between a commodity and the monetary sign of the commodity's value, or the difference or variability of a commodity's value through time in relation to itself or to other objects—there is no value; value requires a relation of difference. I also mean that there was no *exchange* value. Insofar as exchange value is, as Marx put it in one of his simpler formulations, "in the first place, the excess above and beyond necessary use-values," the agrarian economy we are looking at sought to exclude surplus, and, hence, exchange value. The quote from Marx comes from the French version of *Contribution à la critique de l'économie politique* (Paris: Sociales, 1957), 209, and is cited in Goux, *Symbolic Economies*, 27.
32. Smith quotes a document which includes assistance in making rice cakes for the New Year celebrations; the exchange of New Year gifts; performance of the Planting Ceremony; and offerings of ceremonial wine. Ibid., 30.
33. Translations in E. H. Norman's "Andō Shōeki and the Anatomy of Japanese Feudalism," in *Transactions of the Asiatic Society of Japan* 2 (Tokyo: Kenkyusha, 1949), 221–224.

cultivation.... Therefore such a world is called the world of Nature." Exchange in this world consists of the simple swapping of the natural products of each locale, creating a harmonious whole. There is hence no need for money—"no circulation of gold or silver currency"—and no surplus or luxury. So too is there no need for "merchants who pile up profit," and there are no profligate spenders. Likewise desire is confined within this economy closed of all excess: there is no source of greed, no cause for lust or adultery, no drunkenness.[34]

At the level of practical governance, as the dynamics of the commercial economy developed, and the agrarian bases deteriorated,[35] the shogunate tended to become only more reactionary in trying to assert some of these elements as policy. The reforms of the bakufu's chief councilor in the late eighteenth century, Matsudaira Sadanobu, provide only one of the more obvious examples. Sadanobu sought to limit cities and to return peasants to their agricultural districts, offering them funds to do so. Prostitutes, a recurring figure of extra-economic desire, were to be freed from indenture and married off in agricultural districts, presumably to return them to the simple cycle of production.[36] Criminals, also a "wasteful" sector of society,[37] were to be rehabilitated into the order of production through the establishment of the penal colony on Ishikawa island. The colony was first populated with skilled laborers, and criminals were then sent to be their apprentices.

From what we have seen thus far, the economy by which the shogunate was thus landscaping the state was, at least superficially, comparable to the "economy" (*oikonomia*) advocated by Aristotle.[38] Restricted to the management of the family and home, it is an order of self-sufficiency and production for use. The limits of this order are natural and based on the cycles of nature; the difference that intrudes with profit and credit is unnatural, as is money, and therefore these are opposed to and excluded from the economy. The ruling principle of exchange is one of equilibrium and mutual benefit—

34. Not only is there no money in Shōeki's utopia, there is no transcendent equivalent whatsoever. This means there also is no ruler or upper class. This is quite different from the economy of the shogunate, and makes Shōeki's work a radical critique of the shogunate.
35. T. C. Smith provides a detailed narrative view of the way the village unit begins to decompose, by focusing on the *nago*—the position which was in any event closest to opening the closed economy of the *tezukuri* holding. The *nago* holdings gain increasing independence, labor increasingly becomes wage labor, and *nago* develop into the source of an abstract labor force.
36. Takekoshi, *The Economic Aspects of the History of the Civilization of Japan*, vol. III (London: Dawsons of Pall Mall, 1967), 154.
37. Ooms, *Tokugawa Ideology*, 148.
38. See Aristotle, *The Politics* (Harmondsworth: Penguin Books, 1962).

exchange occurs only as a natural process of compensating for naturally occurring imbalances.

By the nineteenth century, when commerce could no longer be thought of in any practical way as being marginal to daily life in Japan, critiques of commerce were being couched in the terms of a natural order and as a problem of the loss of control over natural limits. In *Seji kemmonroku*, c. 1816, Buyō Inshi comments on the transformation of the agrarian farmer base into townspeople and "idlers," and laments the "lost meaning of simplicity."[39] Townspeople, themselves a problem of "overabundance," are referred to as "bugs" who are consuming all the country's products, "maggots" who are "eating the flesh of farmers and warriors." The solution, he said, was to "destroy them and return to the simplicity of the natives" (*domin*, 土民 —literally, "people of the earth"). The problem for Buyō, as well as the solution, is thus phrased as if it were itself a problem of nature (insects that need to be exterminated), in an order the originary foundations of which lay in "native" agricultural production. In Buyō's eyes, the proper source of production had been overturned. Farmers had become townspeople, and so "people at the foundation of the country are now consuming the country."[40]

In Buyō's critiques, the preservation and disruption of the cycles of nature extends across space: Whereas in the past goods did not travel out of the provinces, the new movement of commodities from province to city only disrupts the natural value—adding, by way of the need for concrete mediations like new bridges across rivers and couriers to bring goods across the distances, new expenditures that distort the true value of things. Thus the cycles and flows of commerce across the state are unnatural forms of circulation, and the image of profit "bewitches" people into thinking that these mediations do not create loss (a loss that arises because the bridges and so on add expenses to what must be the fixed value of things).[41]

---

39. *Seji kemmonroku*, 277. (Buyō Inshi was the pseudonym of a masterless samurai of the late nineteenth century.) The version of *Seji kemmonroku* used here is in *Kinsei shakai keizai sōsho* I (Tokyo: Kaizo sha, 1926); Buyō's critical account of contemporary conditions is also discussed in H. D. Harootunian's "Late Tokugawa Culture and Thought," in *The Nineteenth Century*, Marius B. Jansen, vol. 5 of *Cambridge History of Japan* (Cambridge: Cambridge University Press, 1989), 168–258, and Thomas C. Smith's *Political Change and Industrial Development in Japan* (Stanford: Stanford University Press, 1955).
40. Buyō, ibid., 274.
41. Buyō, ibid., 275. More specifically, Buyō's argument is that there appears to be profit in immediate situations—when selling goods to the shipper, for instance, there may appear to be the possibility of mutual profit. But since expenses are added by the costs of circulation, overall there is loss.

Correspondingly, these same mediated movements of commodities disrupt the natural order of time. The labor needed to transport and circulate goods only takes people away from the truly productive activity of farming, and so, for the first time, time itself comes to be "consumed."[42]

These critiques might be read as productivist—that is, based on an image of society as organized around production. But I am not positing an order that, privileging use-value, is separated from what Baudrillard would call a symbolic society (one fundamentally organized around "symbolic" exchanges such as gift-giving, rites and festivals, and so on).[43] Political economy can be taken as a code for economic organization in general, and for a form of modernity in particular. An application of the term "political economy" to the early modern Japanese state must take into account how this involved, or was even founded on, a system of gifts.

Gifts and Governance

Formally speaking, a true gift has no return. Once the calculation of return enters into consideration it is no longer entirely a gift. With no return, there is no institution of gaps or delays—and so no institution of narratives of

---

42. Ibid., 275. Although made from within a reactionary framework, implicit in these criticisms was a perception of agrarian workers' loss of control over their own products, and of the loss of an unmediated relation between workers and their own labor—phrased as a loss of "vitality" (*seikon*). For, Buyō writes, commoners' use of their own energy in the past was limited to the production of their own livelihood. But under commercial conditions, they are allotted extra work, they have to produce a new variety of goods, and sell these goods for money; this money does not stay in their hands either, though, and the result is pure loss, a complete consumption of farmers' (and the country's) vitality.

43. Nor do I fully subscribe to Baudrillard's characterization of Marx. For Baudrillard, Marx endorses use value as the utopian other to exchange value, while failing to realize that use value is itself a construct of the system of exchange value which produces a rationalized system of needs and objects. In this view, Marx's emphasis on production reproduces the binary oppositions of capitalist political economy. A similar argument is reproduced in one strain of anthropological thought on exchange. In Jonathan Parry, for instance, Marx overemphasizes production (specifically pre-capitalist), and such an analysis "inevitably leads to an oversimple contrast between a pre-monetary state of affairs and a post-monetary state of affairs where the former is nothing more than an antithesis to a nightmarish view of commerce" ("On the Moral Perils of Exchange," 84–85). See also M. Bloch, "The Symbolism of Money in Imerina," 170–171; and O. Harris, "The Earth and the State," 236–237, all in J. Parry and M. Bloch, eds., *Money and the Morality of Exchange* (Cambridge: Cambridge University Press, 1989). These are, in my view, reductive readings of Marx's notion of production, related to those readings of Marx which do not see any action by the superstructure upon the base—or at very least based only on his more programmatic visions of history.

The Value of the Stage / 89

temporality, for instance—and no institution of exchange (upon which a social order might be based). From this perspective, it has been argued that Marcel Mauss's famous essay on the gift did not in fact address the problem of the gift at all.[44] It may be that the phenomenal appearance of the gift in exchange annuls it as a true gift.[45] But that is what this chapter takes up: the phenomenon of the gift in the shogunal economy, and, precisely through the annulment of anything emerging from outside the system of exchange, the institution of a closed ritual cycle.

Rice, the measure of value in the shogun's economy, itself played the role of a gift which temporalizes time, organizing through relations of simple exchange an order of pure reproduction, exclusive of events and therefore of history. In the agrarian economy the bakufu had revived, rice was considered a gift from the gods. In annual harvest rites performed by the emperor, grains of the new rice crop were offered to the gods in return for the original seeds given by the gods. There is accordingly a temporality—rice is alienated from its original source—but it is closed; there is always the appropriate return. This cycle, or circle, repeats itself as an endless repetition of naturally set value.

This image would be revitalized, and clearly expressed, in the romantic arguments of the late Tokugawa-period nativists. For Hirata Atsutane, rice was a godly gift, and the return for the gods' blessings was rice cultivation. This work of cultivation, to quote Harootunian, "put people back into 'nature' and established the modes of a natural social reproduction to transform the 'gift' into actuality." And all was based on an annual cycle, in which time was ordered as nature: through an idiosyncratic etymology, Hirata claimed that the very word for "year" (*toshi*, 年), "'refers to cereals and grains. These are the spirits of [the] yearly deities and are formed in the fields.'"[46] In these ways the divine gift of rice, including work as worshipful return,

---

44. "One could go so far as to say that a work as monumental as Marcel Mauss's *The Gift* speaks of everything but the gift: It deals with economy, exchange, contract, ... it speaks of raising the stakes, sacrifice, gift *and* countergift—in short, everything that in the thing itself impels the gift *and* the annulment of the gift" (*Given Time: 1. Counterfeit Money* (Chicago: University of Chicago Press, 1992), 24). However, Derrida does acknowledge the existence of the gift, as part of an exchange, at the phenomenological level: "we do not mean to say that *there is no* exchanged gift. One cannot deny the *phenomenon*, nor that which presents this precisely phenomenal aspect of exchanged gifts" (ibid., 37).
45. Ibid., 14.
46. H. D. Harootunian, *Things Seen and Unseen* (Chicago: University of Chicago Press, 1988), 211, 214–215.

imposed a cycle of sameness on the diversity of even agrarian life: "The reality of production, consisting of countless acts of work throughout the year, became subsumed by simple reproduction and made to appear as a repetitive process culminating in a regular harvest representing the gift of the gods."[47]

Being a closed cycle of reproduction, there would be no waste. Okuni Takamasa put it in organic, bodily terms: tracing the route of rice from its ingestion, through the stomach and back out, "The grain," he wrote "is for man; the wastes are for the subsequent growth of rice."[48] The gift of rice, and its returns, thus organized an order closed to history and to any value beyond the value of production—the value of production is identical to the value of exchange.

The value of rice was thus changeless, completely controlled. This was apparently in contradistinction to the appearance of the commercial commodity. For Buyō Inshi, not only was the circulation of goods disruptive to natural value, it was the very uncontrolled *variety* introduced by mercantilism that was impoverishing. In the past, Buyō says, people had used their "vitality" simply for their own livelihood; now farmers "exhaust their vitality producing various things" for the townspeople and idlers.[49] Thus at the level of production, too, variation penetrates the eternally fixed value of self-sufficiency. Expulsion of the commodity is the expulsion of a degenerative penetration of time.

The shogunate declined suggestions to start levying taxes on mercantile commerce, possibly to keep its system of values free of any involvement in the fluctuations of commerce.[50] The history of taxation may also have some relevance. In the middle ages, rice taxes were not levied on marginal spaces and people such as the *kawaramono* (河原者 or 川原者, people of the riverbed). Known as *sansho* (散所, "scattered places"; Hayashiya Tatsusaburō says this term itself also means "nontaxable")[51] these people and spaces were separate from the *honsho* (本所)—"main," "true" or, in Ohnuki-Tierney's translation, "real" place.[52] Rice and grain taxation, then, contributed to the construction

---

47. Harootunian, ibid., 216.
48. Harootunian, ibid., 339.
49. Buyō Inshi, *Seji kemmonroku*, 276.
50. Merchants did have to pay the shogunate licensing fees, but these were fixed, and applied to guilds which were also supposed to be genealogically fixed.
51. Hayashiya Tatsusaburō, *Nihon geinō no sekai* (Tokyo: Nihon Hōsō Shuppan Kyōkai, 1973), 130–131. Discussed also in Ohnuki-Tierney, *Rice as Self*, 86.
52. Ohnuki-Tierney, *Rice as Self*, 86.

of a space of truth, of "real" experience. In the Tokugawa era this would be the space of the shogunal *kokudaka* rice exchange.⁵³

A centered utopic order emerges through the economy of rice. The divine past was source of value for rice—as in the epic chronotope of noh plays, and as in the more deified representations of Ieyasu. In the present, too, the hierarchical source or center of value associated with rice was first the provincial lords, and ultimately the shogun.⁵⁴ Rice may have been a gift to the emperor, but in the Tokugawa order the center of the state, to whom all surplus of the *kokudaka* system was directed to, was the shogun.⁵⁵ The value of rice thus procured a stable center of value for the state, in a space in which repetition meant the exclusion of difference.⁵⁶ Ceremonial rites also helped to constitute the repetitions at the center of the Tokugawa state.

Many of the regulations on consumption and on behavior in general are listed in the *Ofuregaki*⁵⁷ (the official collection of bakufu edicts and orders), under the category of "ceremonies" *(oshūgi,* 御祝儀*)*.⁵⁸ Ceremony was central to the moral economy of the shogunate. That the arrangement of time was connected both to a system of gifts and to ceremony is already evident in this word for ceremony. In addition to its reference to ceremonial moments, *shūgi*

---

53. To draw a parallel that is necessarily somewhat speculative, but fits with the hierarchy of official time seen in Chapter 1: the higher level the official, and the greater the number of noh performances accorded to him for change of office or other such moments, and thereby the more his existence is acknowledged, the more significant he becomes in the eternal order of time enacted by the noh performances. Time becomes more real, and one becomes more integrated into the order of time the closer one comes to the top and center. Ultimately, time is defined as the time of the very top, Tokugawa Ieyasu.
54. The shogunate was not wholly against participation in commerce. Again, one of the most articulate spokesmen on political economy, Dazai Shundai, said that mercantilism was "consistent with ancient law." But for Shundai, too, it is always assumed that the source of all products for exchange, and the one to whom all returns should go to first, is the daimyo. See Najita, transl., *Keizai roku shūi* in *Readings in Tokugawa Thought*, Select Papers 9 (Chicago: Center for East Asian Studies, 1993), 43–53.
55. This too was phrased as a return, in a system based on personal obligation, not personal economic gain. *Giri* is the best known expression of this gift—debt exchange. In "repayment" for the *on* (favor, grant) given by one's lord in the form of land or stipends, one owed one's life, one's self, to one's lord (and in principle, to the shogun). Suicide at the time of one's lord's death was thus the ultimate closure of the exchange.
56. One could compare, here, Lefebvre's statement that, "the state crushes time by reducing differences to repetitions of circularities." Cited in David Harvey, *The Condition of Postmodernity* (Cambridge, MA: Blackwell, 1990), 273.
57. See Takayanagi Shinzō and Ishii Ryōsuke, eds., *Ofuregaki kampō shūsei* (Tokyo: Iwanami Shoten, 1959).
58. For example, ibid., 92 ff.

meant "gift," and was used when referring to gifts presented at these moments. The calendar was thus organized as a series of repetitive ceremonial moments, themselves constituted by the exchange of gifts. The gift and its return, and the constitutive moment of time, are in a sense the same thing (*oshūgi*).

As discussed in Chapter 1, noh was used as a ceremony both to construct a calendar of ritual cycles, and to construct a hierarchical center of power through exchanges of performances between the shogun and provincial lords. The noh as a ceremonial form of exchange also included payment based on allotments of gifts, rather than salaries for labor performed. The term used for a noh actor's period of duty in Edo itself meant "to offer a gift"—*suehiro kenjō* (末広献上), literally to "give a fan."[59] Having been awarded status comparable to samurai, noh actors were of course given stipends of rice. But they were paid in other gifts, mostly at fixed points throughout the year. They were given "gift mansions" (*hairyō yashiki*, 拝領屋敷) to live in, food and *sake*, and "seasonal" or "appropriate" clothing (*jifuku*, 時服); the clothing that higher ranked actors received at New Year's alone was said to be more than one year's worth, and so, because of these gifts, they "stood far above anxiety over food, clothing and shelter."[60] These were thus gifts of sustenance and practical utility; what was being exchanged, in part, was use value.

Utility, however, was not distinguished from ritual. The gifts of clothing, for example, were integrated into the ritual calendar discussed in Chapter 1. Most of the *jifuku* (literally, "time clothing") were presented at several points in the New Year's festival of the *utaizome*, which was the ritual originary point in the shogun's calendar.[61] In the same way that sustenance was meant to be part of the natural cycles of agriculture, clothing (and sustenance) was united with, and reinforced, the repetitive cycles of ritual time.

Finally, these practices were in keeping with a general political economy of *matsurigoto* (政), a term signifying governance as ceremonial. Espoused by intellectuals from the early Tokugawa Confucianist Ogyū Sorai to the nativist Motoori Norinaga, *matsurigoto* does not separate politics off from ethics or worship, or moral from political action. Thus to behave well is to govern well, and wealth will follow. In accord with this the noh was practiced by all

---

59. Ikeuchi, NS I, 126.
60. Ikeuchi, NS I, 175. See also pages 126, 173, 177.
61. Even among merchants, apprentices were similarly presented with gift clothing (*shikise*), primarily at two ritual points in the year: New Year's and the summer lantern festival.

the shoguns, including those who felt that expenditures on performances of all types should be curtailed; the utility of the noh was a moral, ethical utility.

Governance thus *was* ceremonial.⁶² A literal translation of *kōgi* (公儀), the term for the governmental order of the shogunate, is "public ceremony." In Sakai's words, "the affirmative political process that was imagined [in the eighteenth century] was neither persuasion nor authoritarian coercion, but *choreography*." Sorai makes this clear: "Rites and music are the regulatory underpinnings of human virtues.... Without relying on words, rites and music nourish human virtues and alter the way humans think.... Rites are ... explicit prescriptions of the Way of the Ancient Kings."⁶³ Rites and music meant a good deal more than the rote memorization of dance. However, the principal point is an emphasis on the immediacy of enacting the ethical way of the ancient past—most especially the elimination of language as a mediation between the true ethical community of the past and the experience of this ethical order in the present.⁶⁴

Yet language—ethical language—did intrude at one moment in the shogun's calendar of noh, and this was at the heart of the order. At the very "opening" (*kaikō*, 開口 —"opening of the speech") of the *utaizome*, there was a set place for several lines newly written each year to be inserted into the performance; these were given special importance. In the Tokugawa era, these lines were written by a Confucianist. Thus, ethics and ethical language were integrated into a fixed place within the performative order of noh, in a mode which privileged the performative style (the acting style, not the words, was one of the most important secrets handed down within the *waki* actor families) rather than the pedagogic value of the words performed.⁶⁵ The ethics of Confucianism, itself based on an identity with the values of the

---

62. One might think, too, of the term for the governmental order of the shogunate, *kōgi*, which translates literally as "public ceremony."
63. *Bendō*, Tetsuo Najita, transl., in *Readings in Tokugawa Thought*, 31.
64. For a comparison of this argument for immediacy to Kamo Mabuchi's "idealization of communal spirit" and the absence of the representational uses of language, see Sakai, *Voices of the Past*, 243–246.

I might add that Sorai was ambiguous about the shogunate's privileging of the noh; he preferred the more ancient *bugaku*, but grudgingly accepted certain practices of the noh. The one moment he did expressly approve of was the *utaizome*, the New Year's noh which, I have tried to show, initiated the shogun's ritual calendar. See *Seidan*, quoted in Ikeuchi, NS I, 439.
65. On the *kaikō*, including its pre-Tokugawa history, see Ikeuchi, NS I, 299–303.

Ancient Kings, were made even more immediate through integration into a ceremonial performance which claimed to put into practice the customs and values of the past.[66]

Just as the ceremonial economy discussed above was founded on gift exchange, so too the ceremony of governance was based on gifts. Governance was typically discussed as "benevolence." According to some arguments, the primary meaning of *matsurigoto* was "to make offerings."[67] Similar to the relation of the *nago* to the head family of the agrarian farm unit as a whole, the relation between ruler and ruled in this gift order was also hierarchical. To cite an example of the exchange of gifts in this context, one could look at the machi-iri rites—when townspeople, allowed into the castle for noh plays celebrating events such as shogunal investitures, acknowledged both the shogun's rule and their own position as subjects. These rites were themselves considered "a kind of beneficence."[68] For these performances, townspeople were expected to buy entry tickets. Permission for entry was apparently itself considered a form of return ("for the townspeople ... there was no greater honor than this"[69]), but townspeople also could always expect to receive, upon exiting, an umbrella, some *sake*, and a few coins; the more important the event, the more money given.[70] All of these gifts were announced, along with a statement of thanks, by the town administrator just before the townspeople left, and the townspeople in turn expressed their thanks as they left.

---

66. There is also a bodiliness in this ceremonial governance—an emphasis on the body which could enact the "customs," "etiquette," "rules," and "rites" (*rei*, 礼—Sorai's "rites"—implied all of these) of the past exactly in the present. This is a body free of any material excess, a body which could bring about a precise identity between past and present. In this sense, too, repetition was without difference, so that a bodily repetition of the past, or at least of the shogunate's image of the past, could perfectly reenact the past in the present.
67. Motoori Norinaga, for example, argued that although *matsurigoto* might indeed involve worship and the performance of rituals, its real derivation was the offering of services (in Motoori's case, to the emperor rather than the shogun); "government under heaven" meant "offerings and services"—*Kojikiden*, cited in Maruyama Masao's ahistorical essay "The structure of Matsurigoto: the basso ostinato of Japanese Political Life," in Sue Henny and Jean-Pierre Lehmann, eds., *Themes and Theories in Modern Japanese History* (London: Athlone Press, 1988), 29.
68. Ikeuchi, NS I, 189.
69. Ikeuchi, ibid., 189.
70. Occasions are recounted in Ikeuchi during which whole piles of coins were simply left out for commoners to take as they could (and they did fight over the money). It may be that, paradoxically, these appearances of excess, and the surprise and desire they engendered, helped to bring commoners under the sway of shogun's supposedly fixed economy of power and society. See Ikeuchi, NS I, 13.

The Value of the Stage / 95

The exchange of power—with the acknowledgment of the shogun as true ruler—was thereby completed and supported by an exchange of gifts. Although these included monetary payment, the exchange involved both ruler and commoners in the supposedly fixed moral values of the shogun's order.[71]

The machi-iri performance was, however, more of a gift from the shogunate than it might appear. Townspeople were frequently refunded the price of their entry tickets after the day of the performance. This would suggest that there were other forms of coercion than the simple desire on the townspeoples' part to see the shogun, or to enter the shogun's moral economy; there were more monetary forms of desire, and economy, involved. Thus, considered here from the perspective of monetary economics, one can see that for the commoners the shogun was setting up more a *theater* of an archaic gift economy than its actual reassertion.

What I have described thus far is a shogunal attempt to invoke a place apart from the movements and mediations of commerce, a deliberate effort to banish the economy of value that was emerging with statewide mercantilism. In the shogun's agrarian economy, the worth of goods, ethical or moral worth, and political values all were considered part of the same order, in terms of one single measure (a measure defined by its identity with an originary past). Wealth and utility, therefore, were matters of moral and political good, for society as a whole. "Wealth," accordingly, was *fuku* (福), but also "the good," "public welfare" (*fukuri*, 福利), and "blessing," "bliss"—as opposed to the merchant's *kanemochi* (金持ち; literally, "holding money/gold/coins"). This broader sense of wealth provides additional context for understanding the meaning of the second half of the compound term *keizai* (political economy)—"save the people (*saimin*)." It includes the (spatial) imposition of an unchanging set of values, in which the value of labor and production is not distinct from the value of circulation and exchange. In this view,

---

71. It should be kept in mind that in the case of noh, the purchase of tickets by a wider public, at least until the Tokugawa era, was associated with the *kanjin* "subscription" noh performances. Usually sponsored by temples, the funds from ticket sales were meant for construction of temple buildings, or public works such as the building of new bridges. The tickets therefore were in essence a form of gift, which, it was thought, purchased an entry into personal and public salvation. Tickets, in other words, were not solely a matter of buying a moment of personal pleasure, but rather involved the exchange of moral worth.

surplus is just a matter of obligated alms, a dutiful return to the benevolent source.[72]

Rice, Money, and the General Equivalent

Any discussion of gifts, or of exchange or substitution in general—or even any speculation on the orientation of an order of value—requires an account of the form of equivalent of what is being exchanged, or given.

Goux outlines four stages in the genesis of the transcendent money form: simple barter between two commodities; an extended form of barter; the development of one commodity, such as a grain, which becomes the standard of value for all other commodities; and finally the transcendent money form—gold, for example, in a gold standard economy, separated off in a treasury as the transcendent backing of a cash currency.[73] In the first, elementary form, the two commodities of barter have a specular, mirroring relation of value to each other. The second level of value is just an extension of this: one commodity is placed in this exclusive mirroring relationship with multiple other commodities, although these other commodities still have no standard of measure between themselves. The third level resolves this problem: all commodities find their value in terms of one single commodity, a general equivalent, and their values are all standardized in terms of this general equivalent. At the final, fourth level this general equivalent is separated off in a position of transcendence, as is the case with gold being placed in a treasury as backing for cash, but pulled out of circulation.

The bakufu seems to have been opposed to the fourth, wholly transcendent level of the symbolic value of an abstract money-form economy. Their

---

72. Accordingly, the apparent excesses of the daimyo in Edo might not have been considered excessive. The edicts of frugality issued to daimyo as well as to commoners, as Shively has shown, did not precisely curb expenditure; they *regulated* expenditure (this would seem to be the closest translation for the term *kenyaku*, 倹約, more commonly translated as "economy" or "frugality"). Levels of luxury, like levels of social class and everything else in the Tokugawa era, had their proper places. Therefore not only to spend too much, but to be overly frugal would be, in Tokugawa Ieyasu's words, to "fail in [one's] obligations" (passage from the *Tokugawa jikki*, cited in Shively, "Status in Early Tokugawa," 152).
73. Jean-Joseph Goux's close analysis of the emergence of the transcendent money form, based on Marx, provides a useful framework for approaching the forms of equivalence specific to the Tokugawa economy. I am not trying to integrate the money form of early modern Japan into Goux's evolutionary, and largely universal, history. Goux claims to be describing a genesis of forms of exchange which is "globally patterned" (*Symbolic Economies*, 94), a progressive accession of at once "gold, the father, and the phallus to normative sovereignty" as general equivalent, in a process that is both personal and historical, phylogentic and ontogenetic (24). It is thus a unilinear progressivist account of the history of the money form, and of history in general.

institution of the rice stipend seems to have been based on a more "ancient"[74] identity of exchange, as in the mirror relationship between two items in simple barter. Specifically, the generalized form of this mirror relationship of value perhaps best characterizes the bakufu's economy—a relationship in which all commodities find their value expressed and standardized by one central, nonabstract commodity: rice.

Under the Tokugawa shoguns all goods and possessions were translated into an equivalence to rice. In this way, an aggregate expression could be given to a household's economic position, and the positions of different households, domains, or regions could all thereby be measured (in *koku*—about five bushels of rice) and compared. Rice was thus made the measure of everything, including income, wealth, and social status.

Rice was not, however, simply a representative of value. As a privileged natural commodity, rice *had* value. Rice was thought of as a gift from the gods to the first emperor. Although annual harvest rites performed by the emperor—offering grains of the new rice crop to the gods in return for the original seeds given by the gods—had fallen into disuse by the Tokugawa era, rice was still spoken of as containing *nigitama* (divine soul). Accordingly, with rice, what circulated was a priceless commodity with sacred value—not a substitute.

The same could be said of the use value of rice as a commodity. Itself a circulating commodity and staple food, rice entered into the satisfaction of immediate needs, and was an agent of the process of production. Thus, although it was a representative for exchange value, it held use value, a value which in contemporary representations was also natural. Rice embodied a real material presence of a value that was the source of all value. This was the theory behind policies such as that advocated by Kumazawa Banzan, of *kikoku senkin* ('revering grain and despising gold'). For Kumazawa, "The treasure of the people is grain. Gold, silver, copper and so forth are the servants of grain. They come after grain."[75]

Consequently unlike the abstract relationship that money has as a representative of value, with rice there was an identity between its function as a medium of exchange and its function as intrinsic economic wealth. Eco-

---

74. That this identity was therefore also one between past and present has already been shown—hence it is an identity with an ancient value form which was itself perceived as identitarian.
75. Kumazawa, *Shūgi gaisho*, cited in Morris-Suzuki, ibid., 17.

nomic value thus is undifferentiated from noneconomic value, and the originary rule of all things is natural, essentialist, immediate and unchanging.[76]

At the same time, the bakufu recognized and utilized the more abstract form of coined money. The Tokugawas managed to regularize a system of coins, and advocated their use, in limited contexts. They had firm enough control over gold and silver coins in the late seventeenth and early eighteenth centuries to substantially debase them by repeatedly increasing the content of copper relative to gold or silver, although this did result in strong inflation. Thus some scholars have argued that because the value of the coins was to some extent arbitrarily determined rather than based on the actual silver or gold content, there was a symbolic form of monetary representative in the shogun's economy similar to the abstract currency of capitalism.[77]

However, the bakufu never created a statewide abstract money system, and never separated gold out of the currency system. Although gold was at times nominally the general equivalent of other metals, for the most part the bakufu allowed a dual or even tri-metal system of gold, silver and copper; no real abstract universal equivalent appeared.[78]

Despite the shogunate denying the domains the right to continue minting their own coins, the provinces did continue, to varying and limited degrees, to use their own coins and their own paper currencies (*hansatsu*), just as some domains retained limited use of their own ritual calendars. As the shogunate's power weakened, these domainal monies became more pervasive. So in this way, too, money did not constitute a statewide general equivalent. Coins, furthermore, were still dealt with in the Tokugawa era as negotiable goods themselves, yet another form of commodity rather than a transcendent and fixed representative of value.[79]

As for paper money, in other words money which was purely representational (having none of the use value of a metal coin), the shogun did not allow himself the right to issue money, but did allow this right to domainal

---

76. Law, therefore, by this form of rule was nonjusticiable, being based rather on an eternal natural good.
77. See, for example, Peter Frost, *The Bakumatsu Currency Crisis*, Harvard East Asian Monographs 36 (Harvard: Harvard University Press, 1970), 11–12.
78. To the extent that the coinage systems were regularized at all, the circulations still tended to be localized by class (with coppers circulating more among the lower classes, and among the upper classes, gold) and by region (silver was the principle coin currency in the area around Kyoto, and gold around Edo).
79. On the use of coins as negotiable goods, see Takekoshi, *The Economic Aspects* III, 422.

lords.⁸⁰ Hence in principle the shogun maintained control over rice, the primary medium of exchange, and the right to mint coins; lesser powers were granted the right to use a more abstract form of money. It may be that these levels of representation allowed for different levels of power, creating another hierarchy of similitude and rule. Similar to the hierarchy of time mentioned above, in this case, the closer one comes to a true, embodied, natural or divine representative of value (as rice was taken to be), the closer one comes to the center of rule. A more abstract form of representation such as cash currency thus would imply a more distanced position from the center of value and more separate from a position of rulership.

To further speculate on the quality of this economy's space, because the measure or rule of comparison is a divine center (rice, or Ieyasu's deified being), the relation of things to this center is determined in terms of their place in the theological hierarchy. Depth therefore is a matter of spiritual judgment—everything is represented on a single plane—and is linked to the spiritual quality of the objects; depth is linked more to the quality of the objects themselves than to a rationally measured, homogenous space. This spatial relation is thus similar to what Goux calls medieval or feudal space: "there is no absolute separation between the world of *facts* and that of *values*."⁸¹ This kind of separation arises only with a more mathematical Euclidean notion of space, and the perspectives of independent subjects. This latter form of space is precisely the picture that is presented in the scholar of Western learning, Shiba Kōkan, and his critiques of the typical forms of illustrative representation common until the nineteenth century. For Shiba, too, these two different modes of representation were important not just as modes of art, but in fact were matters of truth and of governance.⁸²

Returning to the relations of space more directly in the terms of the general equivalent we have been discussing: in the generalized form of the mirror relationship of value, all commodities find their value expressed and standardized by one central commodity, and thereby acquire a determination that is both social and autonomous. This neatly describes the relationship that the bakufu had with the domains—a form of centrality against which all other elements defined themselves, including their relative value to each

---

80. On coinage and the issuance of paper money, see Honjō Eijirō, "Bakufu no shihei hakkō," in *Bakumatsu no shinseisaku* (Tokyo: Yūhikaku, 1940), 245–287.
81. Goux, *Symbolic Economies*, 174.
82. See, for instance, "Seiyoga dan," in *Nihon no meicho* 22 (Tokyo: Chūō Kōron, 1971). This is discussed further in Chapter 4.

other, and yet which nonetheless allowed for independent power and simple binary relationships among the various elements.[83]

There remained a tension in this relationship, between a feudalistic dispersal of power in which the bakufu cultivated simple relations of power and identity between individual domains, and a broader, "monarchical" unification based on representations of the shogun as a transcendent center. This relates to the broader conditions of the time, with the bakufu advocating a simple relationship with an agrarian base of production even while the only way they could reenact such an order would be through manipulations of space that already implied a different political economy of circulation and exchange. This may explain the shogunate's policy of privileging rice as the measure of value, at the same time it encouraged the use of coins. Although the shogun cannot be considered an absolute monarch comparable to European kings, the problem was similar. To quote Marx,

> absolute monarchy—itself the product of the development of bourgeois wealth to such an extent that it became incompatible with traditional feudal relations—needs the material lever found in the power of the *general equivalent*; it needs wealth in a form that can be mobilized at any moment, a form absolutely independent of particular local, natural, individual relations: the form that corresponds to the general, universal power that the bourgeoisie must be able to exercise in all parts of its territory. It needs wealth in the form of money.[84]

With rice as the legislator of all value for the shogunate, there was no separate realm of simple economy. As in the self-sufficient village unit, the price of an object would not be distinguished from its moral and social value; all of these were in principle fixed by the unchanging needs of nature, which, in other words, were "priceless." It was a mode of substitution based on a disavowal of representatives, or substitutes, of value. Instead, the measure of things was based on unmediated presence: of natural use value in the general equivalent (rice); of the ancient laws in the present ruler; and of the past values and customs in the present order of society.

---

83. In what were truly more ancient times, around the third century, actual mirrors were apparently distributed by emperors to their outlying lords—material signs of precisely this relation of power. But while some intellectuals associated with the shogunate did argue for the revival of ancient forms of status relations, none that I am aware of made reference to these ancient mirrors.

84. Marx, *Contribution à la critique*, 181; cited in Goux, *Symbolic Economies*, 39.

The Value of the Stage / 101

Even among the more outspoken champions of this value form there appears fairly commonly an expression of the present as a "degeneration" from a true identity with the past.[85] This loss, and the manipulation of this loss, set up the kind of longing seen in the previous chapter. This debasement of value implies a break or disjuncture in the identity between true value and the current appearance of things, matching the debasement of allegory seen in the poetics of the noh. At this point, however, I am emphasizing only that there was a desire for unity with an originary past value.

Noh: *The Reed Cutter*

In the following chapter, I will argue that noh plays typically entail a structure of desire that is shamanic: each play generally proceeds in two acts, with the main character first appearing as someone longing for another person of the past, and then in the second act reappearing as that very person of the past, to dance in brief unity of past and present identity.[86] This fits the bakufu's rice economy, with its claims for the material embodiment of past values, and unchanging identity with them.

A glimpse at another noh play is worthwhile here, in the context of value, exchange, and equivalence as discussed above. *The Reed Cutter* (*Ashikari*) is one of the few noh plays set in the context of a marketplace, although even in this case it is not the market that determines the true value of things. Based on the *Yamato Monogatari* and poetry from a tenth-century imperial collection of poetry called the *Shūishū*, the play concerns a wellborn couple

---

85. Dazai Shundai, for example, sought solutions so that "our degenerate world [could] become one with the ancients." His answer to the problem was trade for profit; though "not the best way to govern," it would bring relief to the present crisis. He was also one of the first samurai to acknowledge that the boundaries of the shogunate's ostensibly closed economic circle was penetrated at the very top (in this case, the closure of the country); "Look at the *Bakufu* today, buying commodities from abroad through Nagasaki and selling them throughout the country. This is, indeed, trade. Why then should the daimyo of the land be at all fearful of trading their produce to other domains?" Ultimately, however, Dazai's solution seems to be a matter of maintaining the proper "ancient" form of passing on rule: giving a domain lord's inheritance only to the firstborn son, and not allowing further distributions to later born or adoptive sons—a form of rule which replicates the unchanging closed value of rice as a general equivalent. See *Keizai roku shūi*, 43–53.
86. This is especially true of what is sometimes called *mūgen* (phantasmal) noh, in opposition to the *genzai* ("contemporary" noh—plays which often were based on real historical people, and tended toward a more linear temporality; these plays too, however, were almost never based in a real-time historical present). The *mūgen* noh include the so-called warrior and women plays, and covers the majority of plays performed in the Tokugawa era as well as today. The distinction of *mūgen* versus *genzai* is itself a modern one. See Komparu, *The Noh Theater*, 76–79.

who have fallen on hard times. The wife leaves to find employment in a nobleman's household in the capital, but returns years later to find that her husband has become a poor reed cutter. He hides out of embarrassment, but they reunite and go to live together in the capital.

The initial setting is of separation from that which is good and true: separation of husband and wife; of countryside (the bayside market place) from the capital, where the reed cutter once lived; of past happiness from present destitution; even of the main character from his own true being—"I myself do not know my own face," he states, "I have forgotten it. In the midst of the market crowd."[87]

The past, and the capital, are figured as the valued place from which things have now fallen.[88] The reed cutter, for instance, commenting on how he had once been a person of "quality" and consequence in the capital of Naniwa, sings "now I have fallen, dew from a leaf, I have withered and faded like a dry reed." The desire, then, to find a unity in the present with that originary place, is expressed as an exchange, and is based on word play—between *ashi*, which means "reed," but also "bad," and *yoshi*, the word for "rushes," which also means "good." So when the principal character sings

> I have withered and faded like a dry reed.
> My reeds (*ashi*) have also lost their color,
> But buy them please, the best I have.
> Imagine they are rushes (*yoshi*) instead. . . .
> Buy my reeds, give me a fair price.

he is asking for a neat exchange, for an imaginary identification between the past and the present state of affairs, which is also an identification of the good (of the past) with the bad (of the present). This would be "a fair price." To the attendants' question "Are reeds and rushes the same thing, then?," the husband replies that they are (and rushes *are* simply dried reeds).

Other, real identities are then discovered, and the husband admits that he is the wife's husband of the past. The whole scene of the play, too, is identified with an explicitly founding past, as the husband and wife are defined by

---

87. James A. O'Brien, transl., 153.
88. The capital, it would seem, was associated with value because it was associated with associations. When the wife's attendants first encounter the reed cutter, for instance, they express delight that he should be selling Naniwa reeds (Naniwa would be well known in poetry as both the name of a fourth-century capital, and of a reed); the reed cutter replies, "It takes someone from the Capital to appreciate Naniwa reeds." It may appear tautologous, but value derives from the association with associations (with value).

quotes from two poems of the *Kokinshū*—two poems which, as the chorus sings, "Are the parents of all poetry. They are the seeds of the poems of every generation.... The first models of our people." Husband and wife are identified with their past true selves as described within the play, and at the same time these characters are identified with the originary models of *all* men and women.

Now discovered to be "a man of quality," the husband is given a nobleman's hat and robe to wear. The play closes with their return to the capital, completing the reunion of value. The husband is reunited with his true self and memory is thereby restored. The proper relations between man and wife are revived, and in general the goodness of the past is reasserted in the present—all in a capital of value which itself defines value as an unchanging, supra-economical good.

Commerce, Capitalism, and Kabuki

Tokugawa Japan—a country of newly defined boundaries and spaces—was yet also a country on the move.[89] The processions of daimyo to Edo; the movement of agrarian workers to the cities; the traveling poets; the circulation of knowledge;[90] and especially the flows of commerce—all these contributed to the emergence of a state space, and to the figuration of that state differently from the controlled boundaries and permanent values affirmed by the shogunate.

It was not simply a matter of commercial flows "penetrating" the boundary lines of the shogun, although this metaphor does arise. In the way

---

89. In the words of a contemporary traveler: "It is scarce credible, what numbers of people daily travel on the roads in this country, and I can assure the reader, from my own experience, having passed it four times, that highway, which is one of the chief and indeed the most frequented of the seven great roads in Japan, is upon some days more crowded than the public streets in any [of] the most populous towns in Europe. This is owing partly to the country being extremely populous, partly to the frequent journeys which the natives undertake, oftener than perhaps any other nation, either willingly and out of their own free choice, or because they are necessitated to it." "Kemperer's History of Japan," in John Pinkerton, ed., *Voyages and Travels* 7 (London: Longman, Hurst, Rees, Orme, and Brown, 1811), 784.
90. The great blossoming of different schools of intellectual thought in the Tokugawa era was accompanied by a good deal of circulation and influence between members of different schools; some nativists were trained by Confucianists, and so on. Furthermore, intellectuals themselves were often literally on the move, leaving domains they were supposedly beholden to, or departing the shogun's service to return to agrarian contexts, and so on—a peripatetic condition which itself belied the claims for closed boundaries and enduring masters made by the shogunate, and by some of these thinkers.

that commercial culture and values were often talked about, it was as if the streams of commerce were somehow floating, like the floating world which defined commercial culture, above the ground of the state. Commerce was in a very literal way dependent on water. The system of canals, waterways, and rivers of Edo in particular led it to be known as a "city of water"; nearly all available shoreline was taken up by merchant warehouses, shops, and markets. The kabuki theater, too, and the pleasure quarters were expressly confined to and constructed in an area accessible primarily by bridge or boat; theaters were often built at the riverside.[91] This floating quality of the surroundings was integrated into the theater, as for example in the spectacular opening of the theater's new season, the New Year's *kaomise* ceremony, when the star actors entered not from the stage, but rather by gliding in on a boat.

Within this merchant economy, value itself takes on a moving, floating quality. This is expressed, for example, in the way the spirit of gold describes itself in a late eighteenth-century work by the novelist Ueda Akinari:

> Just when you think I've gathered in one place, I may suddenly run off somewhere else, according to how my master treats me. I'm like water flowing downward. Night and day, moving ceaselessly, I never stop.... I do not depend on a permanent master.[92]

Value, which in this case is monetary value, has lost the permanence of its moorings, and is no longer identified with any single rule or master.[93] These

---

91. This pattern was followed in other major cities, including Osaka, Hakata, Kanazawa, and Niigata. See Hidenobu Jinnai, 137.
92. "Himpukuron" (On Wealth and Poverty), in *Ugetsu Monogatari*, Leon M. Zolbrod, transl. (Vancouver: University of British Columbia Press, 1974), 201. It may be relevant that the verb used in "water flowing downward" is *katabuku* (傾く), the verb from which *kabuki* is derived and which, literally meaning "to tilt," implied a certain avant-garde expression of difference.
93. This lack of grounding, or loss of social anchor, is evident in Ogyū Sorai's frequently repeated description of the new urban life as one in which "Both greater and lesser people are living like guests at an inn (*ryoshuku no kyokai*)." But for advocates of the shogunate like Sorai, this was the result of a separation from the natural values of the agrarian terra firma: "The basis of the social order created by the ancient sages was that all people, both high and low, should live on the land. As a result a system of propriety was established. Nowadays, these two elements are lacking, and consequently both high and low experience distress and all manner of evils are brought into being.... Both greater and lesser people are living like guests at an inn, which is directly contrary to the way of the sages..." (Cited in Morris-Suzuki, *A History of Japanese Economic Thought*, 21.)

The Value of the Stage / 105

form part of the qualities characteristic of the Tokugawa-era economy of commerce, money, and the culture of kabuki.[94]

Rice was the measure of value for the shogunate; money was central to the merchant realm. Noh actors were instituted into the rice economy. Literally, in the sense that they were given rice stipends to live on, and were restricted from using their art to gain profits outside these awards. And figuratively, insofar as their own cycles mirrored those of rice as a natural value form. Kabuki, however, developed under the patronage of the three principal locations of developing monetary capitalism: the rice merchants, the Edo fish market, and the Yoshiwara pleasure district.[95] Along with the fish market and the pleasure quarters, the kabuki theater itself was popularly believed to be one of only three places in the country where over 1,000 ryō in gold coins changed hands daily.

As mentioned above, the shogunate utilized the country's systems of money and made some effort to centralize and control them. Yet when they took steps toward centralization, and brought in the best-known coin maker, the coins were minted with the name and guarantee seal of the coin maker, not the government. A very wealthy merchant, it was his credit that backed the coins (in this case, gold *koban*) rather than the bakufu's.[96] The value of money, in other words, remained within the realm of the merchants.

---

94. Because commerce was *not* based on the commodification and parceling of land, commerce remained in a very real way separate from the values of the Tokugawa agrarian economy. The shogunate continued to operate a mode of socioeconomic control that was literally land based. Social positions and classes were maintained through officially allotted land holdings, assessed land productivity, feudal levies, residential immobility, and so on. As daimyo became increasingly dependent on money borrowed from merchant lenders, the collateral provided for these loans was made up only of products of the land, such as rice, or paper—a clear distinction was maintained between rights to these products and rights to the land itself. There was therefore no possibility that the capital of merchants could be transformed into territorial ownership. See Miyamoto Mataji, "Daimyōgashi no rishiritsu ni tsuite—Kōnoike ryōgaeshō shihon no kenkyū," in *Osaka Daigaku keizaigaku* 10, No. 2 (Nov. 1960), 1–26. In this way too, the developing geography of commercial space was disconnected from what was represented as the permanent base of production, and value, of the shogunate.

95. This relationship was acknowledged and formalized by a ritual exchange of gifts between the kabuki theater and patronage groups from these three arenas of capitalism. At performances of *Sukeroku* (one of the preeminent plays about the Yoshiwara district), the show would begin with a requisite respectful salutation to the Yoshiwara, and representatives of the Yoshiwara, in turn, made a ceremonial presentation of the headbands, lanterns, and parasols that were central props in the play. Some of the more generous merchant patrons were even allowed the opportunity to play some of the musicians' parts in plays. See, for example Gunji, "Kabuki and its Social Background," in *Tokugawa Japan*, 198–200.

96. Takekoshi, *The Economic Aspects* III, 31–32.

What, then, was money like in the Tokugawa era? Money and its circulation, as the passage above from "the spirit of gold" indicates, seemed to desire new and forever changing pathways, in contrast to rice. As the merchant's apprentice says in Saikaku's *The Eternal Storehouse*, "Tucking away a clever interest-making koban, putting it at the bottom of a deep trunk, and keeping it from outside contacts all these years is not what we expect from a true merchant. If these are your methods, sir, you will never become a millionaire." "Gold coins wrapped up and left are hardly likely to multiply, not by so much as a single ryō."[97] It is precisely this constant need for "outside contacts" that the shogun's agrarian cycles wished to avoid, in order to preserve the closed circle of value on which its rule was based.

The apprentice in this Saikaku story is commenting on the merchant's admission that he has set aside a lump sum of money for his wife to use for temple visits after she retires. By the standards of the rice economy, this would be an appropriate act of setting aside surplus for the return to its godly origins; in Buyō Inshi's terms, a preservation of vitality. But in Tokugawa mercantile capitalism, this is an act of taking "live" money out of circulation, confining it and therefore restricting development. Money was reputed to have a spirit and a voice, and in Saikaku, when hoarded, money's "captive spirits" moan; again, in apparent desire to be sent back out into circulation.[98]

Money, and the commodities in which merchants dealt, seemed to have the power to generate interest on their own, or with only minimal assistance from productive labor. Thus a poor man in *The Eternal Storehouse* wonders, "Can there be no way of making something out of nothing?"[99] Noticing the amount of scraps dropped by carpenters and roof thatchers on their way home from work, the man picks them up and sells them just as they are. These scraps "grow into trees," and he becomes a wealthy man. The only real labor added was the carving of scraps into chopsticks, on days too wet to do anything else; like the gold that craves to reenter circulation, wood seems to increase and multiply on its own. This emphasis on growth and transformation becomes the new nature of value, displacing the natural value of rice.

In these examples, if money *has* value in the experience of those using it, rather than just *representing* value, it is value that nonetheless is separated

---

97. G. W. Sargent, *Japanese Family Storehouse*, 135. Saikaku's work was evidently an exceptionally perceptive account of commercial values and the experience of commerce in Tokugawa Japan—enough so that it was supposedly read by people then as a kind of how-to manual.
98. Sargent, *Japanese Family Storehouse*, 123. Saikaku also equates "breath" with monetary "interest" through a word play on *iki*.
99. Ibid., 61.

from the realm of human production—unlike the representations of rice as embodying value.[100]

A similar point can be made regarding time. In the rice economy, humans are part of the natural cycles of agricultural production in which rice as value is produced, consumed, and the surplus then returned for a renewed and identical cycle. This closed and eternal temporality is based on the godly gifts of a past to which the cycle always seeks to return. I pointed out earlier in this chapter that the commercial world, too, was associated with notions of eternity, but that this eternal temporality was primarily an expression of the temporal distribution of the worth of a commodity. Time becomes separated from the natural world, and from human labor production.

Thus time and value become separated from the human life cycle. This leads to dreams of being reunited with the value of money. The paradox of owning wealth and yet being separated from it at the time of one's death is one of the most common expressions of this problem. Again, Saikaku: "To think that all this gold and silver will be someone else's when I die! . . . What a sad and dreadful thought that is!" wails a sick tea merchant, desperate to keep his wealth with him. He orders a servant to bring the money from his storeroom and lay it around his body, from head to foot, as if he could thus become one with it. He dies, but not before going mad—the madness of an impossible separation of human life from the values it produces.[101] In a sense, Saikaku was describing the effects of early primitive accumulation—here, with the direct producer himself becoming alienated from his own surplus production.

In the capitalistic usages of commercial money, it became difficult to really *have* money at all. The separation of money from its own value was twofold. First, money's need to circulate: this is a problem not only of capital, which needs to be invested in order to produce, but also of money as a representative of exchange value. Money is possessed only when it is withdrawn from circulation, but as Marx has shown, money then loses its character of universal exchange value. Also, as representative of wealth, money becomes real only when it is given up: "As material representative of general wealth, it is realized only by being thrown back into circulation, to disappear in

---

100. One could argue that attributing to gold the ability to breathe and to grow is a perfect example of Marx's idea of fetishism—seeing in a commodity powers supposedly natural that are in fact social powers (Marx himself used gold as an example, and the appearance of value as naturally inherent to it). I am following a slightly different approach, though.
101. Ibid., 93–96. There is an additional problem of value, or money, and the separation from its source in this story: the merchant has made much of his money by adding used tea dregs to the new tea he sold.

exchange for the singular, particular modes of wealth."[102] Unlike rice, which literally could be consumed, hoarded money was exchange value lost. This provides a way to read Saikaku's observations on gold, and is part of the problem of a cat made of gold: In this case, a man so desperately wants to be united with his wealth that he *is* reincarnated as a golden being. But, "although its body was of gold it could naturally not spend it." Fittingly, the cat is then reincarnated as a miser, a man who never spends his great hoard of money, so he gets nothing for it (he could not alienate his wealth from himself as capital, to spend and enjoy it); bored, he dies at an early age.[103]

Secondly, money as capital is also separated from its own moment or place of complete value fulfillment; capital always entails a delay and deferral of consumption through the reinvestment of surplus. Capital is inherently future oriented. It only remains capital if it continues to be invested and reinvested for a future return. This opposes the temporal orientation of surplus in the rice economy, in which surplus is always considered the rightful return to the originary past, with the shogun as embodiment of that originary past.

In this experience of mercantilism, time becomes the time of a commodity's worth. Monetary value takes on a life of its own, and grows apart from humanity and the life of the human body. Because value is defined in terms of a future goal, it is never fixed.

There is evidence of coin exchange merchants minting their own coins several hundred years before the Tokugawa era. Thus, even before the Tokugawa era began, merchant exchanges were geared toward a transcendent universal equivalent and a speculative future. A new possibility for speculation arose and with it the new need for a mediator in storing rice allotments allocated to the Tokugawa domainal lords. Through the use of bills given in exchange for rice allotments, the merchants engaged in something like our futures markets. Despite being outside the law of the bakufu, merchant associations such as the *kō* developed a detailed discourse on future-oriented capitalistic investment.[104] Exchange was thus aimed toward the future.

The whole point of these exchanges was the open aspect of value. The kabuki theater again provides an example. Unlike the officially patronized noh, kabuki theater productions were dependent on the financing of capital investors (*kinshu*, 金主); these ventures were considered a form of risky play, full of future potential for both great wealth and absolute poverty. These

102. Marx, *Grundrisse*, 233.
103. *Japanese Family Storehouse*, 72.
104. Tetsuo Najita, "Political Economy in Thought and Practice Among Commoners in Nineteenth-Century Japan: Some Preliminary Comments," *The Japan Foundation Newsletter* XVI, No. 3.

great windfalls and losses differed dramatically from the fixed ritual cycle of pure reproduction advocated by the bakufu.

Rice as a general equivalent was based on a simple relation of direct exchange. But from early in the Tokugawa era it was said that no exchange of commodities was possible without the action of an intermediary merchant. The shogun himself found the institution of the rice merchant necessary to keep the *kokudaka* rice system operational. This mediation instituted precisely the break in identity between buyer and seller that the bakufu's economy sought to escape.[105]

Being purely representational, money itself and particularly the increasingly varied bills of credit lacked any grounding or essential identity with the value it represented—even for proponents of commerce like Saikaku. In "The Man Who Built the Cenotaph of Debts," people pile up bills of credit without having any wealth, or any intention of paying these bills; they simply "maintain appearances on other peoples' money."[106] The one man who eventually does try to repay his debts is unable to find many of his creditors, and so he builds a stone temple at Mt. Koya, which he calls the Cenotaph of Debts.[107] The cenotaph is the exact figure of a bill of credit, and perhaps of money in general: an empty tomb, holding a body that in fact lies elsewhere. As if to emphasize this, after stating the name of the tomb Saikaku concludes: "One would search history in vain to find a parallel for such honesty." Just as the cenotaph is the vault of nothing—devoid of the deceased body—so too there is no past essence in history to verify, or lend value to, the honesty of the present. History has no body; it lacks the essence of the shogun's claims for an eschatological past.

Kabuki, and the Prostitute as Ghost

Whereas noh's poetics were allegorical and transhistorical, kabuki's were novelistic and, like the merchant world it expressed, valorized the changing time of the present and future. As in the Saikaku stories cited above, money

---

105. Furthermore, as the samurai class fell deeper into debt, the accumulations of rice surpluses which in the shogun's moral economy had their rightful place in the hands of the lords, increasingly fell into the hands, and circulations, of the merchants. Rice as a "priceless" commodity was thus given a price, and entered into a very different system of values—as happened with the lords themselves.
106. *Japanese Family Storehouse*, 72.
107. Given Mt. Koya's status as one of Japan's oldest and most important sites of Buddhism (Shingon Buddhism; the area includes a cemetery with the mausoleums of some of Japan's best-known historical persons), it is likely that Saikaku was also commenting with some irony on the place of capital as Japan's new transcendent representative of value.

itself often figured as a motivating character in the narratives of kabuki, as it certainly did in the everyday lives of the merchants.

The causal force of money in kabuki is evident, for example, in *Izayoi Seishin*, or *Kozaru Shichinosuke*. An example in which merchant money becomes a theme is that of an early version of *Shibaraku*, one of the most popular of all kabuki plays, titled *Kagemasa Ikazuchi Mondo*. At a New Year's day birthday celebration for the young Yoshitsune (a legendary warrior), gifts are presented. The play's hero presents a chest of arms labeled, "Secret Arms for the Felicitous Day." But when the chest is opened, the assembled group finds only a merchant's ledgerbook and an abacus. The hero then proceeds to offer a new lexicology for the word "ledgerbook" (*daifukuchō*, 大福帳): to summarize, the three component characters are taken to signify a realm in which the entire domain—a boundless area including even China, India, and the Heavenly Reed Plain—prospers under the benevolent and eternal good governance of one man. This man is no longer a military ruler. The hero ends his interpretation saying that people must pay special attention to the merchant's ledgerbook, and he then tries to turn away even the emperor's gift (a sword), for Yoshitsune the former warrior now has his "secret arms."

This can be read as an indication that the bakufu's power is being, or should be replaced by the power of the ledger. And in the hero's extended explanation of the meaning of *daifukuchō*, the structure of relations throughout the realm is summed up by the merchants' principle of accounting.

Hence the values arising in mercantile capitalism were also part of kabuki. This occurred within the aesthetics of the kabuki drama, but perhaps the ultimate expression—at least of one aspect of capital—was the great desire among Edoites and people throughout the country to spend huge sums of money on kabuki and the pleasure quarters. Edo guidebooks are replete with descriptions of people of all social levels, "squandering their inheritance, and ruining their names" on kabuki.[108] Great prestige was attached to the idea of casting away every last coin one owned in the pleasure quarters. This fame and prestige are of course in themselves returns of a sort. For example, the eight great *tsū* profligates of late Edo were famous for their knowledge in the ways of pleasure quarters expenditure. But this reckless spending is a nonmoral form of action—like the actions of the *kinshu* investors who funded the theater—which implies a rejection of the all-

---

108. From a 1662 guidebook, quoted in Shively, "Bakufu versus Kabuki," 234.

encompassing sacred moral values of the bakufu's political economy. It is a form of expenditure that opens the eternal, ethical reproductive cycle of the bakufu's economy in favor of a valorization of present and future productivity; and the surplus of this new production no longer falls under the reign of communal moral ethics, instead being part of individual practical action.[109]

The emergence of desire as surplus was also associated with kabuki. This is evident in the plays' poetics, in the appearance of an opposition between social ethics and personal desire—an opposition that becomes the basis for dramatic tension. The love suicide plays are an obvious example. In the moral economy of the shogun, one had an absolute debt to one's lord and to the gifts from the past; one effectively owed one's life to one's lord, in principle making suicide an appropriate expression of return *to* one's lord (at the time of the lord's death, for instance). Desire theoretically would be part of that closed debt—one should desire to follow one's lord in death. So to desire a destiny completely apart from that circle of debt is to create an uncontrolled excess, and a new opposition. Personal and social ties become opposed, and human love becomes separated from morality. Emotions as excess, therefore, and the structural opposition of love (*ninjō*, 人情) to duty (*giri*, 義理) were a product of the culture of kabuki.[110] This shift gave rise to the *ninjōbon*, a genre of books on human love and personal feelings, in the late eighteenth century. Not surprisingly, both these books and the love suicides were eventually banned by the shogunate. Before the suicides were completely prohibited, the shogun required that they be called not "love sui-

---

109. The separation of economy from morality was also visible in understandings of the money form itself. Again, one might turn to the spirit of gold in *Ugetsu Monogatari*: "because I'm neither a God nor a Buddha but basically an object devoid of feeling ... I have no responsibility to judge for people what is right or wrong. It's for Heaven, the Gods, and the Buddhas to praise good and condemn evil. These three make up religion. Their prerogatives are not mine. You must remember that wealth only accumulates where people treat money with respect, because though gold has a spirit its soul differs from that of man. For example consider the case of a wealthy person who for love of his fellow human beings bestows his largess on someone without seeking proper security. If he fails to see when he gives aid that the borrower is a bad risk, then no matter how good his intentions are, his capital will in the end surely be lost. This amounts to knowing the power of money but misunderstanding its essence." Ueda Akinari, "On Wealth and Poverty," 200–201.
110. This is an opposition that is still commonly portrayed as a timeless expression of the makeup of Japanese character. Though elements of contradiction between personal and communal needs appear in earlier tales, as a structural basis of narrative and dramatic tension, it appears to arise first in the culture of kabuki.

cides" (*shinju*, 心中), but rather simply "death by accomplice" (*aitai jini*, 相対死に)[111] —thus removing the excess that love had come to represent.

The space of the city might be understood in a similar way. Briefly, the construction of the pleasure quarters as spaces literally walled off from the rest of the city was an attempt to bring elements outside the control of the shogunate into a confined area. These elements included wanderers who were performers, perhaps prostitutes, but still associated with the religious values of shrines and temples. Their status as *hinin* (非人, "nonhuman") was hence not entirely pejorative. But their incorporation into the body of the city severed those ties, and, while possibly encouraging the acknowledgment of *hinin* as legitimate humans, at the same time allowed for them to become lowly or immoral humans. The bakufu's gesture of creating the space of a moral economy also results in the incorporation, or interiorization, of an emergent immorality. The pleasure quarters comes to be known as an evil or bad place (*akusho*, 悪所), and for the first time prostitution is considered an evil.[112] Thus within the body of the city, desire is interiorized and, opposed to morality, becomes an excess and an evil.[113]

Especially for critics of kabuki and commerce, this desire is part of an economy that is gendered. Buyō Inshi repeatedly cites women and the kabuki theater as the material sources of, and linked figures of, a form of desire that is at the root of the country's ills. Women are for Buyō inappropriate objects of desire partly because their own values are so capricious.[114] But it is especially the *selling* of women that Buyō associates with kabuki, and with desire as excess.

Instead, Buyō believes that desire should be part of the same closed economy, based on the family unit, as agriculture. The bounded love between a husband and wife is the origin of a good body, a good family, and a good

---

111. Gunji, "Kabuki and its Social Background," 203.
112. Shively, "Bakufu versus Kabuki," 242.
113. A notion of the interiority of the human body as dirty also arises in the Tokugawa era, particularly among the members of the pleasure quarters. Edokko were the first to sell toothpaste, and it was especially the lower classes from the country who were considered to have a dirty interior, accompanied by bad breath; thus the slander, "your breath (literally, the interior of your mouth) stinks! Shut up!" (口中が臭いぞ、黙っていろ). White teeth became very popular, as a sign of a clean body. See the *Edo seikatsu jiten* (Tokyo: Seiobō, 1963), 192.
114. Women, says Buyō, change with whatever they see before them, and even in the case of religious belief, it is more a matter of superficial infatuation than true faith. *Seji kemmonroku*, 243–244.

state.¹¹⁵ These forms of limited, bounded desire, however, are exceeded by the charms of women, and kabuki: men begin to spend great sums on women other than their wives, and daughters leave the home and become the family's principal money earners (as prostitutes), no longer hierarchically distinguishable from their parents. Although women are no longer engaged in domestic production such as weaving or sewing, they live in great luxury, "as if meeting with a dream." People come to desire not only the pleasure of women, but great varieties of things in general, all from outside the controlled cycles of production—shops in the pleasure quarters deal not only in love, but also in all kinds of expensive exotica. With the prostitute as the central figure, production in general is displaced by consumption, and consumption is divorced from morality.

The effects of kabuki's poetics, in Buyō's eyes, were similar to those of the prostitute. The music was lewd and excessive, and the plays were a form of unbridled carnal pleasure; it was an art of being "captivated by women's hearts," a captivation that "breaks" loyalty and duty (忠義を破り) and "separates people, friend or foe."¹¹⁶

Like the transcendent money form and the poetics of kabuki, this image of woman, and of desire, disrupted the productivist economy of the shogun. For critics like Buyō, these effects are negative, and could only mean a dissolution of reality. Prostitutes and the theater are aligned with ghosts (*yōkai*; 妖怪); though bewitching, they are mere jokes (*zaregoto*, 戯れ言) of the customs and values of the ancient people (*kojin*, 故人). Deceptive, they are part of the workings of dissipation (*hōtō*, 放蕩) in the world in general.¹¹⁷

Furthermore, Buyō emphasized that it was the whole country, not just the lower classes, that was taken up with the theater and the prostitute.¹¹⁸ Thus, here at the level of economy, we find that the "joking" representation of values of the past indicated that experience in the Tokugawa era was defined by a ghostly, dispersed unreality.

The Gift of Edo

Kabuki, like the noh, had its form of gifts. Gifts expressed and sealed relations between patronage groups and actors.¹¹⁹ The *hanamichi* (花道; literally,

---

115. Ibid., 250.
116. Ibid., 243.
117. Ibid., 252.
118. See, for instance, ibid., 267–268.
119. See note 90, above.

"flower path"), a bridgeway and side stage leading through the audience to the main stage, was originally used for audience members to present actors with gifts (*hana* can mean "gift" as well as "flower"). These gifts were simple exchanges, with actors acknowledging and thanking the audience; they established relationships and identities between presenter and recipient.

There was, however, yet another meaning of *hana*, related to excess. For instance, *hana* was a metaphor for the fights in which a man of the pleasure quarters was always ready to engage. In kabuki, *hana* referred to plays that were excessive and transgressive, and in particular to the play *Sukeroku*,[120] whose main character (as well as the Ichikawa Danjūrō line of flamboyant actors best known for playing the role) was known as *Edo no Hana*—the "flower" or "gift" of Edo. This sense of the gift as an excess—as much as the prostitute—comes to define the economy of the pleasure quarters, and to reorient the values of the shogun. The most relevant figure to this excess is that of the *Edokko* (江戸っ子, "child of Edo"), whom Sukeroku represented,[121] and the great expenditures made by him.

The idea of an excessive gift returns us to a formal problem raised earlier in this chapter—the possible contradiction between a true gift and the return of exchange which annuls the givenness of the gift. In the closed exchange cycles of the shogun, the gift always had a return (*kaeshi*); the very closure of the economic circle depended on the preclusion of any kind of gift as pure expenditure, as something which had no return and therefore would disrupt the circle of exchange. The Edokko represents this latter form of a gift, the prospect of an expenditure which, in terms of the cycles of agricultural value,

---

120. The poetics and story lines exemplify excess, as in Sukeroku's challenging and overcoming a high-ranking samurai. These plays were apparently written primarily for the purpose of presenting whole scenes devoted simply to exchanges of *akutai*, abusive insults and self-aggrandizing bravado, or even menacing-sounding syllables that in fact are nonsense. See Barbara E. Thornbury, *Sukeroku's Double Identity* (Ann Arbor: Center for Japanese Studies, University of Michigan, 1982), 70, and Gunji, *Kabuki—yōshiki to denshō* (Tokyo: Nara Shobō, 1955), 48–50. The props also indicated elements of excess. For example Sukeroku's famous headband, which was ceremonially presented to the actors by Yoshiwara patronage groups before the play, was a color of purple that was itself a sign of externality: illegal in the theater and pleasure quarters, the dye came from China and was supposed to be used only by noble classes. The cherry trees (another reference of *hana*) for which Sukeroku and the pleasure district were very well known, were illegally brought to the pleasure quarters from their confines in the imperial palace grounds, and came to be a preeminent symbol of the pleasure quarters.
121. "Sukeroku's actions, costume, make-up, and speech established him as the ultimate Edokko"—Thornbury, *Sukeroku's Double Identity*, 70. Sukeroku is also described as the quintessential character of the *tsū*, which was quite different from the Edokko, but this incarnation does not arise until later versions of the play, performed by Danjūrō II.

is anti-economic. At the level of the shogun's temporality, this latter form of the gift thus represents the appearance of the event.

The Edokko was, as the name implies, above all a figure of the capital—the first to be produced by, and of, the new city—which as mentioned was itself *the* place of consumption and expenditure.[122] The Edokko, too, was born of the flows of commerce, as a popular description originally from kabuki made clear: he "took his first baby bath in the waterways of Edo... and was raised in the middle of Nihonbashi bridge [the principal trade thoroughfare into Edo]."[123] And although he "kept no money overnight," the Edokko was a figure of money, united with it; he was "gold-leafed."[124]

The Edokko was poor—he had no money—and yet he spent "with generosity."[125] But this was a mostly aimless generosity. He had nothing to give, and no part of himself was alienated—he gave nothing of himself away—that it might come back in a return gift. There was nothing in what he gave, or spent, that compelled a return. Nor did he apparently wish to show generosity to or for anyone in particular. The accounts of spending sprees tend to emphasize simply the outlays of money, rarely listing the objects of consumption.[126]

This is in opposition to the shogun, whose gifts not only always required a return, but also in the very act of giving returned to the shogun an image of benevolence, of the hierarchically placed generous giving being. If the Edokko spent generously, he did not spend out of generosity; generosity with expectation of a return does not seem to have been his motive. This is also different from the *tsū*, who, like the Edokko, were from the commercial world and were prodigious spenders. The *tsū* were wealthy merchants, and their use of money was always a purchase, on fame if nothing else. The outlays of money associated with the Edokko and others in the pleasure quarters

---

122. To emphasize the validity of this birth claim, the designation was only applicable if one were at least the third generation to have lived there.
123. *Suidō no mizu o ubuyu ni abi... Nihonbashi no mannaka ni sodatta...* At the same time, his view toward the shogun was askance: "glaring sideways at the golden dolphins [a reference to decorations on the shogun's castle towers]." Cited in *Edo seikatsu jiten*, 179.
124. Ibid., 179.
125. The Edokko was "no stingy saver of money" (*kane o kechikechi tameruyōna koto o shinai no ga Edokko na no da*). Tanaka Shin, *Shonin no bunka* (Tokyo: Fuji Shoin, 1967), 18.
126. The *Edo seikatsu jiten* says that even if the Edokko had only a small amount of money, he would spend it on buying women; so these expenditures are linked to the forms of desire described above, as in the purchase of prostitutes (see *Edo seikatsu jiten*, 223).

brought no such return. As cited earlier, men in fact were "squandering their names" as well as their fortunes.

These moments of extravagance appear to be moments of pure gift giving as expenditure without a return. They were also, as Buyō Inshi says, of an "instant" (*katatoki*, 片時).[127] That is, divorced from exchange, these expenditures were neither repayments for things received in the past nor payments made for future returns, however immediate. To the extent that these were therefore moments outside of narrative temporalities, they became events. Especially in view of the shogunate's order, based on the repetition of cyclical returns, the Edokko's outlays constituted an interruption, a rupture of the cycle of return; hence, an event. In kabuki, the *ichiyazuke* (一夜漬け)—simple short plays sometimes based on events of just the previous day—emphasize this instantaneous quality.

The place of meaningful experience was accordingly also of the instant. It consisted neither of the retrospective contemplation of the noh's aesthetics, nor the eschatological values of the rice economy. It was also not the deferment of experience into the future inherent in the values of mercantile capitalism, as least as in the depictions of Tokugawa Japan. In capital, as discussed above, any enjoyment of received wealth or surplus must be deferred and reinvested—constituting a debt to the future, in contrast to the rice economy's debt to an originary past.

Thus the Edokko and the expenditures he exemplifies might be understood as figures of a more generalized collapse of economy, apart from the calculations and productions of value seen either in the economy of rice or of commercial capitalism. Spending all that one has, all surplus, clearly did not fit the agricultural reinvestment of surplus demanded by rice. It also denied the separations that arose in merchant value between having money and keeping money "alive" as capital, between the circulations of time as defined by money and commodity value versus the cycles of human life. Consequently the Edokko is similar to the notion of a third term advocated by Bataille—a negation of utilitarian value, and of the restrictions imposed by any need for the reinvestment of surplus (*la part maudite*, or "the accursed share"). In this view the Edokko's expenditures would be liberatory disruptions, in effect positive, creative departures from the limits of the existing economies.[128]

---

127. Buyō Inshi, *Seji kemmonroku*, 254.
128. This also parallels Deleuze and Guattari's creative desire as production, a desire which is not in search of an object it lacks, but rather simply a productive energy that forever moves outward, looking for new contacts.

Furthermore, just as the Edokko might be looked at as an event in the official social order of things, so too the pleasure quarters might be regarded as an "event" within the overall geography of the city. Accordingly, since Edo was the capital, what was at stake was the refiguration of the center of value of the Tokugawa order.

Yet even if there was a refiguration of value orientations, it would not be accurate to view the pleasure quarters expenditures as entirely liberating. For example, although these moments of intemperance did constitute an event, these same events became elements by which a new narrative of time was instituted—as with personal memory. The great losses of money are repeatedly characterized as occasions with which to construct memory, a memory that would last for the rest of one's life.[129] This is not the memory form of the noh, which is always already constituted and of the eternal past. It is more about the forgetting of that kind of memory, which is another way of saying that it is an event. In a final example from Saikaku, a description of spending in the pleasure quarters is provided in the story of a man who finds money, and rather than returning it as he first sets out to do, he decides instead to spend it. Being found rather than earned or received as a gift, the money is already outside of any chain of exchange. So, too, is the moment: the character's decision to spend the found money was entirely unplanned, and the desire to spend "had never previously entered into his calculations."[130] The moment thus had nothing to do with the past, or with received economic "calculations." The purpose, though, is "to make this day serve as a memory for my entire life."[131] Thus it is eventful, based on the erasure or forgetting of past ties. Yet it is also a memory, and becomes part of the narration of a new temporality, in this case the life cycle of a person (in fact it becomes the defining moment of that life cycle), which has its own restrictions.

The Edokko was a figure—perhaps the preeminent figure—of early modern capitalism, and of the experience and values of early modern capitalism. The Edokko's absolute expenditures were present-oriented instants, that appear as attempts at redeeming in the present the deferral of enjoyment into the future that capital required. Similarly, the Edokko's "gold-leafed" body was an exaggeration that indicates this same desire to be united in the present

---

129. See, for example, Buyō Inshi, ibid., 254, and Saikaku (Ivan Morris, trans.), *The Life of an Amorous Woman*, 215.
130. *The Japanese Family Storehouse*, 20.
131. Ivan Morris, trans., ibid., 215.

with a monetary value that always insists on being sent out for other contacts, and future growth. With these characteristics, the Edokko expressed both the separations and the concomitant fantasies of unity that emerged in the experience of commerce and the culture of kabuki.

• • •

The spectacular consumption that defined the capital of the Tokugawa order thus entailed two different orientations of value: one facing back to the eternal past origins of nature, and the other projected into the fluctuating future values of mercantile commodities. This chapter suggests some of the different implications these orientations had for the experience of time, space, memory, and human life in general in the Tokugawa era.

Although the two sets of values had basic differences, both embraced visions of eternity. Eternity therefore becomes a means of juxtaposing the two orientations, and of commenting on the wider historical space of Tokugawa Japan. Furthermore, even if all nation-states are in some way predicated on claims to eternity, then these images of eternity need to be specified, as this chapter has begun to do. Each of the two economies partook in a desire for unity with a base of production perceived to be lost: the rice economy sought to reinvest the "ghostliness" of commodities with the eternal values of the divine (embodied by rice as a general equivalent); and the money economy—exemplified by the figure of the Edokko and his great expenditures or hoarding—yearned to redeem the future value of capital in the present. This perception of a separation from the presence of value is a defining characteristic of the Tokugawa era.[132]

Looking at the different orientations of economy in the Tokugawa era leads to a conclusion similar to Ernst Bloch's notion of nonsynchronicity: the space of social life involved several different times and spaces at once, "as when Nazi Germany simultaneously celebrated its mythic past and technological future."[133]

---

132. This is mirrored by the experience of the capital itself. Edo was a city of consumption, not production, for both upper class samurai, who were by law separated from their agricultural bases, and for the merchant class with their culture of consumption. The creation of a lower class based on their roles as consumers of the shogunal spectacles was part of the policy of the shogunate (as in the machi-iri performances or the appreciation of the shrine at Nikkō discussed in Chapter 1); the shogunate thus created the very separation of production and consumption that they in other contexts critiqued.

133. "Nonsynchronism and Dialectics," in *New German Critique* 11, 22–38.

Although these economies were in some ways collusionary,[134] each also offered the possibility of penetrating critique of the other. Thus, kabuki was not simply critical of the values of the noh. For Buyō Inshi, for instance, the romantic values of the rice economy became a source of critical insight into the separations and contradictions of experience in the commercial world of kabuki.[135] It is therefore somewhat simplistic to locate the possibility for change, critique, or emancipatory awareness solely in the marginal, as is commonly done; critique emerges rather out of a relation.

Finally, as in the case of the commercial values of kabuki, what is taken to be confrontational resistance may not have started out that way. The conditions and even the need for merchants were integral to the shogun's own economy. Merchant culture and values developed positively and creatively on their own, but within the conditions provided by the shogunate. Attitudes of resistance might then follow—as was the case with kabuki, which at times expressed clear resistance to the values of the shogun—but there is a danger in locating, a priori, a conscious resistance or direct opposition in all transgressive or marginal developments.

The layering of apparently opposed world images at the root of early Japanese modern life reappears in the following chapter, in the discussion of the poetics of the noh theater. The orientations of value which I have in this chapter discussed as economic—even while I have also tried to show that these economic regimes were related to more general modes of orienting social form—are in the next two chapters examined as working through aesthetic form.

---

134. As were the material conditions: the circulations of noh actors and exchanges of performances between provinces and the shogun in Edo, for example, provided the material and ideological stability for the growth of commerce; the shogun's ritual cycles were thus good for capitalism. At the same time, the flows of commerce helped to secure the homogeneity of space that was needed for the organization of the state.

135. Accordingly, as emphasized in the introduction, this is not just a matter of residual, older conceptions and practices of time and space still lingering about, as newer forms emerged and eventually replaced them. Also, this was not the sort of dialectical relation that would lead toward a synthetic resolution of opposites. Similarly, I would add that it seems to me of limited use to enter into arguments as to whether the "gift economy" is truly antecedent to market exchange, or that the "gift" as a category (based on an exchange of inalienable objects between interdependent transactors) is universally opposed to "commodity exchange" (exchanging alienable objects between independent transactors). See Christopher Gregory's *Gifts and Commodities* (London: Academic Press, 1982) for one of the clearest examples of this line of thought. Both the shogunate's rice economy and the commercial economy had forms of gifts and market exchange as I have tried to show. The critical point is to historicize them, to show the particular historical intersections of their usages.

3

Longing for the Death of Time: The Poetics of Tokugawa Noh

> A nation may well be regarded as a work of art. Culture is not a reflex, but a progressive appropriation and renewal.... Thus ... are drawn various portraits of man, of man's own works, of modes of life that have already resolved themselves into landscapes and interiors: in short, all that 'forms' space, matter and time.... It must therefore become immediately apparent that national schools of art are not simply convenient frames. For, among these schools and beyond them, the life of forms sets up a sort of ever-changing community ...
> —Henri Focillon, *The Life of Forms in Art*[1]

> A mountain wind blows down Osaka's slope
> To moan the certainty of death;
> [Yet] its message still eludes me....
> My words are all dry, like seaweed on the shore.
> Touching, they once said, but lacking strength—
> My poems lacked strength because they were a woman's.
> Now when I have grown decrepit
> My poems are weaker still. Their life is spent.
> How wretched it is to be old!
> —*Sekidera Komachi (Komachi of the Barrier Temple)*[2]

---

1. Henri Focillon, *The Life of Forms in Art* (New York: Zone Books, 1992), 144–145.
2. See *Yōkyokushū* (*Nihon koten bungaku zenshū*, vol. 33), Koyama and Sato, eds. (Tokyo: Shinchosha, 1983), 433. I have used here the translation by Karen Brazell, in *Twenty Plays of the Noh Theatre*, Donald Keene, ed. (New York: Columbia University Press, 1970), 74.

"Now I return to the Burning House.
But where is the place I used to live?"
Unai calls as through the black night
She searches here and there.
"Where is the Sought-for Grave, where?"
—*Motomezuka (The Sought-for Grave)*[3]

It is certainly possible to claim that social and aesthetic form are not at all the same thing—that even if influenced by economic structures, for instance, the genealogy of artistic forms and practices nonetheless proceeds with some independence from those economic structures. By these standards, the aesthetic form of the noh need not be thought of as reflective of or reducible to the values seen in other realms of social action.[4]

It could further be argued that something approximating an independent, bourgeois institution of "art"—as had already developed in the West when Kant began writing of a separate realm of aesthetics—was beginning to develop in the Edo period. This is evident even in the origins of the tea ceremony in the sixteenth century, with practitioners demonstrating their sensitivity and status through their ability to judge and pay for (or in some reported cases, even steal) the most expensive tea utensils, stones for the attached gardens, and so on. The ability to recite lines from the noh plays, too, became a means of producing class status through the ability to pay for, and learn, this art.

The category of aesthetics, however, did not arise in Japan until the end of the Edo era, just after the Kōka *kanjin* noh performance. Terms such as

---

3. See *Yōkyokushū*, (*Nihon koten bungaku taikei*, vol. 40), Yokomichi Mario and Omote Akira, eds. (Tokyo: Iwanami Shoten, 1960), 74. Translation by Royall Tyler, in *Twenty Plays of the Noh Theatre*, ibid., 49.
4. Henri Focillon's *The Life of Forms in Art* is a seminal work (originally published in 1939), in looking at the dynamics of artistic forms while still emphasizing the historical character of these forms. For Focillon, the realm of art in general, and signs in particular, takes on a life of its own, implying a method which need not necessarily be concerned with questions of representation at all. His work therefore has interesting implications for a renewed interest in the materiality of signs, and is one of those works which points to intriguing possibilities within art history for broader areas of social and cultural analysis. At the same time, from my perspective, even while he does grant history to aesthetic form, this history is nonetheless overly independent of the social, and perhaps the political. However these are issues which deserve subtler treatment than I can provide here. Also it should become clear in the next two chapters that I am interested in little more than the general experience of certain forms, within a specific historical era.

bigaku (美学) and *bijustu* (美術), for fine arts, beauty, or aesthetics, came into use between the mid-nineteenth and early twentieth centuries, and were tied up with display and the use of art as object of display.[5] Aesthetic experience, beauty, and beautiful form only then became more fully disjoined from other modes of knowing, understanding, and experiencing the world. The notion of aesthetic form and the contemplation of beauty as being disinterested is, in Japan, primarily a twentieth-century product.

It is necessary therefore to assume a more extensive understanding of the "aesthetic"—one which pertains not only to artistic forms, or formal, built structures, but also to the practice of such forms in the sense of the existence of certain conditions of experience and subjective agency (self-fashioning) in general.[6] The "aesthetic" is by these terms not at all confined to a narrow realm of art, nor is it delimited to private sensibility, in opposition to public community, or ethical value. The larger moral and social order being orchestrated by the Tokugawa shoguns remained also a question of aesthetic form.[7]

In more practical terms, there was an almost modernist sense that a performative art like the noh was a special realm, more closely involved with affect and emotion than other kinds of social action, and in ways that opposed more rational cognition. The noh, therefore, could be used for the training of desire and emotion. Thus in one of the few Edo-period treatises on the aesthetics of the noh, *Bushogoma*, the author states not only that one

---

5. Early sources include the nineteenth-century writings of Nakagawa Shigeaki, Nishi Amane (in particular, his "Bimyōgaku setsu"—"The Theory of Aesthetics," 1877) and Tsubouchi Shōyō's "Bi to wa nani zo ya" ("What Is Beauty?," 1886). One of the earliest and best known works on the Edo era was Kuki Shuzo's early twentieth-century *Iki no Kōzō—The Structure of Iki*. See Leslie Pincus, *Authenticating Culture in Imperial Japan: Kuki Shuzo and the Rise of National Aesthetics* (Berkeley: University of California Press, 1996). For an English language translation of Kuki's work, see John Power, transl., *Reflections on Japanese Taste: The Structure of Iki* (Sydney: Power Publications, 1997). The idea of an independent realm of aesthetics becomes one of the many highly determined new categories of discussion among early Meiji thinkers who were consciously looking at the West. These debates revolved not only around the parameters of the aesthetic, but also how aesthetics might be brought back into a relation with ethical order, for the purposes of good governance. However this separation and attempted reunification of an independent world of art with an ethical order of governance is also already visible in Shiba Kōkan's short "Treatise On Western Painting," *Seiyoga dan*.

6. There has been some tendency recently, sometimes implicit and sometimes explicit, to distinguish between aesthetics (as a theory of perception) and synaesthetics (as experience, which is more inclusive of the bodily senses, and the cognitive as well); I do not want to make that distinction here.

7. So too, to give one small example, a term like *giri*—which now is taken to mean something like "social obligation," and considered to be a very specifically social term of relation—was used in the Edo period also as a point of aesthetic form.

ought to feel the noh before one thinks about it, but also that in practicing it, even if it seems unpleasurable, one should do as one is expected to and then "it will become pleasurable." So the aesthetic structure of the noh was not conceived of as unrelated to social form. It established a specific relation *to* social form—through the control and disciplining of desire as well as through the ability to create a feeling of consensus, and therefore community.

Yet there is an element of Tokugawa-era noh plays that stands out as anomalous, especially in a world as committed as the shoguns' was to the fixedness and boundedness of identity. There are in effect two kinds of plays that are given special privilege by the Tokugawa rulers. One is the clearly ritual, "godly" type, as in *Takasago* (高砂). These plays typically end in a happily transcendent, divine reconciliation of the present world of appearances with the past world of true identities.

But while these ritual plays were always performed at official programs, and were given special status (*Takasago* was the most commonly used of all by the Tokugawas), the same status was accorded to *Sekidera Komachi* (関寺小町). This nonritual play tells the story of Ono no Komachi, one of Japan's most famous beauties and most revered poets. The play, in other words, raises the image of absolute beauty and of the referential potency of pure poetic language. This, however, is unlike most of the other plays about Komachi, and it is certainly different from the ritual category plays. In brief, the play ends with a decrepit and decaying old Komachi, unable to call back her lost abilities as a poet, and longing, in a state of ugliness, simply for death. So the play results in an aesthetic failure, an inability to revive a good, stable, "beautiful" form. Nonetheless, this play was accorded the highest rank, and at least in theory only the heads of noh schools, the shogun, and top-ranked daimyo were allowed to practice or perform it.

Why would this be so? By most accounts, the kind of state that the Tokugawa shoguns were trying to enforce was premised on firm boundaries, stable identities, and, therefore, a sense of closure and completion. Why then would the shoguns privilege a play that leads instead to an unending dissolution of identity, the ongoing breakup of unity, and perhaps even the impossibility of transcendence? Even if the noh was thought capable of producing an internalization of some kind of moral imperative, what kind of "whole" community could a play like *Sekidera* imply? The weight given to *Sekidera Komachi*, and its apparent contradiction to the ritual plays also valued by the shogun, is central to the discussion of Edo-era noh aesthetics.

Although these are elements that were selected out by the Tokugawa regime, they are present in the noh more generally and lead to an examination of the relationship these general characteristics had with the Edo era. In considering the significance of *Sekidera Komachi* to the Edo era, two qualities are particularly notable. First, a dependency on a poetic promiscuity and multiplicity of meanings and identities as much as on a singular and transcendently unified meaning and identity is definitive of the noh in general. Thus, the possibilities of a multiplicity of times, of temporal experience, and a multiplicity of sites of identity formation were integral to the planned, ordered structure of the Tokugawa world. Secondly, although the noh is typically portrayed as an almost ascetic theater of rigid aristocratic and "feudal" sumptuary control—particularly in contrast to the world of kabuki, which is seen as a site of excess and decadence—plays like *Sekidera Komachi* are premised on excess and decay.[8]

Furthermore, this decadence is framed in the context of death. A specter of deathliness is omnipresent in the noh. The context for most of the plays is a ghostly "dream" moment and the main characters who initially appear on stage nearly always turn out to be mere apparitions of some former self from the distant past. Other than those ritual plays that end in pure redemption of the present in the past, the principal characters are left as mournful "ghosts (or shadows) of death."[9] Yet the result is not necessarily a continuing desire to return to the fullness, youth, and life of the past. Instead, the characters often seem to long for death. In *Sekidera*, as in the ending of the play *Motomezuka* (求塚, "The Sought-for Grave") about a ghost tormented in hell and seeking her own lost grave, it is a real death that these characters seek as much as it is life, and it is their own dead body or grave that they long to be united with as much as with a live one.

---

8. There is of course a simpler, more directly religious reading possible for this desire for death. In many sects of Buddhism, especially at the time when the noh plays were first written, there was an emphasis on enlightenment as a place outside, and after, the cycles of reincarnation. Here, too, death is a positive transcendence of circulations and identities. But the desire for death arises in a variety of plays, including ones with non-Buddhist motifs. More importantly, the Tokugawa regime, as well as society in general in the Edo era, were not as a general rule taken up with the Buddhist worldview, which sought to deny this world in favor of the after life—if anything the reverse was the case. That is part of the point.

9. 亡者の形. See *Yōkyokushū*, vol. 40, Yokomichi and Omote eds., 74 (including n. 17). In *Motomezuka*, the ghost does finally find her grave and disappear—implying some kind of resolution. But the resolution is at best uncertain—apparently temporary rather than final—and it is clear that the woman will continue to yearn for final reunification with her body's place of entombment indefinitely. This ambiguity with regard to resolution is basic to the noh.

So the theater that the shoguns took for their official ceremony, and used as a construct of mastery and eternal ritual continuity, was in many ways premised on a desire for death and endings, on ghosts, vacant graves, and empty or degenerating bodies. The central importance given to *Sekidera Komachi* can thus be considered in the same light as, and part of the same problem as, the "dream" portrait of Ieyasu as the central image of the founding ruler. There too, the purported divine origin of the realm was in effect only a dreamy recollection painted long after his death, rather than a full reembodiment or full image of the Ieyasu as he appeared in life. An emptiness or ghostliness thus pervaded both the geography of shogunal authority, and the poetics of the shogun's official mode of representation.[10] The central question then remains: can this in any way be the basis for a state, particularly one claiming for some kind of eternal integrity?

To further specify the problem, as seen in both *Sekidera* and *Motomezuka* the longing for death is ultimately a longing for the death of time. In formal terms, time is in many ways the critical issue in the noh. It is time that sets up the distances and hence erotics of desire and longing that form the core of the noh's narratives. It is also time that sets up basic questions about identity being found and completed, or lost, dispersed, and left unfulfilled. Accordingly, if the problem for the Tokugawa shoguns of setting up the boundaries of the early modern state was a matter of expanding and fulfilling the Tokugawas' own will or identity, the noh suggests that this would in part be a matter of time.

There are indications beyond the formal level of the noh that in the Edo era, time was felt to be taking on an autonomous role in relation to the movement of nature and the general workings of cosmology. Time was becoming more important, governing all else—in some ways an increasingly modernist structure of time—but its very autonomy also implied the possibility of alienation. The formal tensions that arise in the noh between time and the desire for transcendence of time are part of these general conditions.

This chapter and the next give close attention to the problem of time in the noh, with this chapter providing a more comprehensive view of the aesthetic order of Tokugawa noh. As elsewhere, I will consider basics of the kabuki theater as well, and the literature of capitalism associated with it. The ghosts and empty graves of the noh can also be juxtaposed to the cenotaph of

---

10. Yet another layer of this ghostly incorporeality of Tokugawa life is Saikaku's idea of the cenotaph as an image of the new capitalism.

Saikaku's *Eternal Storehouse of Japan*, for example, or his merchant characters who constantly, but impossibly, long to be bodily united with their accumulated gold. A multiplicity of times is present within both the noh and kabuki. Because these times are potentially in conflict, competition, and struggle with one another, the poetics of Tokugawa theater inevitably involved a politics of time. The noh and kabuki developed distinct aesthetic worlds, however, and the politics were neither a simple matter of opposition between the two, nor one of empowered centers versus disempowered marginals.

One could think of this and the following chapter as an archaeology of two central images: for the noh theater, the aged figure of Komachi or the woman ghost, searching for her own grave—or, alternatively, the dream image of Tokugawa Ieyasu enshrined at the Tōshōgū; and for the kabuki theater, the classic *mie* pose of an actor frozen in action at a critical moment, and glaring cross-eyed at the audience—or, the figure of a man with his eyeballs ostensibly popped out, though still attached to his face by a string of coins, popular at the Ryōgoku street fair. First, a very general description of the noh plays.

The Noh: Contours of Staging and Narrative Form

Because the noh was initially a creation of the middle ages, it is potentially awkward to discuss the poetics of noh in the context of the Tokugawa era. But the Tokugawa shoguns chose to use the noh rather than some other mode of theater or ritual—and there were certainly advisors who argued that a more courtly form, such as *gagaku*, would be more suitable—and more importantly, the shoguns in essence re-created the noh in a form of their own choosing. Furthermore, even within the structure that emerged under the shoguns, certain elements gained broader appeal, and so can be considered as particularly appropriate to, and expressive of, that era. Before specifying these elements, though, an overview of noh plays will be helpful. The general features described here—the very slow pace of the noh, for instance—were in some cases not firmly set until late in the Tokugawa era.

Noh plays take a variety of topics for their subject matter, but nearly all are based on well-known works that were increasingly thought of as "traditional" literary works. The most common sources are the eleventh-century *Tale of Genji*, written by and about the Heian imperial court, and the *Tales of the Heike*, a post-Heian, twelfth-century compilation of oral narratives about the rise and fall of the Taira warrior family. But nearly anything well known could become a source, whether it was a section from the eighth-century national mythology of the *Kojiki*, a poem from any of the better known imperial anthologies, a folktale, or a Buddhist treatise. Only small sections from these works were used, and typically a noh playwright might have based his plays on annotated summaries of the original works rather than attempting to actually read through the often difficult and sometimes nonexistent original texts. These works were, in any event, almost always from the past. This was a tendency which the Tokugawa shoguns made into law; no mention was allowed of current affairs, particularly regarding the samurai class.

The typical noh play can be divided into two parts—some plays are formally broken midway through, with the role of the main character at times being played by different actors in the first and second parts. Generally, the narratives begin in the "present," and move to a world of the past, and often they involve travel away from the capital (or perhaps a shrine or temple). This progress in time and space is formally accomplished by the *michiyuki* (道行, travel or "road going") with which all noh plays begin. The *michiyuki* is by and large only verbally presented: the play opens with a priest (or occasionally someone connected with the imperial court) announcing who he is (the *nanori*, or "naming"; 名乗り)—a passage which itself may clearly indicate, and in some cases ritually invoke, the context of "tradition" in which the play is set. The priest then explains that he is going to take a trip, describes places and scenery he passes along the way, and finally announces that he has arrived. In this *michiyuki*, the priest's explanation is filled with poetic associations, connecting his world with potentially numerous other traditional literary settings.

Having arrived at some "local," usually provincial area, the priest will encounter someone, or some thing, which strikes his curiosity and his memory, and so he inquires of this person about the memory associated with the area. By the end of the first section of the play, this local person reveals that he/she is in truth that very person of the past, associated in popular memory with that locale. In the second section of the play, the local person then appears in his/her true guise as the well-known character of the past, usually to dance out the role that had been verbally described at the end of the first section. The priest has almost no role, other than the critical act of opening up the scene of the play and the narrative more generally—it is after all the priest's questioning that draws out the manifestation of the "real" identity of things. The tension of most plays centers on a longing for unity within the main character (the *shite*), that most often also revolves around a tension between the unity or disunity of present and past—a longing of the main character to be reunited with his/her own former and truer self, or with a lover of the past, or even a lost child. When not centered on a relation of past and present, the plays are almost always set up on a disunity of local provincial setting and the capital. For example in *Kinuta* (砧), a woman's desperate desire to be reunited with her husband who is off in the capital (it should be remembered that in the middle ages, travel out from the capital was still associated with going into the distant past; so this spatial separation is itself not distinct from the temporal disunity of past and present). Some plays end with a clear resolution or reunification, while others do not. The plays are premised on a liminal moment: they often begin around twilight, and although there is a specific category of "dream" plays, plays from any category can end with the chorus describing the waking from a dream, and sometimes the dawning of the sun.[11]

Progression at all levels is ostensibly governed by the principle of *jo-ha-kyū* (序破急, "preface-break-speed") mentioned in Chapter 1. This refers to a set of relations which are neither specifically temporal nor spatial. The *jo*, or preface, is more a term designating spatial origin than time, but in the noh it is also used to refer to a moment of stasis before the introduction of time. *Ha* is a break, tear, or ruin; in the narrative progress of a play it commonly implies a speeding up of tempo, or the introduction of time and narrative, but it can also create a "break" through the slowing of tempo. *Kyū* means speed, and generally plays are expected to end with a feeling of fast tempo. The stage itself is sometimes referred to by these terms, with the rear, backstage area being the *jo*, midstage the *ha*, and upstage front the *kyū*. Within the narrative, each song is (again, ostensibly) organized by this progression, as is the overall development of the play and the progression of plays within a full day's performance of noh. Within a play, the *ha* level is generally the longest, and most important. It is in the *ha* level that the character's true identity is revealed and danced out. This dance itself was considered by Zeami to be the most important moment in any noh play. Called the *kusemai*, it was derived from a form of popular dance in the middle ages. *Kusemai* (曲舞) means "wandering," or "unconventional," "bending," "leaning," "inclining" dance; so the critical moment in the narrative of a noh play is based on the

---

11. It is still common, too, to be told that one of the best states in which to experience the noh is the trance-like moment shortly before you actually nod off.

introduction of some kind of difference. One of the questions here, however, will be what kind of difference.[12]

In the Tokugawa era, five set categories of plays were established, and ordered in a fixed *jo-ha-kyū* scheme. Thus, any full performance should include plays in the following order: first, a "god" (*waki*, ワキ; *shinji*, 神事; or *kami* 神) play; then a "warrior" (*shura*, 修羅) play; "woman" or "wig" (*kazura*, 鬘) play; and either a "miscellaneous," "madness," or "contemporary" (*monogurui*, 物狂い or *genzai*, 現在) play or a "demon" (*kichiku*, 鬼畜; *kiri*, 切, etc.) play—a dance from a god play might then serve as a conclusion. The god plays were considered ritually auspicious. Slow and stately, they end in complete resolution, unlike fourth and fifth category plays, and were considered by Zeami to be structurally "orthodox." So the general trajectory of a program moved from slow paced ritual plays to faster, more irregularly structured plays that typically ended with greater expressions of longing, unfulfilled desire, and little resolution. All of this was cyclical, however: just as the *jo-ha-kyū* principle always implied a return to the *jo* level, a full noh program always ended with some reference back to a "god"-type play, typically in the form of a dance.[13]

The five categories of plays were themselves ordered according to the *jo-ha-kyū* scheme. First category god plays were considered the introductory *jo*; warrior plays were generally the *jo* of the *ha* level; woman plays formed the true *ha*, while the fourth category "miscellaneous" plays were the *kyū* level of the *ha*; and the fifth category demon plays were the *kyū*. Perhaps in part because the five category structure was not created until the Tokugawa era, there is variation in the specificities of how different plays fit the *jo-ha-kyū*

---

12. It is interesting that the meaning of *kuse*—unconventional, leaning, inclining—is almost precisely the same as the meaning of *katabuku*, from which kabuki derived. I will not pursue that similarity here, however. Certainly in the Tokugawa formulation of noh, the "difference" in noh (of a ghost from the past, etc.) will be seen to be quite different from the difference of kabuki.
13. Even the four noh troupes (or really five, counting the unofficial Kita family) were hierarchically categorized by these principles, in the following order: Kanze, Hōshō, Kongō, Kita, and Komparu; the Kanze school in an official program would perform the first category play, the Hōshō school the second, and so on. The two most important schools were first the Kanze, and then the Komparu; the Komparu were presumably placed last not as an expression of demotion, but rather as an affirmation that the final stage in the cycle was also a renewal of the cycle, and therefore equivalent to the first stage. Accordingly, the Kita school (popular even among shoguns but not officially recognized), known for its "fast" and "unorthodox" style, was the school that most often took the *kyū*-level demon play roles which had no association with god-type plays. On the precedence of troupes in a day's program, see Omote and Amano, *Nō Kyōgen I* (Tokyo: Iwanami Kōza, 1987), 128.

order. But designation of the woman play as the *ha* level—and therefore the most important—goes back to the middle ages and to Zeami. "Plays in this category," he wrote, "form the central element in the day's entertainment,"[14] and he accorded them the highest rank: *myōka* (妙歌)—a term which literally means a song/work of "strangeness" or "mystery." It is therefore the figure of the woman, and the increasing portrayal of yearning desire that characterized the woman plays (and "madness" plays, which Zeami grouped together with the woman, *ha* level), that are the central element of noh. There is also a larger argument here too, again with regard to the introduction of difference. This figure of the woman is what "breaks," but also therefore catalyzes, the narrative. Again, the question will be what kind of difference this is.

The noh has little of a dialogic or antagonistic development between independent characters. The drama consists really of just one character, known as the *shite*.[15] There is the "side" character (*waki*) of the priest, and there may be "helpers" (*tsure*), but generally the noh is about the *shite* only. Thus, although the staging of a story is divided among the actor apparently playing the *shite*, a chorus, and the musicians, in fact the *shite* is being acted out by all three elements. Even lines spoken in the first person can be taken, alternately and apparently at random, by the actor and by the chorus—or, the music may indicate a mood of the *shite*. All are contributing to the characterization of the one single being defined as the *shite*, and nothing else. Thus, if there is any difference of perspective at all, it can only be developed from within the character of the *shite*; the chorus and sometimes the actor himself will speak in the third person about the *shite*—but never in terms of conflicting viewpoints. Furthermore, the drama therefore develops as a pure interiority—there is no position of exteriority.[16] This emphasis on the limited perspective of the *shite* only, commonly thought a fundamental charac-

---

14. Rimer and Yamazaki, *On the Art of the Noh*, 84.
15. Royall Tyler's translation of *shite* as "doer" is awkward, but literal, and it conveys the idea that the *shite* is the only one (or thing) who is involved in the drama. Etsuko Terasaki gives slightly greater weight to the importance of the *waki*, or "side" characters, and their role in prompting the *shite* to tell their stories. See Terasaki, *Figures of Desire* (Michigan: University of Michigan Center for Japanese Studies, 2002).
16. It can also be argued that the trajectory of the *michiyuki*, and therefore of the noh plays in general, is a movement into an interiorized world. See for example Thomas Hare, who says that even as a play moves from aural into visual expression, it also moves toward an "internal" world of the *shite*. See *Zeami's Style* (Stanford: Stanford University Press, 1986), 75–77.

teristic of the noh, is a Tokugawa re-creation, and so this, too, needs to be considered as expressive of Tokugawa poetics.[17]

The form of the stage itself was not standardized until at least the eighteenth century. Traits that had become common by the Edo period include a spare stage modeled after shrine stages for performances of rituals; a pine tree permanently painted on the back wall as the only set, and usually some kind of "bridgeway" (*hashigakari*, 橋掛かり)—a side stage connecting to the dressing rooms, but also a "bridge" between two worlds (the present world of humans, and the "other" world of the distant past or the gods). As if to emphasize that only the *shite* actors are truly making this connection, people playing lesser roles enter differently than the *shite*. Stage assistants and often the musicians and the chorus do not enter by the bridgeway, instead kneeling through a small window on the opposite side of the stage. The *waki* and *tsure* "side" or "helper" characters will enter on the bridgeway, but the curtain at the start of the bridgeway will not be lifted for them unless they are accompanied by the *shite*.

• • •

Much of the poetic form of Tokugawa noh did have a direct genealogy to the earlier context of what is called the Japanese "middle ages," roughly from the thirteenth through the sixteenth centuries. In sweeping terms, much of the literary production from this time was dealing with the loss of everyday coherence, and of any social or political center of gravity. Especially for aristocratic classes, prior to the middle ages the idea of life outside the capital had been almost unthinkable. In the middle ages, however, travel became a way of life, and literature tended to focus on both removal from the imperial capital and on the afterlife as the only place of meaning and repose.[18] By the mid- to late-middle ages, when the noh came into being, there was renewed emphasis on this world—but the only possible perspective was still limited, or fragmented. Zen Buddhism is perhaps the most well-known source of this worldview, and this poetics: Zen emphasized that one can and should under-

---

17. It appears likely that in Zeami's own time there was a similar emphasis on the singular position of the *shite*. But by the sixteenth century noh plays had developed such dramatic interaction between characters that there was almost no distinction between the *shite* and the *waki* ("side") characters. On the elimination of side roles in the Tokugawa era, see Oda Sachiko, "Nō no engi to enshutsu: shōzokuzuke, katazuke o meguru shomondai," in *Nōgaku kenkyū* 10 (1984), 63–108.

18. Along with *The Tales of the Heike*, on which so many noh plays are based, another obvious example is Kamo no Chōmei's *Hōjōki* ("Account of My Hut").

The Poetics of Tokugawa Noh / 133

stand the world through physical, bodily senses, but that one could only know things in momentary and circumscribed ways. The Zen rock gardens, designed to be seen only through windows from oblique angles, and the ink paintings often done by the same artists, are typical examples. The poetics of *renga* is another example. In the "linked poems" of renga, the idea is to *not* create a complete picture of a whole, or any totalized statement of meaning. The emphasis in renga is on the links between each poem rather than on the poems themselves, and through these links to create a shift in context, and a shift in meaning, for each poem that precedes the new poem. Rules were created for renga composition, but these very rules demanded "variety and constant change." Even when brought within limits of a set number of poems, the idea was to contain poems within a whole "while resisting comprehensive interpretations."[19] These were thus fragmented perspectives. But at the same time, there was an urge to reunite these views into some new sense of community—hence the fixed numbers of poems, and of poets involved in the renga composition parties.

Zeami, especially in his later years, was a devoted student of Zen, and he was clear about drawing influence from the aesthetics of renga. Even more than Zen and renga, however, the noh embodies the apparently contradictory tendencies toward fragmentation and dispersal on one hand, and yet a movement toward a new whole, and closure on the other. Especially because these two elements become separated out and emphasized in the Tokugawa era, I want to focus here a bit more on unity and fragmentation in the noh.

• • •

One of the simplest and most productive ways to consider the noh as unity might be through Bakhtin's concept of the "epic" chronotope. As a chronotope, this implies not only a structure of space and time, but also an orientation of value. It is therefore particularly apt for my interests here.

To briefly review Bakhtin: the most salient feature of the epic chronotope may be that the sanctioned place of value orientation and point of view—the source of value, the measure by which the worth, moral goodness, and truth of everything is judged (what I have called the point of value)—is located in an "absolute past."[20] In place of the open-endedness of the present,

---

19. Steven Carter on the *Minase sangin hyakuin*, in *Traditional Japanese Poetry* (Stanford: Stanford University Press, 1991), 303, 306.
20. Most of the characteristics I outline can be found in the chapter, "Epic and Novel," in *The Dialogic Imagination* (Austin: The University of Texas Press, 1981), 3–40.

and at the expense of contemporaneity, which cannot become an object of representation, an epic perspective is derived from and looks toward an unchanging past. Bakhtin's three "constitutive" features of the epic chronotope are:[21] a national past (epic is therefore explicitly tied to the boundaries of a nation-state); a national tradition (personal experience is not part of the epic); and most importantly in my view, an absolute distance that separates the epic world from contemporary reality—disjoined and transcendent, the epic past creates an unchanging and unchangeable image of value.[22] The epic past can also be associated with a patriarchal ruling class which is similarly separated from the other classes by a distance that is "almost epic."[23] The epic past is monochronic rather than in any sense dialogic—there is no way of connecting it to the present. Absolute, the epic past is also fully completed, "like a circle;" it contains "the entire fullness of time."[24] Epic characters, too, do not develop but rather are always already completed, "hopelessly ready-made ... [and the epic character] is absolutely equal to himself.... There is not the slightest gap between his authentic essence and its external manifestation."[25] The image one sees of a character therefore completely defines that character. There is no possibility of the epic hero somehow stepping out of character for a moment, and the mask becomes a common expression of that identity. There is, in other words, an epic wholeness of time, of identity and of value in general, which does not permit any excess or any intrusion of difference. Tradition, about which there is a commonly held evaluation, becomes the only means by which the epic past can be revealed in the present.

This absolute, distanced past is precisely the kind of world of tradition and value that early noh drew upon, and that became far more heavily accentuated by the Tokugawa shoguns. Play sources were nearly always from traditional works of literature, either directly or indirectly via well-known commentaries. The language, already archaic, was under the Tokugawa eye made still more poetic, and more "classical," so that even in the Edo era one

---

21. Ibid., 13, ff.
22. "The epic world is an utterly finished thing, not only as an authentic event of the distant past but also on its own terms and by its own standards; it is impossible to change, to re-think, to re-evaluate anything in it. It is completed, conclusive and immutable, as a fact, an idea and a value. This defines absolute epic distance. One can only accept the epic world with reverence; it is impossible to really touch it . . ." Ibid., 17.
23. Ibid., 15.
24. Ibid., 16, 19.
25. Ibid., 34.

would have to have been well versed in earlier linguistic forms to understand a noh play at all. Staging, too, emphasized a distance, or refusal of intrusion by any kind of contingency related to the present. Sets were essentially nonexistent, and only the sparest signs were used as props. A sword or a cup of *sake*, for instance, would equally be represented by the use of a fan. A temple or a mountain hut, if represented at all, would consist of a simple non-iconic frame of bamboo. So, too, the action: in some plays there is almost none. And as I have already noted, the narratives, too, moved from present to past in such a way that, as indicated in the response to the questions of the traveling priest, the identity of what one sees before oneself is "in truth" the identity of the past. The past is the one and true point of value.

The noh's temporality, too, consisted of an epic structure of completed cycles, without possibility of narrative development—at least, this is one way of viewing the noh, and its "god" plays in particular. Likewise, the *shite* can be seen as an epic hero: there to be filled out, completed, but not developed, with any possibility of alternative traits. So too the masks that virtually all *shite* wear: the mask itself is at times described as literally embodying a character, but at the same time the masks are for the most part generic (for example, the "young woman" and "old woman" masks), and are said to be capable of expressing a very wide range of emotions, depending on how they are held. Time, and identity, are filled out, known—on the surface rather than harboring other possibilities—but identity, and time itself, are for the most part generic and of the past rather than individualized and of a changing present.[26]

As with Bakhtin, it is tradition that is the ultimate means for expressing the connection to this epic past, and it is also tradition that figures as the source of authority—or, again in Bakhtin's terms, the source and gauge of value. This was far more accentuated by the Tokugawas, but was evident from the start. Zeami, for instance, though not defining it in terms of tradition, insisted that noh plays must be based on well-known works from the past. He emphasized that within each play, "there must be a scene in which the source of the play is clearly revealed.... This is the most important moment of the entire play. In addition, one must include a quotation from a famous poetic source for the [main character] to recite."[27] The creation

---

26. Especially in the case of the "demon" plays, however, the past can intrude in ways that may actually be threatening.
27. "Sandō," in, J. Thomas Rimer and Yamazaki Masakazu, translators, *On the Art of the Noh Drama* (Princeton: Princeton University Press, 1984), 150.

of meaning through allusion to earlier works was by no means a new invention even then. But what Zeami began to do in a way that others had not, was to appropriate sources from almost any period, and indiscriminately.[28] Works which on their own implied differing and even antithetical worldviews—early imperial poetry, military tales from the twelfth-century *Heike*, tenth-century folklore, Buddhist treatises and Shinto mythology, and so on—were now all being brought together as part of the shogun's, and therefore the state's, collective traditional past. It was the Tokugawa shoguns who began to refer to this as part of their "tradition." Consequently, at an institutional level this newly conceived body of tradition became a new state canon, historically amorphous but all-encompassing, and known by everyone. Hence, just as the traditional sources act as the basis of authority within the plays—coming from a distanced but now newly unified past—at a state institutional level this body of tradition becomes the authorized foundation tying together a new community of people, with a common (and unchangeable) cultural background. It is also an anamnestic totalization, a canonization and bounding off of official memory—in sum, it is both a body of memory (a historically transcendent canon), and a relation to memory (one in which, by virtue of the transcendent nature of this common memory, the group itself attains a transcendent form of common identity).

A few further points on authority and unity: In the treatises of Zeami—which continued to be held in some importance by the Tokugawas—he takes great pains to locate the origins, and authority, of the noh. He does so by citing a sort of divine or ritual genealogy. Yet these origins are not simple. He lists a critical moment from the Shinto *Kojiki* mythology, in which the powers of the heavenly goddess Amaterasu are captured by a dancer using a trick and a mirror; he mentions a performance in "the country of the Buddha" whereby heretics were overcome; he describes a folktale, in which a great ruler of China is born; and then several variants on each of these.[29] That is to say Zeami was claiming for the noh all sources of authority then known: Shinto genealogies to godly power, Buddhist sources, local folk connections and Chinese sources of authority. As with the literary sources, Zeami's gene-

---

28. For example, all imperial poetry anthologies after the first (the tenth-century *Kokinshū*) were actually required to base their themes and vocabulary on poems of the first three—but *only* those, with the *Kokinshū* preface holding a special place of reverence.
29. See his *Fūshikaden*, and in Rimer and Yamazaki, ibid., 3, 31–37.

alogy for the noh claimed a new, transcendent unity of authority and power—truly an epic source of value.[30]

The same point can be made yet again with regard to the Tokugawa organization of noh play categories. In addition to the hierarchical five-category structure of god-to-demon plays, was a ritual play known as *Okina* ("old man," 翁). The most important of all plays, *Okina* was performed before the start of any full program and the part of the old man (a god) was generally taken by the head actor of the shogun's preferred noh family. The play itself was a simple set of dances, involving the appearance, masking, and then unmasking of the old man/god, and was the only noh play in which the mask was openly placed on and removed from the actor onstage; the play in these ways was an open archetype of the principles of noh. *Okina's* place in the hierarchy of noh plays was thus an approximation of the position of kingship: outside and above the regular hierarchy—Bakhtin's epic distance—it yet also embodied the principles of the whole. Itself a divine ritual,[31] it was also directly connected to the shogun through a series of substitutions: it was the "shogun's actor" who performed the play; the place of a noh actor as representative of the shogun, or other high-level official, was often highlighted at the end of plays, when the shogun might remove his own outer robe and place it on "his" actor, as a gift. The play's relation to the rest of the noh thus creates an image of divine kingship, with *Okina* as the ritual source of the noh and the shogun similarly the divine origin of a wholly unified hierarchical order.

Finally, at the level of representation or signification, the noh creates an epic unity of meaning. The question of representation is, for instance, directly visible and explicitly raised with regard to the identity of the *shite;* insofar as most plays revolve around the uncertainty of this identity, the question of representation is itself a fundamental topic of the noh. At a general level, the question is posed in terms of the object, or local person, the priest initially encounters, and its ability to represent the "true" past identity with which it is associated in memory.

---

30. A common approach to the noh has been to claim that it is really about Zen Buddhism, or Mahayana Buddhism, or Shinto, and so on. Clearly it is all of these, but at the same time none of them explain the noh. That line of argument therefore does not strike me as a fruitful means toward an understanding of the poetics of noh.
31. Actors had to go through several stages of abstinence over a period of several days before performing *Okina.*

The play *Matsukaze* (松風, *Wind in the Pines*) is a *ha* level play that was considered a "bread and butter" classic for all schools and so was popular in both the middle ages and in the Edo era. The narrative centers on the ghosts of two sisters, Matsukaze and Murasame; Matsukaze has been driven mad by her love and longing for her lover, the ninth-century poet Yukihira. Perhaps as an effect of this madness, she believes that a pine tree is in fact the lover with whom she so wishes to be reunited. The status of this tree therefore is uncertain: is it just a pine tree, a wind-in-the-pines? Or does it more fully indicate both the presence of the great poet and, by calling out her name, a reunion with his lover? Names themselves become critical questions of representation; here, the question is, what does "Matsukaze" mean? Does it truly unite present, "local" identity with the past, "true" meaning? Or does it fail to do so? In *Matsukaze*, the question is reiterated at several levels. Initially raised by the priest, it again comes up at the moment of "revelation" of Yukihira, in the guise of the pine tree. The still present-day incarnation of Matsukaze becomes convinced that this is not simply a pine tree, but that rather it is in fact Yukihira himself: "Oh joy! Look! Over there! [she points to the pine tree] Yukihira has returned! He calls me by name, Pine Wind! I am coming!"[32] "Pine wind" thus at once indicates the pine tree of the present, Yukihira of the past, and Yukihira's naming of Matsukaze—an act which unites the lovers, past and present, in a complete transparency wherein nothing can mediate or come between the two. Matsukaze's sister Murasame (a "helping" character for Matsukaze, the *shite*), however, is not yet convinced, and reiterates the doubt—it is a delusion, she says; "That is a pine tree. And Yukihira is not here."[33] Eventually, however, she too is convinced, and Matsukaze, Murasame, and the chorus all together sing, "Yes, we can trust his poem: 'I have gone away / Into the mountains of Inaba / Covered with pines / But if I hear you pine / I shall come back at once.'"[34] Yukihira's words and the pine tree are all trustworthy signs, fully indicating the presence of the true past meaning in the objects, persons, and words of the present. All are one.

---

32. 『あら嬉しやあれに行平のお立ちあるが、松風と召されさむらふぞや』*Yōkyokushū*, Amano and Yokomichi, eds., 64. English translation from Royall Tyler, in Keene, *Twenty Plays*, 30.
33. 『れは松にてこそ候へ行平はおん入りもさむらはぬものを』*Yōkyokushū*, ibid., 64.
34. 『あら頼むしのおん歌や。たちわかれ。いなばの山の峰に生ふる、待つと聞かば、いま帰り来ん。』Ibid., 65.

In the play *Yamamba* (山姥, *The Mountain Woman*), the issue of naming is still more clear. In this play, Yamamba is split into two people: one, playing the role of what might be termed the true essence of the character (and considered to be the *shite*, not the *tsure*), is an old woman dancer who wanders through the wilds of the mountainside, seeking to hear her own name, and her own song. The other is a woman of the capital, also named Yamamba, who can do Yamamba's dance, but she has only the name, and the form or dance pattern of Yamamba's identity, and not the essential meaning. She goes off to the mountains in search of this meaning of her dance, and the meaning of her name. In the end, the two Yamambas (form and meaning)[35] are provisionally united; again, representation (naming) is called into question, but only to demonstrate at least a momentary epic unity of meaning within noh's signs.[36]

Beyond the issues of naming and character identity, language, and the ability or inability of language to adequately signify, is a specific subject for some plays, as in *Sekidera Komachi*. I will return to this play below. At the furthest extension of what might be called an epic closure of meaning (a unity created by an absolute distance), however, the noh presents a realm of meaning transcendent of representation altogether. In the ritual play *Okina*, for instance, the lines spoken by the old man/god are an incomprehensible (but nonetheless treated as sacrosanct) string of sounds and words. The sounds are not considered gibberish, simply incomprehensible (noh scholars have therefore devised endless theories as to what the lines "really" mean). Like the position of the play itself, the lines signify a realm of meaning beyond language and transcendent of representation.

Or, one could look at the terms Zeami used to describe the aesthetics of noh. The most common and cliched word used by Zeami and nearly everyone else since, is *yūgen* (幽玄). The term was widely used even before the middle ages, mostly in reference to poetry. Like the lines spoken by the god Okina, *yūgen* was and still is often described as unexplainable. The most frequent definition is simply "mystery." Prior to the middle ages *yūgen* might still imply little more than a special beauty, but later—especially in the context of the noh—it came to be associated with a spiritual, transcendent form of mystery. Yūgen thus describes a realm of meaning beyond representation,

---

35. Also a unity of the capital and the outskirts. There is a great deal more to this play than commented on here. See for example, Karen Brazell and Monica Bethe, *Nō as Performance: An Analysis of the Kuse Scene of Yamamba* (Ithaca: Cornell University East Asia Series, no. 16, 1978).
36. Ultimately Yamamba falls back into a set of earthly desires and divisions.

transcendent of the contingencies of language and the everyday by an epic distance that preserves the unity of that meaning.[37]

Especially when taken as a whole—viewed from the perspective of a full cycle—the noh does then seem to be founded on an epic chronotope (more so than renga, for instance). Yet a tendency toward fragmentation and dispersal is also present. These are characteristics which were there from the start.[38] Noh plays may have depended on past works of tradition, for example, and the Tokugawas may have created a fairly fixed canon of traditional works. But viewed poetically (rather than at the level of the institutional canon), none of these poetic references in any way offer a totalizing view of their traditional source. Plays based on the *Kokinshū* anthology of poetry typically take no more than one or two poems as the basis for the entire play. Furthermore several different plays are in some cases written about the same poem, or the same classical figure, each differing in point of view from the other. The result is an almost renga-like series of extremely limited glimpses, or perspectives, on the original source.

Nor do the characters in all plays end in pure completion, reunited with their object of longing. Especially in the third, fourth, and fifth category plays, the disjunction of identity and of the signifying capacity of language may appear irresolvable. The *ha* level, and even more the final *kyū* level of the *jo-ha-kyū* principle is about such a disjunction; that is the trajectory of noh's narrative. For Zeami the final stage was a state of "agitation,"[39] and the form of movement appropriate there was *saidō* (砕動), or a "pulverizing movement;"[40] "a movement of the body so that it seems to 'break' into many pieces."[41]

In fact even plays that may appear to lead toward a unity of character may be composed of little more than renga-like progressions of perspective. Let me return to *Matsukaze*. There, the question of identity as defined above

---

37. Another of many possible examples might be *hie*, the aesthetics of "chill," or "coldness"—an avoidance of display of any type for the pursuit of a "higher," transcendent purpose. With regard to Zeami's use of *yūgen*, Norma Field has reminded me that his elaborations become more transcendent only late in his career, suggesting that it may not have started out so divorced from representation and language.
38. I am not implying an opposition of perspectives, in the way that Bakhtin in his discussion of epic neatly opposes it to the "novel" chronotope. I am simply trying to indicate some of the ways in which the noh is not necessarily so epically totalizing as it might seem.
39. See *Kakyō*, and Rimer and Yamazaki, *On the Art of the Noh*, 84.
40. This was especially the case for the Kanze school, generally privileged by the Tokugawa shoguns.
41. Rimer and Yamazaki, ibid., 259.

fairly clearly seems to consist of whether the pine is just a tree, or the great poet and lover Yukihira, brought together with his loves, the two women Matsukaze and Murasame—and by extension, whether the present is just the present, or whether it rather represents the past in the present. But just when *is* this "present," and this "past?" Initially, the present is just the seaside at the provincial bay of Suma, and Matsukaze and Murasame are saltmakers—it could conceivably even be the immediate present of the Tokugawa era. Then, early on, a poem written in the ninth century by Yukihira (also on Suma) is quoted, suggesting that the present shore by the sea is, fittingly, meant to be the seaside in the time and place of Yukihira. But shortly thereafter, Matsukaze sings a passage almost verbatim from the eleventh-century *Tale of Genji*, and several additional references follow. The contemporary setting of Suma is in these passages revealed to be the scene from the Suma chapter in *Genji*, set in the mid-tenth century. In that chapter, prince Genji (himself a great lover) meets up with a local woman (the Akashi Lady), whom he would later bring back to the capital with him. Matsukaze/Murasame are, accordingly, now being identified with the Akashi Lady; so the tale of Matsukaze and Yukihira is also the tale of Genji and the Akashi Lady. This identity then is further complicated. In the *Tale of Genji*, Genji leaves the Akashi Lady with his robe as a sign that he will return; Matsukaze similarly has a robe of Yukihira's, which again identifies the two couples, but it also identifies them with yet another set of lovers—Narihira (another famous poet and lover, and the brother of Yukihira) and his lover who are depicted in yet another, related noh play, *Izutsu*. So there are now three sets of lovers being identified at different points. Nor is the present-past just the time of Genji, the time of Yukihira, or of Narihira. In one short passage, the bay at Suma is poetically linked with a whole set of seaside locations associated with salt gathering.[42] After that passage, further place names such as Ojima in Matsushima are mentioned[43] that associate Matsukaze and Murasame not only with other saltmakers, but with *ama* (diving women, popular images of local women with whom one might fall in love); and, later, possibly with *shirabyōshi*—traveling ritual dancers, who at times may have doubled as prostitutes of sorts. "Matsukaze," therefore, refers at different points to a local saltmaker; to a ninth-century lover of Yukihira; to Genji's Akashi Lady; to the lover of Yukihira's brother Narihira; to the romantic image of sea-diving women and the still

---

42. See the translation by Tyler, *Twenty Plays*, 23. This passage is a *tsukushi*, or "exhaustive enumeration"—see Tyler, ibid., n. 6.
43. Ibid., 26.

more erotic image of *shirabyōshi* dancers, and so on. The setting is the "present," but it is also Suma bay in the ninth century, and in the twelfth century; it is also the many related locales famous for saltmakers, and so on.[44] To follow all of these links one would certainly need to be remarkably well versed in traditional literature, but the end effect is, again, as much a scattered series of fragmentary renga-style images as it is a whole, unified identity. Further, if there is any great union achieved between past and present identities in *Matsukaze*, the identities are nonetheless multiple, nearly to the point of excess. It is a multiplicity that would strain against any experience of *Matsukaze* as unified.

Finally, mystery, too, is double-edged. While it can imply an unquestionable epic transcendence, it can also imply an ambiguity that at very least leaves meaning open to multiple interpretations, or worse, can indicate the impossibility of any true signification. At the end of *Matsukaze*, we are told, "Only Matsukaze remains" (松風ばかりや、残るらん).[45] What does this mean? "Matsukaze" means "the wind in the pines," but we have seen all the possibilities that entails. So, does the play end in an epic unity of pine tree, Yukihira, and lover, and so on? Or is it just the wind in the pines? The very ambiguity leaves the answer open.

This fundamental openness to polysemy is one of the basic characteristics that is clearly part of the middle-ages origins of the noh. During the middle ages, however, the noh had not yet become nearly so formally institutionalized as it did in the Edo era, and it is really in the Edo era then that the clear opposition between plays of ritual closure and plays like *Sekidera Komachi* arises.

• • •

It is easy to see the fit between the traits of epic value outlined above, and the models of state being architected by the Tokugawa shoguns. The oneness (or, in noh terminology, the "harmony") of the closed *jo-ha-kyū*-styled cycles of noh plays agreed with the flows of actors and performances that the shogun created to define boundaries and allegiances to their new state. And the *jo-ha-kyū* principle also accorded with the sense of closed, repetitive ritual time that the same performances gave to the shoguns' regime. The absolute epic distance of noh's "traditional" sources helped to represent the transcendent

---

44. If these are not enough, there are also quotes from the poetry (and worlds) of a number of other anthologies, including the tenth-century *Kokinshū*, the twelfth-century *Kinyōshū*, and the *Shūishū*. Most of these poems are cited in the endnotes to Tyler, ibid.
45. *Yōkyokushū*, Amano and Yokomichi, eds., 65.

The Poetics of Tokugawa Noh / 143

structure of authority and unchangeable value that the shoguns were arguing for in their rice economy, and their own position as founders of the state. It is not surprising then that the shoguns would insist on the canonization of the plays themselves as tradition, or that the formal, cyclically ordered five-category hierarchy of noh play styles would have developed under their patronage. More generally, it is easy to see why Bakhtin would define the epic as the chronotope of the state.

Yet in Tokugawa Japan the plays which were most expressive of ritual closure (of time and of meaning) were clearly not the most popular, including within the shogunate. For example, looking at the repertoire of plays for *the* official troupe (Kanze), even among plays listed at the first-category "god" level, only 7 of 22 were considered to be orthodox enough to be used for ceremonial programs. In several cases, less "ritualistic" plays from the third through fifth categories were being used as first category plays.[46] At the same time that the shogun was encouraging a slower tempo in the noh, in actual practice the most frequently performed, and apparently enjoyed, plays were those from the third to fifth categories—plays not only based on quicker, more active roles, but also expressive of a more irresolvable sense of degeneration, disjunction, and loss, and consequently melancholic longing.[47] By the latter half of the eighteenth century, the most popular plays were two "madwoman" (*monogurui*) pieces. *Dōjōji* (道成寺) is an unusual noh play about a woman who wrongly thought a priest would marry her; her desire for him becomes so strong it transforms her into a serpent, hot enough to melt a temple bell.[48] *Sumidagawa* (隅田川) is a play without any

---

46. The list (*kakiage*) of 1784 is provided in Omote, *Kōzan bunkobon no kenkyū* (1965),420; a 1720 list can be found in *Nihon shomin bunka shiryō shūsei* 3. See also Gerry Yokota, *The Noh Drama of Japan*, PhD Dissertation (Princeton, 1992), 284.
47. Even the quieter type of plays of the third (*ha*) level became less popular. *Matsukaze*, for example, though long considered the standard play for everyone to see, was less and less frequently performed in the Tokugawa era. Furthermore, the Kita school, which as noted specialized in the demon category plays, was at several points the most called-upon within the shogun's own castle (even while the shogun refused to officially recognize the school). See Ikeuchi Nobuyoshi, *Nōgaku seisuiki* II, 40, passim.
48. *Dōjōji* is the one noh play that depends upon a realistic prop—the temple bell under which the woman jumps just as it falls (the prop is realistic enough to break actors' legs if they do not jump with the proper agility). Unlike most other noh plays, in the words of Keene, it "depends for its success less on the poetry than on the dramatic situation and the spectacle" (*Twenty Plays*, 239). *Dōjōji* was the most frequently performed play, and when it was performed it garnered the largest audiences—this includes the Kōka performance—and so presumably it was the most popular. I have not seen clear numbers for *Sumidagawa*, but on its popularity see Ikeuchi, *Nōgaku seisuiki* I, 417.

stated source, though patterned after a set of stories in which a mother loses, seeks for, and finds, her child; unlike the stories, however, in *Sumidagawa*, the mother's desperate search ends with the discovery of her son entombed in the recent past by the side of a river.

So, at the same time that the Tokugawa order of things appeared to be founded on the poetics of an ideal epic boundedness, in which the past was fully incorporated within the present, and the signified wholly embodied within signifier, there was yet also—within that very order—a sense of dispersal, of emptiness, and of a body that was no more than a ghost.[49]

Before looking in more detail at some of the elements of this contradiction, if that is what it is, I want to give the barest of sketches of *Takasago*, the most commonly performed ritual god play in the Tokugawa era, and *Sekidera Komachi*. One should be reminded that this is not an opposition of official, government ceremony versus unofficial, popular form. *Sekidera* was a play the Kanze family—the family the shogun chose above all others as its official representative, through most of the Tokugawa era—took as its own, and it was taught only to the school's master.[50] Further, among woman plays there are only five that were given the highest level of "dignity" (*kurai*) in noh, and *Sekidera* was the foremost even of these; both *Takasago* and *Sekidera* were therefore top-ranked, eminently official plays.

Takasago was considered by Zeami to be one of the more straightforward and orthodox of the god plays, and the god plays were the most orthodox of any. In his words, it "had no secrets." At the same time, especially in the Tokugawa era, efforts appear to have been made to accord it a high mysticism: Kō Masayoshi, an early-sixteenth-century noh actor, seems to have invented a kind of number symbolism by which he claimed he could trace what he thought were distinctive percussion patterns (thirty-six, each with their own symbolism) in *Takasago* all the way back to the myth of Uzume in the eighth-century *Kojiki*.[51] Apparently the most commonly used play for ritual programs, *Takasago* belonged to a group of three plays among which one

---

49. One way to understand this would be simply to show that noh as ritual became disjoined from noh as entertainment. In one sense that was the case, within the shogun's castle and outside. Gradually, some programs were being held for what was specifically called ritual purposes, and these would be more formal, while other performances were considered to be only entertainment (See Ikeuchi, ibid., 31, and passim). But I am also trying to show that both tendencies were co-present, and perhaps even in some ways codependent, at all levels.
50. When an actor from the unofficial Kita school did play the role, he was confined for six months for the offense.
51. *Kō Masayoshi kudensho*, in *Nōgaku shiryō shūsei* 13 (1984), 97.

would be chosen for each year's performance of the Tokugawa New Year's rite (*utaizome*). Eternal longevity is a theme within the play, as indicated by the characters themselves (gods who appear as pine trees, the preeminent symbol of eternity throughout Japanese literature). The power of language, too, is a primary theme; in general, as one would expect from a god play, it is a good example of epic unity.

Takasago is only slightly irregular, like *Matsukaze*, insofar as the *shite* is initially divided into two pines, or two gods, Takasago and Sumiyoshi.[52] The two gods explicitly indicate the contexts of the play: Takasago "refers to the distant past of the Manyōshū," and Sumiyoshi to the "present" Engi era (901–923) and the *Kokinshū*. The *Manyōshū* is considered the first anthology of "Japanese" poetry, and the *Kokinshū* the first imperial anthology. Both works were considered to embody the basic principles of all good literary form; the preface to the *Kokinshū* in particular was held to be the fundamental expression of proper poetics. Thus the two gods directly refer to what were considered to be the origins of poetic representation.

Of course they refer as well to the temporal relation of past and present—or given that the play openly states that the "present" is the Engi era, but citations are then included from much later times, it could also be understood to include a relation of past, present, and future.[53] But the relation is also one of space: Takasago and Sumiyoshi are geographical places, but on sea coasts separated by the Inland Sea.

The play accordingly opens with an appearance of disunity. The obligatory priest, in the countryside, finds two local people—an old man and an old woman. When asked about the memory associated with the place, the locals tell the priest of the "paired" pines. The locals also tell the priest that they themselves are husband and wife, but one lives on the opposite shore of Sumiyoshi and the other is from Takasago, where they stand. It then also emerges that the old man comes from the time of the Manyōshū in the eighth century, while the woman is from the tenth-century Engi era, when the Kokinshū was written. "Astonishing!" says the priest, and wants therefore to

---

52. Technically, Sumiyoshi is considered the *shite* and Takasago is his *tsure*, or "helper."
53. In one of the very few treatises by a Tokugawa noh actor, Komparu Anshō in the early seventeenth century stated that *Takasago* does encompass all three times: the past in a central poem in which an old man refers to the pine tree as his old friend; the present in the final auspicious words of praise for the lord's reign; and the future in the priest's decision to travel to the second coast of Sumiyoshi and wait there for the divine revelation. *Konparu Anshō denshoshū*, in *Nōgaku shiryō shūsei* 9, Omote Akira and Oda Sachiko, eds. (1978), 87.

know what it can mean to be "paired."[54] This in a sense is the question of the play: it is asking how the two pines/people can be a pair if they are spatially separated by the distance of the Inland Sea; temporally separated by the time of the Manyōshū and the Engi era; and therefore separated from true representation. That is, can it make sense to say that these are "pairs," when it would fairly clearly appear that they are not? The very ability to signify, or name—and thereby truly realize—epic unity, is being called into question at the outset.

The response is made at several levels: first, it is a question of affect, or love, which can overcome the distance of space: "Though a myriad leagues of hill and stream divide them, hearts truly in touch do not find the way to each other long." But, then it appears to be more a question of representation, or of naming: "The Pines of Takasago and Sumiyoshi bear...the name of Paired."[55] And, "These pines mean unfailing leaves of speech: words whose vigour endures, now as then."[56] "Leaves of speech" is a very basic word play (one that again refers back to the *Kokinshū* preface) based on the phonetics of *kotoba* ("words"), as a conjunction of "leaves of things/speech" (*koto no ha*). In this context the wordplay is being used to combine the enduring "leaves" (needles) of the pine with the stability of words as signs.[57] The pine tree, itself a sign of eternal continuity, thus is also a sign of the stability of language. By linking the linguistic sign with the pine tree, the pine becomes a sign of language's ability to call forth and maintain a single meaning. Fur-

---

54. Royall Tyler, *Japanese Noh Dramas* (London: Penguin Books, 1992), 283.
55. 『高砂住吉の松に相生の名あり』*Yōkyokushū*, 221. The word for "paired," *aioi* (相生), more literally means "together living" ("conjugal" is another word used in some translations of the play), but I am going with Tyler's translation since the term appears in several different contexts to suggest a pairing or union.
56. Ibid., 283–284.
57. This is a far more complex construct than I am allowing for. The sentiment is reiterated in the succeeding passages, when the gods and chorus sing a passage not readily translatable into English, but rendered by Tyler as, "pine bows glow with ever green leaves of speech: dewdrop pearls that in the heart seed polished grace until all beings alive, to the Blessed Isles, they say, draw nigh" (ibid., 285). Here too, the eternal life of the pine is associated with the constancy of language, but also with the ability of language to represent feeling, or "heart." But this ability to represent "heart" is also an ability to represent the feeling, or "heart" of all things in nature, so that poetic representation has to do with the ability to accurately express and create the good proper order of things in nature. Finally, this ability to represent the good order of things in nature also is the ability to create good governance; the proper form of poetic representation is the proper form of governance. All of these quotes refer to the preface of the Kokinshū (or commentaries on it), in which all of these issues are raised. But this is not just independent subjective emotion; it is the feeling of all of the natural order.

thermore, because words are not just words but rather the actual leaves of a tree, it gives language the corporeality and stability of eternally living nature. There is no arbitrariness possible here between signifier and signified, no potential for linguistic instability; these are natural signs.[58]

We can also view this from the perspective of the economics of value discussed in the previous chapter. Here, the pine tree in *Takasago*, as in the noh in general,[59] takes the role of the general equivalent—the general equivalent being a guarantor of value that is both a material embodiment of natural value, like rice, and yet as the sole equivalent of value for all other goods it is transcendent; it is in between pure transcendence and "real" physical embodied value. In *Takasago*, the pine tree acts as the general, transcendent figure for, and yet gives natural body to and therefore guarantee of, the worth of all language.[60]

Having been told the meaning of the pines, the priest then asks if the old man and woman will tell him their names. The couple, saying they have no further need for secrecy, explain that they are the paired pines. With this initial revelation that the old couple themselves are the two famous "paired" pines, which are indeed the gods of the past, the first half of the play ends; the actors and chorus sing of traveling back to the other shore at Sumiyoshi.

There is then a break, and as sometimes happens, a *kyōgen* actor[61] enters to retell the full story to the priest, but in a more colloquial language. This is the one place that something like colloquial language may enter the noh. Rather than an intrusion of the everyday, however, the effect may have been to create one further level of the epic connection between the present with

---

58. The pine tree is thus already at the start of the play an embodiment of the kinds of eternal pairings of past and present that are clearly revealed at the end of the play. This may also help to explain the usage of the pine in *Matsukaze*, in which the tree is not only an embodiment of the lover Yukihira, it is also the power to name, and thereby truly call forth, Matsukaze.
59. The pine is without doubt the preeminent symbol of the noh. It is used in plays throughout the repertoire, and provides as well the permanent setting for all plays (the pine painted on the back wall of the stage, and three pines set in front of the *hashigakari* stage bridge, are permanent fixtures for all stages).
60. Thus, at the end of the above quoted passage, the chorus explains that, "All beings, feeling or nonfeeling, have a voice, and that voice is a song. Plants and trees, soil and sand, wind sounds and water noises: in each one the spirit harbours all things. Springtime woods swaying to east winds, fall insects crying in northern dews—are not both song, our poetry? The pine among them towers, lordly, green through a thousand falls, and shows no hue of new or old: a tree worthy of that title, 'Marquis', the First Emperor gave it, so that in China and in our Realm all men sing its praise." Ibid., 286.
61. The kyōgen actor would otherwise appear in the comic plays that served as interludes to the noh plays.

the past—the contemporary colloquial language of the kyōgen actor somehow adequately representing the truths of the noh play, even while the noh's classical language of the past was privileged over that of the kyōgen.

The second half of the play consists of the expected reunifications: the name Takasago is dropped once they arrive at the shores of Sumiyoshi, because Takasago is now encompassed within Sumiyoshi. As the kyōgen interlude explains, the two are "one in spirit." The epic distances of time and space are transcended, and the Sumiyoshi deity dances a sacred kagura dance, itself the invocation of a god, in which he sings of their arrival at the transcendent[62] point of origin ("for God, for Sovereign, the road runs straight to Miyako in springtime, when the dance is 'Home to the Palace'"),[63] and of eternal felicitous time ("'A Thousand Autumns' brings peace to all, 'Ten Thousand Years' makes life long, while, touched by the wind, the Paired Pines sing, inspiring tranquil joy the paired Pines sing, inspiring tranquil joy").[64]

Takasago thus ends in a complete expression of the epic chronotope, and ties it to the shogun, the "Sovereign" in the lines above; also, as the actor playing the role of Sumiyoshi finishes his dance, which he explains is called "Home to the Palace," he turns and faces the shogun directly. It represents a fixed and well-grounded origin for the state. Like de Certeau's idea of the seventeenth century religious episteme in Europe, the *modus loquendi*, it represents a world in which there is just one semantic system (tradition), in which meaning is everywhere, but it also has a spiritual legitimacy—"a proper place from which to speak."[65] In de Certeau's formulation of the *modus loquendi*, even if meaning is not localizable, there is still real certainty that it exists—

---

62. This achievement of transcendence, and of oneness with the past world of the divine, is indicated by vision and a clear moon (a common sign of unity/disunity with the heavens throughout the noh): the dance starts with the words, "O wondrous, O divine vision O wondrous, O divine vision! Beneath a clear moon the God of Sumiyoshi dances one, while we in awe adore his holy form!" (ibid., 291). Here, Sumiyoshi himself becomes the form, or sign, that is purely and transparently representative of the divine past.

63. This is the name of one of the very earliest *bugaku* (a ritual court dance) dances, older perhaps than Sumiyoshi's own dance, but at the same time another layer of the meaning of the dance Sumiyoshi is performing.

64. 『千秋楽は民を撫で、萬歳楽には命を延ぶ、相生の松風、颯颯の聲ぞ楽しむ、颯颯の聲ぞ楽しむ。』(*Yōkyokushu*, 225). English: see Tyler, ibid., 291, 292. The final pairing of the play is indicated as well by the repetition of the last two lines (the last of several sets of parallel couplets in the final passage).

65. Michel de Certeau, "The Arts of Dying," in *Heterologies* (Minneapolis: The University of Minnesota Press, 1986), 160–161.

The Poetics of Tokugawa Noh / 149

that there is still some kind of nonlocalizable reality. It is in the twentieth century, says de Certeau, that this latter source of authority, localizable or not, is lost; the production of narrative occurs through a "system of phonetic drift," in which the only authorities are verbal. Language itself becomes the referential body, now distanced from both the speaking subject and the "maternal" body—de Certeau calls this new mode of representation the *modus scribendi*. At least in the case of the noh, something similar to these two structures of representation (the *modus loquendi* and the *modus scribendi*) may have been co-present—the *modus scribendi* in other words was already at issue in the early modern noh.

Sekidera Komachi, a third category "woman" play, was already by the 1500s associated with "secret" performance traditions, and by the 1600s it had become an "inner 'mystery' of noh."[66] Like *Takasago*, *Sekidera* takes the preface of the *Kokinshū* as its primary source—and, therefore, signification in general and poetic language in particular is a primary theme.[67] The *shite* of the play is Ono no Komachi, a ninth-century poet renowned both for her poetry and for her radiant beauty.[68]

The play opens with a symbol of separation and impending unification that, in this case, is cosmological: it is just before the Tanabata festival, a popular celebration of two stars located across the Milky Way. The stars are thought to be lovers, who on the seventh day of the seventh lunar month appear to come together for one day. At this time, the priest who is organizing the preparations says that there is an old woman nearby who knows all the old secrets of the art of poetry, and he is going to take the children over to hear these old words; the priest prays for "skill at poetry." So in the context of possible celestial or cosmological unity, a transmission or unity with the secrets of language is hinted at. Right away, the question of representation is thus placed in relation to the question of natural cosmological wholeness: the stars will get together; will the ancient words be similarly united with the new generation of children, across the expanse of time? Also, the name of the temple itself—Sekidera (関寺)—means "temple of the barrier or boundary." In part this may be merely an issue of geography, insofar as the temple seems to have been located at an important mountain pass between Kyoto and Lake Biwa. But

---

66. See Tyler, *Japanese Noh Dramas*, 226.
67. There are quotes from other sources made by both plays that would also indicate this—for example, two verses by Po Chu-i in the *Wakan Rōei Shū*.
68. This is one of a series of noh plays written about her. The others are *Sotoba Komachi*, *Kayoi Komachi*, *Ōmu Komachi*, and *Sōshi-arai Komachi*.

more importantly, it adds to the context indicating the possibility—or impossibility—of the crossing and transcendence of larger boundaries.

The priest and young children travel off to Komachi's hut, a simple frame, hung with prayer-like strips of paper inscribed with poems. There, as an aged woman of the present, Komachi is bemoaning her current condition and mourning the passage of time: "Man has no second chance at youth; He grows old. The aged song thrush Warbles again when spring has come, But time does not revert to the past. Oh, how I yearn for the days that are gone! What I would do to recapture the past!"[69] The visitors explain they have come to hear of the secrets of poetry and of her own story. Two poems from the preface to the *Kokinshū* are cited, and both priest and Komachi acknowledge that these are (as the *Kokinshū* states) "the mother and father of all poetry."[70] The poems, they say, serve as models for everyone—Noblemen and peasantry alike, City dwellers and country folk, Even commoners like ourselves."[71] This poetic pair is the origin, and apparently the guarantor, of all representation.[72] Further, "The words of poetry will never fail. They are enduring as evergreen boughs of pine.... As long as words of poetry remain, Poems will leave their marks behind, And the traces of poetry will never disappear."[73] Poetic words are accordingly stable, enduring, and even natural signs. So far, it would appear things are similar to *Takasago*, and we are headed for epic fulfillment.

Impressed by the old woman's knowledge, the priest continues to inquire. Finally, the revelation that she herself is Ono no Komachi is made. But the phrasing is curious: "You are what is left of Ono no Komachi"[74] (御身 のはてぞとよ, literally, something like, "your body is the end/remnants of Komachi"),[75] says the priest. She seems to be a remainder, and only that—

---

69. Karen Brazell, trans., in *Twenty Plays*, 70.
70. For an English translation of the poems, see Laurel Rasplica Rodd, trans., *Kokinshū* (Princeton: Princeton University Press, 1984), 37.
71. Ibid., 71.
72. As the Kokinshū preface states, these two poems were also used as the first texts for all calligraphy practice; perhaps in ways similar to the noh's insistence on original meaning being literally embodied, or acted out (this too will be discussed below), the truth or meaning of these poems was realized through the material strokes of calligraphic practice. These two "mother and father" poems are also cited as the basis of the noh play "The Reed Cutter," another play, like *Takasago*, based on fixed value with an absolute origin.
73. Ibid., 71.
74. Ibid., 72.
75. *Yōkyokushū*, Koyama and Satō, eds., 231.

hardly a pure sign of her past identity. The succeeding lines[76] also emphasize that the old woman, being one hundred years old, is indeed just the right age to be Komachi. In other words, she has not died at all, and this is not a reappearance. Rather, especially since it seems she cannot become young again, it is in fact death, or an end, that she seeks. Quoting poems she once wrote, she says, "The joy I felt when I composed those lines Is gone forever, but still my life goes on, Attending the months and years as they come and go.... (chorus) And how long must I, who wrote that poem, Live on, like flowers fallen, like leaves scattered?" "To moan the certainty of death; Its message still eludes me."

None of the signs in the present seem adequate representations of the past. At the end of the chorus just cited, Komachi laments, "Look at it now, my mud-daubed hut! Can this be my resplendent room?" Then, "I who used to watch the Festival of Stars... Now stand in shameful hempen rags! A sight too painful for eyes to bear!" She herself, like her room, are no indication of her former being, when she joined court parties to watch the festival of the stars. Thus, the relationship suggested at the outset of the play between the reliable reunions of the stars and the constancy of human signs is broken. The stars may continue their meetings, but not Komachi. This is not the closed cyclical time of the stars, nor the union of *Takasago's* pines. It is a time without end, but continuous in an unhappy sense of being open, and empty of meaning. Even Komachi's own power of language seems to be lost: "Now when I have grown decrepit My poems are weaker still. Their life is spent."

In the end, although the possibility of rejoining with youth and beauty is raised by the dancing figure of a young boy, Komachi is only a ludicrous double, a "madwoman prancing" beside him. As dawn appears, nature becomes both an allegory of Komachi's unhappy condition, and her separation from nature: Terrible sign of her former past that she is, she seeks to hide herself so that she may not be seen; "Where is the forest of Hazukashii [the forest of shame]? There is no forest to hide my shame." Komachi, it appears, will continue in this condition forever, counting up the years ("Has Ono no Komachi reached a hundred years? Or even more?"). Finally, "the hundred-year-old woman you have spoken to / Is all that remains of famed Komachi / Is all that is left of Ono no Komachi." Only a degenerating body is left, an empty sign, of a time of lost origins and also without end.

---

76. (Not in the Brazell translation.)

This is not a portrayal of epic values, nor of the *modus loquendi* of a religious episteme. There is no assurance of an origin of meaning, either localizable or unlocalizable. In *Sekidera*, language itself fails (there is a disjunction of essential meaning from both signs and from time, even while Komachi finds herself caught in both language and time). Unlike *Takasago*, *Sekidera*'s "Barrier" is absolute, divorcing Komachi from the return to an epic origin, and also preventing her from a completed end. And most importantly, time itself can be seen detaching from its relation to the workings of the cosmos, and from nature. The forest, and therefore the world, still somehow manages to express and configure Komachi's condition. For the most part though, she has fallen *into* time, but time has become disjoined from the natural movements of the world.

Yet *Takasago* and *Sekidera*, and the poetics of both, somehow went together in the Edo period. How? What does this tell us of early modernity? I will return to the times, and images of death, in early modern Japan, but first some very general and brief comments on beauty and deformation.

Aesthetics of Deformation

Looking at the built environment of Tokugawa society from the view of art and architectural history, it is possible to see quite varied forms. Emphases on clarity, closure, and monumentality were visible in the way the Tokugawa shoguns orchestrated everything from the borders of state and the flow of people—with new, broad highways, and the system of checkpoints that supposedly would control who moved where—to bureaucratic law; the architecture of power;[77] the architecture of buildings—the castles themselves, for example; to ways of seeing in the theater. Chapter 1 described some of these structures of "beauty" as a rationalized totality that the noh helped to configure—the comments of Hayashi Shihei with regard to the noh performing the "brilliant sounds of Japanese nature," also described this as a "beautiful" order;[78] even the new calendar of time, which brought the various independent ritual and governmental times under the state/family Tokugawa calendar, might by those terms be considered as a rationally "beautiful" monumental figure.

---

77. The neat pyramidal structure of lines of power, by which samurai were removed from their land and independent bases of power and centralized in a single castle for each domain, which was then beholden to the central castle in Edo.
78. See *Nō kyōgen* II:73.

On the other hand, more nonrational forms—forms which were more curvilinear, multiple and multiplying to excess, opaque and disorienting, and indecipherable or open in meaning—were also part of the Tokugawa order. As for example in the architecture of the shrine at Nikkō, which is of a baroque, almost gaudy ornateness and intricacy,[79] and which in fact contained several pieces of European art of the baroque era—including baroque lanterns, that seemed to carry through an architectural theme there on light and the "shining" power of Tokugawa Ieyasu. Or as in the general architecture of power—even while the shoguns created the great open highways as official paths for the cycles of daimyo lords, they at the same time disdained open spaces and panoramic views (very unlike either Renaissance or Enlightenment Europe), and even while they created fixed administrative laws defining straight hierarchical lines of power between lords and shoguns, the shoguns preferred a more labyrinthine and secretive reliance on behind-the-scenes political relations, and on a never-certain but huge network of spies. Finally, the complex and ever-changing networks of mercantile capitalism that were allowed to develop and were even relied upon, including along the many waterways then winding through the city of Edo, also might be described as convoluted and nonrational in "baroque" ways. Even the merchant capitalists, who supposedly were strong proponents of a rational, calculating kind of knowledge, at the same time were part of the audience that made the *kaichō* (periodic openings of temple storehouses for all-night exhibitions of objects considered strange and rare) a tremendously popular form of entertainment, and the merchants of course were also the ones who helped create the great city fairs of exotica, and the pleasure quarters, which gave Edo its "brilliant, unreal, 'dream'"-like character.[80]

There was, in other words, not only a confluence of apparently discordant forms, but of forms that at least in classic Western art history have commonly been thought of as part of different historical moments.[81]

In the poetics of the noh, the same questions emerge. On the one hand "beautiful," totalizing syntheses are evident throughout: following the *jo-ha-*

---

79. An ornateness which tended to bring together and blur the boundaries between painting, architecture, and sculpture, as was also the case in the European baroque.
80. There are a number of works that deal with Edo as dream-like; see for example Hino Tatsuo, *Edojin to yūtopia* (Tokyo: Asahi Shimbunsha, 1977). These last adjectives are from Focillon's description of the European baroque. See Henri Focillon, *The Work of Art in the Middle Ages*, vol. 2 (London: Phaidon, 1969), 141–142.
81. To some extent, this concurrence may be true of the Western enlightenment as well, insofar as the sublime is somehow integral to the conception of rational and harmonious beauty.

154 / Visioning Eternity

kyū principle, as just noted, the music of noh was described as expressing the "brilliant harmony of all Japan." Or in the narrative form of ritual plays such as *Takasago*, taken to be the highest expression of noh, in which the great epic synthesis of past and present becomes the ultimate figure of essence in state rituals. Yet at the same time, these ritual plays were in the Edo period described as, more than just beautiful, being "sublime," as in the term *sōgon* (荘厳).[82] This was especially true of the more official performances and the more important ritual-style plays.[83]

If one were drawing conclusions from this, would one then say that there was a general aesthetic experience of totality? Or not? And does the noh, as the ceremony of state, indicate a state of mastery, or mystery? Or, as in the West, is this already indicative of an order of beauty and reason that, as for Baumgarten and Kant, was also dependent on and delimited by the limitlessness of the sublime?

As a general structure of rulership, one of the first precedents to look at might be the medieval theological formulations described by Kantorowicz in *The King's Two Bodies*. There too, as in the symbolism of the king's funerary procession, Kantorowicz finds "the concurrence of two heterogenous ideas: the triumph of Death and the triumph over Death."[84] And, although heterogenous, Kantorowicz also describes these ideas as coexistent: "We should not forget that the uncanny juxtaposition of a decaying corpse and an immortal Dignity ... was fostered after all in the same ground...."[85] For Kantorowicz, however, this is not particularly a problem. These are two aspects which together make up the single principle of medieval kingship. Crudely put, one aspect is that of the natural body of the king, which dies (and therefore is a temporal being, subjected to the effects of time), and the other aspect is the legalistic "immortal Dignity," the ongoing official, public being of the kingship, which is beyond time and death. The living (and

---

82. *Sōgon* appears to be the most commonly used term. Along with the meaning of "sublime," it can also imply—as in English—awe, solemnity, and grandeur. It is not, however, a directly theological term, and is more associated with "stately" majesty.

83. *Sōgon* was used to describe the shogunal investiture performances of the machi-iri noh, for example (see Ikeuchi, NS I, 188), and was used by one of the principal noh school heads to describe the play *Takasago*. See *Konparu Anshō denshoshū*, in Omote Akira and Oda Sachiko, eds., *Nōgaku shiryō shūsei*, vol. 9, 1978, 26.

84. Ernst H. Kantorowicz, *The King's Two Bodies* (Princeton, New Jersey: Princeton University Press, 1957), 429.

85. Ibid., 436.

dying) body of the king, though of course a critical element in the equation,[86] ultimately is superseded by the effigy of the king, which becomes the privileged site of the "immortal Dignity." Mourning and triumph both are elements of the kingship, though in the funeral they are separated, with triumph located in the king's effigy and mourning attaching to the king's deceased body.

To an extent, this framework does help explain the noh and the Tokugawa shoguns. Recall that the memorial shrines at Nikkō for the first Tokugawa shogun, Ieyasu, were similarly divided, with one shrine holding his natural body and another where the displayed "dream" images of him were venerated. Within the poetics of the noh, the two very general types of plays of the ritual and demonic, or for example *Takasago* and *Sekidera*, could be taken as expressive of these two aspects of the shogun-as-king. Or at very least the imagery of death and decomposition of the demonic plays, which comes at the end of a noh program, are part of the "*kyū*" level of the *jo-ha-kyū* cycle; like the *kyū* level, then, the figure of death could be nothing more than that aspect of the principle of eternal kingship which keeps the kingship regenerating, and therefore eternal. The godly and atemporal *jo*—with its immobile bodies in the *jo*-level noh plays, and the very temporalized ("fast") demonic *kyū*, with its active but deteriorating bodies in the *kyū*-level noh plays, are thus the two principal bodies, or aspects, of the shogun.

This would make for a rather functionalist dualistic principle, as it does for Kantorowicz.[87] This may indeed be an accurate understanding of the Tokugawa shoguns.

Still, it does not seem to account for the Tokugawa privileging of death, including at the most public, official level of the shogun, and of noh plays like *Sekidera*. Even at the shogun's memorial shrine, mourning was associated with Ieyasu's dream image/effigy as much as or more than it was with his natural entombed body (and his memorial image, being a dream portrait, was of course not even a fully embodied effigy). This therefore is not quite the same as a functional dualistic principle of kingship.

---

86. It is important to keep in mind that this is not just a duality of an individual historical king's body in opposition to the public office of the king; this duality exists *within* the concept of rulership itself (see ibid., 171). The implication of this would be that death, too, is part of the public office.

87. In *The King's Two Bodies*, there may be an apparent contradiction, but the contradictory terms in fact work to maintain the structure: the idea of the eternal King helped maintain the fiction of immortality for an increasingly "terrestrial" political institution, while the immortal King was able to act, and will, through the bodies of the mortal kings.

It is instead worth focusing more on the "sublime" (*sōgon*), which seems to have been an important component of the Tokugawa aesthetic attitude. The noh's sublime, insofar as it can be taken as a privileged aesthetic of the shogunate, shows a more complicated relationship between death and immortality, decay and identity, and the aesthetic reverence of power.

• • •

As in some Western formulations, the "sublime" identification within the noh, even while it might create the effect of a transcendent, specified identity, was based on the dispersal of identity. It entailed a movement beyond the self (the identity that appears first as a character of the present, but then is "fulfilled" as a better-known identity of the past) as a means to a more empathetic union with what might be thought of as meaning in general; but this is a meaning, or identity, which itself is mysterious and unspecifiable. Thus, at least one side of the noh's sublime involved the bracketing, or refusal, of difference (since difference depends on specifiable individual identities). If there is any comparison to Western concepts of the sublime, though, there is much at stake, given that the sublime is one of the key aesthetic terms to Enlightenment subjectivity. In the noh, there are two different elements that can be isolated as indicative of the sublime and that can help to clarify its role(s).

On the one hand there are the plays commonly from the first, "godly" category in which transcendence might be thought of as more theological, in which the world in general (including the natural world) partakes of a divinely given universal order of value-as-goodness. The play *Takasago*, which as described above consists of a divine linkage of present with past time and space (the play concludes first with the chorus celebrating the appearance of "the holy image"—all the godly and temporal aspects combined in the image of the Sumiyoshi deity—and then the dancing of the *shite* playing that role), and which uses the pine tree as a sort of natural guarantor for the stability of representation and meaning, would seem to indicate both; this play was explicitly described as a "sublime" (*sōgon*) play. As dictated by the *jo-ha-kyū* cycle, the final moment is said to result in this sublime dispersal of all identity, in a "fast" time that transcends the differentiations upon which identity depends. But this is a transcendence that always is at the same time a return to the first, god-given world of well-defined structure and unicity.

Sekidera Komachi shows another possibility. Even in the basic plot it is clear that there is no return to divine origins and identities. Komachi remains, or rather becomes, an independent being, separated from the world of beautiful coherence and completion. Nature no longer is entirely an element of divine value and meaning—it no longer holds the pure and stable transparency of representation that *Takasago's* pine tree did. To the extent that nature does still serve as the embodiment of a stable sign, and a stable being, it is an unhappy one: the final context is the "forest of *Hazukashii* (shame)," naming the condition of both Komachi and of the world—or rather, nature and the world become Komachi. But Komachi becomes divorced even from that. The end of the play finds her wandering, and crying "Where is the forest of *Hazukashii?*" She thus is alienated from the sign and name of her own unhappy being.

In addition to *sōgon*, there is another aesthetic term translatable as "sublime" that appears in *Sekidera* and elsewhere: the "chaos," but also most "advanced" level of *ran-i*, or *rangyoku* (乱曲 or 闌曲). Literally, movement or music which is chaotic, disordered, deranged (乱曲), this is where one would find the "pulverizing movement" of *saidō* (砕動), in which a dancer's body seems to "break into many pieces." Zeami makes it absolutely clear that these are the aesthetics of the final, *kyū*-level stage of the noh. So also, he writes, is "astonishment."[88]

But this moment of *ran-i* chaos and astonishment is not *just* of the demonic level, and it is not just what noh "descends" into as part of the process leading to a return to the transcendent level of godliness.[89] The moment of chaotic "sublime" is not necessarily part of that narrative trajectory. *Ran-i* is, according to Zeami, itself definitive of the ultimate rank of "virtuosic transcendence" (*taketaru kurai*, 闌けたる位),[90] and rather than a return to the "straightforward style" of the first-category god-plays (*waki*), it is the chaotic moment of *rangyoku* itself that is "*the transcendent* and ... the musical level of singing with complete fruition."[91] So, too, with astonishment: "When the audience can express its astonishment as one with a gasp, *the moment of Fulfillment has come.*"[92]

---

88. *Zeami Zenchiku*, "Shūgyoku Tokka," 191.
89. Just as *Sekidera Komachi* is of the middle *ha* rather than the final *kyū* level.
90. *Zeami Zenchiku*, "Sarugaku Dangi," 26.
91. From Zeami's "Go ongyoku no jōjō." The translation here is from Thomas Blenman Hare, *Zeami's Style* (Stanford: Stanford University Press, 1986), 234. Emphasis my own.
92. If this moment of astonishment is not reached, Zeami says, it would be "the same as constructing an image of the Buddha but never installing the eyes in the image." This is a striking depiction of the sublime as a moment when divine eyes are completed points beyond just chaos. See "Shūgyoku Tokka," 190–191, and Rimer and Yamazaki, *On the Art of the Noh*, 138–139 (emphasis my own).

Thus, unlike the beautiful fulfillment of the sublime of *Takasago's sōgon*, with its always-implicit return to godly origins, the chaotic *ran-i* is not a stage on the way to a godly return; it is itself the point of return—or rather, the point of transcendence. The chaotic body is itself part of the pinnacle of transcendence.[93]

These two types of the "sublime" are close to the kind of distinction that emerges in the West as the difference between the "beautiful" and the "sublime." I discuss the implications of this split below. But representation is clearly part of what was at stake, and so first a few words on that.

Because the narrative of a noh play generally does not employ development, plays are more like the completion of a picture. Like baroque allegory, they are about images, which may or may not be fulfilled at the end of the play; along with "accomplishment," "fulfillment" is one of the basic translations of the word *noh*. The central focus of a play revolves simply around whether or not the identity of a figure will ultimately be revealed or made present in its full plenitude. The uncertainty of the image is also part of the poetics of staging. As a very general rule, the noh proceeds from verbal descriptions of an image, to the visual image of that description. Choral chants revealing the true identity of a character are usually followed by the *shite's* dancing out of that revelation, and more broadly, the first half of a noh play tends to consist more of verbal descriptions of revelation while the second half consists primarily of the actual appearance of the true character.[94] Dramatic tension thus depends in part on the question of whether the verbal descriptions will be fulfilled by the embodied appearance, or revelation, of

---

93. Some of the general characteristics I have outlined are not far off from readings of the sublime in Western aesthetics. These, too, describe a transcendence which has more to do with formlessness than with form. Instead of a simple transcendent moment of understanding and meaningful experience, this sublime leads only to an intuition of the ineffable, and to the awareness of the impossibility of meaningful form; sublime moments are therefore ultimately threatening, and in some contexts horrifying. The sublime, at least by this reading of it, thus is not about the final attainment of knowledge but rather the inevitable failure of knowing. In some ways like the allegorical emblem, it indicates the failed coevalness of an idea and its representation, the certain failure of images (and images themselves are only deathly or ghostly locales of meaningful experience), and it is more about radical incommensurability than about fulfillment. In the sublime, the subject "is faced with a horrifying image of its own lack of totality." See Vijay Mishra, *The Gothic Sublime* (New York State: SUNY Press, 1994), 226, ff.

94. The visual image was described as necessary for full meaning, but the idea seems to have been that the spectator would in effect bring the verbal and the visual together as a unitary "image"—so this was not a simple privileging of the visual over the verbal.

those verbal signs. The physical manifestation in the second half is thus critical, but nonetheless sometimes left ambiguous, as therefore is the image.

The same might be said of the human body, not only in the theater but also in its relation as an expression of and measure of the social. Even in the early Edo era, the sensuous body had become a principal source of measure for understanding the world in general, and a voluminous variety of perspectives emerged on just what the body was. By the late Edo period, to give just one classic example, a hugely popular statement of the low arts of *gesaku* and the pleasure quarters' view was formulated in Shikitei Sanba's description of the public bath (*Ukiyoburo*). There, Sanba argues that it is the physical, material and naked body that is the measure of all and that demonstrates the equality and mortality of all. Sanba neatly goes through a list of supposedly transcendent laws, such as the Five Virtues of Buddhism, and shows them to refer to little else than the mortal human body.[95] He took pains too, to make clear that this was a view that was not only of the pleasure quarters, but of society at large.[96]

The noh of course needed bodies, but bodies only in the most opaque and ephemeral way, contrary to Sanba. This also is part of the tension of noh's poetics. In the interest of portraying an epic meaning and an eternal time, meaning and time are separated from the contingencies of the physical body. The denial of the body is evident in the noh's staging, which consists of bodies without bodiliness: the noh is characterized by beautiful dances and beautiful costumes, but the dances (the only kind of action really possible) are completely stylized and choreographed; the oversized costumes both cover actors' bodies and are stiffened against obvious revelation of movement; and actors' faces are of course covered with uniform stylized masks. Yet there is a continuing need for the body—to fulfill the image, as just described, and (like the pine tree in *Takasago*) as at least the possibility of a natural guarantor of the continuity of eternal past meanings and values.

Hence there is here a tension in the noh's use of bodies, including as guarantors of representation, which might be conceived of in the same terms as the tension in the shogunal economy of the general equivalent. On the one hand there is a desire for the values of an eternal transcendent which are

---

95. For a partial English-language translation see Robert W. Leutner, *Shikitei Sanba and the Comic Tradition* (Harvard: Harvard-Yenching Institute, 1985), 137–165.
96. He tried, he says, to "[leave] out the parts about the licensed quarter and emphasize the humor in commonplace people and events." Ibid., 141.

guaranteed in the figure of a natural body—like rice being the natural measure of all other things in the shogun's economy. Yet there is also this other image of the transcendent, which is beyond the boundaries and identities of the material altogether. This conflict of notions of representation and transcendence was also evident in the way the shoguns thought about using noh as a representation of their own power. At several points in the Edo era, Tokugawa shoguns argued over whether it was appropriate for them to actually get up on the stage themselves and dance, or whether it would be more appropriate for an actor to act on stage as their representative. A number of shoguns did act themselves, but this appears to have been an ongoing point of uncertainty.

Underlying these tensions, and expressed in the sublime of *Sekidera Komachi* and *ran-i*, is an awareness of the failure of the adequacy of representation.[97] Given the failure of representation, the sublime experience serves as its replacement, or at least it points to that which lies beyond representation.

To some extent sublime accordingly works negatively. The "madness" of *ran-i*, in particular, can be compared to Kant's understanding of the *Schwärmerei* (mad) quality of the sublime, and more generally the noumenal aspect of things. The chaotic character of the sublime might risk an infinitely open reflection of the objective world, but it also reveals to us our limits—and in this revelation (another way of putting it is that nature reveals its irreducibility to our interests as sensuous beings), we also feel that which is *not* limited in ourselves; we therefore in a way grasp that as well.

For Kant, the ineffable, out-of-scale "bigness" as well as the chaotic disintegration of the sublime experience are opposed to the experience of beauty (Kant also confines the sublime to an experience of nature, and not to a work of art, but for this context that can be disregarded). Whereas the sublime is concerned with what is unlimited and formless in the world, beauty is concerned with the form of an object, and with coherence, completion, and ordered systematicity. In beauty there is a harmony of imagination and understanding that does not exist in the sublime.

With important qualifications, this split between the beautiful and the sublime is visible in the noh, too, in the conjoined opposition of *Takasago* and *Sekidera Komachi*, and the distinction between *sōgon* and *ran-i*. Whereas *ran-i* consists of a moment of chaotic transcendence, beyond the narrative

---

97. The adequacy of representation to, apparently even the sensuous appreciation of, the universal good (again, as an example one can think of *Sekidera*'s failure to embody even a clear expression of that which she no longer is).

structure of the play, *sōgon* is always part of the process of a return to the "beautiful," completed, ongoing cycles of the *jo-ha-kyū* order, and the godly origins that anchor it.

In the Western, Kantian construct, the sublime actually does bring us to an appreciation of universality and morality, even if this is no longer divinely given. But beauty, too, becomes a symbol expressive of morality. At risk of great reduction, because morality in this schema depends on freedom of imagination, and because the imagination is part of the experience of beauty, it is only through beauty that morality and freedom can become palpable. Although the sublime is opposed to the beautiful, they also work together.

This would be one explanation, then, of the need for apparently contradictory plays like *Takasago* and *Sekidera*, and for the favoring of principles like *sōgon* along with *ran-i*. Without explicit *commentary* this can only be speculation. But these divisions do indicate some synoptic shifts that occur in the Edo era.

First, especially in ritual plays like *Takasago*, the single protagonist that is the *shite* is still not an independent being, or substance, causally acting in the world; it is simply an overarching presence, that partakes of a divine universality. But in plays like *Sekidera*, one can see the emergence of an independent subjectivity, no longer united with a (noumenal) world of value, in ways that make it to be the source and measure of universal meaning and morality. Unhappily caught in the physical, phenomenal qualities of the body, time, and language, in *Sekidera Komachi*'s world—as in some ways for Kant's—the only means of experiencing the universal is via a sublime transcendence. Even if *Sekidera* does not exactly point, as the flip side of the sublime, to reason as the source of systematicity as an ideal, in *Sekidera*—and especially in the context of its opposition to *Takasago*—one can see the grappling with something like what in the West might be called a modern subject.

At very least, the ritual world of *Takasago* no longer sufficed as an expression of the Tokugawa order of things. The need for the sublime already indicates a world in which aesthetics was replacing the divine. But not yet entirely. In simple terms, part of the tension in Tokugawa noh—indicated by the concomitant valorizing of plays like *Takasago* and plays like *Sekidera*, but also by the dramatic tension within the plays themselves—lies in what may be thought of as a historical moment in between religious and more secularized worlds. Tokugawa noh might be thought of in a vein similar to Walter Benjamin's description of baroque allegory. For Benjamin, baroque allegory has to do with the "rescuing of the gods,"[98] which implies not the maintenance of a continuing theological worldview, but rather an attempt at retrieval, or radical reconstruction, of a long lost, mythic past in an already secularized world.

If the sublime is thus a critical aesthetic attitude in Tokugawa noh, however, questions remain as to the possibility of envisioning the unified totalities that Chapter 1 described as being so important to the Tokugawa project of state unification. Part of the idea of the sublime, including in these notions of *sōgon* and *ran-i*, seems to be the recognition of limitlessness, and the ungraspability of things. It implies an inability to distinguish frames of inside and outside, including of time; what Lyotard (from a different, Western context) described as the sublime's "abject failure to totalize." This puts into doubt the monumental view of the noh's ritual order of time as a single and wide-reaching set of closed cycles, described in Chapter 1. The use of the noh to create a transcendent order of unified, statewide time was perhaps not quite so simple a matter as just commanding a set of provincial lords and actors to attend a family New Year's ceremony.

One possible way into an understanding of this might be to look at the overriding presence of mournful longing seen in the noh, and the experience of melancholy. At a very general level, part of the idea of melancholy as a historical trope has to do with the emergence of the idea that the world can only be depicted and understood through representation—that is, through the mediation of signs, which no longer are felt to bear iconic or direct relation to that which they signify. This sets up a desire to represent the unrepresentable, and the yearning for an impossible presence, which can only end in failure. This results in a structure of melancholy.[99]

This mournful remembrance, as well as the empty presence of the world, is one way to describe the form of the first shogun's memorial at Nikkō, and is therefore one of the general attitudes of memory in official Tokugawa life. Although meant to deify the state founder, the image and the memory are disembodied and not fully present (except as a dream). Mourning would therefore be as appropriate as (or more so than) celebration or deification.

In the noh, melancholy is one of the most important dispositions. For example, in the "five sounds"—categories of music which match the five cat-

---

98. Susan Buck-Morss, *The Dialectics of Seeing* (Cambridge, MA: MIT Press, 1991), 168.
99. For similar discussions of melancholia in European history, see Christine Buci-Glucksmann, *La folie du voir: de l'esthétique baroque* (Paris: Éditions Galilée, 1984), and Patrick Camiller, transl., *Baroque Reason* (London: Sage Publications, 1994).

egories of plays—the central form was *aishō* (哀傷, melancholy, or mourning).[100] This is the emotion with which the typical *ha*-level "woman" play ends.

As a form of aesthetic experience, melancholy, too, can be thought of as a problem of time, and of death.[101] In Timothy Murray's view, for example, the melancholic relation is "a representational trajectory that disturbs and unsettles the delusions of mastery over the enigmatic figurations, and folds, and spaces of intertextual and intercultural otherness." It involves a continual remembrance of death, and a continual sense of loss, without any vision of resolution, or end.[102] Assuming this to be a fair description of the noh, then here, also, it would seem that in its poetics, the noh is definitely not in any simple way a normative construct of power. There is no uncomplicated mastery of time, parallel to the image of the shogun as in control of fixed boundaries of time and space.

From a more closely Freudian position, melancholia is the effect of a loss that has gone unmourned. The lost object (or otherness), having gone unmourned, is in fact sustained within the mourning subject, and the mourning subject increasingly identifies *with* that lost object. Mourning is thus distinguished from melancholy in critical ways; melancholy is in part a result of the lack of mourning.[103]

Certainly one does get the sense that there was, in the Tokugawa memorial, an identification with a lost theological totality—as there was in the noh itself and in the attempt to re-create an archaic economy of natural value. From this perspective, it would be the most official, ritual-level noh plays

---

100. Along with *renbo* (恋慕), or "romantic longing." Another term, *aware*, which was one of the two most commonly used words used to describe the general aesthetic of the noh, can also be translated as melancholy. But this word is heavily overdetermined, having been used for centuries to describe a great variety of different forms of aesthetic experience, to the point of meaning almost anything.
101. "The melancholy personality contemplating ruin and death was one of the dominant topics of baroque literature and art." Buci-Glucksmann, ibid., 23.
102. See Timothy Murray, "Translating Montaigne's Crypts: Melancholic Relations and the Sites of Altarbiography," in *Bucknell Review* 35, no. 2 (1992), 122, 124. I am using the structure of melancholy only as a set of relations (as is Murray), which do not necessarily equate literally to the disease of melancholia; this does not, for example, imply a total withdrawal from the world (something one does see in the middle ages in Japan), which is truer of melancholia itself as an illness. See Murray, 123–124. This notion of melancholy is also somewhat different from Freud's, and I am only using here what seems relevant to explaining the noh.
103. See Freud, "Mourning and Melancholia," passim, in *The Standard Edition of the Complete Psychological Works of Sigmund Freud*, J. Strachey, trans. (London: Hogarth Press, 1935–74), XIV.

that would be the most melancholic (and conservative of whole temporalities, to the extent that they claim to transcend the disjuncture from the divine past with which they identify), while the later woman plays, more explicit in their expressions of separation and loss, would be about the process of mourning. To give just one example that might back up this line of thought, in *Shūgyoku tokka*, Zeami does write of the importance of "fulfillment," as mentioned above, and in this work describes it as the result of the proper completion of the process of *jo*, *ha*, and *kyū*; "If this natural process toward completion is not carried out, no feelings of Fulfillment can arise." If indeed carried out properly, the process "surpasses any question of mere skill, and represents an unconscious Fulfillment." But the feelings this completion gives rise to are sensations of "Melancholy Elegance."[104] Melancholy in this context thus clearly does have to do with an incorporative completion and wholeness of a sort, not simply a mournful impression of loss and disjuncture. Mourning and melancholia, central to the noh, thus are also foundational to the experience of the early modern state. The experience of melancholy, furthermore, might accordingly be as much about the support of an empowered identity as it is about the expression of loss or death.

The destruction of identity described by the noh's aesthetics of the sublime, and the emphasis on melancholic longing, both describe an aesthetic attitude that yearns for transcendence and totalized identities at a time when it is felt that these are impossible. This sublime aesthetic was itself part of the basis of Tokugawa power.

• • •

There is still one last point to make regarding the problem mentioned at the outset of this chapter, the longing for death and for dead bodies. To make an obvious point, this is also a longing for a "body" outside of circulation altogether. Plays like *Sekidera Komachi* very clearly thematize the impossibility of a full and complete return to the past, and the past as *the* source and measure of real value. In both *Sekidera* and *Motomezuka* (in which Unai may indeed have united with her body—but as a dead body, not as a return to the full life and value of the divine past), the dream is for a place beyond all circulations of meaning, time, and value, as constituted at that time. The discussion thus far has described some of the ways in which this impossible relation to the world of the epic past is brought out in other aspects of Tokugawa life as well: in particular, the "dream" image of the founding sho-

---

104. See Rimer and Yamazaki, *On the Art of the Noh*, 137–138.

gun as the foundational shrine for the entire Tokugawa regime is based on this relation of impossibility, and the infeasibility of carrying out a fully rice-based economy.

But what then of the relations of capitalism as a potential factor, here at the level of aesthetics?

By some arguments, such as Karatani Kojin's, the general idea of the sublime as a state of experience beyond difference arises historically only with the development of a commoditized monetary economy—"a place where all differences are unconditionally bracketed."[105] Further, the category of aesthetics is tied to the development of an object which cannot be represented by anything else—that is, the work of art—but this idea of an object that cannot be represented by anything else is itself tied to the emergence of the commodity form. Those connections, too, are visible in early modern Japan.[106] Since the noh took on its more ossified form in tandem with the development of capitalism, should we read the emphasis placed on the "sublime" experience (already present in Zeami's treatises), and on plays like *Sekidera Komachi*, as a product really of a consumer capitalist culture? Perhaps, although these traits can be understood through the dynamics of the noh's epic values, and the uncertain possibilities of that value orientation in the Tokugawa period. Capitalism certainly was a fundamental catalytic factor in Edo-era life, and undoubtedly helped contribute to the formation of rational, reasoning subjects that the sublime also depended on. And capitalism's very status as illegal, but functionally necessary, in itself may be part of the formation of a realm of value through instrumental reason. Nonetheless it remained a very separate economy of goods and people, and a few words can be said from that perspective.

One of the readings of the aesthetic of capitalism is that it leads toward what are often generically called "gothic" forms: as capitalism becomes an invasive economic form, the argument goes, it decodes earlier notions of time, space, and value—especially when it produces inflationary spirals, as were seen in the late Tokugawa era. These decodings become embodied in works of art focusing on the human body; this aesthetics is therefore part of the capitalist failure of corporeality and of the corporeal as a guarantee of stability. It entails destruction, but at the same time fabulous growth: as Marx put it, "the capitalist...converts value, i.e., past, materialized, and dead

---

105. Karatani Kojin, "Uses of Aesthetics: After Orientalism," in *Boundary 2*, 25:2, 1998, 147.
106. Critiques of something like a commodity form, including by critics like Buyō Inshi, do not appear until the late Edo era.

labor into capital, into value big with value, a live monster that is fruitful and multiplies."[107]

It would however be overly simplistic to think of capitalism as merely decoding and deterritorializing the noh, as if it somehow came, logically or historically, after the noh. Rather than looking at the noh, it is more appropriate to consider the conditions of capitalism in the similarly "gothic" aesthetics seen in Tokugawa-era kabuki, especially late Tokugawa kabuki—a time both when mercantile capitalism had become well developed, and furthermore when inflationary uncertainty had become very widespread. I mention here only a set of brief examples.

The murder and ghost plays of the kabuki playwright Tsuruya Nanboku are famous, and were hugely popular then.[108] It was not only Nanboku, however; by the nineteenth century, one sees throughout kabuki an increased development of the use of blood and disfigurement: the *teoi goto* (手負いごと, "wounded" scenes, emphasizing a gruesomely realist use of blood); the *semeba* "torture" scenes, which developed into a large genre (including, for example, *yukizeme* (雪責, snow torture): stylized torture scenes, in a "strange atmosphere evoked by stylized tormenting of a young girl amidst a stage setting with snow";[109] *hebizeme* (蛇責, snake torture); even *kotozeme* (琴責, torture by being forced to play the *koto*, and other musical instruments—the music must be played beautifully, but in such a way that it is a terrible excess of beauty); and so on. The monstrous growth and uncertainty of capital's bodily basis here finds expression in the mutilations of the human body. This is seen, for example, in openings-up of the tidy circulations of a body's life-

---

107. Karl Marx, *Capital, A Critique of Political Economy*, vol. 1 (New York: International Publishers, 1967). On capitalism and the gothic, see, for example, Vijay Mishra, *The Gothic Sublime* (New York: State University of New York Press, 1994).

108. Also in the nineteenth century there is some possibility of seeing the "gothic" aspects of kabuki as being tied to nationalist identity in the face of increasing encroachment and apparent threat from a number of countries abroad. For example in Nanboku's play *Tenjiku Tokubei*, a play based on a real merchant marine who traveled abroad (to India and elsewhere), there is an evil sorcerer who has the power to transform himself into myriad forms (including a giant toad). The play makes very clear that this magic power to transform things comes from abroad: specifically, the sorcerer's father was a Korean warrior, who taught his son this power so that he might overthrow the Japanese government. (The play also contains some remarkable "fast changes" of identity underwater—as if the very crossing of oceans to other nations was a dangerous act, potentially destabilizing one's identity.) So in this case, it appears that threat of deformation has to do with projecting a fear of one's own instability onto a national other. But this play is almost unique in this kind of nationalist undertone.

109. Samuel L. Leiter, trans., *Kabuki Encyclopedia* (Westport, Connecticut: Greenwood Press, 1979), 115.

blood. Spurting blood becomes the circulations of life, like the circulations of capital, gone monstrously wild.

These may be considered as examples of the sublime, though I have found no reference to them in those terms. Certainly in these cases, as with the noh, the basic possibility of a rational or "beautiful" order of value depends also on moments of something like the sublime disintegration of unified identities. Also similar to plays like *Sekidera Komachi* are the Saikaku stories in which people die mournful deaths, lamenting that they cannot take their riches with them in death, and even rolling in their coins (their world of value) as if to somehow reunite their bodies with the time and value of those coins. More generally, it may be that the rational instrumentality of capitalism helped develop the secularized tensions of the sublime seen in the official Tokugawa noh plays. Clearly there are also basic dissimilarities that distinguish the two, including the noh's desire for a divine past in opposition to kabuki's privileging of a secular, open future. For the moment, it is merely worth noting that in both of these separate economies, the search for full meaning, experience, and value leads also to a position of alienation, and a desire for transcendence from the overall structure of exchange. In both, there is at least a dream of a value that is outside of circulation: a dream for a value outside of the circulations of alienating time in which both the longing women of the noh and the kabuki capitalists seem to find themselves, and a dream for, if not a means into a more meaningful or "valuable" experience of being, then a way out of the contradictions and alienations that arose within these orders of meaning and value.

• • •

Although early Tokugawa shogunal advisors recommended that the traditional ritual of *kagura* be appropriated as the official rite of state, the shoguns instead opted for the noh. Even if the immediate precedent was Hideyoshi's use of the noh for a brand of self-deification, and even if the Tokugawas, too, fashioned the Tōshōgū shrine as the seat of a Tokugawa divinity, the noh was part of a world that saw the dissipation of a theologically legitimated social order, and the gradual replacement of god with beauty.

The use of the term noh, which developed mostly within the Edo era, may be part of this process. Along with the idea of fulfillment, noh has also been glossed as "skill." The notion of skill (generally as *gijutsu*, 技術) was for Nakae Chomin the precursor to the separate sphere of the fine arts (*geijutsu*, 芸術). The shoguns used the noh, too, to create the image of a world apart from all else—disinterested, and yet as capable as anything else of effecting a contemplative moral community.

Official performances of the noh related to the shogun inevitably involved a moment of transcendence. But, judging from the official weight given to *Sekidera*, the "ritual" moments of official noh depended as much on a kind of sublime transcendence as they did on a more properly divine experience.

The contradictory valuing by the shoguns of the ritual play *Takasago* and the nonritual play *Sekidera* can be resolved, to some extent, as the cooperative workings of an aesthetic split between the beautiful and the sublime. But it also expresses tensions of orientation and horizon seen elsewhere in Edo life—not only between a divinely and a secularly legitimated society, but more generally between a world whose guarantee of coherence is godly, and one in which individual perceptions no longer can rely on that guarantee. These tensions then underlie others, such as the use of rice as a natural value that would ground all other values, at a time when the economy could not work without also using cash; or the use of a deified portrait of Tokugawa Ieyasu as the divine founder of the regime, but a portrait that could only be a dream-memory rather than a divine incarnation or embodiment of that founding figure; or even the arguments over whether it was appropriate for a shogun to physically dance out a noh play himself, or instead use another actor as his representative.

As an aesthetics of power, these tensions do not bolster the idea of the shogun as a divinely transcendent figure. Aesthetic form in Edo-era noh does not yield up the image of an eternal fullness of all time, of the full presence of the past in the present, or an entirely completed and fulfilled world in those senses—it does not create that kind of utopic space. If there is a utopic urge, it is also dependent on the sublime, and on a transcendence of all given structures of time and exchange.

In privileging plays like *Sekidera Komachi*, it seems that the Tokugawa rulers were acknowledging that the closed, repetitive ritual cycles that the noh was helping to put into practice were only an ideology, in the simple sense—that is, a belief that was put into practice, but was nonetheless "false" to the overall conditions of the times. The images of closed and unified time and history that came from the ritual practices of the noh and the aesthetics of its more ritualistic plays were part of the larger meaning and experience of the noh only within a new context. This context included an acknowledgment of the inevitable failures of any simple belief in those images.

Yet the noh was a theater of power nonetheless. The poetics of noh in the Tokugawa period express contradictions, which mirror the contradictions that were produced in the value orientations of the rice economy on the one hand and capitalism on the other. Power and the experience of unity in Tokugawa noh emerges out of the expression and transcendence of these contradictions—in the image and experience of the unidentified "sublime"—rather than in any claim, for instance, of a return to a world truly founded on an archaic, divine past. The sublime, by these terms, becomes a specifically early modern form of aesthetics, and of transcendence. It is the ability of these sublime moments to negotiate the contradictions of the era, including the experience of transcending these contradictions, which forms the site of power and authority. Power and authority do not then lie in the claim to have achieved the value orientations of either the rice economy or of capitalism, and state form should not be thought of as founded on either the economies of rice or of capitalism, alone, either. Tokugawa power lies in the ability to negotiate the contradictions of these value orientations as much as in the value orientations themselves.

4

Times and Visions of the Instant

Performances such as the Kōka *kanjin* noh of 1848 were moments that mediated time, or temporalities. Thus the era name could be changed in the middle of 1848, after the *kanjin* noh performance of that year. As I began to indicate in the previous chapter, the orders of time being mediated were implicated in wide orientations of value, including economic value. Different ways of orienting the values that formed the basis of the state, and state power, were therefore at stake and at play in these noh performances. Time, however, took on a privileged role as an autonomous force and ground of action, just as vision gained new status as an independently dominant sense. Time as a ground of action, and vision as a means of relating to the world, were in fact related.

(Double) Layers of Time

Both the noh and kabuki can be thought of as fragmenting time, each in their own ways. Judging from theater poetics, one can look at Edo as an era composed of many times; this raises the question of how the different times related to each other. As outlined thus far, there were two different trajectories of value and of time, and therefore two different modes of relating to the past and two different modes of memory. One possibility—but by no means the only one—is that this would lead to the kind of "double consciousness" that Michael Rowlands describes, a feeling of the world as divided, with two separate images of the world coexisting, but in contest.[1]

The noh privileges the past. That is where the opening "travel scene" (*michiyuki*) generally points. And more specifically, the appearance of the

---

1. Rowlands, "Inconsistent Temporalities," in Daniel Miller, *Worlds Apart* (New York: Routledge, 1995), 37. Rowlands in fact makes an interesting claim for the interpenetration of inconsistent temporalities, but says this results simply in constraint.

172 / Visioning Eternity

main character (*shite*) is, to quote Jameson on epic forms, a "wedge, or opening, through which a hitherto aimless but lively . . . narrative suddenly falls into the deeper past (or that deeper past into it)."[2] The appearance of the *shite* thus temporalizes the narrative, but as has been shown, in a structure of time that valorizes an essential past.

Kabuki in many obvious ways had an opposite relation to the past and to the memorializing capacity of the material of "tradition." The shogunate prohibited reference to contemporary events, as if that in itself could legislate a noh-like attitude toward the past. Kabuki playwrights followed those injunctions to some extent, and certainly used traditional material a great deal. Kabuki was inventive, however, and continued to invent "slants" on the tradition-oriented official view. Chikamatsu Monzaemon's play *Sagami nyūdō sembiki inu* (*The Sagami Lay Monk and the Thousand Dogs*), about a fourteenth-century military ruler known both for his cruelty and for his love of fighting dogs, is a well-known example. Using devices such as a punning use of the Chinese characters that made up the names of the play's protagonists, Chikamatsu managed to convey that the play was referring to the eighth Tokugawa shogun, Tsunayoshi, who had only recently died—a double crime, referring not only to the present, but also to a shogun. Like the protagonist of the play, Tsunayoshi had a fanatical love of dogs (under his rule, the killing of a dog was a capital crime), and he was popularly rumored to have died in a syphilis-induced madness.[3] Although the play focused on traditional material, it was therefore a contemporary parody. The valuation of the past as the focal point of truth was redirected toward the present, and for parodic purposes; memory of the past thus served as little more than a means of focusing on the present, in critical ways.

This revaluation of the past can be seen as an institutionalized trope in kabuki, known as "*jitsu wa*": "in fact," or "in reality," implying that the sign or image one sees of the past is "in fact" a reference to the present, and that the present is therefore the site of true reality. Additionally, this use of, but reversal of, the noh-style traditional "originary" stories of the past is indicated by one of the words used to describe these origins. Whereas in the noh one of the basic terms for the origin of a story was a "seed" (*tane*), in kabuki the two syllables that make up the term were simply reversed, as *neta*. The very idea

---

2. *Postmodernism*, 288. For Jameson, this is a filmic form; a comparison to the noh in that sense would be productive.
3. A classic description of this is Donald Shively's "Chikamatsu's Satire on the Dog Shogun," in HJAS 18, 1955, 159–180.

of having a fixed, canonical origin is here parodied (*neta* is otherwise a nonsense term) even while it is continued.

Further, along with those plays that did focus on traditional material, there were the plays that more simply and obviously referred to the present: especially, for example, the *ichiyazuke* (一夜漬, "overnight pickles") that were based on very current events, especially scandalous ones, and hence were also known as "living newspapers" (*kiwamono*, 際物).[4]

Thus, even when kabuki used traditional material, the "wedge" of the traditional image opened time out onto the present, not the past; the present now became a *constitutive* present. Kabuki, it seems, thus created a political and epistemological overturning of the concept of the present, and, if not a forgetting of the epic past, at least a different kind of remembering.[5] In terms of value, in the noh it would seem that the only means to finding "true" experience would be through finding redemption in the past, while in kabuki, only a redemption in the future-oriented present could equate with true experience. At this point it therefore seems clear that there are two opposing images, almost mirrored, including two different relations to the past (as exemplified in the kabuki term *neta*).

These are not necessarily contested opposites, however, and the relation does not imply a "double consciousness" that is simply defined by two separate worlds in contest with each other. The kabuki play *Sukeroku* is a good example to consider.

Sukeroku (助六) was one of the "eighteen favorites" and one of the most popular plays of the Edo period. The central character, Sukeroku, is part uncontrollable Edokko and part all-knowing man-of-the-pleasure-quarters

---

4. With regard to these kinds of plays, Brandon cites an Edo-era comment: "Lately it has become the rage to stage, the following day, adulterous affairs and scandal which occur in the city the preceding day. Not even the names of the people are changed and the audience finds this very interesting." In James Brandon, *Kabuki Five Classic Plays* (Cambridge, Mass: Harvard University Press, 1975), 4.

5. Some writers connected with kabuki and the pleasure quarters did argue for a kind of forgetting. In another classic and immensely popular work of the late eighteenth century, *Hizakurige* (*Shank's Mare*), Ikku Jippensha begins a long comic tour of Japan with a parody of classic memory: the characters "remember" an epigram that states "We remember we've forgotten / When we get to Takinawa." "But," the narrator then adds, "they have nothing to forget." Memory serves only as a reminder that there is no need for citations from the past and for that kind of memory; there is nothing there, and the present and future are therefore open. This story is also a kind of re-memberment in the sense that it too, similar to *Ukiyoburo*, is an attempt to redefine classic Japanese aesthetics, as well as the body of Japan itself (the work is a travelogue that takes the characters around Japan), in terms of the material human body.

tsū,[6] and the play was therefore one of the quintessential expressions of the mercantilist capitalism / pleasure quarters nexus of values.

The basic narrative form superficially appears to oppose the noh's. Sukeroku, though a lower class character, is a man who knows the pleasure quarters. He knows the power of slang (his *akutai*, 悪態, "abusive language" can defeat any samurai), his style of dress attracts geisha women more than the money of any samurai could, and the most beautiful woman of the pleasure quarters is in love with him. Sukeroku's antagonist is a samurai, of the upper class and wealthy, but portrayed as evil. Both men love the beautiful and stylish prostitute Agemaki, but Sukeroku is the real hero and he wins her love. Sukeroku murders the samurai, and the play ends as the bloodied Sukeroku promises to meet up again with his love Agemaki at a future time.

The play in these ways privileges low class in opposition to samurai, and contemporary fashion-style knowledge over samurai inheritance. It also hints at the classic kabuki ending of a "love suicide." In love suicide plays there is a *michiyuki* "travel" scene like the noh's, but the travel occurs at the end of the play instead of at the start, and it points toward the future (the after-life, where the two lovers will be reunited) rather than the past. Consequently this kind of play finds redemption, or unity, in the future rather than in the past. All this would point toward *Sukeroku* as being a nice opposition to the typical noh play.

That, however, is only one layer of the play. First one could look at the staging.[7] As the play opens, the setting is an elegant house of prostitution in the Yoshiwara pleasure quarters, and the setting is further punctuated by occasional notes of *sugagaki* shamisen music. The shamisen is an instrument specific to kabuki, and *sugagaki* is a style associated only with the pleasure quarters. But at the same time, there is another set of musical instruments playing offstage: a *taiko* (large drum) and flute, both from the noh, and these are playing a "stately" song of kagura ritual. The noh ensemble continues, and as the great heroine makes her entrance, it plays *a watari byōshi* (渡り拍子, "crossing over") song. Thus, while on the one hand the heroine's appearance is clearly being made in the midst of the pleasure quarters, on the other hand it is being staged as a noh-style "crossing over" of some larger-than-human being. Like the "bridgeway" on which noh actors make their entrances, the kagura crossing over implies a shamanic-like bridging of the

---

6. The character was modeled after one of the well-known *tsū* of the time.
7. For an English language translation that indicates much of this, see "Sukeroku: Flower of Edo" in James R. Brandon, trans., *Kabuki Five Classic Plays*, 55–92.

other world of the divine past with the contemporary human world. This is further emphasized by the flute music, which generally indicates a divine presence. Thus if there are not yet two different visions of the play's setting, there are at least two different possible temporalities in the opening mise en scène of the play: the simple present, possibly opening into an unknown future; and a noh-like appearance of a being that may pull us into a transcendent past.[8]

The same staging is repeated for Sukeroku's entrance. The noh instruments play another *watari byōshi* "crossing over," and, in a classic noh-style statement of an opening into the divine world, the moon is said to reflect purely in Yoshiwara (despite it being a moonless night), and the divine noh flute alone then sounds as Sukeroku appears. Already one might begin to wonder whether the present is really just the present, or rather in fact some more transcendent past.

The play continues, however, and the plot appears to follow a non–noh-like trajectory that is not so focused on the past. Sukeroku contends with the evil samurai (Ikyū) for the woman (Agemaki), and, in his uncontrolled Edokko-style excesses, he continually prods the samurai to fight, ultimately murdering the samurai. Because the murder is witnessed, at the end Sukeroku must flee from his love Agemaki after all; he can only hint at rejoining her at a later time and world. Thus, the pleasure quarters' values of love and excess have spurred the narrative, but they have also led to separation, and their redemption is found only in some other place, located in an unknown future.[9] All this seems to follow the narrative timeline of kabuki's constitutive present rather than noh's emphasis on the past.

But like the staging, the play's present- and future-oriented narrative is not so simple as it first appears. Sukeroku's constant antagonizing of the samurai Ikyū, forever egging him on to fight, may not be merely a symptom of Sukeroku's "Edokko" excesses. Sukeroku has been trying to get Ikyū to draw

---

8. This second layer of time is further indicated by the tolling of a temple bell in the opening background. Temple bells were generally used to mark a religious order of time, and often the time of the other world in particular.

9. More straightforward love suicides illustrate this more clearly. In *Sonezaki Shinju*, for example, a man wishes to buy out the contract of his prostitute-lover so that they may marry. However, he is cheated out of his funds by a greedy friend and so cannot marry the woman. Greed is thus the catalyst for the narrative, and the only possibility for redeeming the love of the two protagonists in this kind of context is suicide. The two lovers accordingly take the only route they can, and kill themselves at the end of the play so that they can be reunited in the future world of the afterlife.

his sword, he claims, because he suspects that Ikyū has stolen a sword that is rightfully Sukeroku's. The sword is in fact a famous one: it is the named sword owned by the famous Soga Gorō, a twelfth-century hero who needed the sword to avenge his own father's wrongful death. In other words, suddenly the play seems to have shifted, or to have added another layer: Sukeroku may be "in fact" Soga Gorō of the twelfth century, now trying to recapture the sword so that he might avenge his father's murder, and the play may be a version of one of the most well known of all vendetta stories, the classic *Tales of the Soga* (*Soga Monogatari*).

The revelation of Sukeroku as Soga Gorō occurs toward the end of the first act, as Ikyū switches from calling him Sukeroku to calling him Soga; Sukeroku acknowledges that the samurai "knows his [true] name." The play then seems to switch to the mise en scène of the twelfth-century story; Ikyū continues his conversation in this new setting: "Your [Soga's] father perished ignominiously. While you without the spirit to avenge him debauch with drink and whores, your father's murderer, Suketsune, lives in pomp at court..."[10]

All this is reemphasized with the start of the second act. Temple bells toll, indicating again a more other-worldly time, and it is revealed that not only is Sukeroku in reality Soga Gorō, but the samurai Ikyū is in fact a great general of the Taira clan, and Sukeroku is therefore also—along with being Soga Gorō—a general of the Minamoto clan. This accordingly also brings the play into the story line of another classic twelfth-century warrior's tale, *The Tales of the Heike*, and it molds the play still more in the form of the noh.

Sukeroku thus is built of several layers. First, it is set in the present world of the pleasure quarters, is based on a known merchant of that time, and is classified as a "*genzai mono*" (現在物, "contemporary" play, as opposed to a *jidaimono,* 時代物, "history" play). It stages a temporal structure that seeks resolution in, and therefore ultimately values, a future world rather than the classical past. This is the narrative time of Sukeroku the townsman and it is impelled by the pleasure quarters' values of excess, irreverent "abuse" of authoritative rules of language and society, and desire for personal aggrandizement and personal love. But the play also enacts the world of the noh. It follows a classic two-part noh play structure, with Sukeroku revealed at the end of the first part to be "in truth" a famous character of the classical past, and then appearing in that guise in the second part. Like many noh plays, the

---

10. Brandon, *Kabuki*, 87.

story refers both to the *Tales of the Soga* and the *Tales of the Heike*. This other narrative time, which says the truth of the present is really in the past, takes as its narrative catalyst the more traditional authoritative values of vengeance in the name of filial piety. One must always remain loyal to one's leader or father even after death, and if one's ruler is wrongfully killed then vengeance will repay that past misdeed. The aim of this narrative of vengeance is to make the value of the past, and of one's ruler, whole again. Rather than an excessive desire for self-aggrandizement in the present and future, it is about the absolute suppression of one's own feelings and the patient waiting to fulfill one's debt to the leadership of the past.

Judging from this play, the reorientation of the present seen in some genres of kabuki does not necessarily mean that kabuki opens up or decodes the times and values of the noh. *Sukeroku* is not a parody of the noh.[11] Nor is it simply a mise en scène of the noh, in the sense of "staging" another worldview as *just* a theater of that worldview, instead of a material embodiment. There were such kabuki plays, which restaged actual noh plays in a more kabuki-like mode. Instead, in some ways *Sukeroku is* a noh play, utilizing the aesthetic form of a noh play and seeking a noh-style fulfillment of a more epic time and experience.

So, which time was the real time and which identity was the real Sukeroku? This very question is one that does not seem to have applied to the Edo era. To use a kabuki term, there was a sense of *nijūsei* (二重性) — a "doubleness," or "double-layeredness." Judging from this kind of evidence, early modern Japan was made up of several orders of time, layers that coexisted and overlapped.[12] This is not the same thing as saying that time was fragmented. These layers were both opposed *and* similar forms of experience. While they may have pointed toward very different values, some of the conditions appear to have been related. The desire for epic transcendence in the

---

11. There are small moments which could be taken as parodies of the noh's aesthetics. At one point, for example, Agemaki inquires about a poetic line, "Whose sleeve stirs the fragrance of plum blossoms?" (See Brandon, ibid., 58). The reference is to the thirteenth-century imperial poetry anthology. But instead of being an invocation of the past typical in the noh, in this case the reference is to the brand name of a popular medicine for hangovers; Agemaki at that point is drunk.

12. Another, related technique that became more prevalent in the late Edo era was *naimaze* (綯い交ぜ). This was an "intermixing," or overlaying, of two plots in one larger play. These may have been two stories from two different "worlds" (世界) of the classic canon, or, more likely, either a combination of a classic story with one or two contemporary stories brought together. Regardless, the result is a doubling effect, or a world that seems to consist of parallel and multiple narratives, rather than a single coherent time and experience.

ritual plays of the noh, for example, may in form be not all that different from the kabuki love suicide's desire to escape the time of the present and find some place of unity in the future (and in capitalism, to escape the constant alienating need for capital to circulate). This too, after all, is a form of transcendence.

Plays like *Sukeroku* seem to acknowledge both the double layeredness, and the confluence in apparently opposed forms of value. For example, look at how *Sukeroku* ends. Sukeroku has murdered the samurai Ikyū, and now, having been seen, must flee; if he and Agemaki are to be brought together again, they must seek some other place. Agemaki tells him she will wait, "by the great gate, near the river bank," and Sukeroku's last words are, "until... we... meet." They could of course just be planning on meeting by the entry gate to the pleasure quarters, sometime later in the evening, say, or later in the week. But the images of "the great gate" and the bank of the river also can refer to the gate and the river one crosses on the way to the other world. Is this then the noh's narrative, implying a reunion in the other world of the classic past? Agemaki in this same moment does congratulate Sukeroku on having procured the great Soga Gorō's sword ("*Tomokirimaru*"), so maybe the play has in the end brought us into that past world. Yet Agemaki and Sukeroku have reverted to calling one another by their contemporary, pleasure quarters names (Sukeroku, not Soga Gorō). Does the future meeting at the riverbank therefore imply the then-popular *michiyuki* ending of a love suicide, in which the two will cross the river to the afterlife together, thus pointing to a reunion and fulfillment in the future rather than the past? The lack of specification leaves it possible that it may be pointing either to the past or to the present. But it also conceivably brings both structures of time together, allowing both to be co-present. At this point it may not matter, since in a way the endpoint and solution of each is the same. The noh's tremendous longing to be reunited with the body of the past,[13] and kabuki's goal of fulfillment in the future somehow come together in a desire for transcendence. The play dramatizes just this confluence.

Furthermore, here too it is the ability to bring together and negotiate the differences of times, values, and identities that brings real power. In *Sukeroku*, the characters who are weakest and mocked the most are those with the

---

13. Along with all the usual noh themes of wishing to reunite with a lover from the past, that is also what the system of vengeance was about. In the middle ages, a lord was considered to own the body of his retainer, and if a lord was wrongly killed, the retainer could repay this "debt" with his own body—it is thus a process of redeeming a debt, and fulfilling a body of the past.

most superficial and unidimensional identities. This includes the samurai Ikyū. By all traditional standards if anyone should have been able to play the double role of a contemporary hero and a traditional warrior bent on revenge, it should have been him. Yet it is Sukeroku who, as the hero, is able to layer a whole set of identities. He is a strong but composed "rough" *otokodate* (男達) hero, but he is also the out-of-control Edokko; he is a fireman (something almost like a street thug), and he is also a widely known lover within the pleasure quarters; and he is alternately one of the eighteen great *tsū* (powerful merchants of the pleasure quarters); a monk; and the great samurai hero of the past, Soga Gorō. He also brings together the ostensibly opposed aesthetic and regional styles of the "rough" *aragoto* (荒事) associated with Edo, and the softer, romantic style of *wagoto* (和事, or *nuregoto*, 濡れ事) associated with Kyoto. In contrast to Sukeroku, characters like Ikyū reveal their impotence through their inability to enter even the "second" world of the pleasure quarters. As soon as they try to use the language of the pleasure quarters, or to take on the simplest of customs, they only make utter fools of themselves. Their characters must, then, remain singular and weak, while it is Sukeroku's ability to successfully act out and bring together the multiple layers of identities that makes him so powerful.

The layered quality of time—the layering of different kinds of time—is less visible in plays of the noh; it is important to keep in mind that most plays were written long before the Edo era. Still, some of the noh plays that the Edo audiences selected out of the traditional canon do seem at some points to thematize the contest, if not confluence, of different temporal structures. *Dōjōji*, one of the two or three most popular noh plays among all classes, is one such example.[14]

Although a product of the middle ages, *Dōjōji* was unusual as a noh play. It became famous for its very realistic temple bell prop, and the almost comic use of "side" actors created a more dramatic sense of antagonism of perspective within the play (as opposed to the more transcendent lack of alternative perspective created by the typical noh play's focus on the *shite* alone.)

To summarize very briefly, *Dōjōji* is sort of a story within a story. It tells of a young woman who, while still a girl, misunderstands her father. The girl and her father are often visited by a generous young priest as he travels home,

---

14. Evidence indicates that *Dōjōji* was the most popular noh play in the Edo period, including among the shoguns. Its popularity reached an apex around the time of the Kōka noh performance, in which it was included and outsold all other plays. See Iiura, *Nihon engeki shi* (Tokyo, 1964), 1089, 1095; and Ikeuchi, NS I, 18.

and the father one day jokingly says the priest shall someday take the girl as a wife. Not realizing it was said jokingly, the girl takes the statement at face value and then some years later attempts to consummate the marriage; the priest nonetheless escapes. The woman's desire quickly swells into a jealous rage causing her to transform into a serpent. She finds the priest hiding under his temple's bell; she wraps herself around the bell, and her desire is so hot that it melts the bell, killing the priest. This is the end of the first story, and basically the end of the first part of the play. The play then reenacts these horrific events in a new, parallel form. Two servants are told by a temple abbot to raise a new bell which has not been hung for years. There will be a celebration, but they are told not to allow any women in. A woman dancer arrives, however, and by hypnotizing the two servants with her dance she is able to enter the temple grounds. She attacks the bell, leaping up into it as it falls to the ground. At this point the abbot tells the original story, and it becomes clear that the woman dancer is the serpent woman of that original story. However, prayers are recited, and the serpent woman appears in her true form, seething in her desire. But this time, when the bell is lifted she flees off into the river, her body "burning in her own fire."

The story clearly has origins in Buddhist themes but it is by no means clear that those themes account for its popularity in the Edo era. Its popularity among merchant capitalists in the later Edo period would seem to indicate otherwise. The play is often considered to be about the desire of women,[15] but it is also about time. It opens with the abbot consulting the calendar, and finding the day to be auspicious, he decides to "restore ancient custom," and have the bell rebuilt and raised. In a sense, without the bell the temple has been without time. The play thus opens with the question of time, and with the prospect of reinstituting a particular kind of (religious) temporality.

Then, the dancer appears. She is there, she says, to attend the service for the new bell so that "[her] sin and [her] guilt might melt away." She is there for a kind of redemption. But to get into the temple compound, she must dance for the two servants, and at this point we see the effect of her dance: she does a *ranbyōshi* (the "chaotic" dance discussed in terms of the sublime in the previous chapter), which leaves the servants in a hypnotic dream. She turns to the bell, and, crying "This loathsome bell, now I remember it!," she

---

15. For an interesting psychoanalytic reading on this, see Susan Blakeley Klein, "Woman as Serpent: The Demonic Feminine in the Noh Play Dōjōji," in Jane Marie Law, ed., *Religious Reflections on the Human Body* (Bloomington: Indiana University Press, 1995).

begins to strike it. It is only after this that the servants wake up, returning from the hypnotic reverie to their time, and they are told the story of the serpentine young woman who, in her lust, had melted the first temple bell.

So it becomes clear that it was the young woman's desire that, by destroying the first bell, had destroyed one kind of time and instituted another. That is the effect of women, or the desire of women. This is the time of longing in the extreme, of transforming bodies and deforming, "melting" time. Her "remembering" of the bell is directly opposed to the abbot's, and her striking of the new bell would presumably create a very different temporality than the abbot had intended for it. It is when she strikes it that the new bell falls down.

The first part of the play concludes with the retelling of the first story, which ends with the serpent's encompassment and melting of the first temple bell, and the death of the young priest. This would appear to be the death of ritual time, and the triumph of the time instituted by desire.

But in the second part of the noh play, the woman is trapped within the bell rather than wrapped around it, and in the end she is sent off by the priests' prayers, her own breath and body in burning flames. With the temple bell raised again, we are given a second ending that opposes the first story. One can now assume that it is the priest's archaic ritual time that has been put back into place, although an ambiguity remains.

Thus, while the play does not show a confluence between the two perspectives in the way that *Sukeroku* does, *Dōjōji* is unusual in showing at least a contest between two different possibilities. Most noh plays, including the demonic plays that might end with a burning serpent, only raise one perspective at the start and then simply reiterate or deny it at the end. Furthermore, as the preeminent emblem of time, the bell in *Dōjōji* becomes an image of both possibilities.[16] It is on one hand the material of the woman's terrible memories—something that she "remembers" in her own way, and strikes in her own time of desperate desire. It is the emblem of time defined as monstrous desire. On the other hand, it is also the emblem of transcendent ancient custom, an image of ritual time based on the recasted and restored image of an unchanging past. The same might also be said of the allegorical use of the sun. The river that "swells" with the woman's desire, and in which her burning body floats away at the end of the play, is called Hitaka, or "sun on high." Yet also at the play's end, the final appeal of the priest's prayers is

---

16. This bell became a famous emblem not only for the play, but for the noh in general. Noh theaters still reverently make a special place for the *Dōjōji* bell backstage.

made to the sun, so that the sun is implicitly instrumental in detaching the woman from the bell and preserving a more ritual form of temporality. Accordingly, like the bell, the sun (a natural image of time) is here an emblem both of the woman's time, and the priests'.

There is in these ways a double layeredness to one of the most popular noh plays of the Edo era. Although *Dōjōji* does not as clearly show a confluence between the two perspectives in the way that *Sukeroku* did, it at least shows how two very highly determined objects of time—the temple bell and the sun—embody two very different orders of time. It is hard to discount the usual reading of this play as containing a Buddhist critique of desire. But its critique of desire and the temporality of desire, as figured by women, is so close to the kinds of critiques of pleasure quarters women and the commodity form that one sees in Buyō Inshi—critiques coming from members of the late Edo merchant class that formed the new popular audience of *Dōjōji*—that it would be hard not to read the themes of *Dōjōji* in that context as well.[17]

Even if kabuki's values were different than those of the noh, kabuki should nonetheless not be viewed in any simple way as being liberating or enlightening vis à vis the values of the noh. Nor was it necessarily a logical or historical successor to the aesthetics of the noh—it is not a matter of the "traditional" versus the "modern." The aesthetic forms and times of both coexisted, but in a layered form that did not necessarily imply a simple contradiction between times or values.[18]

Morphologies of Time: Change and Transformation

In this section I look at the problems of time from a slightly different angle, focusing more on qualities of embodiment and change.

In practical use, official performances of the noh functioned to bring moments of change (events) into a more ritualized order of repetition. This was part of the shogun's economy of unchanging, "archaic," natural value.

---

17. The play does not resolve in any kind of victory for either view. Although the priests do manage to send the woman off in the second telling, even there the woman is not killed, but rather continues in her burning rage, off "Into the waves of the river Hitaka."
18. There are many other ways one might look at the coexistence of the two theaters. At a practical level, for instance, one might consider the undying popularity of the noh among the merchant class—citations are common remarking on well-built, though illegal, noh stages found in commoners' houses (e.g., see NS I, 36). Contrariwise, one could look at the popular Edo period vogue of inserting current events into the "short songs" (*kouta*) of noh, in the same way that kabuki used events of the time, even though this too was quite illegal.

What then of the narrative structure of the noh plays? Is there any notion of change, or of transformation? What is the time of eternity?

The same can be asked of kabuki. The discussion above shows that kabuki was not simply noh's opposite. Nevertheless, the "newspaper" plays and the general tendency to refocus things onto the world of the present are in clear opposition to the orientations of the noh's world. Kabuki terminology is replete with the vocabulary of change and transformation. Forms of staging include *henge* (変化物, transformation pieces); *hayagawari* (早変わり or 早替わり, quick changes); *hikinuki* (引抜き, an instantaneous ripping off of one costume, to reveal another identity underneath); *bukkaeri* (打つ返り, roughly the same as *hikinuki*, though the costume in essence is turned inside out); *hayaguke* (はやぐけ, yet another form of the *hikinuki*); and so on. Further, the kabuki-related economy of capitalism was of course founded on the idea of value as uncertain and mutable. Does kabuki therefore have an opposing notion of change—and does kabuki, as is often claimed of capitalism, therefore inaugurate a new kind of temporality? This is a problem of time, but also of materiality, or material bodiliness—in Edo theater, change, transformation, and value seem to have to do with the stability of form as much as the stability of meaning, and with the materiality of form and time. Temporal change is accordingly partly defined in terms of the continuity, exchange, and transformation of materiality.

It should be noted that the noh was associated with more than one kind of ritual, "eternal" time. As mentioned in Chapter 1, the most basic use of the noh in the inauguration of time was the New Year's performance. A critical moment of these performances was the *kaikō* (開口, opening words). Because this was the one moment in the ceremony for which new lines were written each year, it is the one point at which there is a possibility of the intrusion of the new, and the present.[19] But for now, I will simply point out that it was in the *kaikō* that specific reference is made to the new time being instituted, and so it is here that one might look to find an idea of what kind of time that was. The *kaikō* was also used in contexts other than the shogun's official New Year's ceremony, and although the form remained the same, the vocabulary apparently underwent subtle shifts. The noh *kaikō* was also used for imperial ceremonies. In these situations, the "time" that the *kaikō* refers

---

19. Prior to its use in the noh, the *kaikō* was connected with more specifically ritual purposes, and in those contexts was associated with humor. Presumably these moments of humor were like other ritual moments of comic "entertainment" of the gods, that in fact were meant to break the godly presence and reinstitute the time of humans.

184 / Visioning Eternity

to is *miyo* (御代): time in the sense of a "world," or "reign." This refers to the time of the emperor, of course, but it more generally implies a full, complete eternal world largely transcendent of any kind of ongoing time. Next, the noh's *kaikō* was also used at ceremonies in important Buddhist temples. Here, time becomes *nori* (法), or the Buddhist "law." This too is a nontemporal reference, here to the eternal rules and processes of the Buddha. Finally, in the case of the shogun's New Year's rite, time is referred to indeed as *toki* (時), or what is now the word for ongoing "time"; by this, it would seem that the shogun's was the most temporal of powers, and times.[20] Yet on closer inspection, in the remainder of the shogun's *kaikō* the references are to the "time" of pine trees, evergreens, and ever-reviving plants. Accordingly the shogun's temporal order may have had more of a quality of being *in* time than the others, but this was nonetheless a time without end, and eternal in that sense (or, one might say that the Buddhist and Imperial were orders of eternal temporality, and the shogun's was by this view more of a durational, sempiternal temporality). In all of these cases, then, the one moment of the "new" (the *kaikō*) was in fact a moment whereby the permanent would be reinstituted. Change was excluded from all of them.

Another term, used by Zeami and translated by Rimer and Yamazaki explicitly as the "eternity" of noh performances, is *jōjūfumetsu* (常住不滅).[21] Literally, this means something like "continuity" or "constancy," "always," and "that which is not extinguished/ruined/dead." Here, too, the emphasis is on a sempiternal lack of change or death. Because this sempiternal order is something which must be renewed, it is also cyclical (the *jo-ha-kyū* principle is another indicator of this cyclicity: one starts in nontime, then breaks into fast time, eventually then returning to nontime),[22] and this cyclicity implies a sense of closure—even without death—and the possibility of "fulfillment."

Eternal duration, or continuity with closure, is thus part of the temporality of the noh, and change, or newness, is primarily a matter of reinstituting the same—change is defined mostly as pure reproduction. None of this should be

---

20. For brief citations from *kaikō* of the era, see Ikeuchi, NS I, 301–304.
21. Rimer and Yamazaki, *On the Art of the Noh*, 259. Rimer and Yamazaki give as a literal translation of the term, "unchanging and indestructible."
22. Yet another example might be the term Rimer and Yamazaki translate as the "modes of cosmic change" (ibid., 78), but which more literally mean something like the "melodies/rhythms of time" (*toki no chōshi*). This was a concept of the middle ages, and referred to the temporal cycles of the hours of the day and the four seasons; Zeami applied this concept of change-as-natural-cycles to the structure of dance and voice. See "Kakyō," in *Zeami Zenchiku*, 87.

surprising, but still it at most only describes the ritual level of noh (and ultimately not even that), and does not account for the exchange and transmutation of bodies and images that makes up so much of the noh. Another example may help, this time from the play *Izutsu* (井筒, *The Well Curb*).

Izutsu is a classic noh play that was popular both in the middle ages and the Edo era. It is a third-category "woman play," and related to *Matsukaze*. Because it describes two lovers, initially just kids, who measure their comparative growth against the curb of a well, it thematizes the issues of time and change.

Izutsu is based on an episode of the tenth-century work, *The Tales of Ise* (*Ise Monogatari*). In the play, the story is relatively simple. A traveling priest meets a woman, offering a prayer and flowers to the grave of the legendary ninth-century lover, Narihira. The woman tells how Narihira and his lover (the "daughter of Aritsune"), while still children, pledged their love to one another by the side of a well. Then, as they grew older, they measured their comparative growth against the curb of the well, and their commitment to one another by viewing each other's face in the well water. The woman narrator reveals that she herself is Aritsune's daughter, longing to be reunited with Narihira, and at the end of the first half of the play she vanishes into the well. In the second act when the monk lies down to dream, reversing his robe to restore the past, she reappears. Wanting desperately to be with Narihira she puts on Narihira's hat and cloak, thereby "changing" into him. As the play concludes, however, the dancing figure becomes the ghost of the woman, Aritsune's daughter, now wilting away.

Within the play, there are several different images of time, change, and embodiment. At a number of points the play brings up the image of time as contingent, progressive, and entailing change in the sense of decay and loss: "Swift as arrows have months and years of intimacy passed (年を経て), And no longer alive is Narihira."[23] The figure of the well curb, which shows both man and woman to have grown old (*oi*, which means not only to grow but to grow old), and apart, is also emphasized at several points. Even here, though, there is no simple idea of the well as an emblem of material consistency through an unchanging time, against which the aging of the two lovers can be seen. When references are made to growth and aging, they are phrased in ways that make it uncertain who, or what, is aging; it could be the woman,

---

23. 「真弓槻弓年をへて、今は亡き世に業平の」The English translation is from Chifumi Shimazaki, *The Noh* Vol. 3, 64–7.

the man, or even the well itself—or all of them.[24] But a generalized sense of aging as change, separation, and loss is present.

In tandem with this, though, there is the usual desperate attempt to reunite with the world of the past, wherein lies the true identity of the woman and her lover, Narihira, and thereby to achieve some kind of eternal stability and fulfillment. Initially, therefore, the story finds the woman, somewhat as in *Motomezuka*, giving her prayers to a grave mound. But she is at this point trying to unite with a living (eternally so) body, not a dead one as in *Motomezuka's* ending. For the woman, the grave is at very least a "trace," or "impression" of Narihira. The word used at this point is *ato*, which implies not only a reminder, but a physical trace. The question then becomes, what kind of materiality does this "trace" have? Is it only a shadow, or at least a material emblem that nonetheless implies the passage of time as loss, or, more felicitously, does it actually embody the past? "Something here remains," says the woman, "till today."[25]

The attempt to reunite with the past accordingly has to do with filling out a trace, and giving it material body. This is what the second part of the play attempts to accomplish. After the woman reveals in the first part that she herself is Aritsune's daughter, in the second part she attempts to realize the fullness of the past not just by trying to be *with* Narihira again (to dance with him, whatever), but rather she attempts to *be* him herself—to embody him, and fill him out, by putting her own body into the traces of his. She takes his hat and his robe—"souvenirs" of him (形見, *katami*—another word which implies some kind of physical trace, as well as image; literally it means something like "form-looking")[26]—and "puts them about her body" (*mi ni furete*, 身に触れて).[27] The costume the actor wears here is a special one, combining the courtier's hat and specially patterned coat that identify Narihira with "her" own kimono. It is a "half-man, half-woman"[28] combination, which shows that while she is still Aritsune's daughter, she is also now Narihira.

---

24. This is captured in Shimazaki's translation, as for example: "The Well curb round, on the well curb oft leaned I To measure my height. It seems to have grown—It has grown old indeed." 『筒井筒、井筒にかけしまろが丈、生ひ、老いにけるぞや。』 (*Yōkyokushū*, ibid., 279).
25. *Ato wa nokorite sasuga ni imada.* Shimazaki, ibid., 54.
26. Still another term used to refer to Narihira's remainder is *shirushi* (印). *Shirushi* also implied some kind of physical presence, but is generally used in the sense of the "mark" of someone—it is the word used for the impression of one's seal (the Japanese version of one's legal signature), and so also has the implication of being one's guaranteed representative.
27. Shimazaki's "The robe he left behind I now put on" glosses over these points. Ibid., 164.
28. Shimazaki's terms. Ibid., 46.

The culminating point comes when the woman then dances a dance, known as a "shifting dance," or "changing dance" (*utsuri-mai,* 移り舞): "Hesitant and bashful," she sings, "Into Mukashi Otoko [Narihira] I change-dance myself."[29] "Change," in this case, as well as transformation, implies the ability to embody a more eternal time, and to transcend the changes and transformations that the time of aging might bring—to reincorporate the past in whole body. It is also a moment of doubling that implies a very brief moment of unity.

This of course is not all there is to it, though. The "souvenirs" are not necessarily so stable after all and not so effective as embodiments of past memories. Immediately after saying, "Wearing his hat and robe, A woman it cannot be, a Man it is indeed, Narihira's image—," the woman then adds, "I see with deep yearning" (*natsukashii,* 雲かしい; a word implying nostalgia, and therefore separation). Immediately thereafter, the woman is herself only a ghostly image.

What has led to this more ghostly sense of an embodied past is the woman's own great desire to "recall, and turn back to, the past" (*mukashi o kaesu,* 昔を返す). This is supposedly the desire of the noh in general, too. The effects of this desire are acknowledged even by the woman herself. Speaking allegorically (her own longing for the past figured by "memory grass"), she says, "Long into oblivion has faded the past, but The memory-grass seems still to grow, for how long, with nothing to wait for? Indeed nothing happens but Its memory Long clings to one In this earthly life."[30] Ultimately, in other words, this initial desire to reunite with the past, and this focus on the past, leads to a falling-out of time. "Nothing happens." Caught in a time defined by desire for the past, one loses the time of meaningful experience.[31] This is part of the structure of desire in the noh.

Thus, as in Narihira's hat and robe, the matter of time, memory and body is made clear in the status of the "trace," or souvenir in noh. While offering the possibility of lasting, complete and immutable form, ultimately

---

29. *Hazukashi ya Mukashi Otoko ni utsuri-mai.*
30. Ibid., 50–52.
31. Furthermore, it becomes a time of almost pure interiority. The initial means of "turning back into the past" consists of two acts: first, one turns one's kimono (or at least the sleeves) "inside out" (despite the term, in actual stage practice the sleeves are often merely flipped over)—this seems less a matter of turning outward one's own inner being, than of folding the outer world in. Second, one lays one's head down, to dream. Even if this is not "just" a dream, and truly accomplishes some kind of reembodiment of the past, it is still within the confines of one's own dreamworld.

in these plays one tends to be left with nothing more than the trace. As only a trace, the souvenirs and souvenir images are furthermore caught in a time of endless longing and decay. There is at least a formal correspondence between this alienation of experience figured by the souvenir, and Benjamin's reading of the capitalist commodity as souvenir: "Experience is 'withered,' a series of 'souvenirs.'"[32] That is what one is left with in *Izutsu*. At the end, the dancer is nothing more than the "spirit-ghost of the deceased woman" (*bōfu no hakurei*, 亡父のはく霊); "Like a withered flower, Its color gone, only the scent lingering"[33]—that is, she is neither the woman of the present, nor the Narihira of old. She is only the "souvenir" of Aritsune's daughter and trapped in a disembodied time of "withering" (*shibomu*, 萎む) decay.[34]

While the narrative of desire in the noh may thus typically lead to a more ghostly, disembodied kind of time, there is a secondary element of desire even within this kind of noh. This is the desire to escape circulation, and to find some kind of "dead matter" that is of much more stable body and value precisely because it is outside of circulation or exchange. In the first kind of desire, as in *Izutsu*, the hope is to make a full "return" (*kaesu*, 返す—"return" in the sense also of "repayment") to the past, a purely closed exchange of the woman's body with Narihira's (*utsuru*, 移る, as of the "changing dance" whereby the woman's body embodied Narihira's, can also mean "exchange"). This exchange is also phrased in terms of circulation and flow, especially of desire: in *Izutsu*, the outflowing of the woman's desire for Narihira succeeds in bringing him back from a long absence, and so the chorus sings, "Her heart flew, won back his love, and the errant outflow elsewhere was now a dying trickle."[35] In other words, there is a good, closed circulation between man and woman, past and present. Even the mirroring that occurs in *Izutsu* and other noh plays can be thought of along these lines. At several points in the play, the man and woman look into the well water, which is also their "heart-waters," to see if their vows will remain consistent, and, accordingly, if

---

32. Quotation cited in Buck-Morss, ibid., 189.
33. Shimazaki, ibid., 68; I have altered the translation. Shimazaki also notes the reference in the final line of the play to a passage in the Buddhist *Yuima-kyō*, discussing the "breaking" or "bending" of a body which is like a plantain tree; the result is, "There is nothing solid inside. . . . This body is like a dream. . . ." Ibid., 68–9.
34. This idea of "withering" or "bending" could nonetheless also return the discussion to the idea of the sublime (Zeami considers it at some length, in terms of a beauty that cannot be captured in explanation, in the *Fūshikaden*).
35. Shimazaki, ibid., 58.

their images of one another will remain stable. Past and present hopefully would be neatly mirrored, in a pure exchange of imagery, and their present images would hopefully remain true to their bodies and vows of the past. But in fact the mirroring does not hold true. Again, there is a distortion or anamorphosis[36] of the relation between past and present.

These exchanges hence are not so pure, and the circulations not so closed. There are therefore two different visions of the bodies, or material "souvenirs" of the past, and so two different bodies of time, and of change in the noh. One is a body of completed and controlled circulations, with qualities of fullness and of desire satisfied; "change" can only mean a reproduction of the same.[37] The other involves an inability to give material embodiment to time. It is a time of disfigurement and disembodiment, a "withering" time in which there is only a distorting exchange between past and present. It is a time of eternal duration, but without any points of closure that might give it wholeness and meaning.[38] This second kind of body and change leads at least

---

36. Anamorphosis did begin to become popular by the nineteenth century in Japan, but technically it is of some question whether it applies to the noh. Literally, it means something like "to form again," and herein lies the question: what is the stability of the process or re-forming? Anamorphosis is a process of imaging and distortion, but in anamorphosis, generally it is the mirror (a nonplanar mirror) that takes an already distorted image and makes it whole or normal again. In the noh, the moon, or other images, in some ways take a "distorted" image of the present (i.e., a ghostly figure of the present) and make it whole again, but in the case under consideration, the reflection more simply works the other way around: it distorts a once-whole image. Either way, the process of imaging and embodiment (that is, I am looking at the mirror as a process) creates an unstable exchange, or reflection—a transformation.

37. This may help to explain the tremendous emphasis placed on straightforward bodily imitation in the transmission of knowledge on how to do the noh. In one of the very few Edo-era written commentaries on the noh, it is explained that words and theory are "useless" for noh actors—it is the body itself which transmits this knowledge. For document quotations see Ikeuchi, NS I, 304, and Omote, *Nō Kyōgen* II, 389.

38. There are many possible examples of the two bodies of the "souvenir," and of the difference (and relation) between the time of unity and the endlessly repetitive time of unfulfilled desire. One is a play closely related to *Sekidera* (and also about Ono no Komachi), called *Kayoi Komachi*. This play recounts the story of how Komachi's love came repeatedly to visit her. For ninety-nine nights he came, as she notched off the visits on a carriage wheel shaft; on the hundredth visit, if he really came, their love would be requited. The tension builds, and the lover hands Komachi the wicker hat he once wore; the end is ambiguous, but all hinges on the hat and the counting: if the hat truly embodies his past, then he has returned and the end of the repetitions has been reached. Time, body, and desire have all been fulfilled. Of course if the souvenir is only a hat, then the longing will continue, and the time of repetition will be without meaningful end.

implicitly to the second kind of desire, in this case for death.[39] In this way too, the noh was made up of an interrelation between a durational but ghostly time of longing for impossible fulfillment, and a more transcendent time of unity and embodied completion.

Both kinds of time may be related to power. They need not necessarily be understood in terms of continuing control, on the one hand, and loss of control on the other (so that the transcendent, ritual aspects of noh would be appropriate for the shogunate, for instance, while the deformations of the "woman" plays would not). For example, while the ritual kind of embodiment of an eternal unified time was surely an aesthetic that would be in agreement with the institution of the shogun as an ongoing representative of a unified state, the more alienated time of decay may have been relevant to the form of state power as well. Alienation implies distance. So too distortion, and anamorphosis, may imply the creation of two different images or bodies, with a distance between them. This distance, at least in the noh, is nonetheless connected by the irrepressible longing (as in any nostalgia; it is the separation that allows for the longing). In other words, the time of decay creates a spectatorial relation to the time of ritual unity. There is a feeling of alienation from that time of unity, but nonetheless there is a longing for that time. This parallels the structure of spectatorial power in official performances like the shogunal machi-iri investiture. There, the shogun himself claims a sort of ritual connection with the gods, yet this ritualism is also dependent on spectators—thus the importance of having townspeople present on the first and most official day, even though they cannot fully see the stage. Their desire to see this performance which they cannot understand, and hence are alienated from, confirms the power of the shogun (from both sides: the commoners find their own place in this point of ignorance and alienation, and the shogun too sees them as those who are excluded from full participation in the knowledge, identity, and power of the official rulers). Or, in aesthetic terms, the appreciation of and longing for the noh's ritual time confirms its "beauty" as a transcendent and unquestionable good. Accordingly, it seems quite possible that the distortion and decay did not just create an alternative image, which would then subvert and de-center the pos-

---

39. One could read the often crazed focus on the "souvenirs" of the past (almost every noh play focuses on an object/remainder from the past) as a form of fetishism, an emblem that takes the place of this impossible exchange with the past. This works in many cases, though not all, and I am more interested in the different kinds of memorative bodies the souvenir can act as.

sibility of having a unified subject of power.[40] In fact, just as the shogun seems to have needed the flows of capitalism, so too it appears to have needed the apparently uncontrolled flows of excess desire as much as it depended on the control of closed circulation.[41]

Still, I am reluctant in this context to reduce the discussion to a simple construct of state power alone. To finish the discussion of the times of change in Edo theater aesthetics, and to get a picture of the larger cultural landscape, what of the striking theatrics of change and of gory and ghostly bodies in the kabuki?

Kabuki displayed and even reveled in times of change and transformation. From the mid-Tokugawa era on, one of the more popular genres was a dance scene that consisted of nothing more than one or more actors doing a series of quick "transformation pieces" (the *hengemono*). These initially became popular in the first period of the floating world's efflorescence in the late seventeenth century, and then became still more popular in the nineteenth century around the time of the Kōka noh performance. Furthermore, kabuki was connected to things "new" in a way that the noh generally was not. The "living newspaper" (*kizewamono*) designation was broadly applicable, and one of the principal reasons people went to see kabuki plays was to plug into the news. News in the kabuki, however, was defined in part as the flow of gossip. People went to the theater not just to find out what all the latest events were, although this was part of it, but they went also to find out what was being considered "news," what was being talked about, what was current and in popular circulation.

The connection here to fashion is obvious, and as has been explained, kabuki also became the privileged location for fashion. Nearly everyone, including the samurai, wanted to get into the kabuki theaters to see and show off the latest in clothing fashions and to stay in touch with the latest slang. Kabuki was thus integral to the institutionalization of a notion of time that

---

40. Some have argued that this is what happens in the context of distortion and decay, as in anamorphosis. See for example Martin Jay, *Downcast Eyes* (Berkeley: University of California Press, 1993), 48.

41. Consequently there seems to have been some risk, more commonly associated with the desire of commodity capitalism, that even the shoguns themselves might become overly attached to the noh. There are commentaries at several points in the Edo era saying that while shoguns should continue to perform the noh for such purposes as reviving their own physical health, they nonetheless were errantly becoming "addicted" (*tandeki*) to the noh, and thereby becoming "dissipated." See Ikeuchi, NS I, 437.

included an emphasis on newness and change—the temporality and newness of fashion in particular.

Fashion, generally speaking, values the eternal occurrence of the new, but always in the same way. It therefore denies the occurrence of the new as a real event, a real interruption that might truly change things. It does away with any end—it "protects from death"[42]—but because it has neither event nor end, it too (like the noh's time of endless desire) risks emptiness and meaninglessness. This is one way of reading kabuki's transformation pieces: a set of random changes that are visually exciting, and which people did come to see precisely for fashion's purpose, but which were in essence simple repetitions of one another, and without narrative development or end. Change in this case is a random repetition of the same.

Unlike the noh, in kabuki these changes were relished as a source of pleasure and so were valued. The *hengemono* transformation pieces are one example of this delight in the mutability of form. In Tsuruya Namboku's *Osome Nanayaku (Osome's Seven Roles)*, one actor played seven different roles, with transformations of gender, age, social position, and social role—the instability of society itself seems here to be depicted and enjoyed. Many others could be cited.[43] The enjoyment of mutability fits the capitalist privileging of unnatural metamorphosis, as described by Saikaku. For example, the chopsticks which on their own transform into trees, and lumber, and these then transform into ships and an ever-growing fortune for a clever merchant. This is far from *Sekidera's* terrible melancholy in the noh. Desire here is *for* change. This is a temporality of *transformation*—a time of change—as opposed to the noh's time of fulfillment, which is a temporality of stasis (and in which hopefully the one true value of things is re-fulfilled in the present, so that present and past are identical—there is no development, no change, of character or anything else).

Saikaku also describes the effects of that desire. Meaningful value—both the economic value of a thing and the possibility of enjoying or experiencing that value and that thing—increasingly is associated with material commod-

---

42. Osborne, *The Politics of Time*, 166.
43. Another popular play of the nineteenth century was *Rokkasen sugata no irodori* (first performed in 1831). It consisted of five dances, portraying the five unsuccessful lovers of Ono no Komachi in comic form. Whereas the noh play *Sekidera Komachi* presents change as mournfully sad, the kabuki play delights in it.

ities, and commodities take on a life of their own. The time of meaningful change, in other words, or more simply meaningful time, is attached to the commodity, and this grows apart from humans. Even gold, for a capitalist, can forever increase in value, but a person dies; the life of a commodity is no longer part of the lifetime of a human. The importance of this as a general experience of time is indicated in Saikaku's stories of people on the eve of their death, desperately longing to become of one body with their fortunes, or of the terrible greed of one man resulting in his reincarnation as a golden, but frozen, cat. Thus while the desire for transformability in kabuki opposes the noh's desire for stable form, the effects are similar. Here, too, one ends with an alienation from meaningful time, and a desperate longing to somehow find a way to reunite with the materiality of that time—to reembody it. And here too, a more final death, apart from the circulations of value, seems to be an ultimate solution. The Edokko's overnight exhaustions of all wealth, ending all possible future circulations, is a symptom of this. In a more limited way, any spending was a kind of bodily death. Thus, *jibara o kiru* (自腹を切る, suicide by "cutting one's belly") also meant "to spend one's money."[44] In both, redemption implies death. Accordingly, while kabuki's transformations and capitalism's values may have found enjoyment in change, in contrast to the noh, the end effect is not only a time of repetition, but a time that is alienated, disembodied, and consequently seeks either some kind of reembodiment of meaningful time or else death. Like the noh.

Ultimately, especially in the late Edo era and the time of the Kōka noh, kabuki's increasing absorption with transformations actually seems to come closer both to the noh's longing for pure exchange and closed circulation, and to the desire for death as a way out of these longings. One example will illustrate these points.

Henge (変化) is probably the most common and basic word for change in kabuki. Literally it simply means "transformation," and was applied fairly generically to the wide variety of change images that emerged in kabuki, from metamorphosing plants to humans that turn into animals. In the late seventeenth century, *hengeshin*, or "transforming bodies," also became popu-

---

44. Kabuki played with this double meaning. For example, in the play *Sugawara Denju Tenarai Kagami*, there is a famous character named Sakuramaru who thus commits suicide; because of this association of the name "Sakuramaru" with belly-cutting suicide, the name was also invoked when one was spending one's own money.

lar.[45] But *henge* also means "ghost";[46] the effect of transformation in this case implies a ghostliness. This use of *henge* is most obvious and widespread in the nineteenth century, and perhaps the most popular of nineteenth-century ghost plays was Tsuruya Nanboku's *Tōkaidō Yotsuya Kaidan* (東海道四谷怪談, *The Yotsuya Ghost Story*).

Yotsuya Kaidan was based on two actual murders, but like many later kabuki plays, this story was layered onto a much older tale, of a samurai who finds that his wife is having an affair with their servant and so murders her. The play is therefore a fairly complex interweaving of several different murder plots. Throughout, it depends on constant exchanges and substitutions of bodies, most of which fail, and broken circulations. Transformation is at the heart of this.

The basic plot, insofar as it can be shortly summarized, centers on the samurai, Iemon, and his wife, Oiwa. Iemon is masterless (a *ronin*), and so "floating," he is eking out an honor-less living making umbrellas. His unhappiness with this situation carries over to his wife, who has weathered a recent pregnancy poorly. Wanting more for himself, he decides to kill her and marry the granddaughter of a wealthy neighbor. Accordingly, when Iemon is encouraged to give medicine to his wife Oiwa to help her recover, he substitutes poison for the medicine. The poison is not immediately effective, and he gives her further potions, a form of "torture." Oiwa discovers the effects when given a mirror: the mirror reveals that rather than restoring her body, it has horribly disfigured her face.

Iemon then realizes that the servant knows what he has done. He therefore attempts to substitute the servant as culprit for himself. He accuses the servant of stealing a treasured family medicine, and murders the servant too. He then crucifies the servant and Oiwa on opposite sides of a door, and sends the door floating off in a river. Themes of this double murder are then played with in the other subplots. In another murder, a traveling seller of medicine wants Oiwa's sister Osode for himself, and so he kills Osode's husband and goes to live with her. But he has gotten the wrong person, and the man he has killed was in fact his own previous master. Osode's husband, whom all

---

45. See Gunji Masakatsu's "*Kabuki to nō no henshin, henge*," in *Shizen to bunka* No. 19, 1988 (Special Issue: *Henshin henge*), 4. Gunji sees *henshin* and *henge* as originally connected to the Buddhist concept of transformation (*keshingoto*, 化身事), but there is little of that theological import in the kabuki of this time.

46. As opposed to *henka*, another reading of the same characters (not used for these kabuki plays) which more neutrally means transformation, variation, mutation, or metamorphosis.

thought dead, eventually returns, and in order to find redemption and repay her husband for her own treachery, Osode has her husband's would-be killer kill her instead (in still another permutation of identities, it then turns out that the man Osode was living with was actually her own elder brother). The lover, in turn, to redeem himself, kills himself.

Meanwhile, Iemon begins to find himself haunted at every turn by the ghosts of his wife and servant. Their bodies return too, nailed to the door and floating in the river. Iemon takes refuge on Mt. Hebi (Snake Mountain), but even here he is haunted, and though there are several different endings to the play, all conclude with his own death.

Identities are thus unstable throughout and one is never sure who a character "actually" is. Osode's lover, for instance, is also her brother, and her dead husband turns out to be his former master, and so on. The play also contains quick changes and bodily exchanges throughout. This is part of the staging: when Iemon's servant and wife are nailed to opposite sides of a door, they are both played by a single actor, using a specially built door and some very quick makeup changes. It is also part of the plot. When Iemon is about to marry his new bride, for example, he lifts her veil and finds the head of his murdered wife, Oiwa. He cuts off her head, but then realizes that it was the head of his new wife-to-be that he has cut off. He runs then to the wealthy grandfather of the new bride, but runs into his murdered servant and cuts off his head (again); but it is the grandfather after all that he has decapitated.[47] Also, just like the mirror-water of *Izutsu*, which shows the lovers grown apart (a failed exchange of past and present), so in *Yotsuya Kaidan* the mirror shows Oiwa to be a disfigured body of her former self rather than a restored one.

The instability of identity through time, and the impossibility of a happily fulfilled identity in time, is also thematized in terms of broken or uncontrolled circulations. This is phrased literally, as in the river on which Iemon discards the servant and woman whom he murdered, but which brings these bodies back to haunt and destroy him. It is also expressed as the circulations of time itself, which as can be seen constantly returns a surprising and unhappy failure of identity (murdered people never seem to really be the hoped-for victims). And, somewhat like the uncontrollable flows of desire in the noh's woman and demon plays, it is visible in the uncontainable desire

---

47. These are extreme cases of *migawari*: "body switching" (身代わり), that in earlier plays more commonly was a matter of substituting one body for another to fool an enemy, or in some cases to surreptitiously give one's own body up for death in order to save one's master.

not only for money but for women outside the proper bounds of family. Men in *Yotsuya Kaidan* constantly crave women beyond their own, and are willing to destroy the proper bounds of a family (in Iemon's case it is his wife and child, and in Osode's lover's case, her own husband) in order to get the objects of their desire. But the stability of a good, fulfilled embodiment, and its connection to the value that can or cannot accrue in circulation, is most clearly portrayed in this play by the role of medicine.

Medicine is that which is meant to make a body whole and healthy, with properly controlled circulations of blood, and so on. Iemon's substitution of poison for medicine has the opposite effect, instead, changing Oiwa in a deformed way. Yet medicine is also the life-blood of the family, and literally so in *Yotsuya Kaidan* (families in the Edo period did have their own medicines). The medicine which Oiwa is supposed to get is called "blood-road" medicine, indicating that it is meant to restore her own blood circulations, but also the "blood road" circulations of generational continuity. As if to underline these functions, the most popular way to prepare medicine in kabuki was to mix it with one's own blood before giving it to one who is sick; a loyal servant could prove his own worth by committing suicide in order to thus give enough blood to save his master. Further, medicine is also connected in kabuki to the desire for money. A common scene entailed a passerby, potentially a good samaritan who, while looking for a sick person's private bag of medicine in order to help him, finds instead the man's bag of money. The choice then becomes: save the man or take his money (money and medicine are thus opposed sides of the same value—with one, medicine, renewing the proper flows of healthy circulation, and the other, money, the subject of uncontrolled circulations of desire and health). In a sense medicine is a purer form of money: it could be used as an especially valuable gift, particularly as a present for the terminally ill or the blind.

What does all this mean? First, as one might expect, the play proceeds through a series of transformations, mutations, and unequal exchanges of bodies and identity. It also is founded on what might be called capitalist desires for excess, as seen in men and women who want more than what they have, and who are willing to go beyond fixed social boundaries of reproduction to achieve this. None of this is the least bit happy, though. The play takes at most only a perverse pleasure in mutability. It is clearly not the pure enjoyment of change for change's sake that is more broadly seen in kabuki up to this point. Increasingly, in other words, even while kabuki still accepts the world as a place of flux and unequal transactions, and even while it accepts the portrayal of human desire as a desire for excess (unlike the noh), the effects of this are increasingly destructive of social form and result in a time that is ghostly and haunting and divorced from any possible fulfillment.[48] The circulations of desire, like the circulations of capital, do not return any clear sense of embodied, materialized fulfillment or completed identity. As for all of the characters in *Yotsuya Kaidan,* the only possible means of redemption is a more transcendent kind of death.[49] Thus, kabuki starts from an entirely different point of value, and a different appreciation of the changing bodies of time than the noh. Kabuki seemed to be founded on a privileging of change, of bodies that truly transform, of the need for uncertain value, and therefore of a time that must be constituted by change. This contrasts to the noh's vision of time as fulfillment, implying an eternal body of value and a time that endlessly reconstitutes rather than developing into something new. But kabuki ends up at a point very nearly that of the noh's.[50] In both theaters, time itself, like the bodies that are produced in and of time, ends up as ghostly and unfulfilled.

---

48. Yet another example one might look at is *Kasane.* In this play, a man in a boat with his lover finds a skull floating by with a hatchet in it. The man had been a lover of his mistress's mother, and in order to be with the mother had killed the father; this skull is the father's. When the man removes the hatchet, miraculously the mistress's face is immediately disfigured. The man's desires have led him to excesses in the past, which come back to create a disfigured present. The only thing he can then do is kill the mistress too.

49. There are many possible sites for looking at this privileging of time as ghostly, but of death. In kabuki, says Halford, *hitogoroshi* (murder) became "one of the regular climaxes" (*Kabuki Handbook* (Tokyo: Charles E. Tuttle Co., 1955), 427). Also by the nineteenth century, one of the most popular forms of memento in kabuki were prints of famous actors. *Yakusha-e* (prints of actors) were hugely popular throughout the Edo era, but in the nineteenth century one of the most popular forms were the *shini-e*: "death pictures," which provided the month and day on which the actor died, along with his Buddhist (i.e., death) name. The great variety of death pictures that spread through Edo included portrayals of actors in their roles as ghosts; these are discussed later in this chapter.

50. Ghost plays such as *Yotsuya Kaidan* were earlier considered of poor quality and lesser importance than other kabuki plays, and they were confined to the off-summer months. People would then go to see a ghost play just to get a "chill," and hence relief from the summer heat. It might consequently be argued that it is unfair to accord *Yotsuya Kaidan* as much weight as I have here. But by the early decades of the nineteenth century the ghost plays had taken on a much larger importance, to the extent that in *Yotsuya Kaidan's* case, the play was presented at the finale of the New Year's performance, the most highly valued time of the season. In this case, the calendar is instituted by a play of ghosts and death.

Speed, or "Making a Clock in Slow Motion"

At the same time that the kabuki theater was preoccupied with change, it was also fascinated with speed. Changes generally had to be fast, or almost immediate. In the noh, from the start of the Edo era the shoguns carefully encouraged a radical slowdown in performance speed. Although no precise figures for performance time are knowable, the average number of plays given in a day's performance prior to the Edo period was seven, and some programs had as many as twenty plays. The shoguns then legislated the number initially at four, and since the overall day's performance time apparently remained the same, one can presume that under the Tokugawa shoguns' patronage, the noh slowed to almost half its previous speed. It continued to slow throughout the era, reaching something close to its present pace by the nineteenth century.[51]

Why? What importance could performance time have? In the quest for value, and for the embodiment of meaningful time, speed was as important an element as change.

When looked at in terms of speed, it would seem that kabuki and the noh are inarguably unlike each other. Kabuki's greatest enchantment with speed came at the same time that noh reached its final, ossified slowness (the early to mid-nineteenth century, the time of the Kōka performance), indicating the possibility of some kind of relation between the two.

In the Edo era, there were institutions of regular, measured and even technological time keeping. Temple bells had long been used as time keepers tolling the hours, and in the Edo period mechanical clocks also came into some popularity. These were not, though, the same as Western clocks. In the Edo period, a day was given twelve hours, with six hours each given to periods of lightness and darkness, regardless of season. This meant that nighttime hours were not precisely equal to daytime hours, and none of these remained consistent over the course of seasonal changes. Clocks were accordingly made that allowed for easy and constant adjustment. Time was hence not entirely defined in terms of technological measure—it was more to the contrary. Western clocks were well known, but considered remarkably com-

---

51. Omote Akira, who has researched these figures as closely as any, states that the average time of a noh play in the Edo period was likely about 77 minutes while in the middle ages it was about 33 minutes (that is, more than twice as fast as in the Edo era). According to Omote, in the early Edo period the noh had reached about 66% of its modern rate of slowness, by the mid-Edo era about 70 to 80%, and by the nineteenth century, it approximated 95% the current rate of slowness. See Omote, *Nō kyōgen* I, 223–236.

plex and cumbersome—their inflexibility did not mesh well with Edo time—and they remained objects of exotica throughout the era.

In kabuki, nearly all the concepts of change and transformation are also connected to speed. *Hayagawari* ("quick change") was one of the generic terms for change in kabuki. There were numerous other words for change, all roughly similar, and in nearly all of them the point was for the change to be as fast as possible. Even the word *hikinuki*, which means simply to "pull out" the few strategically basted threads holding one costume together, so that another might be revealed underneath, was so closely associated with speed that it became a verb for "sudden change." Intricate sewing and stage technologies were also invented to enhance the appearance of speed. The idea of speed was as important as, and helped to define, the idea of "change."

Like the *hengemono* transformation dance pieces, this aesthetics of speed can be linked to the time of fashion and commodity capitalism. It is not necessarily just that either though, as Saikaku once again shows.

Saikaku's work on mercantile capitalism, *The Eternal Storehouse of Japan*, can also be looked at as a study on speed. The form itself—a series of very short stories within which one story will suddenly become another story, and so on, so that a number of stories may be told within the space of two pages—assumes a mode of reading that required readiness to make rapid connections between very quick shifts of plot and theme.[52] Speed is also part of the theme of the work, as in the story, "Making a Clock in Slow Motion."

In that story, time and qualities of time are clearly connected to methods of production, as the title itself announces. It begins with a description of the Chinese, a "self-composed" people, and the way they make clocks. Chinese people "spend their time strumming the *koto*, playing chess, making verses, and drinking wine. In autumn they stand by the sea admiring the moon, and in spring ... they make trips to the mountains to view the wild apple in bloom." In this context, the story relates, the clock was invented. "Year after year a man thought about it, with mechanisms ticking by his side day and night, and when he left the task unfinished, his son took over. ... At long last,

---

52. As one of Saikaku's translators puts it, Saikaku "does not labour his points ... He proceeds rapidly from topic to topic, expecting his readers to follow as best they can—and if his readers were already schooled in the twists and turns of rapid *haikai* verse, they probably experienced little difficulty." Sargent, *The Japanese Family Storehouse*, 210. Most of the arts of the pleasure quarters incorporated some notion of speed. "Woe to the slow gesture," says Focillon in describing the painting style of the famous printmaker Hokusai (*Life of Forms*, 176). But Focillon attributes to this style the intrusion of accident—i.e., the appearance of true difference, and that is not the argument I am making here.

after three lifetimes, the invention was completed."[53] Thus, the time of clocks is here represented as following the slow cycles of nature. It follows the flow of the seasons, and is completed in three generations—three generations being considered a completed natural cycle. Hence the cycles of this time form a completed whole. It is also slow. The Japanese title uses the term *mawaridōki,* or "slow-turning," and this refers both to the speed of the clock, and to the speed of its production. So, this clock time is a natural, cyclical, and slow time of closed reproduction.[54]

"But this," says Saikaku, "is hardly the way to make a successful living." He then goes on to describe an episode that focuses on finding a new mode of production in order to make a better living. A poor townsman of Nagasaki wishes to produce a Chinese confection, currently being imported at very high prices, but he cannot figure out how to make it, nor will the Chinese tell him their secret. At last, after much experimentation, he finds that the trick lies in how the sesame seeds are prepared. The process turns out to be simple and cheap, and because he can still sell at high prices, he quickly profits.

Others, however, quickly learn the process, so he does not sit still. He abandons the confectionery business, and opens a fancy goods store. Continuing thus to "exercise his gifts to good purpose," he makes a fortune, "all made within his own lifetime."

Saikaku thus shows the basic capitalist impetus toward ever-speedier change. Whoever comes up with a newer and cheaper production process will inevitably stay ahead, but he/she must then continue with these innovations, presumably at an ever-quicker pace. "Good opportunities seldom wait."[55] Further, time is now structured by ever-changing processes of production, rather than the cyclically closed time of an unchanging reproduction seen in the Chinese clock.

This new temporality of speed is therefore definitive of a new kind of "clock." Unlike the natural clock invented in China, this is a clock, and a time, that wants more ("only a fool would try to imitate the lackadaisical Chinese approach"—natural time is here almost parodied). In a way, speed seems to be part of an attempt to overcome natural time, and the almost endless waiting that that kind of time implies. In the time of speed, rather than wait the full duration of three generations, one can have one's own fortune

---

53. Sargent, ibid., 105.
54. *Mawaridōki* also was described by Saikaku as "not useful." See *Nippon Eitaigura,* 127, in *Teihon Saikaku Zenshu* vol. 7 (Tokyo: Chuo Koronsha, 1951).
55. Ibid., 105.

"within [one's] own lifetime." Speed, accordingly, is a means to timeliness—to living *in* a meaningful, and valuable, time.[56]

It is also evident that there are overtones of nationalism implied in the different qualities of time. Speed is a more productive kind of time, and the basis for the new, Japanese way of making a living and a clock. The closed cycles of nature are "slow," and Chinese (*Morokoshibito*, 唐土人), or at least foreign since "Chinese" in the Edo period could still be a generic designation for foreignness. The distinction between speed as Japanese versus slow cycles as an increasingly foreign time adds another layer to the contrast between kabuki and noh. The noh's temporality would presumably be increasingly alien.

Speed, too, then becomes an issue in the question of controlled circulation; shogunal control of circulation was not just a matter of maintaining spatial boundaries. For example, the shogun Tokugawa Tsunayoshi, himself given to great flaunting of luxury and a proponent of large public displays, especially of the noh, admonished against the "swift flow of seductive luxury."[57] The government advisor Ogyū Sorai saw this as part of the new conditions of "urgency,"[58] in which even the samurai class was increasingly caught up with the necessity to buy more, and buy more frequently. Sorai's critique of Edo life as being like "living in an inn" referred not only to the qualities of instability and transiency, but also of speed. Edo houses, he said, "true to the bustling fashion of the city," "are erected in great haste." This is in *Seidan*, a treatise on government; apparently for Sorai, good governmental form was defined in part in terms of the flows of time—a sort of economy of time. Sorai also criticized the ukiyo-e woodblock prints that were one of the better examples of the frenzied flows of fashion. Ukiyo-e, he said, which could be rapidly produced and distributed (more rapidly then even than moveable type), were not a proper method of printing, and to this he opposed as better the process of making rubbings from stone, which was a slow and painstaking process of taking rubbings from ancient stone markers.[59] Speed was thus a question of production and reproduction for Sorai, too, and he envisioned a method which appears to have come as close as pos-

---

56. Also, this is not just a spatialization of time, or the imposition of regularized technological measure, as is commonly described of the nineteenth-century time.
57. In Ikeuchi, NS I, pp. 27, 29.
58. In *Seidan*. See J.R. McEwan, transl., *The Political Writings of Ogyū Sorai* (Cambridge: Cambridge University Press, 1962), 37–8.
59. Ibid., 47, 49.

sible to closed reproductions—prints based on unchanging originals, and made through material contact with the lettering or iconography of those originals.

That is one way of looking at where the noh fit in. The ritual cycles, the *jo-ha-kyū* principle that returns from speed to nontime, the ritual aim of completing an ancient material body—all were structures of unchanging natural flows of time and value. In these, as noted in Chapter 1, were said to be found "the sounds of Japanese nature," and "the sound of harmony in Japan." This "Japanese" order of time is clearly opposed to the time of Saikaku's "Japanese" clock.

Speed, for Saikaku and kabuki, was a means of not only approaching full value, but also of overcoming the slow and "useless" time of generational cycles. The noh's slowness was in these respects similar.[60] The painfully slow movement on stage in the noh, for instance, can be compared to the gestures and movements of the noh performances on the national level, in which the noh was used to create a mastery over time. Even *Sekidera*, which narrates the terrible loss of stable time, is comprised of the *shite* sitting motionless on stage almost until the end of the two-hour long play. There is thus no movement to temporalize time at all. Nor is there movement to create difference within space (spatial alteration), movement that might create some possibility of time, or of change, even within the realm of space. In this way the noh's motionless bodies create something like a mastery over time through the institution of a motionless space. This becomes the preferred aim, and the slow movements that do arise are in a sense only longings for, and reinforcements of, the value of that timeless space.[61]

Hence, as opposed to kabuki's speed as mastery and means to value, the noh controls time and approaches value through slowness and space. The result is that kabuki ends in a time without place—that is, without a single

---

60. There is no large vocabulary of "slowness" in the noh the way there is for speed in kabuki. In Zeami's treatises of the middle ages, the distinction is more a matter of the nontemporal "preface" of the *jo* level versus the "fast" tempo of the *kyū*. The focus on slowness is more a Tokugawa construct.

61. To say that the noh could thus control time through a kind of spatialization, or (lack of) movement, also assumes that space was already connected to time. One might read the noh as making this connection of space and time, only then to use space to control time. This same relation might of course also then invite movement and conquest *by* speed—as seems to be the case with kabuki's trajectory. On the baroque as an era which newly associates space with motion and time, see Lewis Mumford, *The City in History* (New York: Harcourt, Brace, and World, Inc., 1961), 364.

place of stable value—and noh ends in a place without time. We are back to the simple opposition of fast change versus closed cycles.

However, the noh was not always only about slowness, or final fulfillment. Zeami privileged the final, "fast" (*kyū*) level over the return to the timeless *jo*. In terms of narrative progression, the most important moment was the almost instantaneous *ha*, or break, and it was the "woman" plays of interminable longing that were most important to nearly all audiences.

In kabuki, on the other hand, the critical scene in many plays was the *tachimawari* (立 回 り, fight) scene, which was staged as a dance in "slow motion." Although a form of slow-motion,[62] the *tachimawari* sequences were also dependent on a feeling of remarkable speed. The idea was to show the fast parries of a hero against attacks from one or more opponents. When there are a group of attackers, in the staging they approach the hero one by one not because they are stupid, but as a matter of motion. Breaking the fight sequence into a series of fights allows the audience to see the various moves against the various attackers that the hero would in real time be making all at once. It is in other words a very cinematic approach to motion and speed, both assuming a temporality of speed and assuming that time might be broken up into images, the better to understand and depict it.[63]

However, while the need to thus break up speed in order to really see it, taking the fastest moment and breaking it into a series of sequential movements, can be thought of as simply the slowing down and fragmenting of what is in reality an intensely fast and complete moment, nearly all other scenes of quick change lead to an openness and a lack of completion. Neither kabuki's urge for speed, nor the noh's drive for slow immobility generally had a complete endpoint, even though both seem to have desired a complete ending and resolution. Saikaku's story of the clock is unusual insofar as, in all three episodes that make up the story, people not only devise new methods that bring them riches and find these riches "within their lifetimes," but they also retire so that they *can* partake of these riches. This is Saikaku's one statement of the dream of speed—that there would be an endpoint that one could reach, within the span of one's own lifetime. Otherwise, the exhilaration

---

62. All *tachimawari* consisted of tightly choreographed movements, but not all were really played in slow motion.
63. See, for example, Stephen Kern's discussion of 1870s film pioneers and the cinematic attempts to capture speed and motion—in particular, E.J. Marey's "photography of time." In this case, it seems that it was the speedy temporalities of capitalism that set the conditions for cinema, rather than the technology of cinema creating a new vision of time.

from speed and change in kabuki, and the enchantment with slow immobility in the noh, both lead only to an endless seriality.

This confluence of the two problems of seriality explains the structure of another pleasure quarters work, by Ikku Jippensha. In *Shingaku tokei-sō* (心学時計草, *Thoughts on the Time/Clock of Shingaku*), Ikku tells a series of typical tales of a popular courtesan. But she is unusual in two ways: first, she brings in a clock (albeit the Japanese, adjustable kind) and allots all clients an identical amount of time, despite protestations from her employers that special patrons should continue to receive priority; and second, along with her pleasure quarters profession, she is also a leader of what was then something like a new religion—the religious-ethical system of *shingaku*. There is thus an overlap of the pleasure quarters and theology. Both the pleasure quarters and the divine, though, were beholden to the newly defined time of perpetual seriality (*mannen*, 万年 —perpetuity, which is the label then used for the time of Western clocks). This is also visible in the narrative form of the work. Although it is a typical series of fast-moving tales of the pleasure quarters, the work is at the same time framed in the preface as being of the "pillow-time of *Kantan*." *Kantan* is one of the more messianic noh plays, and the tales hence include expressions of both pleasure quarters time and the godly time of the noh. These are all ordered by perpetual clock time, insofar as each section (there is one section per page) is, on the corner of each page, allotted an hour—Ikku drew a picture of the traditional sign of the hour on the corners of each page. Thus, in this work too there is a layering of different temporalities expressed as the time of Edo, and in this case, the overlap of noh time with pleasure quarters/kabuki speed meets under the sign of the serial clock.

It is the ghostliness of this seriality—the disembodied, devalued aspect of time, from the perspective of both times—that leads also to the appearance of death. Even the *tachimawari* was, as Brandon puts it, a "grotesquely beautiful dance of death."[64]

Instants and Intensities

One of the paradoxes of time in the Edo era is that from the perspective of both the noh and kabuki, the time of one's own activity, and one's own desire, tended to lead to the disembodiment of time—a time apart from one's own material being. This is not to say that people were no longer "in"

---

64. Brandon, Malm, and Shively, *Studies in Kabuki* (Hawaii: University of Hawaii Press, 1978), 93.

time at all; just that time had a ghostliness to it. This led to a sort of crisis of the present, especially as a crisis of the time of "now," and to a desire for some other quality of time. Both the noh and kabuki privileged a moment of the instant—a point neither just spatial nor just temporal[65]—as an expression of this crisis and as a point of redemption, or a way out. Very much akin to discussions of postmodern time, these instants were described as times of intensity, moments of strong and even rapturous affect, but also in some cases as moments of death. These moments represent the possibility of fulfillment, of truly achieving a moment of value and of meaningful time, and so a fulfillment of the temporality that the initial desires and actions instituted. At the same time, however, these instants are moments that not only punctuate time, they also present the possibility of puncturing, or "tearing" (the noh's *ha*) the very structure of time and value of which they are a part. They therefore are tied to the problem of difference, to the appearance and experience of a truly constitutive present, and to the emergence of change (that is, change of a system, from within that system).

On the one hand, in the Edo period this was a theological problem. This can be seen in the example of *Kantan* used by Ikku as a reference to messianic time. In *Kantan*, this messianic time is beyond the epic longing for reunion with the past. Briefly, *Kantan* tells the story of a man in search of a "master," a person and place of true and eternal fulfillment, and initially he finds this fulfillment in all the epic ways we might expect. The man ("Rosei") at first finds himself in the wasting time of everyday life, not even seeking enlightenment: "I do not aspire to follow the Buddha, but instead only fritter my life away." Traveling, however, on his way to finally find a sage of truth, he stops at an inn where he is given the "Pillow of Kantan." This is a pillow from an immortal of long ago, upon which anyone who dozes will be awakened to "the truth of past and future."[66] In other words, this pillow is the object or souvenir that all noh plays seem to focus on, and in this case the pillow-object offers the possibility of uniting with the most eternal time of all—a time incorporating *all* time, past and future included.

Rosei then crosses the mountains, and finds Kantan (a village in China), "once simply a name," lying there before him. Here, the name, or sign, is materially fulfilled. Heaven has "vouchsafed" the "sacred dream"—the trans-

---

65. The instant need not be thought of as instantaneous time literally—it is the experience of an instant, an effect of time but a point outside of time, so that the effect of seeing a whole noh play (all two hours or so) might still be considered as the experience of an instant (as it often was).
66. Tyler, *Japanese Noh Dramas*, 135.

action is heavenly—and he has arrived. Once arrived, Rosei truly seems to be united with the place of truth and value and rule. He is astonished by a royal envoy who comes to tell him that for unknown reasons the king has decided to cede his throne to Rosei. Rosei will therefore himself sit on the seat of value, and he becomes King. He is brought to the Palace (the vocabulary here indicates an idealized seat of rule, at once as the Chinese emperor's throne, the Buddha Amida's Western Paradise, and the Tōri Heaven at the summit of Mt. Sumeru), which is a place of value in several ways: lords "pour in, bearing a thousand or a myriad of gems, treasures innumerable, as offerings." The mountains are of the purest silver and gold, surmounted by a sun of gold. It is also a place of eternal time and changelessness, a place where one finds the "Hall of Eternal Life," "before the Gate of Everlasting Youth, sun and moon barely move." To maintain this state, all Rosei needs to do is drink an elixir. This will keep the pure flows and clear circulations of eternity streaming along in their proper courses: "O pass the cup, I say, that clear, chrysanthemum waters speed on down the stream, till eager hands dart from sleeves gay with chrysanthemums to pick it up again . . . Never shall these blessed waters fail, flowing as the do from healing springs that yield all their bounty, without end. O how they gush forth, with might renewed! . . . as pleasure merges night into day. Happiness, delight, brilliant success: all these here attain their pinnacle."[67]

Rosei has reached that final point of eternal value, goodness, and truth for which most noh plays dream. The pillow really has embodied that wonderful past. This is good, but the play does not end there. The beauty of what Rosei sees is then expressed as the beauty of the changing seasons—cyclical, but in fact indicating the passing of time: "time passes and the years slip by . . . till fifty years of glory reach an end." Thus, time has passed, and even ended, but the ending is one of decay rather than fulfillment. The years "melt away to nothing." With this realization, Rosei does a curious thing for a noh play: he rushes with great speed to lie back down and place his head on the pillow of Kantan again. He then awakens to the realization that the entire fifty years of glory was nothing but a dream—an instant of sorts, "a dream that lasted the short while millet takes to cook upon a stove." At this point, the dream of epic value is a vain and fleeting one, and no great moment of meaningful enlightenment and eternity would seem possible. The pillow is little more than an everyday item.

---

67. Ibid., 137–139.

Yet at that same moment, Rosei comes to realize the whole point is that "all things are a dream while millet cooks"—that one should give up on all desires for "glory or great age." This itself *is* enlightenment, and so the pillow has been an effective embodiment of truth after all: "Now he understands: the sage he sought, bent on liberation, was this pillow... How great the gift it gave him at Kantan, where he has seen the world to be a dream, and finding his hopes met, now journeys home."[68] Rosei's journey for the point of truth has been completed, all in the instant of connecting his head with the pillow. But the truth is not in the epic value of eternal time, with its glorious wealth and immortal circulations. It is a second definition, both of the truth embodied in the pillow, and of the dream instant his connection with the pillow entailed, in this case phrased in roughly Buddhist terms, of a messianic moment of liberation and truth beyond all circulations of past and present, and beyond all desire entirely.

This is a generally religious solution to a theologically phrased problem of finding enlightenment. Nonetheless, although it leads to transcendence, it is in a sense a transcendence of life itself, and of time—a moment that gives up on and so is beyond even the theological image of the eternal heavenly castle. Accordingly, this kind of play privileges something like a form of death (as in the idea of death as beyond all circulation and exchange) as the real guarantee of truth. Here, we are at a moment after theology, in which death becomes the guarantee in place of a failed image of eternity. More simply, the problem of the instant in noh was connected to a crisis of time, value, and meaning after theology—in between a theological and a nontheological frame. This may be an overly general example, and the decrepitude of the aging woman in *Sekidera* is probably a more common expression of the noh's endings than the clear moment of revelation and resolution seen in *Kantan*. The point is that the noh had two different notions of the instant, and of the kind of interruption the instant constituted, just as it had two differing notions of the souvenir.

It is clear that kabuki's "capitalist" time emphasizes fast and even instantaneous change. But the noh, too, privileges the time of the instant. Both the effect of a full play and critical moments within a play—the *ha* of the *jo-ha-kyū*, and the *kusemai* dance in particular—were often described as instants. At a general level, privileging the time of the instant in itself has the potential of breaking up the continuous homogeneity and harmonious

---

68. Ibid., 141.

flows of an epic time, even allowing for multiple instants with no connection between them—a plurality of times, and possibly even different worlds. To the extent that this is so, there is a contradiction of qualities of time in the noh, being a more flowing, continuous, and unified type that is homogenous and all-embracing, and the other a time of singular and independent instants.

While this singular instant time is independent of a homogenous time of duration, it should be kept in mind that it might also be independent of the repetitive time of seriality. Though continuous, seriality may be a time of decay, as in *Sekidera* where history itself, as serial, is a time of disintegration.[69]

There are several terms for the "instant," and the effect of the instant, in the noh. First, one of the more obvious and critical points of the instant is the *ha*, the moment in a play which "breaks" or institutes time in the overall *jo-ha-kyū* sequence. At least at the ritual level, as for example in *Takasago*, the *ha* only opens the instant out into an eternal time and space. In *Takasago* at the *ha* (generally the point at which the *shite* makes his first appearance, opening the play into its possible relation with the past), the *shite* sings of the "stretching/spreading out of our thoughts/mind" (*Omoi o noburu*, 思を述ぶる). Just before that, the traveling priest has described the road of "the capital as it stretches far to its end," (*sue harubaru no miyakoji*, 末遙ばるの都路), and the many days they have traveled, and the many days until they reach the end (*ikuka kinuran atosue mo*, 幾日来ぬらん跡末も).[70] Thus this "instant" brings the play into an eternally "stretching out" space and time. Although the *ha* "tears" open time, it is an instant-time that in fact is eternal and all-encompassing, and identical in form to the ritual time of the narrative.

---

69. There is therefore a parallel of these conditions with the typical claims regarding what have been called postmodern times. In the latter, too, of course, the emphasis on the instant is connected with a weakening of historicity (part of which involves the emergence of the image itself, apart from any referent, as the site of the real); and an empty repetitiveness of time, with no clear point of value to ground a more meaningful narrative of time, or to act as the ground from which to point to something different and better. In this context, the instant becomes a unique moment of feeling and emotion—intense but also strangely euphoric (it is not, in other words, necessarily the climactic moment of a narrative that has led to this point, or that will lead somewhere else from it). They are, then, moments that are often thought of in terms of the sublime—moments emerging out of a temporal shapelessness, and only possibly indicating a point of transcendence of that shapelessness, and so a point of difference, and a way out. Accordingly there is a theological element (or rather, the quandary of a world in between the theological and something else) in the postmodern instant.
70. *Yōkyokushū*, 220.

In the treatises of Zeami, the instant is also tied to the moment of coming-into-consciousness of the "highest level of the art" (this comes "instantly"—*oboezu ni*—"without [time for] knowing," or "instinctively"), and this highest level is therefore called an instant of sorts—*itten tsukitaru* (一点付きたる, a term difficult to translate; literally, something like, "the addition of a single point," or "marking" or "achieving a point").[71] In this case, the instant is described as a coming-into-consciousness in a theological sense: "It resembles the instant when a vague smile without self-awareness [appeared on the face of the Buddhist disciple Kasyapa],"[72] says Zeami, then also comparing it to the critical moment of the founding myth in which the sun goddess, Amaterasu, comes out of a cave in order to see her own face. This coming-into-consciousness is hence a fully transcendent moment: a "Feeling that Transcends Cognition."[73] As the highest level of the noh, it is also the true point of value: "Thus it is that the very highest of the nine levels of excellence . . . is assigned the characteristics/qualities of gold [*kinjō*, 金状]." Thus far, the instant primarily has to do with an eternity, in the sense of an expanded space, time, and consciousness, or an arrival at the time of true value, and although a "point," it is not a point of difference.

There are two additional things worth noting here about the instant from this eternal perspective. First, it is also an "interval," "when nothing happens." In this case Zeami uses *hima* (暇, now meaning "free time," in the sense of a time or moment in between required activities).[74] It is a time of "doing nothing," that "signifies that interval which exists between two physical actions." Here, too, we are confronted with a spatialized view of time, and one in which there is no motion which could temporalize things even in that realm of space. It is nonetheless not an empty time: for Zeami, it is a time of "concentration," in which an actor "binds together the moments before and after that instant when 'nothing happens.'"[75] This too thus points to an absolute concentration of all time and history into one eternity. All movements as well: "Such a process constitutes that inner force that can be termed 'connecting all the [physical] arts through one intensity of mind.'"[76] Second, the noh's ultimate eternal instant is the moment of real fulfillment that comes at the

---

71. "Shūgyoku tokka," in *Zeami Zenchiku*, 188.
72. *On the Art of the Noh*, 133 (Rimer and Yamazaki's translation of this passage is loose, at best, and I use it here selectively).
73. Ibid., 134.
74. "Kakyō," in *Zeami Zenchiku*, 100.
75. *On the Art of the Noh*, 97–97.
76. Ibid., 97.

end of the *jo-ha-kyū* sequence—the moment (*shunkan*, 瞬間—an instant, or "blink") in which one "becomes" (*naru*)—as opposed to imitates (*monomane*, 物真似).[77]

All of this points to an emphasis on the instant, but only as an epiphanic point that condenses all of time and space into a single point, and so stretches into an eternity (thus, the noh was described as a "stage art of no blinking";[78] see the section on visuality, below). It is neither a point that breaks time into a repetitive series, nor a point of difference that might alter the smooth unity of a more homogenous eternity. It creates a "now" time of fulfillment and value, but only in an eternal and unchanging form.

That is not all there is to it with the noh's instant either, though. First, Zeami attaches at least some notion of difference to the final instant of fulfillment: "It is that instant of Fulfillment in an artistic work that gives the audience a sensation of novelty;" "The fulfillment of *jo*, *ha*, and *kyū* provides the spectators with the sense of novelty." However I think it would be misleading to carry this notion of newness and difference very far.[79]

Part of the problem with the eternal space-time presented by the noh's more ritual order is that precisely because it is all-encompassing (there is no outside, no beyond the borders), perspectival difference and "newness" is really impossible. Value here is pure and absolutist. Difference, in other words, cannot arise in a contestatory or oppositional form.[80] The same, however, might be said of the noh's time of ghostly and repetitive absence: in the separation from or absence of an absolute value, there is nothing to anchor an oppositional view for or against things, in time and space.[81] This is where

---

77. "Shūgyoku tokka," ibid., 190–191.
78. Certain actors in particular from the Hōshō school were renowned for appearing never to blink, even in roles that required them to sit on stage for hours. When asked how this was possible, one replied that they don't particularly think of not blinking, but that they had made this a practice of everyday life. See Ikeuchi, NS I, 170.
79. Furthermore, Rimer and Yamazaki's use of "novelty" is itself suspect. Generally they use novelty as a translation of *mezurashiki* (unique, rare), which fits, but in this case it is a translation of *omoshiroki*—more commonly translated as "fascination," and a term that by no means necessarily implies either newness or difference.
80. That seems to be part of the ideological effect of the two preferred concepts used to describe the aesthetic of the noh (*yūgen*, often simply glossed as "mystery," and *aware*—"sadness," "pathos," "beauty," "interest"). Both terms already had long histories as the expression of typically noble/imperial aesthetics. Both are so generic, and almost always described as transcendent and therefore not definable by any single idea or feeling, in such a way that they encompass nearly all aesthetic form. There is no clear boundary that says what they are not.
81. Again there is some parallel with so-called postmodern conditions (really an element of modernity), and the trap of being in between absolutism and the pure absence of fixed values.

the sublime enters, as a kind of intensity that emerges out of a perspectivalless world.

Zeami writes about the moments or instants of eternity in ways that lead to transcendence, but this is not always a transcendence of pure resolution and unity—these are moments that do not, in other words, always accord with a totally bounded space, time, and "mind" (*omou*) of eternity. Some of Zeami's writings resemble attempts in our own time to conceive of moments of desires and intensities which are bodily, and somehow pre-representational—"primordial," in Deleuze's words—and which therefore are potentially outside of any totalizing representational order (including of time or space). Certainly for Zeami, the experience of the instant was at very least pre-conscious.[82] In discussing that point in which the audience feels the highest level of "Peerless Charm," Zeami states, "it can be said that this moment of Fascination represents an instant sensation that occurs before the rise of any consciousness regarding that sensation, a Feeling that Transcends Cognition." He then goes on to give a further etymology of this "feeling," describing how the written character (*kan*, 感—"feeling," or "sensation") was written by excising the bottom section of the character (*kokoro*, which can mean heart, but in this case something more like mind or consciousness). This, he says, describes "an intensity of pure feeling that goes beyond the workings of the mind"; the response to a performance embodying this feeling "is such that there is no occasion for reflection," and "Such a state might be referred to as 'purity unmixed.'" It is therefore a preconscious, and pre-representational, point of intense feeling or sensation;[83] it also describes a temporal economics of purity, in which there is no gap between body and value.

These instants were described by Zeami as times of intensity, but if anything this quality of intensity becomes far more pronounced in the Edo era. The shortening of the texts, the elimination of "side" roles in favor of the focus on the *shite* alone, and the reduction of speed were all part of this increase in concentration and intensity.[84]

This intensity was associated in many ways with a general lack of respect for borders and frames—as much or more so than it was with a condensed but bordered moment of eternity. The end result of a play was supposed to

---

82. Though as Norma Field reminded me, it should be kept in mind that for Zeami, one could only reach this point through a tremendous emphasis on practice and craft.
83. See "Shūgyoku tokka," ibid., 188, and *The Art of the Noh*, 133; as well as "Kakyō," 95–96, and *The Art of the Noh*, 91.
84. See Yokota-Murakami, ibid., 261, 269, 271 passim.

leave one in a sort of intoxication. The final, *kyū* level, too, it should be remembered was the stage of "madness." Another term used to describe the final point at which one was left was *yūkyō* (幽境)—generally meaning solitude, but more literally, "on the border line of indistinctness/vagueness;" *yū* is also the character used for *yūrei*, or ghosts. As B. L. Suzuki says, the aim was "to play as far as madness, an ecstasy in which the self is forgotten."[85] In these cases, the instant entails far more of the attributes of deformation than of eternal stability.

The same might be said of the *kusemai*, the critical dance scene at the end of the central *ha* level, in which a character's "true" identity is finally revealed. The *kusemai* was a popular dance mode brought in from outside the noh and, as its name indicates, it was thought of as an "unconventional" set of dance types. Furthermore, when performed, Zeami and others of his time stress that both melody and words should be "slurred and altered."[86] Thus at the critical moment of revelation, both temporal structure and meaning *do* have some form of difference interjected, or at very least their frames of continuity are "twisted" (*kuse*, 曲). The sharp but meaningless cries the chorus utters periodically, too, are often described as emotive interruptions in the otherwise smooth flow of meaningful time. They were part of a "crisis of feeling;" they were "disconcerting," and involved a "quickening of emotion."[87]

There are many such examples. The most important point is that the last and preeminent instant of "fulfillment" in the noh, for actor and audience, was described as the "borderline of astonishment" (*odorokikasu sakai*, 驚きかす境).[88] This moment of astonishment is, as described above, tied *not* to the "straightforward" style of the *shūgen* god-play style, but instead to the chaotic form of *ran-i* or *rangyoku*; this point of chaotic astonishment is the moment of transcendence, not the ritual-style return to the godly state of unity. It may also be relevant to remember that although the more epic ritual play *Takasago* was of course given eminence in specifically ritual situations, *Sekidera*, with all of its terrible bodily withering, and its longing for death,

---

85. B. L. Suzuki, *Nohgaku* (London: John Murray, 1932), 34.
86. *On the Art of the Noh*, 196–197.
87. B. L. Suzuki, ibid., 26. As Benjamin put it, in such moments "the contrast between sound and signification remains something ghostly and terrible." In Tiedemann and Schweppenhauser, eds., *Gesammelte Schriften* II, 1 (Frankfurt/Main: Suhrkamp Verlag, 1972), 139. Translation from *Baroque Reason*, 71.
88. "Shūgyoku Tokka," 188.

was considered the hardest to do and accorded the highest rank. Furthermore although *Takasago*, as a god play, might be expected to be slow, in its Edo-era form *Sekidera* was far more extreme insofar as the *shite* remains entirely motionless until nearly the end—it was also therefore considered more "intense."

There is accordingly this other side to the instant, just as there are two sides to the noh's emblem-souvenir. In a way, at least in terms of time, the instant is all that a noh play is. It is a dream-instant that one then wakes from, and the question (as posed in *Kantan*) is simply, what are the effects of that instant? What kind of time did it institute, and what kind of time does one therefore wake into? The noh, furthermore, poses two possibilities with regard to the form of its time. First, it represents a time-space of infinitude—bordered, but the borders are forever stretching out, so that one is totally caught within this eternity. It is a state at once of pure immanence and pure transcendence, so there is no possibility of any position of difference. Yet secondly, this eternity is revealed as impossible, and the time of experience is consequently an endlessness of a different sort—an empty seriality that can only view the time of value from a distanced spectatorial position. Again, difference, or involvement in a truly constitutive, participatory time, is impossible. From either side there is no real way of redirecting the flow of time. The intense instant is the alternative to these times, offering the chance of entering active and embodied time.

Difference, in this context, cannot be a function of direct, contestatory opposition. It is more a matter of radical, chaotic deformation, or at most, of opposition in the sense of using the instant to interrupt the supposedly boundless flow of epic time. This opposes the time of the independent unit to the time of homogenous continuity, thereby creating a different form of time. Also, the instant—even when described as a time of immediacy and direct emotion—is not necessarily a point in which all the "true" contingencies of the present intrude; difference, that is to say, is not necessarily a question of the enlightenment of the present. From this perspective, eschatological times that focus on death (as in Sekidera's desperation for a final death), even when messianic, can be as disruptive of claims for eternity as might a more secular form of serial time.[89] In any event, the fascination with the instant in Edo-era noh, along with the increasing focus on intensity

---

89. Another way of looking at this would be to say that the immediacy an instant of "death" brings is also an eruption of "nowness"—a meaningful interruption—and so the problem of now-time is not necessarily precisely the same thing as the insertion of present-time.

and immobility, was both a symptom of the period's eternal times, and one of the only possible alternatives.

The flows and conditions of time in capitalism and kabuki were different from the noh. One might assume for example that where kabuki did give precedence to instants, this might indicate the presence of mercantile temporalities—the need to break down homogenous flows of time into independent units, for example, so that they could be brought into a rational system of measure. One might also look at the brief popularity of kabuki actors acting in a mechanical style, like puppets, as expressive of the increasing technologizing of and mechanization of the body and of time (as well as being a method of trying to regain popularity from the puppet theater, as it more immediately was). Even if kabuki's temporality was defined more by the conditions of capitalism, I have argued that between the forms of noh and kabuki—in their effects—there are meeting points. This commonality is evident in kabuki's temporality, too. The concern with the instant, the increasing limitation of experience to elements split off from the whole, and a turn to the intensity of the body, was still more evident in Edo kabuki than in the noh. I summarize only a few salient points here.

As mentioned above, the quick changes of "transformation" plays were considered to be instantaneous. These, though, while at first sight appearing to truly emphasize a time only of the instant, end up as a repetitive series, a kind of seriality which itself seems to beg for a moment of more meaningful time—a way out of the repetition that would more truly change the continuity of this repetitive time. Within the structure of kabuki's narratives, the most obvious example of this second kind of instant is probably the *mie* (見得, 見栄, or 見え)— a frozen pose of fierce, concentrated, but silent expression that periodically halts a play's progression for several seconds.

One of the more important moments of a *mie* was as the culmination of the *tachimawari* fight scenes described above (scenes of great speed, but which entailed sequential, slow, and even flowing dance-like movements). There were eventually a great variety of types of *mie* developed, but in general, they were used to "capture the moment;" "like a visual exclamation point [the] *mie* momentarily halts the action of the play and intensifies its emotion."[90] The *mie* accordingly is both a climactic moment within the narrative, and a point of intensity independent of narrative time.

---

90. James Brandon et al., *Studies in Kabuki* (Hawaii; University of Hawaii Press, 1978), 86, 84.

Times and Visions of the Instant / 215

Depending on how it is written, *mie* would literally mean "seeing profit/advantage" (the second written character of the compound, *e* or *toku*, generally refers to capitalistic profit). One could infer from this unlikely choice of characters—though this etymology has to be taken as more playful than certain—that the moment of the *mie* is somehow like the capitalist seeing, or realization, of profit—a single point of stasis and enjoyment in an otherwise continuing movement of capital's time. This would imply that the *mie* is no more than a fleeting interruption, and part of ongoing time—much the same way that capitalist profits are no more than brief, at times intense moments that give rhythm to the otherwise ongoing flows of capital reinvestment. In this case the instant always contains within it a view toward the ongoing future.

Also, the *mie* could come at any time in a play; it did not act as a final point of conclusion, or resolution. In contrast to the importance of a *mie*, the play's conclusion was almost insignificant. Consequently the overall temporal form of a play depended less on a clear final endpoint, and it consisted more of a series of relatively random but intense moments.

This kind of time is atomistic more than flowing. As Brandon says of the dance form, "while the word 'dance' suggests in the West a fluid, continuous movement, Japanese kabuki dance leads from one dramatic posture to another"; "the kabuki play is more a series of striking climactic images [*mie*] as the actor holds a pose to show an intense emotion, rolling his head ... grimacing, flinging out his arms and legs"; "All sense of motion is eroded as the static figure is caught ..."[91] On the one hand, these are almost like the eternal instants of the noh: complete unto themselves, they capture the full meaning of the characters and the plays within themselves. Yet they are viewed as part of a series, and so form a serial temporality. As long as it forms a repetitive series, atomistic time in this way is just as homogenizing as the continuous flow of a unified narrative.

At the same time, though, as the most important moment of a play, the *mie* privileges a time outside of ongoing temporalities. These are the moments of greatest affect and greatest intensity (and the better the actor, it was said, the longer he could hold these poses of pure intensity in absolute stillness). They are like the "punctum," or puncturing of time, to use the analogy that Martin Jay describes (in his case, though, for haiku—Jay is also referring to Barthes' notion of the photograph): "Like a Japanese haiku, the

---

91. *Studies in Kabuki*, 45–46.

'punctum' could produce a higher order of emotional intensity.... [It has] the ability to take the viewer out of the frame into a 'blind field' charged with the desire of the unseen..."[92]

Especially later in the Edo era the *mie* was also associated with death, and in this association the *mie* instant becomes increasingly independent of any kind of continuity, seriality included. It punctuates the *tachimawari* fight dances mentioned earlier. These dances, consummate moments of death, were of an intensity and a speed that itself seemed to "capture" motion and thereby in a way end ongoing time.[93] The dances were also known as *tate*, and the character compound for this means "battle array of murder/butchery." This referred to the content, of course, since the dances were scenes of numerous killings, but the thematization of speed and death also appears to indicate the wish for a more final moment of complete ending.[94]

More telling is the way that these *mie*, as moments of frozen motion, were then circulated beyond the pleasure quarters in the form of ukiyo-e prints. The *mie* which arrested the action on stage were themselves captured as images on prints; these *mie*-prints of famous actors were then widely circulated as mementos of those supreme moments of onstage intensity. The print in this case, even while focusing on a unique and discrete time of stasis, becomes part of an ongoing (and consumer capitalist) flow of exchange time. Thus while the images of these moments of singular intensity increasingly gain wider penetration of everyday time, they are nonetheless integrated into a capitalist order of repetition.

However, at the same time that kabuki's absorption in speed, torture, and death grew, a new kind of actor print became even more popular. These

---

92. Martin Jay, *Downcast Eyes* (Berkeley: University of California Press, 1993), 453.

(In psychoanalytic terms, the punctum is like Lacan's *tuché*—the return of a traumatic encounter with the real, that has the power to pierce a symbolic structure of repetition; if one were going to pursue this line of thought, it might be more appropriate to look not only at kabuki's emphasis on immediate events (scandalous, but repetitive nonetheless), but also on murder and torture.)

93. One could also read these as, ultimately, instants of eternal expanse, insofar as the slow motion is meant to capture a moment of pure speed—speed becomes the temporal expanse almost like the spatially "stretched" eternal instants of the noh. I have seen nothing to verify this reading, however.

94. There is also a pulling apart of sense associated with these times, somewhat like the "slurring" of language in the noh's *kusemai*. At emotional high points in kabuki, the hero would make exclamations of nonsense—as, "*yattoko tottcha, untoku na!*" (quoted in Brandon, *Studies in Kabuki*, 71). While tied to the *mie*, these verbal exclamations were kept separate from the images, generally either just preceding or just following the *mie* pose.

Times and Visions of the Instant / 217

were the "death pictures" (*shini-e*) of actors. When a well-known actor died, a print would be produced of him that marked the date of his death, his age at death, and listing his Buddhist name—his death name, that is to say. These prints were hence themselves images of fame, but also souvenirs of grief,[95] and of moments of a final point of real death. As if to emphasize this, there are some in which the actor is portrayed in one of his roles as a ghost. All of these elements are brought together in Figure 1. This is a *shini-e* print marking the death of actor Nakamura Utaemon IV, portraying him in a ghost role, holding the instantaneous frozen pose of a *mie*.[96]

The ukiyo-e prints of these death instants are particularly telling as to the content and role of that moment. The frozen instant act of the *mie* they show is the most difficult kind, known as *nirami* (睨み). In this type of *mie* (performed only by male characters), the actor would not just cross his eyes, but rather leave one eye forward-focused and cross only the other eye. This was thus a doubled look, both cross-eyed and not. The point, in other words, is that this instant moment is a privileged point of negotiation, a time outside of specific temporalities, when everything, including different looks, could come together. This was the look of Sukeroku, who as we have already seen was a character of overlapping world orders. To some extent this same negotiation can be seen in the prints reproduced here. In Figure 1, the *nirami* moment brings together a character apparently split into states of life and death, or ghostliness and full bodiliness; it mediates past and present, as well as the identities of the actor Nakamura Utaemon with the ghostly role of Iga Shikibunojō, and it hints at uniting a Buddhist concept of transcendence (the ghost is forming a *mudra* with his hands) with a more popular and even spectacular idea of death. All this comes together in the instant look of the *nirami*. In Figure 2, the printmaker Kunisada overlays a whole set of worlds, in complex ways. Here, the legendary lover and poet of the ninth century, Ariwara Narihira, is shown in the guise of the contemporary actor Danjūrō VII (not the other way around), who is also playing the role of the famous

---

95. When Ichikawa Danjūrō VIII killed himself in 1854, large numbers of death prints were produced, apparently a testament both to his popularity and to the grief over his death. Especially for the more famous actors, great varieties of death prints were produced. On Danjūrō, see *Kabuki Encyclopedia*, 129.
96. The print is from 1852, by Utagawa Kunisada. It is reproduced in Stephen Addiss, ed., *Japanese Ghosts and Demons* (New York: George Braziller, Inc., 1985). Unfortunately the ghostly blues and silvers are not evident here.

218 / Visioning Eternity

Figure 1. The Ghost of Iga Shikibunojō Mitsumune (Death Print of Nakamura Utaemon IV)

Courtesy of the University of Kansas Spencer Museum of Art.

Figure 2. Ariwara no Narihira as Seigen

Courtesy of the University of Kansas Spencer Museum of Art.

monk Seigen.[97] Here, too, the various worlds and times are brought together in the flash of the *nirami*, and in this case the one body of all of those times and worlds.

These death pictures are no longer just images of great emotion, or speed. Nor are they attempts to hold onto a living image of that which has passed. They are more accurately attempts to capture death, not the ongoing time of life, and to give image to that moment of a final end. The pictures do go out into circulation like the earlier actor prints did,[98] but at the very least they introduce a *memento mori*—a souvenir, and an image, of that desire for an instant beyond the ongoing circulations of time.[99]

Kabuki, too, thus has its elements that nearly approximate the eschatological aspects of the noh. In the aesthetics of both noh and kabuki, ongoing, continuous, durational time had become problematic. Both theaters increasingly hinged on the autonomous instant moment. In both theaters, the instant offers the only possibility for attainment of true value. In face of the failures of transcendent fulfillment, the instant appears also as the only point on the temporal horizon wherein a true, more meaningful difference might appear—a transcendence of the whole structure of temporality, phrased as the "death" of time. As indicated by Edo-period theater, the instant is thus a critical form of time in Japan's early modernity, and a point of negotiation of different times.[100]

---

97. See Stephen Addiss, ed., *Japanese Ghosts and Demons* (New York: George Braziller, Inc., 1985), 54.
98. It is not clear whether these prints, once purchased, were treated similarly to other forms of ukiyo-e or not. Most such prints were considered of little lasting worth and discarded often, so that there was a relatively fast and ongoing circulation of new prints. It would not be surprising if these death prints were held onto, and kept outside of any ongoing circulations.
99. One might return to the popular image of the Edokko townsman, going off and in a single euphoric night spending every last *sen* he owned, as a parallel example of the inherent desire for "death" in capitalist culture at that time.
100. It is important to keep in mind that this does not preclude the importance of the time of homogenous flows and universal sameness. The question was, which kind of time the instant would guarantee. This also shows that—in some ways parallel to the West—the early modern ambiguity of time as universal and whole, or as punctual and potentially diversified, was a political-economic problem of value in the widest possible sense. On Western polemics of time as consisting of homogenous flows versus time as atomistic and diversified, see Nancy Munn, "The Cultural Anthropology of Time: A Critical Essay," in *Annual Review of Anthropology* 1992, 21: 93–123, and Stephen Kern, *The Culture of Time and Space* (Cambridge, Mass: Harvard University Press, 1983).

Vision: Specularity, Spectacle, and the Eyes of Money

In the official performances of noh (and technically, in the Edo era all performances were official since anything done outside the purview of the shogun was considered illegal) lines of vision were fairly carefully controlled. Principally by regulating who sat where, a set of views were produced that created an assemblage of perspectives—an arrangement of controlled lines of vision, that focused on and thereby created a centered site, or originary point of reference, for everything. This point was located on the place of the shogun. Yet these lines of vision were not necessarily all of the same order. They involved different kinds of vision, including in general terms both "gazes" and "glances," as well as different "eyes"—different looks, which see different kinds of values, entail different kinds of desires, and are comprised of different kinds of temporalities. This heterogeneity of views nonetheless did not necessarily imply the breakup of an empowered structure of vision, or scopic regime, although it certainly raises that possibility.

This section looks at the set of relations of vision within which the audience—both ruler and ruled—found and saw themselves as such. I focus on the great public "town-entering" machi-iri noh performances in the shogun's castle as a central model of vision and of seeing and producing rule and order in Tokugawa Japan. As will be seen, structures of vision were not distinct from the problems of time.

Looking across the Edo period, one could in fact find a remarkable array of kinds of vision, none of which were confined by any simple or stable tie to either class or economics. The subject positions implied by these orders of vision, and the social space they helped produce, were at least as complicated in early modern Japan as in the West. Traits of all three categories of vision described by Martin Jay as characteristic of Western early modernity[101] are easy to locate in Edo-era Japan. This includes not only the rational, mathematically understood space of Descartes, with its intellectualized observational looks separating subject from object, but also the "northern," descriptivist view,[102] as well as the "madness" of baroque vision. These characteristics are all evident in Tokugawa times, and others are as well. Although

---

101. Outlined in Hal Foster, ed., *Vision and Visuality* (Seattle: Bay Press, 1988), 2–23.
102. As in Jay's formulation, the "descriptivist" view referred to here emphasizes surfaces and immediate but fragmentary description. It is therefore in a sense photographic. It is also objectively empirical, but without the Cartesian hierarchy of a privileged monocular viewing subject; it assumes a prior existence of a world of objects, indifferent to the beholder's position; and it is more interested in surface mapping than in allegorical meaning.

perspectival space was known in Edo Japan, the perspectival ordering of a unified and mathematically homogenous space cannot be used to describe Edo-era subjectivity as a whole. Perhaps even less so than in the West, there was no single unifying order of visual space in early modern Japan. At least not until very late in the era, around the time of the Kōka *kanjin* noh.

The history of Tokugawa vision involves a genealogy, including the Zen reorientation of medieval apocalyptic visions toward a new focus on knowing the world through immediate bodily truths. Thus in the early Edo period one finds poems like Onitsura's, "In the front of the garden It has whitely blossomed—The camellia." In response to a Zen priest's request, "truth" is defined in this poem as a surface reality that lies before one's eyes: a camellia in the sun is seen to be white, and that is what should be said about it. Part Zen koan, in the Edo era this becomes the basis for an increasing empirical, descriptivist attitude toward the world.

This new idea of "truth" (*makoto*, 真) was yet also tied to the supposedly more plebian comic forms of poetry, especially *haikai* (俳徊). *Haikai* poetry typically opened with a traditional statement, but then, as in the linked poetry of renga, twisted that opening by finishing with a parodic refocusing. Thus for example a poem playing with the more traditional statement of the medieval court poet Saigyō ("I gazed so long at the blossoms they became dear to me, and when they fell, leaving me, I was sad"), becomes "From my gazing I got a pain from the blossoms In the bone of my neck"; the truth of the gaze in this case, too, comes from the material experience of the body. Vision in these cases is descriptivist, and tending toward quick, immediate observations of what lies before one rather than a more intellectualist and distanced view of space as some kind of larger whole. Although empiricist, it is therefore not perspectival in the sense that it does not claim to yield a more unified, integrated view of everything. And because of the often comic emphasis on re-viewing and re-thinking everything that one sees in front of oneself, while there is a new emphasis on the immediate world of the present, continuity of perspective is fragmented in time, too.

On the one hand, this mode of seeing develops into Basho's descriptive haiku. In *The Narrow Road to the Deep North* (*Oku no hosomichi*), these supposedly brief glimpses increasingly come to imply a more unified way of seeing the whole country. In Basho's case, this descriptivism is still very much a product of the subjective, even bodily authority of each viewer. These are *his* views of the country. The bodily sensorial aspect is emphasized in Basho's borrowing of the classic aesthetic of *nioi,* or "smell"—the various sites, and the poems Basho uses to describe these sites, are united by a common sense of "smell."

Yet this stance of descriptive-vision-as-truth is also tied to madness. As the poet Soin put it, "The art of *haikai* places madness (*kyō,* 狂) ahead of reality (*jitsu,* 実) . . . it is a joke within a fantasy." This same madness, nonetheless, is "a means of expressing truth" (*makoto*). *Kyōka,* or "mad poetry," attained remarkable extension throughout Edo society, from kabuki actors to samurai, who in some cases were joining groups to compose these poems together.

A similar descriptivism characterizes the mid-eighteenth century, with the idea of *shasei* (写生)—a simple "reflection" of nature (*shasei* means sketch, but literally in the sense of "a reflection of life"). As in the poetry of Buson, it is increasingly empiricist (in Buson's case, his poetry implies a distance of observer from object to the extent that, when writing even of his own children's death, the poetry consists of little more than impassive observation). *Shasei* is also tied to comic perspectives, and to the "low art" of *gesaku* literature. By the nineteenth century a more Cartesian perspective also emerges out of this, Shiba Kōkan being an obvious example. Shiba's discussion on Western painting and print forms argues for a method of "reflecting true form" that is in part descriptivist: "in reproducing a flower . . . unless the picture resembles that flower, it cannot be said to be a picture of the flower." Shiba here uses the new term *shashin* (写真, which later comes to mean a photograph, to talk about this kind of image).

But while Shiba's essay starts from this empirically descriptivist position, it develops into an argument for something more like perspectival space, with an active, a priori viewing subject who looks out on, and therefore truly knows and has command over, a perspectivally homogenous space. Using Dutch perspectival painting for comparison, Shiba complains that Chinese and Japanese methods depict a sphere as only a flat circle. Western methods, he says, use a "three facet" system,[103] including the use of shading, to portray what is in fact a globe—in other words, he is arguing for an understanding of space as three-dimensional. This understanding of space, he continues, should be founded on scientific foundations (although in a very specific sense; Shiba uses an interesting metaphor likening painting to the mental

---

103. Shiba felt that these modes of vision were different enough from local forms that, even after having seen a Japanese "perspective print" (*uki-e*), Japanese people are disoriented if suddenly shown "the vividly exquisite works of Western painting."

attitude of a medical doctor). As in Cartesian views, space in Shiba's formulation becomes homogenous and empty of qualitative difference. This is in opposition not only to nonperspectival understandings of vision and space, but even to some three-dimensional modes of perspectival space that continued to be practiced in Shiba's time. Maruyama Ōkyo's print work, for example, borrowed from Chinese styles that appeared to be perspectival, but in fact implied qualitative differences (not just the neutral difference of distance) between the spaces that were near, midway, and distant to the observer. In earlier, more spiritualist understandings of space and spatial expanse, space itself was a matter of essential qualitative differences and gradations of value; in Shiba's newly perspectival space, all space was of the same qualitative order of value.

As in Western perspectivalism, Shiba's space is mathematical, and it includes a mathematical relation between observer and observed objects. He provides a fairly detailed statement of the correct way to view a picture, including the lines within a picture that must be assumed, and the distance and height at which a picture should be placed. Also, as in the classic Western perspectival observer's relation to the world, the observer here is both distanced from the world, and yet very much of it (that is, the observer is alienated from but not in any way transcendent to the world that she/he sees). Thus, Shiba says that there should be a direct correspondence between the picture and the observer's viewing position, such that the viewing subject sees the painting/object "as if one were looking at a reflection in a mirror." The viewing subject here finds him/herself as subject in direct relation to the inert and distanced object.[104] Nor is this just a subjective view that might differ from one person's position to the next. There is only one correct way to view things in this kind of world, for Shiba, and so "it definitely would not do to look at [these perspectival paintings] just as one pleases." Not only is the correct viewing position therefore objectively accurate (one just needs to find the right position to view things from), but the accurately depicted image therefore takes on a greater truth value than either the subjective idea of the object held by the observer (including as memory) or the organic characteristics of the object itself. Accordingly, in writing about what he took to be the preserved specimen of a mermaid, he noted that because the stored specimen

---

104. Shiba also emphasizes that these are framed—and therefore presumably unified.

would inevitably change over the months and years, "ultimately, if it were not pictured, one could not know the true reality of the thing."[105]

The world that Shiba is describing is thus the most stable sort of perspectivalist order. It is a space defined by just one homogenous order of value (everyone should see things the same way, in a world without essential qualitative differentiation), just one kind of knowing subject, and just one true way of seeing the world. Furthermore, Shiba makes it clear that this is not just a discussion on good methods of painting and seeing. Western painting, he says, "is truly a technique of real utility, and a tool for governance and education as well."[106] Shiba is laying out the grounds for a social and political order based on a newly homogenous landscape.

Still, even in the early nineteenth century, along with these varied beliefs in the legibility and stability of material surfaces, the more "baroque" concerns with inconstant bodies and uncertain frames of vision were omnipresent. Often the same people were interested in both general forms of vision. Hiraga Gennai would be one example among many, but so would Shiba Kōkan. Although Shiba used a camera obscura to create perspectival drawings, he also worked in classical Chinese as well as Japanese woodblock print styles. This confluence of visions will be returned to below.

What I have described only hints at the remarkable variety of forms of vision present in the Edo era, as well as their interconnectedness.[107] At that time, empiricist descriptivism and even Cartesian-type perspectivalism had a genealogy leading back to Zen Buddhism, but were also closely tied with a "madness" of vision, and even with the kind of baroque reemphasis on an uncontrolled bodiliness that so often is considered in diametric opposition to Cartesian forms of space and sight. Science in this case therefore has a genealogy that includes Zen, as well as comic perspectives and especially madness; and none of these should in any easy way be thought of as emancipatory ways of seeing, or even necessarily counter-hegemonic.

---

105. Quotations from Shiba Kōkan, *Seiyōga dan*, Looser, trans., in *Readings in Tokugawa Thought* (Chicago: University of Chicago Center for East Asian Studies, Select Papers vol. 9, 1993), 159. There is clearly a temporal disjuncture here as well: the time of the accurately observed image becomes eternal, while the time of the corporeal and subjective is fleeting and therefore untrue. This work was written in 1799.
106. Ibid., 160.
107. Martin Jay's broad claim with regard to the "absence of such scopic regimes in Eastern cultures" strikes one as somewhat hasty, to say the least. See *Vision and Visuality*, 19–20.

In order to be more specific about how some of these forms of vision might, or might not, have been part of the same space, and might or might not have contributed to the same order of power in early modern Japan, I want to consider a few terms and conditions more closely.

I am in this section concentrating on the noh, but there are elements of kabuki that are important as background to understanding vision in the noh. Within the pleasure quarters/kabuki theater/merchant world, one of the principal forms of vision was defined by *ugachi* (穿ち). Literally a "penetrating" look, *ugachi* was a skilled mode of seeing, associated with Edokko knowledge, that claimed for a kind of empiricism—it was a learned mode of observation. Theoretically anyone, the shogun and otherwise, could learn it, but it focused on the world as a place of material surfaces which nonetheless held a truth that could be penetrated, or uncovered. It also implied an angle of observation: *ugachi* was said to always be a posture of looking awry, focusing only on the side (*soba*) or sometimes on the back *(ura)* of things. It was thus never a mirroring gaze, in which subject and object are directly reflected, and reflexively constituted. This is not, then, a Cartesian mode of vision, or of subject constitution. It is furthermore a look of or in time, at least insofar as, like the parodic *haikai* poetry with which it was associated, it was ostensibly based on very brief, speedy glances. Finally, it also became associated with a mode of power. The best example of an *ugachi* look in this sense is the famous poem describing the Edokko as a man who gives "a sideways glance" at the golden dolphins atop the shogun's castle towers, and in doing so pierces the power of the shogun.

In the kabuki theater, this look from awry was undoubtedly associated with the critical frozen instant of the *mie*. Even the simple crossing of eyes left no possibility for a transcendent mirroring gaze.

The possibility has already been raised that this look is also associated with money (the *mie*, for example, as a moment of "seeing profit"). The *ugachi* look from awry was in very practical terms associated with money in general, and with the relations of spectacle that capitalism is so typically connected with. This association is most clear in the massive, bustling *misemono* (見世物 , "showing things") fairs set up as a new kind of spectacle specifically to make money. In these fairs the idea of *ugachi* becomes not so much a specific angle of observation as it is more generally a need for constantly new and different perspectives on things, and new forms of seeing. Sights—both things to look at and new modes of looking at them—are what sell, and in order to keep selling, these sights must keep changing (Saikaku describes this too). Objects and bodies of vision themselves take on the capitalist qualities of mutation already discussed (examples include displays of the woman whose neck seems to stretch endlessly; the armless "bottle-boy"; the giantess; the "feejee mermaid"; hairy "demon girl"; and so on),[108] and new technologies of seeing arrive here first (the telescope, the magnifying glass).

It has been claimed that in the West, Cartesian perspectivalism (especially the divide between subject/viewer from object of vision) emerged with the buying and selling of oil painting. As the visual field of the canvas entered the circulations of capitalism, the argument goes, it became detached from its context and separated from both buyer and seller, thereby creating the Cartesian separation between viewer and visual field as object. Although this line of argument is somewhat simplistic, it is relevant that the first Western-style perspectivalist prints in Japan (the *uki-e*, 浮絵) did appear in the misemono fairs. Also extremely popular were the *nozoki* "peep" shows (the *uki-e* perspective prints were generally viewed through the peep show lenses). And more generally, and importantly, all these forms of vision were spectacular—meaning that they entailed a disconnection of viewer from viewed. Consequently, despite the claim for temporal immediacy of *ugachi*-style perspective, in its association with the capitalist misemono fairs (and despite all the glaring bodiliness of the misemono images) this perspective also involves a gap separating the subject off from the object of vision.

As in other forms of spectacle, this look is also defined by a mode of desire, which involves an alienation (an obvious example may be the misemono booth in which men were allowed to come and view, as well as blow air through a bamboo tube toward, a woman's genitalia—but they could never go beyond a restraining wall). It is as well a form of history, or really an alienation from history, such that one cannot be part of the temporality of the thing that one observes. This is no different from the separation from the time of the commodity that Saikaku described. Here too the immediacy or temporality of the *ugachi* glance, with its focus on the present "truth" of things, turns out to also entail a mediation. Much of this is summed up in yet another misemono exhibit, from 1840. There was at that time a man who was supposedly able to extract and reinsert his eyeballs, at will. Not only did he do so, however, but to make it interesting, he attached large strings of

---

108. Most of these are described in Andrew L. Markus, "The Carnival of Edo," *Harvard Journal of Asiatic Studies* vol. 45, no. 2, 499–541.

228 / Visioning Eternity

coins to the filaments of his optic nerves—as if he was seeing through the strands of money.

Vision in this case is mediated by, and assumes the value of, money (and all that this implies).[109]

This "eye," seeing the present world through the perspective and values of money, describes one aspect of the pleasure quarters views.[110] The noh was in some ways quite different.

One of the most important locations for the formation and manipulation of visuality in the noh was the public machi-iri performances. This was entirely a Tokugawa creation. Even the noh stages we see today were not really concretized until around 1700, and these were patterned after the stage form created by the shoguns within Edo castle, and used on occasions such as the machi-iri. The noh stage commonly portrayed today as an apolitical site of traditional Japan is also a historical model of vision and power.[111]

The noh stage was set up directly opposite a veranda-like room for the shogun. Both the stage and the shogun's room were raised, and a divider of gravel-covered ground separated the two. Connected to the shogun's room (to his left) was a series of additional rooms, separated by sliding doors mostly left closed, in which the principal daimyo lords sat. The higher the rank, the closer the room to the shogun—the room next to the shogun's was reserved for the *fudai* daimyo (lords considered to be genealogically related to the Tokugawas).[112] This hierarchy was also constituted as an organization of angles of observation: because the shogun's room was opposite the stage, and about the same height and size, he had the only direct view of the stage; then, the farther one sat from the shogun, the sharper the angle from which

---

109. Saitō Gesshin et al., *Bukō nenpyō* (Tokyo: Heibonsha, 1968), 2:217, and Markus, ibid., 530. Markus reports this example as fact, though it is difficult to believe there was not some ruse involved. I am not concerned with whether it was factual or not, so much as I am interested in the concept of eyeballs connected through nerves of money.
110. In kabuki, the mediating role of money in a spectatorial relation between audience and stage is evident in the practice of expressing one's appreciation for specific moments, or actors, in a play by throwing coins wrapped in paper on stage.
111. Although stages were modeled after the shogun's, the structure used by the shogun was already present by the mid- to late-sixteenth century. A wide variety of stages were used prior to that time, but even the large public performances were typically held on stages with the audience circled around, so that everyone had a roughly similar perspective. See Figure 5.
112. In the case of machi-iri held for shogunal investiture, the *fudai* daimyo attended only the first day. The second day was then reserved for the nonrelated *tozama* ("outer") lords, the third and fourth days for various shogunal officials, and on the fifth day the "priest-prince" of the shrines at Nikkō came.

one could see the stage. These lines of vision were also reinforced by paths of gift giving (see Figure 3). The lower ranking lords would bring robes up to the actors on stage from a more obliquely placed stairway and path, and there was a separate set of stairs for the shogun, again immediately opposite the stage, by which actors and shoguns could make gift exchanges with one another in a single direct path. All of these officials would typically watch the

Figure 3. Paths of Gift Giving

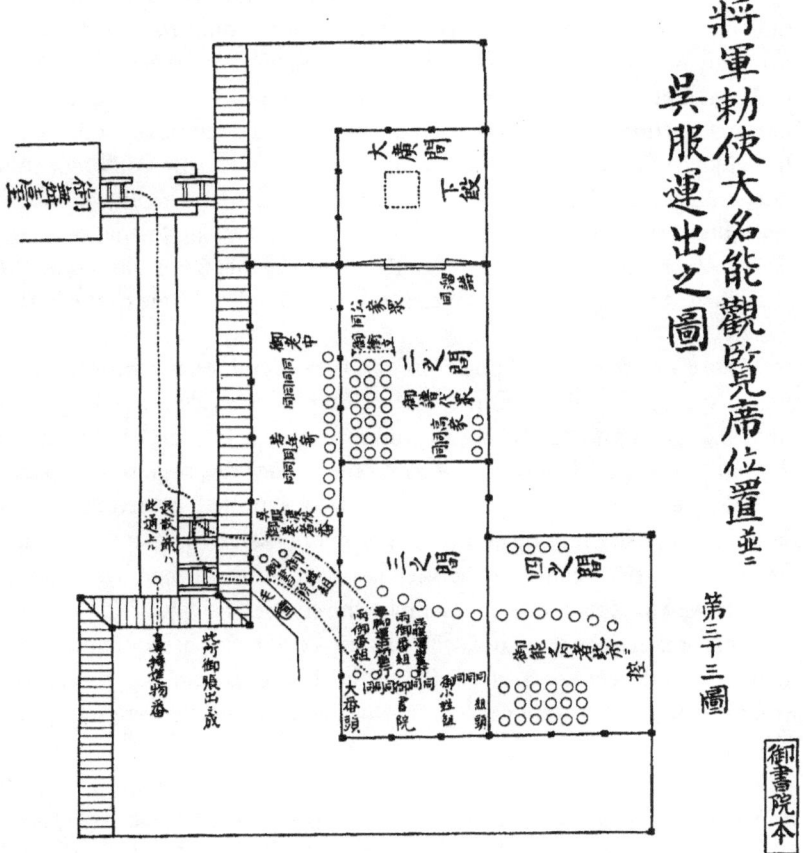

From the *Yanagiei gyōji*, reprinted in part in Ono Kiyoshi, ed., *Tokugawa seido shiryō* (Tokyo: Rokugodan, 1926).

full day's performance, which lasted from around or before sunrise until sunset, so only they had a full view in both a spatial and a temporal sense.

Along with the shogunal and court officials, commoners were allowed into the castle grounds to see the performance. Members of the imperial court as well as commoners were specifically invited to attend only the first day's performance, but this was considered the most important, or "weighty." Unlike any of the officials, however, the commoners were placed in the lower ground-level area that formed the gap between the stage and the rulers' rooms. This was considered a temporary space: they were tightly packed within a temporary bamboo fence (see Figure 4), and forced to sit or stand on the gravel-strewn ground. Even the best view of the stage they could have was set off to the side, and much of this section would have had only an extremely oblique view, or none at all. At the same time, placed in between the stage and the lords' rooms, the commoners watched the goings-on in both spaces (this seems to have been intended), and documents indicate that they enjoyed the spectacle of both actor and shogun equally. Although commoners lined up for performances long before sunrise (generally at about 4 a.m.), they were allowed to watch only half of the day's performance, with a second group coming in for the second half. Hence they were allowed neither a full view of the space of the stage, nor of the completed time of the performance.

Those are the principal positions of observation for a machi-iri noh, but there is still another, third audience. The closest lords of all to the shogun, the three Tokugawa families (*Gosanke*), did not sit next to him, but instead sat "*behind*" the stage. They therefore could see neither the stage nor the actors at all. Rather, from behind the stage they were expected to directly face the shogun, in a position of obeisance that was supposed to be maintained until the very last performance of the very last day. Different members, though, were allowed to replace one another over the course of a day.[113]

This overall stage structure, with its varied audience positions and lines of sight, is an Edo-era construct. Prior to the Edo era there was no uniform structure for a noh stage, but larger performances generally were set up with

---

113. This is described in documents of the Matsudaira family (one of the genealogical branch families of the Tokugawas), compiled as part of the *Yanagiei gyōji*—reprinted in Ono Kiyoshi, ed., *Tokugawa seido shiryō* (Tokyo: Rokugokan, 1928). See p. 515. It is possible that at least in some cases, sitting "behind" the stage may have meant sitting at the back of it, or parallel to the back of it, but the general structure of viewing positions remains the same.

Figure 4. Commoners' Fenced Viewing Area (Machi-iri Noh)

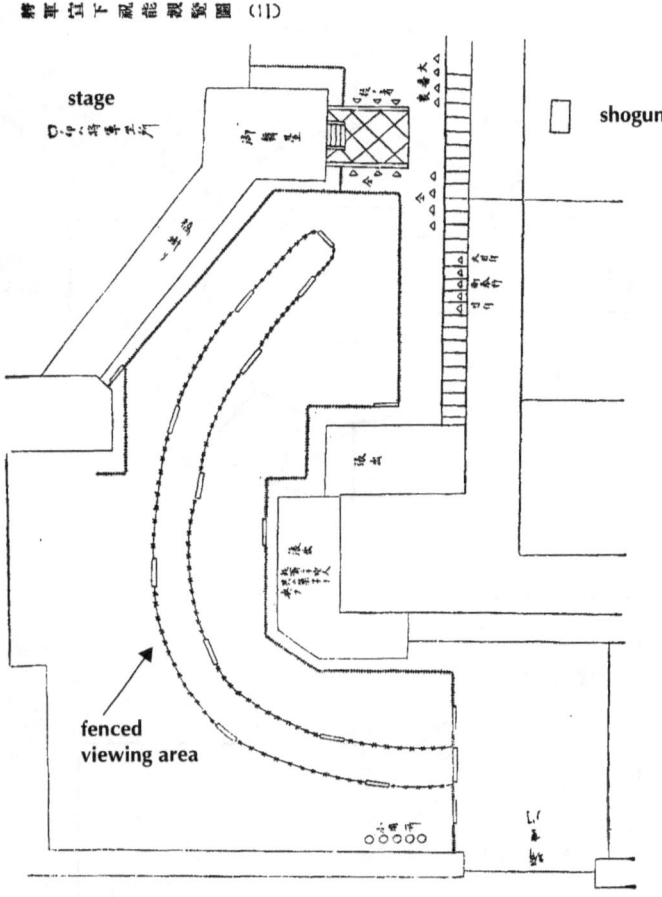

Map of shogunal proclamation noh as reprinted in Ikeuchi, NS I, 185.

viewing stands almost entirely circling the stage, so that most members of the audience had roughly similar positions of perspective (see Figure 5).

To varying degrees, all of the views in the machi-iri noh fix themselves on the shogun at one point or another. This is true even of the actors onstage: Zeami wrote that actors should always play to and focus on the most noble members of the audience, and in the Edo era the one form of improvised look allowed the actors was a sort of unobtrusive glance toward the shogun

Figure 5. Noh Stages: Middle Ages (top) and Edo Era/Modern (bottom)

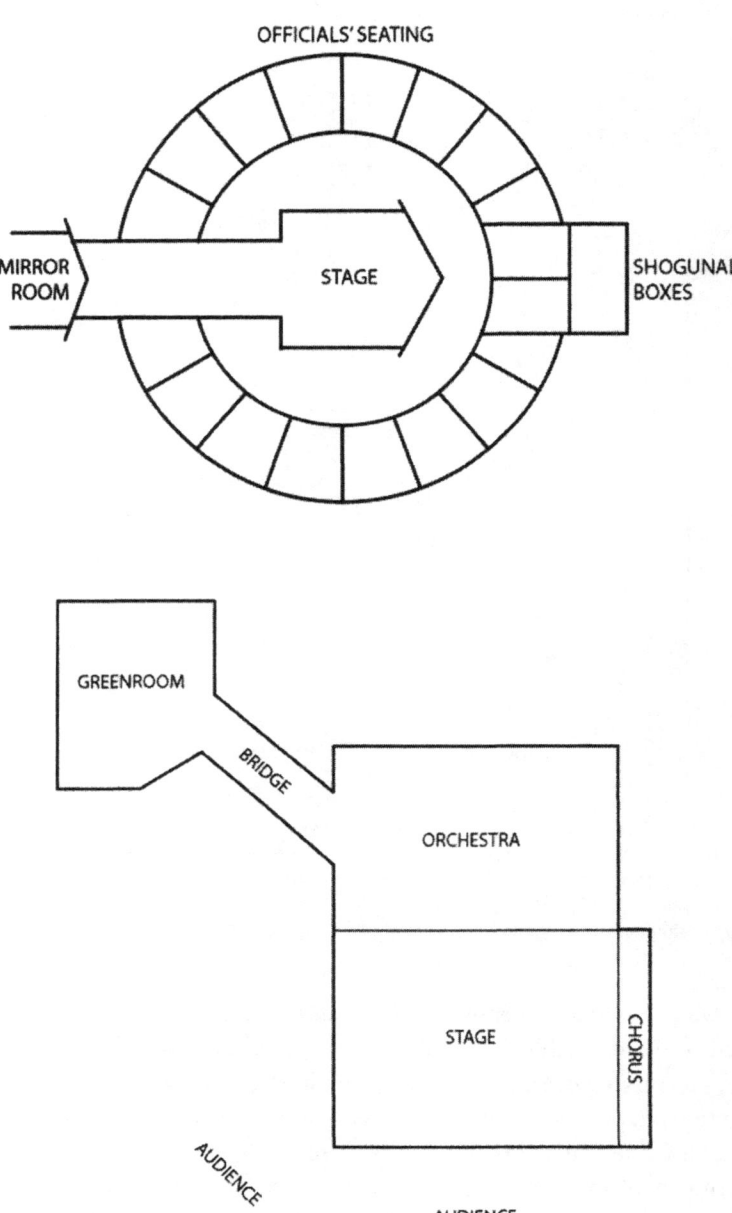

(or other high officials) as a means of flattery.[114] There were also times when the sliding doors were opened so that the shogun was visible to all, including shogunal officials. On one level, then, the machi-iri as a whole was a monocular model. All the various views came together on the place of the shogun, thereby constituting him as the point of reference for, and in a sense the origin of, the whole. At this level, all views are part of a single homogenous space—a space of authority—not all that unlike the Western Renaissance order of perspectival space.[115] Space at this level accordingly might be thought of as relatively abstract or homogenous, insofar as it was all organized by the monocular view of the shogun as focal point.

The shogun himself was part of this, and in a sense what he saw was himself. His was a "gaze" as opposed to a "glance," as in the terminology of Jay, Crary, and others, but it also involved a kind of mirroring. As a gaze, the shogun's were the only eyes that had a direct view of the stage as well as a panoptic view of the entire structure of theater and audience. This was thus the only transcendent form of vision. The shogun's eyes also were the only ones able to connect directly with the actors', thereby connecting fully and directly with the absolute epic past embodied therein (much in the same way that within the plays, moments of divine, transcendent unity are expressed by the image of a purely reflected full moon). Therefore when thinking of Zeami's ideal instant in which the audience realizes the "pure feeling" of Peerless Charm, an instantaneous view of pure experience in which one has no time for reflection, it is really the shogun in particular who realizes this. In this sense, the space of these various lines of sight was already not abstractly homogeneous. The closer the space to the shogun, the more direct the observer's gaze toward the stage would be, and the more transcendent that space would be. The quality of each view, and the position of each view, would differ from the next.

---

114. See Oda Sachiko's discussion of Edo noh actor's stage manuals: "Nō no engi to enshutsu: shōzokuzuke, katazuke o meguru shomondai" in *Nōgaku kenkyū* 10 (1984), 63–108.
115. "Monocularity, like perspective and geometrical optics, was one of the Renaissance codes through which a visual world is constructed according to systematized constants, and from which any inconsistencies and irregularities are banished to insure the formation of a homogeneous, unified, and fully legible space." Jonathan Crary, "Modernizing Vision," in *Vision and Visuality,* 33. These lines of sight can also be thought of in the context of the increasingly secularized notion of rays of light that were related to the formation of renaissance structures of visual power. Descriptions of the machi-iri by Matsudaira Nobuyoshi tell of how the commoners and others, upon seeing the shogun, felt a deepened sense of his "authority." The term here used was a new one, *ikō,* literally meaning the "power of light." In *Tokugawa seido shiryō,* 514–515.

234 / Visioning Eternity

The shogun's gaze thus is without mediation—as Zeami put it of this instant, it is "purity unmixed."[116] Recall also that the moment of Peerless Charm had "the quality of gold"—here, the pure, immediate gaze of the shogun can be contrasted to the mediated "eye of money" described just above. The gaze therefore also entails a temporality, which in this case may be an instant, but is nonetheless that nondiachronic instant which is really the compressed space and time of a forever-stretching-out eternity. In the noh's staging, the eternal gaze may be reduced to a single point (the shogun), but it sees into and opens up the distant landscape of the eternal past. And as Jay says, "the pull of the eye into the distant landscape seemed to grant the view the all-important 'prospective' capacity for foreknowledge."[117] This explains why the shoguns repeatedly commented that by gazing out over the townspeople during these machi-iri performances, they were able to "judge the condition" of the people, including both present and future.

The image of this gaze into distant space and time can be found in Zeami's own drawings. In his treatises, Zeami sketched three ideal role types (old man/god; woman; and warrior; see Figures 6–8), as well as six others.[118] Of these, only one is portrayed with uplifted eyes. This is Okina, the old man/god figure after which the ritual play *Okina* was named, and the role which Zeami said "represents the pinnacle of our art."[119] The principal characteristic of this image seems to be this fact that he is looking up, off into the infinite distance. The actor playing the role accordingly was to "keep his soul at ease and look off into the distance," continually "looking afar."[120] As if to emphasize this eternal gaze and the importance of vision itself in constructing this eternity, Zeami drew a dotted line from the figure's eyes off into space, with the written character for vision (*miru*, 見る) at the end of it. This also expresses the eye of the shogun. And this eye, which sees without mediation straight into the eternal past and reflects the full plenitude of the "Peerless" quality of gold, might again be opposed both to the mediations of the man with an eye connected by nerve strands of coins, and to the crossed gaze of the *mie* moment in kabuki.

---

116. Rimer and Yamazaki, *On the Art of the Noh*, 91.
117. Martin Jay, *Downcast Eyes* (Berkeley: University of California Press, 1993), 25.
118. See "Nikyoku santai ningyōzu," reprinted in *Zeami Zenchiku*, 121–132.
119. Rimer and Yamazaki, ibid., 11.
120. *On the Art of the Noh*, 11, 141.

Times and Visions of the Instant / 235

Figure 6. Okina (Old Man) with "Eyes Looking Afar"

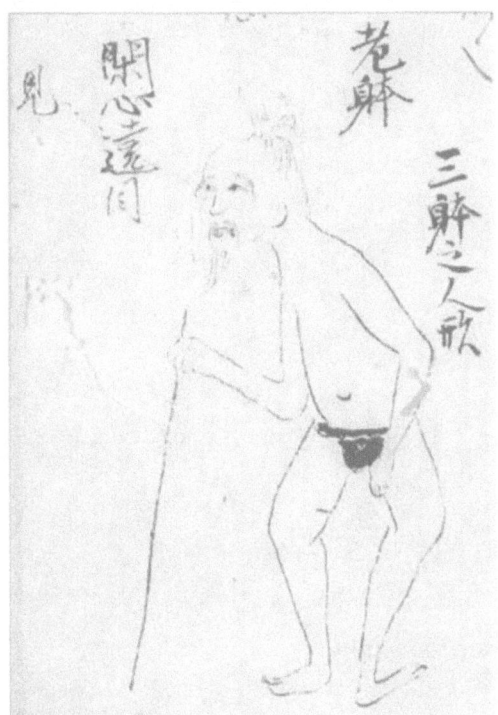

Courtesy of Hosei University Nō Research Institute.

As a look of pure unblinking reciprocity,[121] however, the machi-iri is also a case of the shogun in a sense looking at himself. The shogun's gaze was specular, in that it not only looked clearly off into the distance, but that it involved a direct mirroring relationship between viewer and viewed, or subject and object. This relationship was built into the stage itself: the wall at the rear of the stage, painted with the divine pine tree, was known as the "mirror board" (*kagami ita*, 鏡板). It should be emphasized that this backboard is an Edo-era creation—though almost never recognized as such—so it does express a specifically Edo-era structure of visuality. In fact, according to a lecture given in the early 1930s by the noh actors Kongō Iwao and Umewaka Rokuro, Edo-era shoguns also always had a folding screen painted with the

---

121. Great actors were said to be able to practice "the art of not blinking," hence returning the shogun's regard with a look of their own, uninterrupted by even the blink of an eye. See Ikeuchi, NS I, 170.

236 / Visioning Eternity

Figure 7. Woman Role

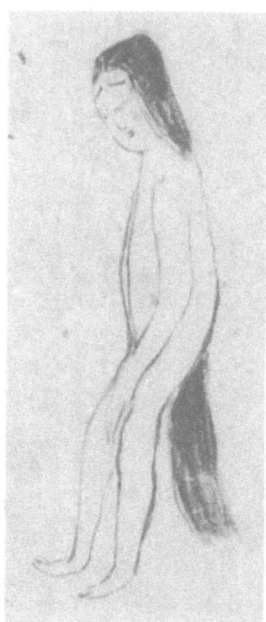

Figure 8. Warrior/Man Role

Images courtesy of Hosei University Nō Research Institute.

same pine put up in their viewing room, and the stage backboard pine was a reflection of this; there thus may have been a double process of mirroring going on.[122] Additionally, the room just offstage, behind the entry curtain, was called the "mirror space" (*kagami no ma*, 鏡の間), and contained a mirror set up next to the curtain.

In part this may simply express the absolute reciprocal reflection of the shogun and the values of the noh's epic past. The shogun himself, gazing directly across from the mirror board and directly at the actors who are acting out that divine past, wholly and absolutely reflects those values, without material remainder outside of himself. It is an act of self-contemplation, in which the shogun's being is reflected as a whole, and that being, or body, itself reflects the whole, complete value of the past. Further, it is an act of knowledge. In this gaze, the shogun sees and therefore knows the epic truth of the divine past, and this knowledge, too, as we have seen in other contexts, is therefore embodied in the shogun himself. As an act of pure knowledge, the shogun's viewing of the noh is thus also a form of self-knowledge, and the shogun knows himself fully, as a complete reembodiment of the values and knowledge of the past.

Thus the shogun might be said to be looking at himself in watching the noh. But it is more than just that. By watching the play, he finds himself as transcendent, as the very image of those divine values. That is to say, it is almost like the Lacanian notion of a child who, while still lacking an understanding of his various body parts as being all connected in one organic being, then gains an image of himself as whole by seeing this image in a mirror. Similarly, the shogun as a mortal (and in the investiture, as not yet a "great barbarian-quelling shogun") looks at the noh and thereby has an image returned to him of himself as a greater whole—the body of the divine/epic past, stretching from here to eternity. This process is also evident in the way that the "mirror room" was utilized by the actors themselves. Particularly for the more important "god" roles, an actor would take up the mask from its special box (for plays like *Okina*, this should be preceded by several days of ritual abstinence, and a ritual fire in the mirror room), and once having put the mask on, he would look in the mirror. In so doing and seeing his masked

---

122. See their compiled lectures in *The Noh Drama* (Tokyo: Kokusai Bunka Shinkōkai, 1937), 9. There are stages older than the Edo era, still in existence, which do have the "aged pine" painted on the back board; the stage at the Nishi Honganji is one example. But these apparently had the pines, and most likely the back board itself, added after the Edo era began (this is what Amano Fumio speculates; personal communication).

image in the mirror, he was said to literally *become* that god (more than just an actor with a mask on). The mirror thus returned an image to him of himself as a new, more divine being.[123]

But what of the three Tokugawa families? What are they doing sitting "behind" the stage?[124] As documents from Matsudaira Nobuyoshi indicated, this was an act of obeisance, but still, why not allow them a room next to the shogun's, where they could bow in his direction? If it was a matter only of not allowing them a view of the stage, the curtains for their room could easily have been drawn, with the sliding doors facing the shogun instead left open. One likely element of this may have been that, as Tokugawas, they too should partake of the plenitudinous reflection of value that the shogun's gaze did. The only position from which they might do this, however, without actually then becoming equal to the shogun himself, would be on the opposite side from the shogun. They were thus the reflection of the shogun's reflection (in this context, one might think of the pine-painted screen set up in the shogun's room, the equivalent of the "mirror board" the shogun faced on stage—here the *sanke* may have been a mirroring of the shogun's mirroring), and their gaze would thus constitute them in the same image of eternal value, even while it also paid allegiance to the shogun.

But this structure of vision is also reminiscent of another example from Renaissance Europe, the *tavoletta* experiments of Brunelleschi. Brunelleschi had taken a small perspectivalist painting and placed a small hole in the canvas. One was to look through the hole from behind the canvas, to a mirror on the other side which reflected the painting's surface therein. Thus viewing the picture through the mirror, one's gaze met directly with the point of view that formed the basis of the painting's perspective. By at least one reading,[125] this has two effects: it reveals and verifies the "truth" of the gaze (that is, in a self-referential way, it shows that the painting is constructed through lines of perspective, and so must be viewed from the proper perspective—and the single "point of view" is then indeed "true"). Perhaps more importantly here,

---

123. Perhaps a moment roughly equivalent to this within the narrative structure of noh plays was the time when the god first appears, often called (the term is borrowed from Buddhism) *kaigen* (開眼), or the moment of "eye opening."
124. While I think the question to be critically important in understanding the structures of vision, I have only found the barest of mention of this practice and so can only speculate on its implications.
125. There are quite a variety of readings of Brunelleschi. The ideas here are from Hubert Damisch's extensive account. See John Goodman, trans., *The Origin of Perspective* (Cambridge, MA: MIT Press, 1994).

Brunelleschi's *tavoletta* setup also implies a symmetrical structure of perspective which may locate a second point of view, and a second vanishing point, somewhere far behind the viewer's head. Even without this assumption, it is clear that for Brunelleschi, the only way the subject could verify the painting's plane of visuality, and therefore his/her own gaze, was by placing himself behind that plane of vision—again, in a sense, the viewer looks behind his/her head.[126] The most important point here is that this takes the apparently finite structure and gaze of a single point of perspective and brings it into a connection with infinity and ubiquity.

That, then, parallels the shogun's secondary gaze—a gaze coming from his own closest representatives (the *sanke* families), from behind the mirror within which the shogun sees himself. The *sanke* thus express and verify the shogun's gaze as the look of truth. It is an outside position which acknowledges the shogun's gaze as the originary point of reference, but it acknowledges it from within the same logic of the gaze (this is sort of like trying to find a way to verify one's own view of oneself in a mirror—the only way to see oneself gazing into the mirror would be to stand behind that mirror, and thus the shogun has his own representatives in that position). Second, and more importantly, the *sanke's* position connects the shogun's view with an all-seeing eternity as described above, or in the idea of infinity as "an idea of what's behind one's head."[127] Zeami expresses a quite similar idea in his outline of the ideal form of sight an actor should aspire toward (for Zeami this is a self-image): "For an actor to grasp his true appearance implies that he has under his control the space to the left and to the right of him, and to the front and to the rear of him. In many cases, however, an average actor looks only to the front and to the side and so never sees what he actually looks like from behind.... Therefore, an actor must... examine his appearance with his spiritual eyes.... Such an action truly represents 'the eyes of the spirit looking behind.'"[128]

All of this, including the *sanke's* view from behind the stage, thus still involves a reflectionist model of vision and of the constitution of power. It also involved an organization of points of view which ultimately are constrained to just one point of true sight, and this point of sight was also a reduction of the perceiving subject (the shogun) really to just his eye.

---

126. For a detailed outline of this possibility, see Damisch, *Origin of Perspective*, 121–122.
127. This idea, mentioned also in Damisch, is Louis Marin's. See *La Critique du discours* (Paris: Minuit,1975), 394–396.
128. *On the Art of the Noh*, 81; "Kakyō," in *Zeami Zenchiku*, 88.

240 / Visioning Eternity

To a degree, the townspeople are part of this order of specularity, even though they were not allowed a total view of anything. Packed into the confines of the bamboo fence, these people could view the stage, and the shogun, at best only from a partial, sideways glance rather than a full gaze; and because they were allowed in for only part of a performance, theirs was a more fleetingly temporal look, caught in the passing moment. Still, in a way it was images of those very structures of incompletion that the noh performance returned to these people. That is, in a way, they too looked and found an image of themselves, and in this limited sense it can be considered a specular relation. As mentioned in Chapter 1, in their appreciation of the performance these townspeople saw and realized their own position as not full members of society, as excluded from full participation in power and in the eternal value of that power. They saw that they could not completely see, that they did not entirely know what was going on, and that they were excluded from the shogun's place as well as from the stage.[129] Furthermore, they enjoyed it, and even, from an exoticist position, found it interesting. As one quote from the time puts it, "For people who know [the noh], it is as interesting as they have knowledge, and for people who don't know it is as interesting as they don't."[130] In their enjoyment at watching this theater which they could not understand and in their pleasure at being given restricted glances at the shogun, the commoners effectively reaffirmed the shogun's eternal, all-knowing and all-seeing position (and the shogun took care to be "magnanimous" in providing occasions when his screen was lifted, so that the townspeople might peek at him and offer rowdy praise).[131] Thus in this sense the

---

129. There is also a contrast visible in the participation in more official, genealogical time of the shoguns, and the lack of participation in this time on the part of the townspeople. This was also apparently a relation of something like ritual versus theater, as well as "real" versus "artificial." For example, members of the nobility as well as daimyo or shogunal officials would wear formal clothing with their family crests clearly emblazoned thereon. Their viewing rooms were also hung with purple crepe curtains, onto which these crests were dyed. (See Yokoi, Nōgaku zenshi, 394.) Reports of the commoners, on the other hand, tell of some who, at least half in fun, attached play family crests made out of paper to their crude outerwear (which would otherwise have no crest), and tied straw ropes around their waists in place of the upper class silken obi belts. (See for example Ikeuchi, NS I, 197–198.) While it might be argued that this played with the idea of the fixity of hereditary social class, however, one could as easily claim that this too ultimately has the effect of emphasizing the commoners' exclusion from permanent or "real" membership in those classes and the official time of genealogy; the commoners' artificial crests are mere theatrical play at legitimate participation in that time.
130. Yanagizawa Kizen, in Hitorine, reproduced in Omote, Nō kyōgen II, 395.
131. See quotes in Ikeuchi, NS I, 199: first, the town magistrate is ridiculed, and then when the shogun's screen was lifted, "the boss was praised; it was rowdy and outrageous."

reflectionist mirroring model of vision in the machi-iri still holds, even for the glance of the townspeople. They looked at and valued the same reference point (the shogun) as the others, using it as a mirror against which they might see and gauge themselves, even though in this case the image that was reflected—that of the commoners—was an incomplete and devalued one. So the overall space of the machi-iri noh was in this limited sense too comprised of relatively monocular, homogenous lines of sight.

Still, the commoners' sideways glance was in some ways closer to the sideways *ugachi* view described earlier, and this is a look of a different order for several reasons. Above all, it is spectacular rather than specular. Part of the Edo-era spectacular vision involved an eye for money (looking toward speculative capitalist value; looking through the mediation of money, etc.), and this implies a different set of values, and a different order of vision from the shogun's specular modes.

On the one hand, even if this other mode of seeing entailed a different set of values, it was still used by the shogun as part of the overall process of the machi-iri. The spectacular and capitalist eye for something that is objectified (the commodity), and that is part of a system of circulation of value from which one is to an extent excluded, would work well in this context. Shoguns, after all, wanted commoners to acknowledge that as shoguns they were indeed of a fundamentally different and unattainable order of being. Descriptions from the time would seem to indicate that that was the way commoners viewed the proceedings, as in one quote (this one regarding the great Kōka performance), in which the shogun and officials, set up on the raised platform of their own viewing rooms, were said to be "set out on view, like one *mon* dolls."[132] Here the shogunal officials are objectified, clearly separated from the commoner observers, and seen through eyes accustomed to monetary, commodity value (eyes which look admiringly, and appraisingly, at the shogun, on display). In this case, the alienation created by consumerist desire seems to work in favor of the shogun's need for a position of distanced but privileged value.[133] Capitalist spectacle here reinforces the shogun's "ritual" position of difference and power.

Accordingly, the bakufu went to some lengths to encourage the appearance that this very mode of seeing *was* present, rather than discouraging it as

---

132. Ikeuchi, NS I, 271.
133. This form of spectacular interest is also connected to the idea of "sightseeing" (*kenbutsu*), as in the shogun's wish to have commoners come as sightseers (only) to the shoguns' divine shrines at Nikkō.

an unwanted element of the capitalist values which the shogun ostensibly refused. For example, rather than simply announcing a performance and letting the townspeople in, the shogun went through a process of having them buy tickets. This was a sham of sorts, both because the "requests" that the commoners buy tickets were in truth demands, and because these commoners were nonetheless given quantities of money (apparently worth a good deal more than the minimal price of the tickets) both at the end of the performance and again several days afterward. Money, therefore, was one of the real motivations for going. Descriptions tell of the townspeople shoving and fighting one another and finding ways to take more than their allotted shares of money and minor items of luxury. Money was in some cases even placed out in piles, for people to come and grab.[134] Through these machinations, the shogunate both explicitly exhibited the desire for money, and by having tickets bought, created the appearance that people wished to see the performance enough to pay money for it—that is, that the people gave it the (capitalist/consumerist) value of money.

Hence the commoners' perspective did introduce a different kind or different value of vision into the overall performance space, and so an element of heterogeneity. But just as the shogun's archaic "gift" economy of rice in practical fact needed the flows of capital, here the shogun's pure specular mode of sight and value not only allowed for, but actually needed the outside confirmation of the spectacular spectator. At very least, the shogun's image of transcendence was bolstered by the overlayering of that image with the commodity image, as seen by the townspeople. Or, put in different terms, the shogun's eyes of gold received outside confirmation from the commoners' eyes of money. To the extent that the shogun actually depended on this outside confirmation of his authority, one might then argue that the whole structure depended on alienation: in a world of already theatricalized, reinvented state divinity, even the *sanke's* position of obeisance to the shogun was not enough to validate the shogun's transcendence. This could only come from a position outside that "eternal" view—i.e., the temporal, broken, and alienated glance of the townspeople.

The same matters of time, memory, and embodiment considered earlier in the context of play structures, above, accordingly also reappear here in the more everyday contexts of spectatorship and the circulation of objects at the

---

134. Typically they were given bottles of *sake* rice wine, cakes, and umbrellas as well as the various forms of monetary gifts and remunerations.

machi-iri performances. I can cite here only a brief and tentative example. The shoguns, as noted, engaged in a ritual exchange of robes with the actors as part of the more general exchange between shogun and actor as representative of a divine past. The robes therefore serve a role similar to that of the object of memory in a ritual noh play—they are complete materializations of an epically transcendent past. In contrast to this, like the everyday objects in a kabuki play, the commoner spectators of the machi-iri engaged only in the procurement of commodities and souvenirs from the performances—not in ritual embodiments of the past, and not therefore in ritual reconstructions of a divine time. Still, one story indicates the commoners' souvenirs worked in some ways with the shoguns' ritual order of time. In this story, apparently widely known, a servant of a townsman (himself too old to endure the uncomfortable conditions of the commoners' graveled viewing area) came home slightly drunk from the morning half of a performance—the segment he had been allowed to see. Along with the *sake* wine and cakes the servant had managed to grab, he pulled out of his kimono sleeves a large piece of the bamboo fence used to confine the townspeople within the castle grounds. The family valued this piece of bamboo fence enough to hold it as a keepsake (it was made into a brush holder), and the chronicler of this story, years later, said "even now this old man treasures it and boasts of it."[135] What has become a treasured body of memory in this case is a piece of the fence that kept those people partitioned off. It acts as a fetishized object of their own exclusion, a physical memory of their separation from the more eternal time and memory of the shogun. It may be just an everyday object, but it becomes more than just a commodity, and as a fetish fills in for what was in fact a real social alienation; these people remember themselves as being legitimate (but excluded) members of that machi-iri world. Consequently, although this was an object very much unlike the robes ritually exchanged by the top officials, it nonetheless worked just as much as the ritual objects to bolster the unity of the shogun's world.

    Is all this therefore a paradigm of visual mastery? Proof not only that the Edo-era concern with controlling time was connected to a very much visually constructed (and theatrical) mode of power and social form, but that this theater of visions was indeed a model of total shogunal control?

    The commoner audience of the machi-iri performances, packed there within the tightly uncomfortable confines of the bamboo fence, really does

---

135. Ibid., 198.

seem to have constituted a qualitatively different kind of time, and vision. Before concluding, it is worth looking just a bit more at this audience.

The position from which the shogun allowed himself to be seen by these people, and the kind of vision with which they apparently looked at him, was, as noted, the *ugachi* angular view from the side. *Ugachi*, however, referred to more than just a look from awry; it also implied a particular form of knowledge. Literally, *ugachi* means to penetrate, or pierce. As an angle of observation, the *ugachi* view was considered a means of seeing into the *ana*, or "holes" of things, and this in turn meant seeing into the hidden truths or facts of things. This was in clear contrast to the direct, reciprocal gaze of the shogun: here, the *ana* holes could be seen *only* by a sideways glance; otherwise these holes would be invisible and one could not see truth.[136] This knowledge was also typically sought for in the partial, fragmented details of things, so there was little desire for the overarchingly unified perspective of the shogun. Accordingly, this is an angle of vision and a kind of knowledge that the shogun could not have, but the commoners did. The position of spectatorial alienation in this case is not disempowering, and does not at all reflect an image of unknowing disenfranchisement to the commoners. Rather than an incomplete act of knowing, the commoners' glance by this definition was fully perceptive, penetrating the "ritual" truth of the shogun. The image of the free-spending Edokko townsman, peering sidelong at the golden dolphins atop the shogun's castle as an act of defiance and power, is one example of this different kind of knowing subject, and different kind of view. Whether or not it was planned this way, and whether or not the "piercing" of the shogun's ritual world worked for anyone other than the commoners, this was the place the commoners held in the machi-iri.

There is also what might be called an *ugachi* order and quality of time. The shogun's gaze, recall, was eternal. Like the "art of no blinking" that the noh actors themselves practiced, the shogun's tranquil observation of the full noh play saw into the fullness of the eternal past, without the insertion of any break or blink that might divide up this eternal temporality and allow for the emergence of different times. In contrast to this, the *ugachi* view was temporal, fleeting, even saccadic, as if composed of brief, blinking views. *Ugachi* views were premised on the idea of only a quick but nonetheless penetrating glimpse, unlike the studied contemplation of the shogun. This of course was

---

136. It was explicitly stated that one must look from the side (*soba*), or even from behind (*ura*). See Jo Nobuko Martin, *Santo Kyōden and His Sharebon* (PhD Dissertation: U. of Michigan, 1979), 52.

the way in which the commoners were allowed to watch the machi-iri noh performances. They were effectively placed in a position of visual and temporal interruption. They were allowed only partial views of the stage and of the shogun; they could see only part of a full program of plays, and only occasional glimpses of the shogun (when he chose to have his side screen raised, to allow them brief views of himself); and within these moments their glances are described as flitting back and forth between the stage and the shogun.

Furthermore, the *ugachi* perspective, and the "eyes" that these townspeople brought with them to the machi-iri performances, always were closely allied with the view toward profit. In this case, the townspeople most likely (I do not have clear quotes to confirm this) looked forward not only to the performance and to the gifts that they would receive at the time of the performance, but they also most likely looked forward to the monetary remuneration that they would receive some days after the performance. This desire for and look toward a future repayment ruptures the idea of any fully immediate time of repayment, or full value. One might oppose this interrupted vision and time to the shogun's (and the noh actors') eyes which saw, without a moment's pause for thought, the "qualities of Gold"—eyes which seemed to directly, immediately, and completely see into, and thereby unite with, the eternal time of pure value.

Accordingly, in the *ugachi* view of the commoners, one finds the same emergence of durational and future-oriented time that has been encountered in other contexts. It entailed a different set of values, and not only saw the shogun from a different perspective, but also carried the structure and flow of time (and value) out and away from the confines of the machi-iri grounds toward a future, monetary return. In these ways it was a mode of vision, and of time, that was qualitatively different from the shogun's.

One might even argue that within the machi-iri performance space, the emphasis on bodiliness and on the instability—even decadent instability—of bodies, reappears in this context. The physical conditions of the fenced viewing area themselves seemed to emphasize this: the "seating" area was intentionally covered with rough gravel, and spectators were not allowed to bring in cushions; toilet facilities were inadequate and a constant source of discussion; and the area was crowded enough that the jostling and shoving of bodies was also a problem. None of this would allow for the comfortable, speculative contemplation enjoyed by the shogun and other officials and the transcendent "swooning" appreciation that went with the officials' view, and all of it would in very concrete ways reassert the grounding of the spectators' vision in material bodiliness. This too is the way it seems the shogun perceived this commoner audience. Whereas quotes from the townspeople with regard to the official audiences indicate a spectatorial and consumerist attitude (seeing the shogun as a one-*mon* doll on display), quotes from the officials reveal a perception of the commoner audience as a space of crude and decadent physicality. In contrast to the elegance of the shogun, the typical person of mention is, for example, the "yellow-toothed woman." These spectators are described as "vulgar" (*biro*, 尾籠), their cries to the actors and to the shogun are lewd, and under these conditions, the noh becomes a place where one "cannot imagine a serious or austere [*genshuku*, 厳粛] spectator."[137] The smell of urine is prevalent.

This latter, corporeal aspect of the machi-iri noh could easily be overstated, and I do not want to push it too far. But it does further underscore the impossibility of seeing the machi-iri performances as constructing a single, unified subject of vision, at least in any simple way.

In sum, within the larger ensemble of audiences in the machi-iri, there were at least two general kinds of "eye," with two different kinds of flows of value, time, and desire. The shogun's eye was the unified gaze of a specular mirroring. Like the moments within a noh play when the full image of the moon was clearly reflected here on earth, as an indication of union with the world of the divine past, the shogun's full-on view of the noh actors and of the "mirror board" (and the eternal pine tree painted thereon) was a position of complete reciprocity with that divine past.[138] This was also the sight of, as Zeami put it, the "Peerless qualities of Gold": in economic terms, this would seem to be the equivalent of the natural value of rice discussed in Chapter 2, and the belief in the unbroken exchange between past and present of fixed value. The shogun's line and quality of sight thus placed him in the position of unmitigated reembodiment of unchanging value; he therefore is the basis of all economic and moral value. This line of sight is then hierarchically graduated, such that lower officials are given increasingly oblique positions from which to view the stage. These lines, or flows, of sight are furthermore reinforced by the actual pathways of gift exchange: lower officials have indirect pathways set between themselves and the stage, along which they must travel in order to exchange robes and other gifts with the actors. The shogun alone

---

137. These quotes are reprinted in Yokoi Haruno, *Nōgaku zenshi* vol. 2 (Tokyo: Wanya Shoten, 1938), 394.
138. This in some ways is reminiscent of the "divine mirror" of late medieval Christianity, in which only perfect truth was reflected. See Jay, *Downcast Eyes*, 32.

has a direct path, and separate stairway, between himself and the stage, so that he might literally have a straight and unmediated path of exchange between himself and the world of the noh stage. Everyone participated in this specular order of vision and exchange, even if by increasing levels of exclusion and incompleteness.

The commoners, along with being placed in a still more oblique point of vision, were nonetheless physically bracketed off from these paths of exchange. They could see the stage at best only from the side, and the shogun only when he was willing to lift his screen. They had no path of exchange whatsoever either to the stage or to the official viewing rooms, and insofar as these gift exchanges (especially the exchange of robes, which would typically be put on immediately) implied a kind of exchange of embodiment, then the commoners were entirely excluded from this kind of embodiment by anything other than a spectatorial relation. But their eyes looked toward a different kind of value, with a different structure of temporality. They were given gifts, including the piles of coins, the *sake* wine bottles, cakes, and so on, but these were placed within their fenced compound and by the castle doors beforehand or from elsewhere. That is to say the gifts were placed there, but not brought there by any path of exchange that would break the barriers between the two spaces. Furthermore, along with these gifts, the townspeople looked toward a future moment, when, outside of the castle, they would receive an additional monetary repayment (often in fact gold). The flow of exchange, and the time of fulfillment of value—even, in a sense, the flow of affect[139]—is thus in contrast to the eternal unbroken flow of exchanges that constituted the shogun's gaze. Like the townspeoples' line of sight in the machi-iri performances, the structure of time here is broken, durational, and saccadic (and assuming a return or fulfillment located in the future), and it was presumably with these eyes, and these values, that they looked at the shogun and at the noh stage. By these terms, the commoners were participating

139. It is not that these flows for the townspeople are somehow blocked off from the shogun completely and instead redirected out toward the coins they will receive later, outside the castle. In many ways both the commoners' obstructed path toward the shogun, and their view toward future monetary repayment outside the context of the castle, are part of the same kind of interrupted affective "flow." The townspeople did of course have some real affection for and desire to see the shogun. This view they had of the shogun—in particular, the "peeps" they gained of him—and the desire it involved, might be compared to the erotics of the *nozoki* "peep" shows that had become so popular at the market fairs of these same townspeople. In both the *nozoki* peep show booths and in the townspeoples' view of the shogun there was a real flow of desire, or affect, but it was at the same time in both cases always blocked off, with real fulfillment always postponed to some later place and time.

in an order of vision, value, and time that was very different from that of the shogun. The performances did not consist of a monocular space.

It is also important to note that along with the apparently two different kinds of desire here—the shogun's specular desire for stable value and ritually fixed form versus the commoners' desire for monetary and consumerist reward—there was an overlayering of two different modes of power: power as force (as in the shogun's ability to command the townspeople to buy tickets for and come to the machi-iri; and power as reception (playing, that is to say, with consumerist desire, both to see spectacle and to gain monetary return). The coercive power of the state (and the power of production) here already meets the coercive power of mass culture (and the power of reproduction).[140]

Returning to the discussion of vision, if one does acknowledge that there were these very different ways of seeing going on at the machi-iri noh performances, it might be tempting to then ask, which eye, and which structure of desire and affect, was *really* operative in the machi-iri performances? Or at least, which was more operative? These questions then would go hand in hand with the problem of whether the townspeoples' mode of vision was or was not effectively contestational to the shogun's eye, the shogun's values, and the shogun's power. In the end, these are questions which I do not think are all that productive to ask. These differing "eyes" were all operative, including along lines that could be contestational in some ways and effective modes of subjectification in others. I have been more concerned to show that there are convergences, and it would seem that these convergences themselves could work both for and against the shogun.

Especially, it is the confluences within these converging forms that are important to an understanding of how, or if, the Tokugawa world cohered *as* a world. Although it is not as clear in this context as I think it is in other contexts already discussed, there are confluences in these two modes or types of "eye" as well. While I have tried to show how each looks toward a different kind of value, and this implies different forms of temporality, different modes of desire, and so on, each, first of all, in some way needs the other. Both, furthermore, seem to have the same longing for a moment or instant of fulfillment—a moment outside the mobility of duration—in a structure that no longer seems certain of that possibility.

---

140. In some ways there is a parallel here to the conjoining of attitudes of religious, "ritual" devotion on the one hand with touristic spectacle on the other, that was described in Chapter 1 as encouraged both at the shoguns' shrine at Nikkō and in the machi-iri noh performances.

Times and Visions of the Instant / 249

This section has not addressed the modes of seeing in the kabuki theater, but the problem of confluences of vision is apparent in elements from the world of kabuki. The best example raised here may be the *nirami* look, considered to be the most powerful form of *mie* (the frozen instant interrupting a kabuki play). As noted above, unlike the usual cross-eyed *mie*, the *nirami* consisted really of two looks at once, with one eye crossed, and the other eye looking straight. As has been described, the *nirami* was an especially important moment of mediating worlds, both in kabuki plays and in prints related to them (see Figures 1 and 2). It is also possible that the two looks it combined constituted a unity of the two basic visualities outlined here—the shogunal gaze and the commoners' *ugachi* (or more simply the kabuki *mie*, a related stance). This would be the ultimate act of power, and it may be that this is why the act of *nirami* was associated with power. The term *nirami* itself also meant, "to command respect."

In the machi-iri, those moments when the shogun lifted his screen to allow the commoners a peep at him, were, for him, the moment when his position of transcendence was spectatorially recognized and thereby fulfilled. That is why he needed the commoners there on the first, "weightiest" day of the machi-iri shogunal investiture performances. At the same time, for the commoners, these peeps were more than just the unfulfilling erotic glimpses they might get at the *nozoki* peep shows in their market fairs. These may also have been, firstly, moments of *ugachi*-like perception—a brief look from awry that is precisely the look of complete knowledge. Even without that, it would seem that at the level of visuality, one glimpse of the shogun truly was a fulfillment of sorts. Here it becomes almost like the moment of "seeing profit"—the frozen but intense instant of kabuki's *mie*, that breaks the narrative temporality of the play yet also transcends it. And to the extent that this was indeed an *ugachi*-like moment of penetrating perception, then it is directly tied both to the Edokko's defiant act of looking *ugachi*-style at the golden dolphin on the shogun's castle roof, and, by extension, to the Edokko's act of absolute expenditure (spending all of one's fortune in one night) that held the promise of a momentary transcendence of capitalist time.

More simply, the commoners' point of view could both participate in the shogun's ritual gaze, helping to confirm it as transcendent and ubiquitous, while also opposing it—but still recognizing the shogun as leader, even if only in the more secular valuation of a commodity world. In the same way that the ostensibly natural value of the rice-based economy could only effectively operate in conjunction with the general equivalent of money, the shogun himself could only be an absolute, ritual ruler (which he therefore to an extent truly *was*) through the theatrical view of this absolutism as just a spectacle. This interaction of worlds of vision is apparent in occasions like the machi-iri noh.

Thus, the moment of confluence or convergence between the two different lines of vision—the same moment which confirms the shogun's position of transcendence—this moment is also the point of possibility for seeing something else. For the shogun, it was the ability to bring all these perspectives together within the single space and time of the machi-iri noh performances in Edo castle, and thereby to negotiate these differing perspectives rather than to impose one over the other, that put him in the position of power.

Movement, Flows, and Capitals of Value

It is tempting to compare the melancholic inward-turning world of the noh plays—plays which seek perfect unity with the past by turning toward a twilight "dream" world—with the early Tokugawa shoguns' decision to radically regulate flows between their country and the outside world, in what came in the nineteenth century to be called the policy of *sakoku* (鎖国, closed country; *kaikin* and other terms were used earlier). It is in dream worlds, perhaps, but especially in melancholic inwardness, that one can seek complete knowledge and control. Separated off from the wider world of history and materiality, but also from an older belief in connection to the divine, this dream world is potentially an inner site of utopic perfection. This comparison of the noh's often melancholic dream world with the shoguns' policy of tightly controlled borders would be complicated to argue for in concrete terms. At the very least, one can say that there was a dream-like, ghostly quality to the Edo era. One might point to the dream-portrait of the first shogun, Tokugawa Ieyasu, revered by succeeding shoguns, as expressing the foundational importance of this dream-like quality, with perhaps the melancholic elements of disembodied lack of, and yearning for, an impossible presence. The policy of closing off much of the world with new borders, too, was part of the underpinning of the new state. It was not as if Ieyasu took an already constituted state and then simply decided to close it off to the wider world. Here too it is almost as if these acts of perfection were premised on something like a melancholic attitude. The noh, after all, with all of its melancholy, was part of these same state-making gestures. This was the "melancholy" of an already secularized image of divine rule, and of an economic image of natural value that worked only in relation to the capitalist money form of general equivalence.

At risk of confusing the analysis provided already, this final section looks at some of the ways in which the aesthetic form seen in noh and kabuki was also, in very practical ways, built into the rhythm and order of Edo-era daily life. In this case, the emphasis is more on general aesthetic tendencies—an opposition between clear rational organization versus a use of dark secretiveness, for example—than on the specifics of noh versus kabuki.

The noh that I have described here was a specifically Edo-era aesthetic creation, and this aesthetic was formed within the context of the Tokugawa shoguns' larger attempts to organize and maintain the new, early modern state of Japan. Whatever the shoguns' strategic needs and conscious intentions, the noh presents us with what might be thought of as gestures of history: by this I mean real, historical forms and enactments, which also embody and materialize in their form notions of history, of change, of time, and of social value. These "gestures" may be real flows of goods, or people, inscribed on the physical geography of the state (indeed in some ways thereby giving body to the geography of the state). But they are also flows of value and desire, as well as notions of material fullness or emptiness, that are inscribed onto and as the bodies of people themselves.

The rigid choreography of movements in the noh all would seem to accord with the economies of movement (straight lines, grand open vistas leading to those in power; regularity, etc.) associated in the West with baroque state power,[141] and then more clearly still in the early modern national orders of power typified by Haussmann's Paris. These qualities can be seen in the noh's emphasis on smooth, unbroken flows of the body (feet which slide in always unbroken contact with the stage, except for final "demonic" moments; hands which move only in slow, graceful patterns; eyes which gaze into an unchanging imaginary distance, so that the mood of a mask is consistently maintained); the preservation of regularity and conformity in movement; and predictable, cyclical repetition in time.

In the shoguns' new state one can also think of the great open highways built across the country to guide the great processions of lords and the traffic of noh actors between their home provinces and the new capital, and to bring goods and tribute directly to the foot of Edo castle; similarly one might point to all the regularized cycles of people and performances spread throughout the state, as described in Chapter 1. Or one might consider the

---

141. See for example Lewis Mumford's discussion of "The Structure of Baroque Power" (especially on "Movement and the Avenue"), in *The City in History* (New York: Harcourt, Brace and World, Inc., 1961), 367–371, ff.

first-ranked noh plays, required for all official, "ritual" situations. The route that *Takasago* maps, for instance, right from the opening:

> Unfolding long, the Miyako [capital] road
> Unfolding long, the Miyako road
> calls us forth today; waves lap the shore
> and ship lanes lie at peace, while spring's mild airs
> waft away the count of passing days.
> Behind us and before, clouds hide the path
> that stretches on and on, until at length . . .
> . . . we have arrived.

And as the twin pines from opposite shores and opposing ends of time unite, at the end:

> For God, for Sovereign, the road runs straight
> to Miyako in springtime,
> when the dance is "Home to the Palace."[142]

Even fourth- and fifth-category plays at times allow for this possibility of clear and straight paths that lead directly to the capital, and the place of pure value—as in *Kantan*, described earlier. In that play, at the point at which the *shite* has apparently found the "Hall of Eternal Life" and place of "purest gold," he is urged to first drink the Elixir of Immortality; then and there, all times flow together, as the chorus sings of a "feast of meandering waters" (*kyokusui no en*, 曲水の宴):[143]

> "O pass the cup, I say,
> that clear, chrysanthemum waters
> speed on down the stream, till eager hands
> dart from sleeves gay with chrysanthemums
> to pick it up again: a swaying dance
> of graceful, sweeping gesture, as of light . . .
>
> Never shall these blessed waters fail,
> flowing as they do from healing springs

---

142. Translations here from Tyler, *Japanese Noh Dramas*, 281, 291.
143. A kind of poetry party practiced among the nobility, and a scene common to noh plays, in which the participants sat along a stream bank and, as a cup of sake rice wine floated downstream toward them, had to quickly compose an appropriate poem before picking up and draining the cup.

that yield all their bounty, without end.
O how they gush forth, with might renewed!
One who drinks, savours the dews of Heaven . . .
as pleasure merges night into bright day.
Happiness, delight, brilliant success:
all these here attain their pinnacle.[144]

In the previous section, too, we have seen that the shoguns' own gaze followed a similarly uninterrupted flow toward the noh's originary, true "Peerless Charm," and "qualities of Gold." Even knowledge and secrecy are defined by these terms, insofar as ritual plays like *Yumiyawata*, and to a lesser extent *Takasago*, were described as "without curves," or "without secrets," meaning that the narrative followed an orthodox and predictable structure, as "known" by the shogun and the heads of the noh schools.

All these straight lines and smooth flows were thus very much part of the shogun's aesthetic economy. Even the waterways that crisscrossed Edo were constructed by shogunal mandate, and in some cases led directly to the castle (high ranking daimyo, too, constructed elaborate gardens that ideally included an area for incoming tides to flow directly into the landscape). These may look like the open, linear, and rational order that characterized Haussmann's reorganization of power in early modern French city form. But especially as seen in ritual noh, the clear lines of sight and travel were more divine than secular or rational, and more part of a transcendent eye of the gods than a panoramic perspective of a merely human ruler.

Yet I have tried to show that these flows were also the foundation of the merchant economy and the "floating world" of kabuki. If the tide flowed into samurai gardens, kabuki actors used the water to literally float into the theaters on ornately decorated boats for opening day performances. The opening day, too, was called *norikomi shonichi* (乗り込み初日), or *noriuchi* (乗りうち, "getting on board," or "embarkation"), as if the entire time of the performance run was a period of "floating." As part of this experience, people would often rent boats on which to party, and float to the theaters.[145] The same system of rivers and canals that brought goods to the shogun was used to develop the remarkably intricate and very well-organized merchant econ-

---

144. Tyler, *Japanese Noh Dramas*, 139.
145. In one diary from the late Edo era, a writer describes boating to the theater as "the most wonderful thing you could do; it was like floating on air." Cited in Hidenobu Jinnai, *Tokyo: A Spatial Anthropology* (Berkeley: University of California Press, 1995), 100.

omy. Most banks of the canals and rivers were lined with warehouses and shops, and river traffic was congested with the flows of commodities. These shops themselves were often thought of as temporary and transient, and the goods that were ferried between them were known to travel with great speed. Thus, the waterways constructed by the shogun laid out an economy of time, space, and value onto the shogun's castle-centered cities that was very different from the shogun's own economy. The same is true of the great, state-traversing highways built by the shogun to allow for the annual processions of daimyo between the capital and their hometowns. The paths laid out to create and maintain absolute control of the lines of connection between capital and province, according to a controlled cyclical time, and for a kind of display based on sumptuary notions of hierarchically fixed wealth, proved to be ideal for the development of another economy altogether. They encouraged the rationally organized flow of goods of consumption, which created wealth for lower classes, along with market-oriented structures of time, and the flows of different, more consumerist types of desire. The very same structures of clear linear connections laid out by the shogun accordingly could also be part of a rational and even Haussmann-like world of secular control and ungrounded capital flow. In this case, two worlds neatly overlap in the same gestures of infrastructural state-making.

There consequently was an overlayering of economies in the physical landscape, much like the double layering of time described above in the play *Sukeroku*. These were flows of different economies, and different value orientations, but they often were literally following the same structure of roads and paths.

The shogun did not rely on the straight open vistas of the large highways, or of the ritualized gazes alone, however. When planning the new city of Edo, the original idea was to indeed use a classic grid structure patterned after the very early imperial Heian capital (Kyoto). Based on still earlier Chinese models, this grid model was meant to embody an "ancient," godly cosmology—so it would still fit with the ritual structure of clear lines that were somehow divine. But city planners then reconsidered, thinking that a spiral plan would instead more easily allow for ongoing growth, and also offer protective barriers to the center. The very opposite of clear sight or divinely rational control, this was a new structure of barriers, secrecy, and secular guards. It furthermore was constructed using canals, which were themselves used for mercantile trade. This was not a matter of one idea of the city winning over another, however. Rather, the shogun chose to keep the early grid

Times and Visions of the Instant / 255

plan, and simply superimposed the spiral plan over it (see Figure 9). The shogun's capital city was hence constructed in such a way as to combine an early, divine cosmological structure with a newer form with no claim to ancient orders, and only an openness to change.

The capital city of the Tokugawas in this way consisted of the same uneasy position between a claim to absolute presence of the past, and yet an acknowledgment of the impossibility of that and the need for something else. The haunted quality of that condition is visible in perceptions of the city, too. To cite just the most obvious example, the description of the pleasure quarters as the "floating world" (*ukiyo*, 浮世) was, as is well known, a double entendre. It referred to the happily "floating" quality of capitalism and all the pleasures in this world that money could bring, but it also referred to an earlier, Buddhist term (*ukiyo*, 憂世) referring to the sad emptiness of this world. This was not a replacement of one term by the other, or a complete parodic redefinition (though it is at times referred to that way in scholarship). The sense of sad-

Figure 9. Grid and Spiral Form of the Capital

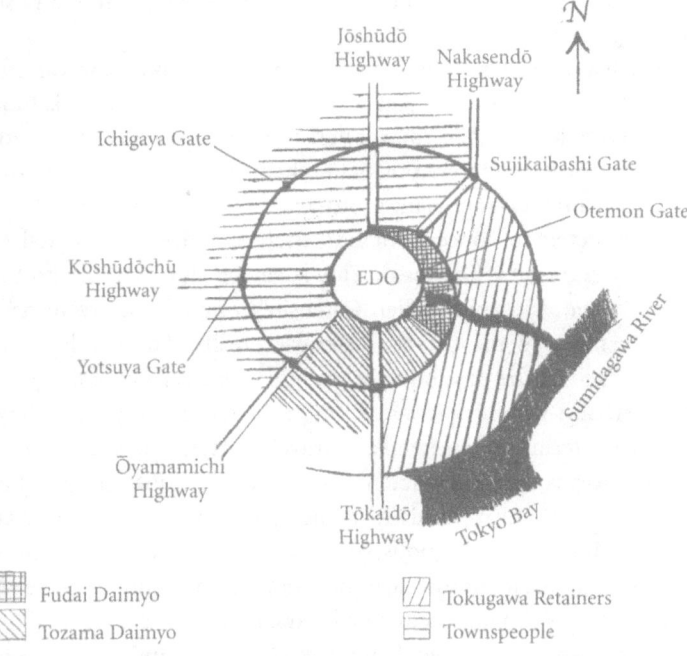

Adapted from Naitō Akira, *Edo the City That Became Tokyo*. Tokyo: Kodansha, 2003, and "Planning and Development of Early Edo," in *Japan Echo* Vol. XIV, Special Issue (1987).

ness, and of ghostly emptiness, continued to be a critique of the socioeconomic conditions of the pleasure quarters throughout the era. In many ways, this parallels the common, melancholic attitude of ghostliness that one sees throughout much of Edo noh and kabuki.

Some of the same aesthetic traits that define Edo-era theater thus also apparently pervaded daily life, as well as the design and experience of the city that was at the center of that life. Conditions such as the well-ordered lines of the highways cannot be reduced simply to a determinative reading as either modernist rationalism or divine cosmology. These same conditions gained a kind of doubled materiality, based on what was at least a doubled set of orientations, or valuations. One might think of the capital city of Edo as itself composed of two contesting poles, or capitals, of value: the shogun's castle (with the noh) as a center of official, semidespotic authority and power would be one, and the pleasure quarters (with the kabuki theater) as a point of attraction and mercantile power the other. This has real explanatory power, and is in a sense true. Like the opposition of the rice economy and mercantile capital, or the aesthetics of ritual noh to the structure of kabuki, there clearly were opposed views of the same geography, from different positions within this geography.

But it is worth another reminder that *all* people in the Edo era to varying degrees participated in *all* of this. Samurai not only sneaked into kabuki plays, they also wrote them, while commoners were not only attending shogunal noh performances, they were practicing the noh themselves (and buying samurai status with their merchant profits).

So it may be better to conceive of Edo itself as indeed *the* capital of Japan's early modernity, albeit doubled. This is similar, for example, to the kabuki play *Sukeroku*, discussed earlier. Ostensibly one of the preeminent expressions of the townspeoples' values, *Sukeroku* is really a "double-layered" play, entailing in its form the possibility of reading it as a parody of the noh's focus on the past, and yet also reconstructing that past in very traditional fashion. By the same terms the *michiyuki*, or travel scene, that is basic to both of these theatrical forms and leads each narrative form to a different point of redemption (the noh of course finds it in the epic past, and kabuki in an unknown future), thus is an ambiguous, or "double-layered" (*nijûsei*) icon of Edo-era narrative; one could almost take this *michiyuki* as a model for reading the experience of the shogun's actual highways. Edo itself, as capital of the shogun's order, was composed of overlapping temporalities and structures of value, and *that* is the real capital form of the Edo era.

This chapter has considered the problem of value orientations, and aesthetics, especially in terms of structures and qualities of time and temporality—and, literally the vision of such. This includes differing notions and qualities associated with the idea of change, differing ideas of "now"-time, and more broadly, differing ideas of the way in which time might be fully experienced—that is, the means by which the full experience of and involvement in time (time as meaningful experience) might be achieved. While the early modern state in Japan may have been comprised of different temporalities, each of which had a different vision of the moment or point of redemption (a different view of the "capital" of time)[146] wherein "true" experience might be had, both nonetheless resulted in a notion of time as durée—a time of durée-as-repetition, in which the realization of meaningful time was forever deferred, or precluded. Time itself thus became ghostly, from both ends. This is a problem of both the time of fulfillment (the noh's more epic form of time, which seeks simply a reembodiment or fulfillment of the time and values of an epic past) and the time of transformation (a more capitalist time, which depends on the ability of capital value, in time, to transform, so that it produces more than itself). Here, the two meet.[147]

If one were able to give a definitive attitude of Edo-era social and historical conditions, melancholia and the aesthetics of the sublime would seem to be close—these are attitudes built into and loosely definitive of the material world of Edo Japan. As explained in Chapter 3, melancholia helps to explain

---

146. The idea that there might be a "capital" of meaningful experience is evident, in the most concrete ways, even in Zeami's writings. In *Kakyō*, for instance, in writing of an actor's abilities, he states first of all that the only place of worthy evaluation is the capital, and further, that if one should leave the capital, one will inevitably fall away from meaningful appreciation—leaving the capital will result in "a stagnation of experience," which "must be shunned" (Rimer and Yamazaki, 95). Literally, to be in the place of value, and of meaningful experience, is to be in the capital.

147. It may be worth noting that the haunted quality of time in the Edo period does not result in a more modernist sentiment of nostalgia. The desire to get "back" into meaningful time was a desire to get *into* a meaningful time in early modernity—not back to some prior early modern Japan. This is just as true of the noh, which arguably depends on a more nostalgic structure of desire. Thus, in the shoguns' basic ritual play, *Takasago*, the ultimate epiphanic moment of unity with value comes in the final dance, as the chorus sings of what is usually translated as a "return to the palace" (or, "back to the citadel"; *genjōraku*—for example, see Hare, *Zeami's Style*, 102). But in fact in the Edo period, any reference in these last lines of *Takasago* to a "return" was considered taboo, and a more appropriate translation would be Tyler's, whose lines read "Home to the Palace"; it is, in other words, a simple arrival, to a point of origin which is immediately present.

the atmosphere of noh, as a world that may entail loss or lack of full presence, but nonetheless does not involve resorting to a nostalgic desire for some other, prior origin. Instead, there is an identification with this world, despite its lack of completion. The same can be said of the shogun himself, as central authority, especially as figured by the dream-death portrait of Tokugawa Ieyasu. Ostensibly the divine anchor of the entire Tokugawa realm, he could not fully be a god; although worshipped as the eternally present founder of their world, he was present more simply as a dream figure. The portrait itself, one might argue, is what the shoguns themselves were about: a representation that is for the most part *only* a representation of a god, implying the death of the possibility of real reembodiment of absolute or divine value.[148]

That "melancholic" atmosphere, or condition of less-than-full presence, is furthermore visible in central elements of Edo life already described: in the shogun's shrine at Nikkō, which depended on both religious worship and secular sightseeing; in the split of Edo castle from the shrine at Nikkō as seats of Tokugawa potency; in the machi-iri performances, which were rituals depending on theatrical spectacle; and of course in rice as a partially transcendent general equivalent of economic value and the grounding of an only loosely stable flow of people and social positions.

It makes sense, therefore, that the sublime was the most appropriate aesthetic mode in the context of Tokugawa power, and the most adequate definition of transcendence in the Edo period. However much Tokugawa power may have been based on an urge for absolute boundaries and total mastery—an assertion of will and state power as absolute—absolute power itself was not a true possibility. In an era that was already separated from the sacral immobility of pure, whole, and transcendent value and time, the grounds for that kind of absolutism was for the most part gone. The sublime emerged in the empty image of a more spiritual and truly divine presence. It served as a mediator between a post-theological but nonetheless epiphanic form of transcendence.

That is why ritual plays like *Takasago* were not enough for shogunal noh, and do not by themselves explain the aesthetics of Tokugawa power. *Takasago* may have been in a word "clear"—without any secrets—and a narrative of

---

148. As conjecture, it is worth considering that the portrait, as a representation of the death of pure godly presence—and even of the death of Ieyasu himself—borrows that very magic of death rather than being just a "dead," empty sign of Ieyasu. That quality of death then could become a mediating factor between a fully bodied image of power, and one more ghostly. Taussig makes a similar argument. See *The Magic of the State*, 94. This might also be thought of as enhancing the commodity value of the kabuki actors' *shini-e* death prints.

absolute and divine legitimacy. But *Sekidera Komachi* in many ways made better sense of the Edo-era form of power and quality of time. *Sekidera* still retains the figure of the divine, but it is caught in a temporality of endless and repetitive longing and desire. *Sekidera's* transcendence, as we have seen, arrives not through a return to the divine, but instead through the interrupted moment of "astonishment" and "pulverization." It arrives not through the completion of divine time, but via instantaneous transcendence of ongoing time. *Sekidera's* aesthetics thus are predicated on an alienation from the divine, and a ghostliness, and the play instead uses the secularized moment of awe as the only means back to transcendence and power. The congruence of this mode of transcendence and this temporality with Tokugawa power is indicated by the privileged "weight" given the play by the Tokugawa shoguns.[149] Not only was *Sekidera Komachi* considered the most "sublime" of plays, but so too the machi-iri performances for investiture of a shogun and the "once-in-a-generation" public presentations such as the Kōka noh were called sublime.

This chapter has focused on ways in which aesthetic discords were expressed in the Edo era especially as problems of temporality. Both melancholia and the sublime can be viewed as conditions of time. The problem of power and the possibilities of difference in early modern Japan were therefore tied to these tensions of temporality. Temporality, though, remained of course not only tied to spatial orders, but also consisted of modes of value, and qualities of materiality.

It may be evident that the conflict of times was, first of all, a conflict of historicity, or of histories. This should be clear in the two play types favored by the shogun (as seen in *Takasago* and *Sekidera Komachi*): it is as if there are two different notions of history at work. The ritual plays like *Takasago* present a character who returns to us from the past to say that there is in fact no departure at all—or at least no absolute return—and so there is in effect no history. The latter-category plays like *Sekidera*, on the other hand, present the story of a failed return; in that limited sense, at least, they are stories of the intrusion of history, and history as excess. The shogun may have claimed

---

149. The rulership patterns I describe are generally true not only of the shogun, but also at lower levels of "central" power. Other, powerful domain lords were using the noh in similar ways, and privileging the same kinds of plays. To give just one example, records from the Sendai daimyo Yoshimura clearly show licenses granted him for the learning of the sacred ritual play *Okina*, but also what were called the "secret" plays *Sekidera Komachi* and *Dōjōji*. A very brief translation in English from one of these records (the *Sarugaku-den kuketsu no bensho*) is in Nishiyama, *Edo Culture*, 183.

a position of divine transcendence for himself, beyond history, but this image was created from within an already secularized time. Furthermore, the shoguns needed this historical time, or at least they had to acknowledge its presence in the everyday understanding of life, and so they needed to work with this as well. Thus the shoguns not only privileged nonritual plays like *Sekidera*, they also brought the commoners in to the first and most important day of shogunal investiture noh performances, so that they could acknowledge the shogun's engagement in ritual time with their own more everyday time of spectacle and history. In the machi-iri performances, the shogun relied on history in this way, even if the time of history was being used to retrospectively reaffirm the shogun's image of transcendence. And the shogun, accordingly, himself embodied (or became the place of) views of time that were at once ritual and historical.

In more formal and fundamental terms, there were tensions in the conditions of experience and power that defined the worlds of noh and kabuki. As described above, both worlds met in a structurally similar problem of repetition (experience falling into a temporality of meaningless repetition) and transcendence (finding a point of meaningful fulfillment, and full or embodied materiality). The problem of repetition and transcendence was thus figured in the Edo period as a double problem, with one temporal orientation (the noh's) forming an endless duration that could no longer attain the past, and the other (kabuki's) a duration that could not ever attain the future.

The framing of power and of difference in Edo Japan therefore could not so simply be a matter of opposition, in which (as is often portrayed) the values of kabuki would be in contest with the values of the noh, and one would merely have to decide which one wins.[150] It was certainly not a case of kabuki being liberating vis à vis the noh, as if kabuki somehow reveled in losses, temporal excesses, and the inevitable failure of the past to equal the present, and this would then constitute a real enlightenment[151] in the face of the noh's false claims to epic values. Nor was it a matter of "double consciousness," as Gilroy,[152] Rowlands, and others have argued for, wherein one has the feeling that the world is divided, and there are two whole, separate worldviews often from two sequentially different historical eras that meet up—and

---

150. This is a line of argument that goes back at least as far as Shively's otherwise still useful article, "Bakufu vs Kabuki."
151. Enlightenment here meaning, as Mumford put it, "freedom and the re-establishment of the dignity of man." (Mumford, ibid, 345.)
152. See for example *The Black Atlantic*, (Cambridge, Mass: Harvard U.P., 1993).

Times and Visions of the Instant / 261

in the meeting, revealing the contingencies and artifices of each. Rather, the noh and the kabuki theaters formed two concurrent worlds which were separate, but which met under structurally similar contradictions of value formation in the same historical moment.

This is not to say that the Edo era was, finally, one big shared conceptual space. To the contrary, the era was made up at once of very different temporalities, as well as very different value systems. But at the same time, an understanding of the era must include an understanding of the way difference involved a point of mediation—what Peter Osborne, after Benjamin, calls a "switch between circuits"[153]—between these different times and values.

Ultimately, in an era in which rigidly bounded identities and ordered cycles are founded on ghostly repetitions and incomplete materialities, transcendence of these empty repetitions can only be found in the instants, or moments of astonishment, or interruption and breakup, that both the noh and kabuki held out as the most valued points in time. These moments, as a means of transcendence, *do* apparently work for power, including state power.

But transcendence is not the only issue. Part of the basic description of this power was the ability to enact the mediations, or "switches between circuits," successfully, and so to *maintain* layers of identity. One can point back to the discussion of the kabuki play *Sukeroku*, in which the fundamental heroic characteristic of the title character is his capacity to assume to his person a whole set of identities and times, and the various and in some cases competing value orientations that these implied. The samurai character's weakness was defined through his inability to navigate any of this kind of "depth" of character. His impotence was not a result of his being a samurai, but rather his unidimensionality—his inability to be anything other than *only* a samurai.[154]

The great public machi-iri noh performances, as I have tried to show, similarly were moments in which differing orders of vision, time, and value were brought together, and negotiated by the shogun. Within his own space of the castle grounds and the time of the machi-iri noh, the shogun brought together different temporalities (including the epic focus on a traditional

---

153. Peter Osborne, *The Politics of Time* (New York: Verso, 1995), 151.
154. This makes a political statement of sorts, giving potency to the world of the commoners and the pleasure quarters over the ruling samurai class, and to the kabuki theater over and against the noh. But this is not simply because of Sukeroku's ability to defeat Ikyū the samurai in sword fights, in love, or in any other simple contest of identity.

past and a temporal narrative that instead looked toward an ever distant future); different economic values (for example, the use of rice versus the use of capital as modes of measure); different ways of seeing; and even different modes of power and subjective identification (the power of command versus a mass culture-like power of spectacle; and, in association with these, the devotional identification with a leader who is a divinity incarnate, versus the consumerist, or touristic mode of identification with a flamboyant spectacle). All this came together as a strategic organization of visual orders, or "eyes." The machi-iri was not the homogenous perspective space of subjectivity, or rule, that could be seen in the West, or in the writings of Shiba Kōkan.

If the machi-iri noh performances constituted in any way an epiphanic experience, which brought together very different orientations of value and transcended their contradictions, then these experiences of transcendence and even epiphany were also experiences of the state. In effect they were experiences of the shogun's power.

Nonetheless, it is just as important to keep in mind that these were encounters of real difference in orientations and regimes of value. One should remember that, first of all, the Edo era and the Tokugawa state really were made up of multiple and contradictory times and value orientations. Because power seems to have lain in the capacity to accrue and negotiate these differences rather than to wholly impose one mode over the others (and thereby impose a simple homogeneity), the state form was built on a multiplicity of affiliations and allegiances to these different regimes of value.[155]

Secondly, moments such as the machi-iri noh may have created a sort of ritualized moment of negotiated transcendence out of these different affiliations and their contradictions, but at the same time moments like these created opportunities for things to be renegotiated, for people to see things differently, and for reevaluation. They were opportunities for a different

---

155. These multiple affiliations are more complicated even than just a conglomerate of class differences that each have their own value orientations. For example, it was not just a matter of bringing together low-class merchants, who generally were capitalists, with upper-class samurai, who generally were part of the rice-based economy. Instead, even these class and economic affiliations were layered and mixed. I have already pointed out that some of the best writers of the "low" literature of the pleasure quarters, of kabuki plays, and of capitalist practices were from families of the samurai class. Similarly, merchant class families also worked to add, through purchase, samurai status to their family identities. These were not, therefore, singular and exclusive solidarities.

experience of, and a different way of identifying with, the state and state power. Thus, although public performances such as the machi-iri noh were surely rites of power, they were also potential sites in which one might see the transformation of power.

Put in more formal terms as a problem of time, while these "instant" moments may have returned some kind of transcendence, at the same time, especially insofar as they were real interruptions, they did create the possibility of interjecting a time of truly meaningful experience into the structure of time-as-repetition, and accordingly a fuller material existence in time—and with it the possibility of difference, and of change. This would more truly be a time of history,[156] and here—in the confluence of these moments and instants generated from within both noh and kabuki rather than in their simple opposition—is where history as much as power in the early modern period lies. In a context such as this, therefore, change as well as social and political opposition should be sought *within* those moments of power and transcendence as much as from outside or elsewhere.

---

156. Materiality, in other words, in a secular, linear idea of history might be thought of as tied to the time of real change, and hence to the intrusion of history; materiality in a way *is* being in the time of history.

5

In the Event: The Kōka *Kanjin* Noh Performance of 1848

The 1848 performance was a truly unique event. With an overall ticketed attendance documented at 57,721, it was by far the largest of any noh performance ever, and at least by this standard, one of the most successful such shogunal expressions of power of the Tokugawa reign. It was also, however, the last such event.

As described in the introductory chapter, for the shogunate this period was a time of catastrophe. Punctuated as well by a series of natural disasters, it was a time in which control of the state, and of society in general, was rapidly and finally falling out of the shogun's grasp.

In the Kōka performance, therefore, one can see a moment of catastrophe, with an event marking that moment of catastrophe, but an event that was meant to overcome the destabilizing elements of the moment. Was the performance therefore really an event? That is, an event in the sense of something that truly inaugurates real change, and difference? Or was it instead a further, successful development of the Tokugawa order of things?—was this noh program an event that brought a time of rupture and difference back into the order of official, ritualized repetition?

Catastrophe generally implies a calamitous time of destruction, ruin, and fragmentation that would indicate at least the possibility for a real historical break, and for something truly new and different to arise. From this perspective, the general conditions of 1848 as well as the Kōka performance itself would inevitably be read as a fundamental break. But catastrophe also means, as in Webster's, "the culminating event of a drama, especially of a tragedy, by which the plot is resolved" In other words, it could also be interpreted as an "event" that finds its meaning entirely *within* a given narrative

266 / Visioning Eternity

structure of time or of history, and furthermore is precisely the moment which *gives* that narrative its closure, and meaning. In this case, the catastrophe would be a very different, nondisruptive form of historical event, which in fact provides narrative closure and meaning rather than disruption and difference.[1] Thus, like the very definition of catastrophe—and like the possible structures of history visible even within the structure of the noh itself—this moment and event of the Kōka performances might be thought of in at least two different possible ways—as either rupture or recuperation.[2]

Context: Changing Economics

The Tempo-era (1830–1844) economic crisis that formed the background context of the Kōka *kanjin* noh performance was only the latest in a series of such crises, and economic practices had in any event been transforming throughout the Edo era. The complex interrelationship between the shoguns' stated sanctioning of an exclusively rice-based economy on the one hand, and a practical dependency on the structures of capitalism on the other, was if anything still more evident as the era progressed.[3] In the Kansei reforms enacted toward the end of the eighteenth century, one can see both continuing attempts to maintain a "natural" economy along the traditional lines espoused by the shogunate, and new attempts to utilize mercantile capitalism as a means of reasserting control for the shogun and for domainal lords.

For example, late eighteenth century responses to economic distress included apparently traditional, conservative steps toward the kind of natural economics sketched out in Chapter 2. The chief minister, Matsudaira Sadanobu, ordered recent immigrants to city areas back to their rural villages, and in theory back to agricultural production. Moves were also made

---

1. For example even if the time was seen to be disastrous, the Kōka performance might be understood as having celebrated that moment as the kind of melancholic or sublime ending that the noh, and the Tokugawa state, had incorporated in its orders of space and time all along; evidence for this is ambiguous. But more simply, the event was meant to mark the overcoming of the ruptures and invoke a broader reconciliation (just as noh plays incorporate dissolution and destruction into their larger cycles).
2. Implicitly connected to this question of the event is the matter of whether the performance was a successful theater of power. If, for example, the program truly reasserted the same old order of official ritualized time, with all the social forms implied by that kind of ritualized order, then certainly it should be thought of as a successful theater of power. It revived the general order of things, and form of value, that helped form the basis of the shogun's power.
3. It should be recalled that this interrelationship went back to the very start of the Tokugawa regime. As mentioned earlier, even the first Tokugawa shogun was using a merchant as one of his principal advisors at the same time that he was formulating the rice economy.

to weaken the merchant guild monopolies, and thereby the power of the merchants. Attempts were made to control the fluctuation of monetary value through controls placed on interest rates, on rent, and elsewhere, and currency itself was strengthened through a recoinage that increased the proportions of precious metal—that is, an increase in the "natural" value of the currency.

Yet at the same time, Sadanobu's reforms selected out certain major merchant houses to be the shogunate's fiscal agents; it was only through the merchants' networks that the shogunate could lower the cost of transporting rice and other goods and services. Furthermore, by the late eighteenth century the capital city of Edo had transformed from being an importer and consumer of goods from Kyoto and elsewhere, to a central producer of economic as well as cultural life. Increasingly, it would seem that the shogunate had to rely precisely on being a central economic producer and arbiter in order to maintain its own centrality of power. But in order to maintain this kind of centrality, the shogunate had again to rely on merchant structures. Hence Sadanobu's reforms were meant to encourage local production and sale of goods by local merchants, and this in turn only further strengthened the merchant economic structures.

By the early nineteenth century, many of the outlying domains no longer were following the shogunal orthodoxy of reliance on traditional agricultural production. Many were active in developing not only new crops and new agricultural methods for increased agricultural production, but also new industries and capitalist practices. Typically, this was done in collaboration with merchants from the castle towns.

By the early 1840s, new economic reforms were announced. Initially, these reforms were once again designed to turn back what was recognized as a general shift away from agriculture. Orders forbidding villagers to engage in nonagricultural work, or to seek such work outside the village, were repeated annually from 1841 to 1845 (the same time when applications were being made for the Kōka *kanjin* noh), though to little effect.

Other methods of control were then attempted, but more through involvement with the mercantile infrastructures. The shogunate gave new emphasis to the further development of production of local goods in the eastern region around Edo, and to the marketing of these goods in Edo, thereby furthering a new kind of centrality to the city. At the same time, the shogun withdrew support for routes from Osaka and elsewhere. Furthermore, the monopoly privileges that had been given to select, chartered trade

268 / Visioning Eternity

associations to distribute goods was abolished; this may have hurt certain merchant houses, but it set up the possibility for the shogunate itself to play that role. Orders were also issued, in 1842, for the domains as well to dissolve such trade associations, although not all domains followed through on this. Some, like Chōshū and Satsuma—domains that would eventually rebel against the shogunate—worried that the shogunate might be setting up its own monopoly trading system or even be moving toward a form of statewide control of commerce, and so instead strengthened their own systems. So new contests for power between domains and the shogun emerged, but these contests were now increasingly being fought through the practices and structures of mercantile production and distribution. The shogunate in particular was setting out new possibilities for reterritorializing and recentering its own power, through a new utilization of, rather than a simple rejection of, these structures and practices of mercantile capitalism.[4]

The general economic context of the Kōka *kanjin* noh performance thus involved new kinds of mediations between what were supposed to be opposed modes of economy, for the creation of an accordingly new kind of political centrality. But let us return to the way the performance itself was structured.

The Kōka Performance: Event of Repetition?

The Tokugawa shoguns had continued to use the kinds of official practices of the noh outlined in Chapter 1—practices which utilized the noh to mark moments of change and bring them back within a cyclical temporality of repetition—and they maintained these practices with remarkable consistency throughout the entire length of their three-hundred-year reign, right up to the very last shogun. In this sense, the Kōka program was indeed perhaps the final, majestic, and validating culmination of that structure of repetition.

In many ways the shogun's organization of the Kōka performance seems to have dramatically reenacted the same sort of gestures seen in the actions of the very first shogun, Tokugawa Ieyasu. Actors were called from each of the

---

4. During this time the bakufu was also, however, still trying to restrict the relative attractiveness of industry and trade as opposed to agriculture. This is only a very simplified summary of complicated economic changes. For more, see Sydney Crawcour, "Economic Change in the Nineteenth Century" in Yamamura Kozo, ed., *The Economic Emergence of Modern Japan* (Cambridge: Cambridge University Press, 1997); Maurius B. Jansen, "Japan in the Early Nineteenth Century" in Jansen, ed., *The Cambridge History of Japan* vol. 5 (New York: Cambridge University Press, 1989); Hayashiya Tatsusaburō, ed., *Kasei bunka no kenkyū* (Tokyo: Iwanami shoten, 1976); and Nishikawa Shunsaku, *Edo jidai no poritikaru ekonomii* (Tokyo: Nihon hyōronsha, 1979).

In the Event: The Kōka *Kanjin* Noh Performance of 1848 / 269

official noh schools, and from major provinces around the country,[5] to make the journey in to Edo as participants. All were expected to obey without question; as one actor put it, it was "an important bakufu duty."[6] Already, here, one can see the same kind of gestures of geographical unity and obeisance that Ieyasu had first put into practice. Furthermore, Kaga, the domain to which Ieyasu had paid greatest attention because of its status as the most powerful *tozama* domain, was again made the center of attention. The grounds on which the Kōka performance were held were owned by the Maeda family of Kaga, and the principal actor of the whole program was himself an affiliate of Kaga, and after the performance retired to that province. It was as if the shogun, in 1848, wanted to return not only to the old form of state unity, but also to the old lines of alliance and allegiance.

The image of unity was emphasized in other ways as well. Official documents comment on the "infinite variety" of people who attended: not just the shogunal or the imperial officials, nor just the merchants, but Confucianists; Western-style physicians; Shinto priests; Buddhists; renga poets; and others. *Everyone*, in other words, was united within the confines of this *kanjin* noh— as one document put it, this was a "momentary convergence of high and low"[7]—and this made it, according to yet another report, "an unparalleled greater Edo success."[8] A similar attempt at all-inclusiveness can be seen in the plays themselves: in the course of fifteen performance days, approximately ninety noh plays were presented—almost half of what had by then become a canonic repertory—and over half of all the kyōgen plays were included. All play types were represented.

The Kōka *kanjin* noh was thus a place of unity, of having *all* the world together within those confines (just as the poetic structure of the noh seemed to claim the eternal inclusion of all time). Ieyasu's advisors' view of the noh as a performative aesthetic in which the "mindset of monetary profit must

---

5. For lists of some of the provinces, see Omote, *Nō kyōgen* I, 144, and Ejima, ed., *Kōka kanjin nō to Hōshō Yūkan* (Tokyo: Wanya Shoten, 1943), 38.
6. Document published in Ejima, ed., *Kōka kanjin nō to Hōshō Yūkan*, 40. This indicates not only that actors were doing this for the shogun as much as for the main actor of the Hōshō school, in whose honor this performance was ostensibly being held. It also shows that rivals were meant to come together in obeisance to the shogun; the Kanze school was the principal rival of the Hōshō school in seeking the top position of patronage from the shogun. In this somewhat rare case, the Hōshō school had been privileged by the shogun over the Kanze school, but the Kanze school was expected to perform nonetheless.
7. Quoted in *Kōka kanjin nō*, ibid., 30.
8. See Ikeuchi, NS I, 271.

not arise"[9] is also still apparent in the Kōka noh. The shogun, as I have mentioned, gave the majority of the proceeds to the principal actor of the Hōshō school. Additionally, before the performance, some tickets were distributed without charge to people in every section of Edo; the government itself had already paid the fees for these tickets, directly and formally to the Hōshō actor, and the government then distributed these tickets on clear weather days to the townspeople. This may have helped to generate interest and assure good attendance figures for the shogun, but it also changed the dynamics of the shogun's relation to consumerist or capitalistic order of values, including monetary gain. If nothing else, it appears to indicate more of a concern simply to have as many people in attendance as possible, and less of a concern with demonstrating the participation of a separate, capital-oriented segment of the population. And for the most part, the majority of tickets appear to have been sold on an equal basis, with each person simply paying for whatever they chose to see.

The Kōka performance itself might accordingly be seen as a utopic construct, emblematic of the larger Tokugawa order. Within the very high-walled confines of the performance grounds (see Figures 1 and 2),[10] representatives from provinces throughout the state, from all social classes and all religious and intellectual outlooks, "converged" before the shogun. This would give the appearance, at least, that within this enclosure all of Tokugawa society assented to the shogun's order of things. While not composed entirely of just one value form as a true utopic space would be, it was approaching a homogeneity.

In terms of the way the people actually watched the Kōka performances—and the shogun—the layout of the audience was similar to the machi-iri performances described in the previous chapter. However, there were some fundamental differences. The shogun's room, or *zashiki*, was on the second floor of a large structure of viewing rooms set up across from the stage. The second floor was the most honored position, and the shogun's room was directly across from the stage with lower ranking rooms extending to his left, as with the machi-iri performances. The first floor was for still lower ranks of officials. Immediately in front of the stage were "boxes" bounded off with bamboo: these seats were not as official as the two-floored *zashiki*, but were still for people of the upper class (or wealthier people: here

---

9. Cited in Ikeuchi, ibid., 437.
10. Unless otherwise noted, all figures in this chapter are from the *Hōshō taiyu kanjin nō no maki*, held at the Edo Tokyo Museum. A second copy exists at the Hosei University Noh Research Institute.

Figure 1. Exiting the Kōka Performance Grounds

From the *Hōshō tayū kanjin nō no maki*. Courtesy of the Edo Tokyo Museum.

Figure 2. Kōka Performance Grounds (Entrance)

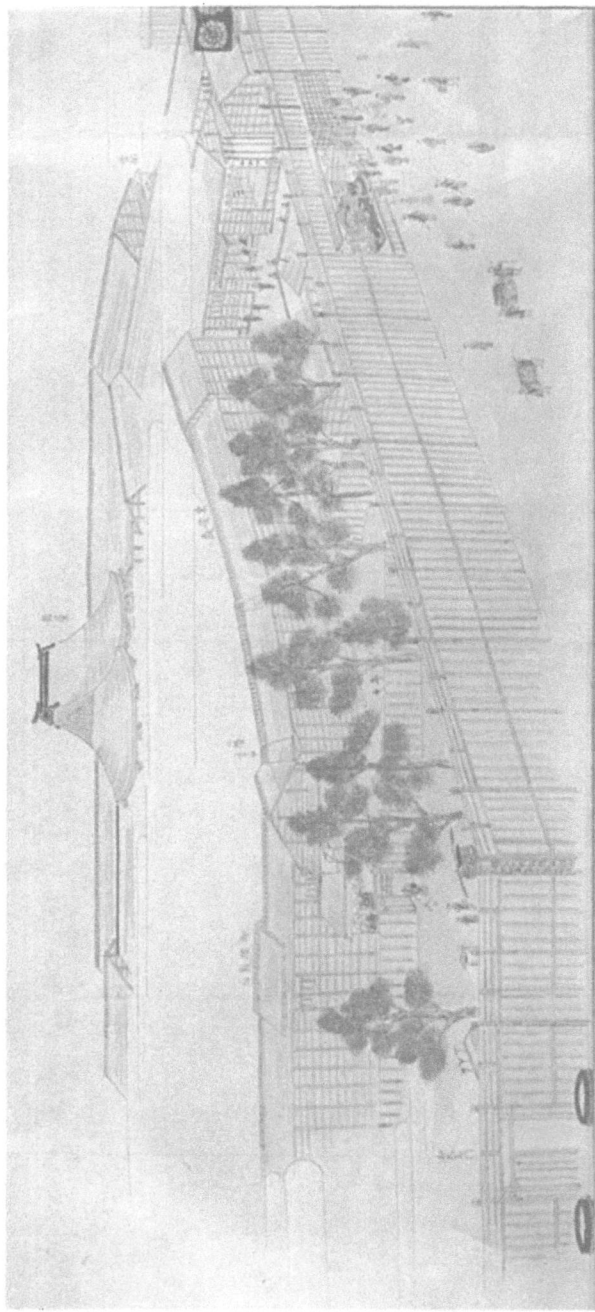

From the *Hōshō tayū kanjin nō no maki*. Courtesy of the Edo Tokyo Museum.

the distinction begins to blur). This area was also roofed. The cheaper section for commoners consisted of a fenced off area, not roofed, between the boxes in front of the stage and the officials' *zashiki* across from the stage (see Figures 3 and 4). So the commoners were again in an intermediary and more "temporary" area, and as with the machi-iri performances, all nonofficial spectators were said to have enjoyed looking at the display of the officials as much as the performances on stage. Thus, in this sense too, one can see that while the *kanjin* noh was ostensibly being held in honor of the head of the Hōshō noh school, it was certainly also about the display and affirmation of the shogun's position.

Even if the convergence of all social groups before the shogun was "momentary," it was a moment that could reposition the late Edo-era time of rupture back within the closed structures of time that the noh had been used to mark for so long.[11] It furthermore brought back many of the same old modes of allegiance, and possibilities for difference, at a time when those lines of allegiance and possibilities for difference were themselves changing in such a way as to imply a full breakdown of the shogun's order.

Without going into the smallest details, it is clear that the shogunal officials in 1848 were using the noh to bring a moment of great historical disruption back within the fold of the same repetitious cycles of spatial and temporal closure that could be seen even in the earliest Tokugawa uses of the noh. They furthermore were doing so in a radically conservative way, insofar as the Kōka program reenacted the same gestures, with the same order of value, as the first shogun. To the extent that all this came about, the Kōka noh as an event can itself be viewed as having effected a form of history very much like that seen in the noh theater's temporal structure (at least the first-category, ritual/god plays): a ritually repetitive time that indeed incorporated the present into a "fulfillment" of the values of the past.[12] From this perspective, the 1848 performance was a culminating moment of Tokugawa history—of the Tokugawa form of history; the shoguns in this view were remarkably successful in creating a very specific form of society, which embodied a very specific mode of time (cyclical), and of change (based on the image of fulfillment rather than transformation). Further, one might

---

11. This may be why the shogun decided to change the reign name midway through the Kōka performances.
12. Ritual repetition does not necessarily mean no change at all. In this case at least it implies a notion of change, but it is a mode of change that leads to fulfillment, not to transformation of a social identity.

Figure 3. Kōka Seating

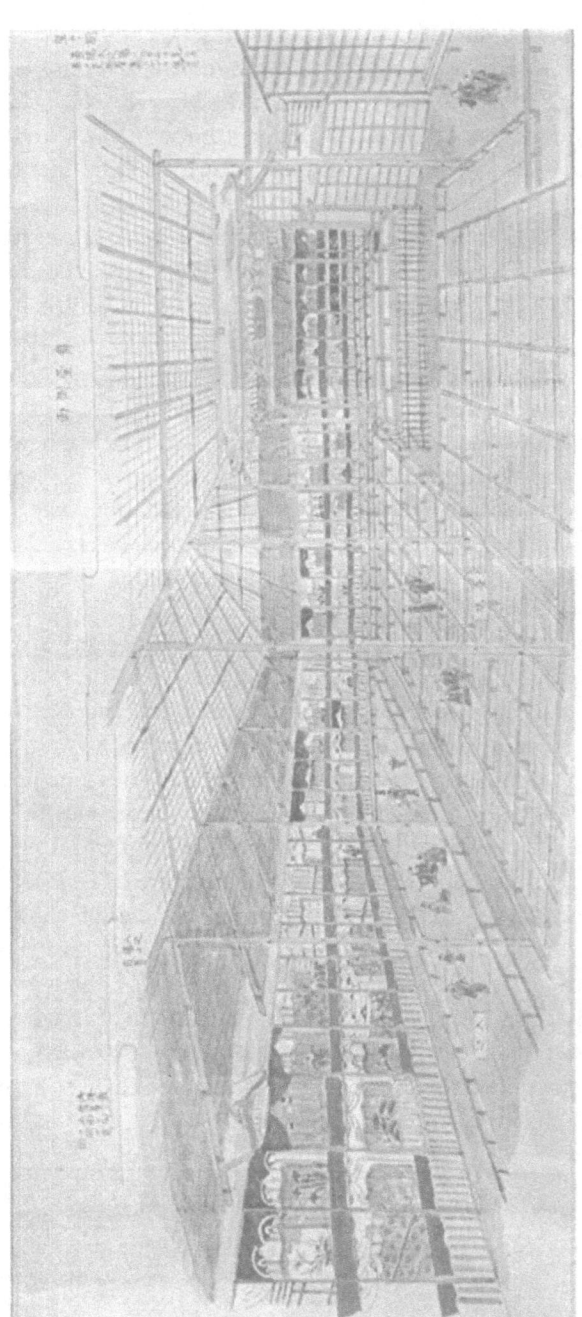

From the *Hōshō tayū kanjin nō no maki*. Courtesy of the Edo Tokyo Museum.

Figure 4. Kōka Seating (Official Rooms at Rear, Intermediate Area for Commoners, Front Box Seats)

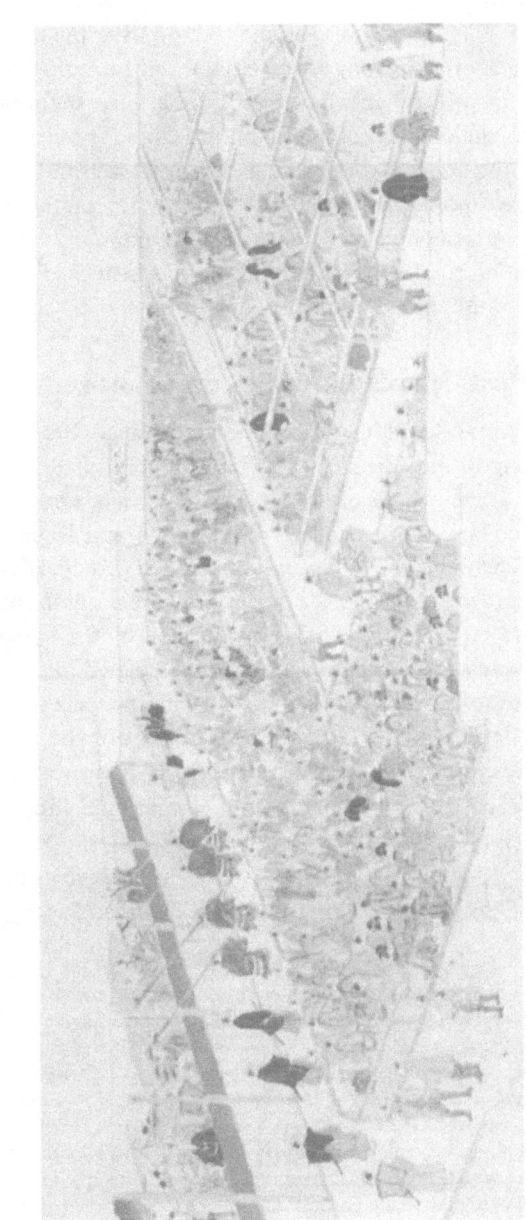

From the *Hōshō tayū kanjin nō no maki*. Courtesy of the Edo Tokyo Museum.

276 / Visioning Eternity

even say that the Kōka performance itself truly achieved the founding, or perhaps recapturing, of an autonomous, authoritative space through the surmounting of time.

Finally, from this utopic perspective, the Kōka program might be thought of as turning an external event (a moment outside the authorized view of history) into an inward time. Like the Tokugawa rhetoric, if not always the practice, of maintaining a closed country—a country bounded off from the outside world, so that flows of space and history might not intrude on the ostensible perfection within the state's borders—the apparently unnecessarily high walls of the Kōka compound helped re-create an inward space of sociality into which all the historical exigencies then crashing around the shogun might not enter.

Context: Spaces and States of Enclosure

The physical architecture of the high-walled *kanjin* noh enclosure, and the turning of outside event into inward, controlled flows of time and value—these are indicative of practices and a kind of symbolic space which can also be seen beyond the confines of Edo-era machi-iri or *kanjin* noh.

The walled housing compounds that provincial lords built, both in their own provinces and in the city of Edo, are a significant example. These compounds consisted of enclosures formed by the surrounding row houses of retainers and by walls. Even relatively isolated lots would be walled off. This attitude of closure, especially along with the specific forms of gardens and the noh stages which nearly always were part of the gardens inside these compounds, created a semi-independent,[13] interiorized, even privatized realm and a space of transcendence not all that unlike the "instant" times depicted in the previous chapter.

By the start of the Tokugawa era in the seventeenth century, a wide variety of garden genres had been developed, and many of these garden forms

---

13. These permanent mansions were truly almost sovereign spaces under the control of each daimyo, even though they were within the space of the shogun's capital city—in some ways parallel to the way the individual domains retained some degree of sovereign independence within the space of the Tokugawa state. Yet at the same time, each mansion was built in ways very similar to the others, and each utilized the garden and in particular the noh stage in the same way—again, parallel to the ways in which the mode of power (and the orientations of value this implied) was becoming increasingly uniform throughout the Tokugawa state. Furthermore, because the noh was ultimately considered to be the shogun's rite of state, by using the noh theater all were in effect abiding by the shogun's rules of social and political interaction.

were continued throughout the era. Nonetheless some generalizations can be made with regard to the typical house of a shogunal or domainal official; basically, their gardens were a mix of palatial aristocratic forms and the gardens of tea houses.

Palatial gardens tended to be carefully cultivated to include microcosmic references to an all-inclusive world. This included elements of longevity (such as evergreens) and of the fleetingness of time (annuals, deciduous trees, and so on), and as in the related "touring" gardens, attempts were sometimes made to include miniature references to all the famous places in the country; thus, these gardens were enclosed universes, with paths of controlled movement through these universes. At times, however, they utilized real scenery from the world beyond their walls—for example, views of Mt. Fuji—as part of their space.[14]

As they had developed by the start of the Edo era, tea houses and their gardens were still more enclosed types of spaces. The windows and verandas that had once been built into the tea huts were dispensed with, in favor of simple walls, and the gardens were not really meant to be looked at much at all; they were only part of the path to the separate world of the tea hut. The tea huts themselves were spaces of transcendence and even death. They seem to have been patterned after the early medieval Buddhist practices of rejecting the everyday world of humanity in general by retiring to remote mountain huts to live a spare, ascetic existence focused instead on the world after life.[15] The effect of a separated world was further enhanced in the tea huts by the small door opening, which required all to crawl in.

The tea ceremony garden was, among other things, referred to by the term *roji* (露地, or 路地). This can imply a kind of "Buddhist utopia," "a spiritual state of perfect selflessness and purity, a state away from the burning mansion of this three-fold world...."[16] In this sense too, then, the tea hut and garden were utopic spaces, and insofar as these were places for the tran-

---

14. Such gardens include the Rikugi-en, built by Yanagisawa Yoshiyasu, which contained the eighty-eight scenic spots considered to comprise the entire pantheon of scenic spots in the canonical traditional literature of Japan; the Hama Goten, built by Tokugawa Tsunashige, which also included four tea houses; the Toyama So garden, which included everything from rural houses to Buddhist temples and shrines mentioned in classical literature; and others.
15. Sen no Rikyū, revered as one of the founders of the early modern tea ceremony, thus wrote of the garden, "The tea garden is as a passage to a house deep in the mountains. Where there is no path, then the scenery should emerge..." Cited in Teiji Itoh, *The Japanese Garden* (New Haven: Yale University Press, 1972), 186.
16. *The Japanese Garden*, ibid., 183.

scendence of the cycles and circulations of life in general, they called up something like the notion of "death" described in the previous chapter. Here, though, the deathly transcendence would seem to have been in Buddhist form.

Yet as used in the Edo era, the term *roji* was not always a Buddhist concept—it could also simply mean a path, or way. Tea huts were not merely places of spiritual repose and selfless transcendence in the Buddhist sense. The tea ceremony in general was by no means a specifically Buddhist ritual, and so in this creation of a new kind of space of "deathly" transcendence that was not necessarily religious at all, the tea huts and gardens can be thought of as very much like the moments of transcendence depicted in the previous chapter as emerging out of the noh and out of kabuki.

In fact, even in its pre-Tokugawa time of incipient development, the experience of the tea ceremony was also closely tied in with the values of consumerist display (though this is not commonly acknowledged). The sixteenth-century warlord Nobunaga used his tea huts to display his expensive tea implements, as did the first Tokugawa shogun, Ieyasu. Hideyoshi's portable tea hut, which he carried along with his portable noh stage, was famous in part because of its gaudy display of wealth—the walls of the "hut" both inside and outside were entirely of gold. Hideyoshi too was proud of his expensive, famous-maker tea utensils, and put them out to be seen both in his tea huts and elsewhere; then, as now, the experience of the tea ceremony involved not only a spiritual transcendence, but also the appreciation of fine and pricey objects valued as commodities.

Large sums of money were also paid for stones that were well known, so that they could be part of the "beauty" of one's tea garden—as objects of monetary value. There are, for example, stories of thefts of such stones from gardens, and of illegal appropriations by higher ranking officials. In these ways the tea hut and garden may have constituted a utopic space, but it was one which incorporated a mediation of differing orientations of value, and a "transcendence" that was not entirely religious. Further research would be needed to back this up, but it may be that the overall form of the tea huts and gardens involved the same kinds of mediations of contrary value orientations, with a "deathly" transcendence out of the circulations of exchange implied by each orientation, that one sees happening in the public noh performances.

The samurai estate gardens with their noh stages, which brought together this kind of tea garden with the world-encompassing structure of the palatial styles, was just as much a space of negotiations. The gardens within the samurai villas were almost invariably built to include a noh stage, and the most elaborate reception rooms used to entertain the highest ranking guests were set up directly facing the stage. The structure and use of these stages largely reflects what can be seen in the more public noh event spaces. A "large" reception room (the *ohiroma*, 御広間) was built directly opposite the stage, and at the back of that room one often finds a painting of the pine tree, as on the "mirror screen" in the shogun's box at public performances. One author states that as audiences gazed in obeisance across the great room toward the lord of the house, who would sit on a raised platform, the pine tree "would have subsumed the figure of the [lord or shogun], creating an unmistakable visual equation between the personage of the [lord/shogun] and the everlasting power of the pine."[17] (Figure 5 is a Meiji-era print of this same mirror screen behind the shogun, in the interior of Edo castle, at an *utaizome* New Year's noh performance.)

Because spectacular paintings such as that of the pine tree were in the Edo era already thought of as within what we might categorize as bourgeois art—art as object of monetary value first and foremost—it is possible to think of this blurring of the shogun's figure with the painting as again accruing to the shogun a doubled, mediated form of power: both the divine figure associated with the eternal pine tree long considered a locus for the appearance of the gods, and a great figure embodying the power of wealth and money. But this is speculation.

At the same time, at least in the case of the shogun, lighting and customs of obeisance were apparently arranged so that audiences could not look directly at the shogun.[18] Furthermore, seating was arranged so that guests to the villas would have increasingly oblique views of the stage and the lord— just as in the public noh performances.[19] In all of these ways, noh performances within the private villas were used to set up the same kind of negotiations of visions, and social hierarchies and allegiances, and perhaps even

---

17. William H. Coaldrake, *Architecture and Authority in Japan* (London: Routledge, 1996), 151.
18. See ibid., 151, including the remarks from the late seventeenth-century visitor to Japan, Engelbert Kaempfer.
19. These arrangements were further formalized by the rooms used. In the case of the shogun, as in his castle in Kyoto (at Nijō), he used the larger and more formal *ohiroma* to receive the non-Tokugawa *tozama* lords, and the more informal, smaller *kohiroma* for audiences with the Tokugawa-related *fudai* lords.

Figure 5. Shogun's New Year's Noh Performance

Courtesy of the Edo Tokyo Museum.

orientations of value, that one sees in the official, public performances.[20] All within an enclosed, utopic space of controlled paths, controlled visions, and, as in the tea huts, transcendence.

The notion of closure in this context, from the emphasis on walls around the performance spaces and the samurai villas to the idea of a "closed" country *(kaikin, sakoku,* etc.), is a complicated one. Walls around gardens and villas became newly important in the Edo era at the same time as the early Tokugawa shoguns placed new emphasis on setting up barriers *(sekisho)* on roads throughout the country, and set up severe restrictions on the flows of trade and people between Japan and foreign countries. Large castle towns were even built around the perimeter of the main island, as if to create a physical barrier to the outside, and according to the *Nihonshi daijiten,* the *sekisho* barriers served among other things to set up a "wall" around the city of Edo.[21]

Yet trade with foreign countries under the first Tokugawa shoguns actually increased. Barriers within the country, and between Japan and elsewhere, were set up more to control flows than to create a truly enclosed and independent space. In some cases, even the idea of controlled flows seems to have been only marginally enforced in practice. At some of the barriers on major highways, for example, there were paths trodden from people simply walking around the barrier houses. Within the city of Edo, too, wooden gates were set along the main thoroughfares, but these served primarily just to create visual partitioning; they were only fully closed—if at all—at night. As has been pointed out, the Japanese term for a closed country *(sakoku)*

---

20. This use of the noh performance space for hierarchies of vision, etc., has a long history. As noted earlier, one of the more interesting cases goes back to the sixteenth-century castle of the pre-Tokugawa warlord, Nobunaga. His castle at Azuchi was then an entirely new architectural form, and not entirely built for military purposes. Projecting out into the space of a central atrium from the second floor apparently was a noh stage, so that angles of vision could be dealt with not only from the sides (the *ohiroma* reception room was also on the second floor), but also from below. This atrium, according to some scholars, may have been patterned in part after European cathedrals. For a now well-known debate on the overall architecture of Azuchi castle, see Naitō Akira, "Azuchijō no kenkyū," in *Kokka* nos. 987–988 (Feb-March, 1976), and Miyakami Shigetaka, "Azuchijō no tenshu no fukugen to sono shiryō ni tsuite. Naitō-shi Azuchijō no kenkyū ni taisuru gimon," in *Kokka* nos. 998–999 (March-April, 1977).
21. *Nihonshi daijiten* vol. 4 (Tokyo: Heibonsha, 1993), 185.

that is often used to describe the Tokugawa era in general was not coined until 1801.[22]

It is not, then, that the shoguns had attempted to construct a realm completely closed off to the flows of influence from the outside, whether it be trade with foreign countries, or even perhaps the demands of history. Rather they were creating the conditions under which these flows might be controlled,[23] and in such a way that the shogun was placed in the privileged position of mediator of these flows. Along with the Kōka noh event, the late Edo-era appearance of the term *sakoku* would indicate that if there was a desire for real closure in relation to an outside, it arose especially in the nineteenth century. If this was an element of the utopic gestures of the shoguns' noh in general, it was intensified here.

Negotiations

The public noh performances themselves were not simple presentations of a single set of values, even for the shogun, but rather were points of negotiation, of differing temporal, spatial, and social orders. A brief look back to the discussion of visuality will help to evaluate the Kōka *kanjin* noh.

In the official, public noh performances, there were basically two separate audiences: the assorted officials and the townspeople. These separate audiences were associated with different orders of visuality, and each of these orders of visuality entailed differing conceptions of value and differing temporalities. The epic, past-facing values of the archaic rice economy were part of the shogun's look toward the "pure golden" time of the gods in the noh, while the commoners for their part watched the shogun with their consumer-oriented visions of value. The temporalities associated with each of the two economies were part of these two visual orders, too. Just as the shogun's rice economy located the redemption of full value in a narrative of a

---

22. See Ronald Toby, *State and Diplomacy In Early Modern Japan: Asia in the Development of the Tokugawa Bakufu* (Princeton: Princeton University Press, 1984), 13; and Itazawa Takeo, *Mukashi no nanyō to Nihon* (Nihon Hōsō Shuppan Kyōkai, 1940), 145. Along with *kaikin* (maritime restrictions), other terms indicating closure that had been in use earlier include *tozasu*—closure in the sense of a door which can be or has been shut.
23. Thus when the early seventeenth-century shoguns restricted foreign trade to the bakufu-controlled port of Nagasaki, and principally to trade with the Chinese and Dutch, it was in order to ensure a shogunal monopoly of control over trade, rather than to shut it down.

return to an unchanging past, so the shogun's mirroring relation with the stage created a look that connected present back to that divine past, in a look characterized by the "quality of gold." So too, official audiences were expected to attend the full length of the noh programs, thereby involving themselves in the full, complete cycle of noh-time that entailed a return to and resolution with an epical past, while the commoners' attendance was broken off at partial segments. The future orientation of capitalism (finding redemption of full value in a future return), on the other hand, was part of the commoners' mode of spectatorship—they were encouraged to look forward to a different kind of resolution, even in simple practical ways, such as the monetary payment they would receive well after the performance date, and outside of the performance grounds. Thus their lines of vision were carried away from the space and temporality embodied by the shogun. In part, the shogun was, through the payment of money, negotiating a space of power for himself that gained approval as well from the capitalist order, even while claiming to keep that space free of capitalism. The ability to mediate, and perhaps layer together, such differing orientations was one of the characteristics of power. In all of these ways, the opposed temporalities and economics of the official rice-based archaic value of the shogun, and the future-looking trajectory of merchant capitalism, were both built into the context of the public noh programs.

These different visions of time and value were part of different modes of power as well, including traits of a divine despotism on the one hand and the spectacular attraction of something like mass culture on the other. Public, Tokugawa noh performances thus would seem to have been negotiating these modes of power and social ordering, too.

Even from fairly early on, then, not only was the Tokugawa state made up of differing understandings of space, time, and the "valued" forms of these, but these differing understandings were co-present and interposed within the official noh programs. Accordingly, to say that the public noh performances were attempts on the part of the shogun to just impose his "official" view of things on the wider world would be reductive, at best. The shogun did not seem to expect an absolute acquiescence by either audience to any single form or image of society. The shoguns utilized and even encouraged both of the forms described, and so if these noh performances enacted power for the shogunate, they did so only through this very negotiation of the two different narrative forms, and the points of conjunction between them.[24] This is in some ways parallel to what was happening in the kabuki theater. The ability to bring together and navigate between distinct worlds, rather than simply imposing one over the other, was the real grounds of power.

Taking all this into greater consideration, can one see in the Kōka noh a cultural and historical breach, a moment of real change? Or just a continuing, at most evolutionary and conservative development of the same old patterns of negotiation? How did it negotiate the times, as an event?[25]

In many ways, the Kōka program does appear to have redramatized what by 1848 was a classic, official format. As already noted, much of the overall organization reiterated even the first Tokugawa shogun's strategies. There was still at least some attempt on the part of the shogunate to continue the interplay of value structures seen in the machi-iri.[26] The shogun, for his part, continued his transcendent gaze into the eternal past, and, as part of this identity of past and present, the "mirror" board eternal pine trees were painted on both the rear stage wall and on the screen in the shogun's box (as evidenced in the official picture scroll—see Figure 6; the painting of the mirror board pine was celebrated with a special ceremony and payment, further emphasizing its continued significance). Meanwhile, for the commoners, the

---

24. This is therefore not quite the same thing as what Appadurai calls "tournaments of value." For Appadurai, tournaments of value are periodic events which, while having to do with the "central tokens of value in the society in question," and while having some consequence on the "more mundane realities of power and value in ordinary life," are nonetheless confined to very special times and participation is limited to those who are in power. The kind of interactions I am talking about were not simple "contests" of value. Also, while they were exceptional moments having to do with the representation of power, the interrelationships of differing orientations of value were nevertheless also part of the experience of society at large. See Appadurai, "Commodities and the Politics of Value," in Appadurai, Arjun, ed., *The Social Life of Things* (Cambridge: Cambridge University Press, 1986), 21ff.
25. There is some need for caution in making any comprehensive claims about the performance, partly because of the paucity of primary material on it (there is one official diary which reportedly discussed it, but the pages from the time of the Kōka performance are lost), and partly because, as a purely public noh held first of all in the name of the head of the Hōshō noh school, it was of a somewhat different order than the more official machi-iri noh. Nonetheless the shogunate invested greatly in it, and attached great importance to it after the fact. It may be significant that each of the great "once-in-a-generation" *kanjin* noh performances were held around the time of severe economic crises—that is, times of potential historical rupture. However this cannot be verified.
26. Some of these differences can be attributed to the differences in form between the machi-iri noh performances held within the castle, and the larger *kanjin* style noh performances. Machi-iri noh performances were, after all, still being held up to the last of the Tokugawa era. But the critical point is the investment of importance on the part of the shogun in this (*kanjin*) form, at this time in the era (1848).

285

Figure 6. Stage with Pine Tree Mirror Board at Rear

From the *Hōshō tayū kanjin nō no maki*. Courtesy of the Edo Tōkyo Museum.

recognition of a more consumerist, monetary vision was not entirely absent. Most were required to buy their own tickets.[27] Also, as with the machi-iri noh, the shogun provided moments for the commoners to look at him, and approve of him with the eyes of consumers—and to see the shogun and the noh with "the eyes of kabuki."[28] Accordingly, all of this would suggest the presence of some kind of continuing interaction and negotiation between the money-free values of the shogun and the more merchant capitalist perspectives of the commoners.

The basic form, and place,[29] of the shogun's traditional performative order in these ways persisted. Certainly by many standards it was a success, with a reinstitution of the official, traditional forms, and with the largest audience ever for a noh having come to this production.

But some of the actions taken by the shogunate were, if anything, reactionary attempts to return to an earlier, *more* "classical" and official form of the noh that in fact never really existed. For example, even though the organizers managed to cram in the great majority of what had become the canonical repertory of noh plays over the fifteen days of performances, *Sekidera Komachi*—the "weightiest" of all but also the play which hints so strongly at the inevitable impossibility of fulfilling the traditional cycles of time—was not included. In fact, already in 1808, the shogun issued an edict banning the performance of all ghost stories. This, furthermore, was at a time when ghost stories were reaching a new peak of popularity, both in noh and in kabuki;[30]

---

27. According to Ikeuchi, at least in some cases this purchase was considered only "temporary," with the price "of course" in fact refunded (Ikeuchi, NS I, p. 205). This would mean that the complex involvement with capitalism and consumerism seen in the machi-iri performances was still in effect at the Kōka *kanjin* noh as well. However, although documentation is scant, it appears that this practice was minimal, and most attendees were either simply given free tickets, or more likely bought them outright. See for example Ejima, *Kōka kanjin nō to Hōshō Yūkan* (Tokyo: Wanya Shoten, 1943).
28. 歌舞伎劇の目で能楽を見. Iura, *Nihon engekishi*, 1090.
29. After all, the shogun was able to get all these people to come to *his* performance grounds, as opposed to the kabuki.
30. As discussed previously, earlier uses of ghostliness, and images of death, were fundamentally part of the order—death being in some ways a means out of the ghostly failures of a true "ritual" cyclicity on the one hand, and capitalism's future-pointing times on the other. Death in that case is associated with a certain kind of eternity, which is beyond or outside of endless cycles of meaningless repetition. By the nineteenth century, however, ghosts seem increasingly to be indicators of the impossibility of even that "deathly" way out; ghosts are now deathly aspects of that failure, and hence a falling into the eternity of endless and meaningless repetition (again, both for the shogun's and for the merchants' economies—capitalism after all was also falling into terrible cycles of uncontrollable inflation). It may be these latter ghosts that the shogun was trying to exorcise.

the edict was largely ignored. At the level of aesthetic form, it would seem that the performance sought a more straightforwardly closed, fulfilled cycle of time, without the intrusion of any failure or break in that cycle.[31]

The machi-iri noh's differentiation of audience positions, both in relation to each other and to the plays, was similarly streamlined: although there may have been some attempt to give presence to consumerist values, the presentation of the shogun to the commoner audience was informal and minimal if done at all, and the practice of a future payment—and the temporal order that implied—was limited. Because tickets were distributed without charge, there was no need for repayment. Furthermore, all audience members—not just the aristocratic classes—were allowed to and expected to watch for the full length of the day's performances,[32] as if they were all truly part of the whole *jo-ha-kyū* cycle of time that underlay a full day's program. Nearly all the interwoven complexity and heterogeneity of the machi-iri seating organizations was absent, including the practice of having the three Tokugawa families (*Gosanke*) sit behind the stage and bow in obeisance to the shogun. One could additionally look beyond the performance grounds, to the space of the city. Prior to opening day, the shogunate took the unprecedented step of issuing edicts calling for the complete closure of both the misemono spectacles of the merchant market fairs, and all kabuki theaters in the city of Edo, for the entire duration of the Kōka performances (something which proved impossible to do with kabuki, especially given the several postponements of the Kōka program).[33] Hence at this larger, citywide level, it was as if the shogun actually was trying to cut out the presence of the capitalist merchant economy entirely, and to impose one single, monocular way of looking at the world.

All of these steps, however, were returns to, or reenactments of, something that never was. The single, unified cyclicities of the ritual style noh

---

31. It might be noted that *kaei*, as a classical Chinese compound meaning "eternity," also implies this kind of return to an earlier mode of time reckoning. It was certainly not unusual for reign names to express notions of eternal time (it would seem obvious that a reign name might want to indicate this), but other modes of time had appeared even in the reign names long before 1848. For example, in the mid-eighteenth century an astronomer by the name of Nishikawa Joken, under the patronage of the shogun, had managed to build an observatory and, on the basis of his calculations, issued a new and corrected calendar. At the same time that this new calendar was put into use (1754), a new era was proclaimed and named Hōreki, or "Treasured Calendar."

32. It was considered a problem that they did not; concern in particular was expressed that they were leaving early on, and wandering off to the kabuki theaters.

33. See *Nōgaku zenshi*, vol. 2, 389, and *Nō kyōgen*, vol.1, 144.

plays were always evident in shogunal noh, for example, and important, but never by themselves alone. The irony of some of these actions taken by the shogunate was that, in the reactionary gestures of a return to something that had never really existed, the effect was in many ways the creation of an order that, in its general form, was at least as close to the homogeneity, unity, and centrality of a new modernity as anything else.[34]

However, this still begs the question: was this then a successful continuation of the shogunate's order, and a status quo of sorts, as one might expect and assume of such a performance in a time of tremendous instability? Or was it in any way a moment of real change (did it have any of the dissociative force that one sees in the critical moments of recuperation within the noh plays), one in which one might even see other, new modes of existence?

Clearly it was both. The Kōka program was a successful, if momentary, enactment of shogunal power, which brought time itself, and Edo society, back into the performative mode of official noh. It served as a structured, but utopic, point of transcendence—a sublime instant, by the terms of earlier noh performances—in which a community of consensus emerged out of the immediate contradictions of history. Surely it was therefore a continuation and fulfillment of the noh's "eternal" order, and the shogun had good reason to declare the start of a new, if old, order of eternity.

Yet one can also see in it something fundamentally new and different. Despite the official importance of the performance, for instance, and in contrast to the attempts at closing down the kabuki theaters, some of the noh actors themselves for the first time took the remarkable and highly illicit step of going to kabuki actors prior to the performance for training in kabuki styles of acting (presumably to create a more popular dramatic form). Thus not only the commoners, but the shogunal officials as well ended up watching an aesthetic form increasingly distanced from the slow, "eternal" forms that had been developing over the course of their three-hundred-year reign. And despite the attempted preclusion of the aesthetics and values of kabuki outside of the Kōka grounds, these aesthetics were intruding into the heart of

---

34. In the case of the closure of the misemono spectacles and the kabuki theaters, undoubtedly there were more immediately practical concerns as well. This includes the possibilities that the Hōshō school might have asked the shogun to close the kabuki theater and related entertainments in order to ensure a bigger box office return at the noh plays, or that the shogun himself might have wished to ensure a larger attendance in order to bolster his own image. But these practical concerns are themselves part of a larger picture, and the specific ways in which practical considerations are organized make all the difference.

the official order itself. Hence, while the organizers may have left out the nonritualistic play *Sekidera*, the more classically structured "bread and butter" noh plays such as *Matsukaze* turned out to be box office failures, and the most popular plays were those that were also performed on the kabuki stage. The play *Dōjōji* was by far the biggest draw of any play, and this even on a rain-dampened day.[35]

Furthermore, if the commoners were given the traditional chance to see and evaluate—attach a general sense of worth, and implicitly, legitimacy as well as power to—the shogun during these plays, their appreciation seems to have changed. One patron is quoted as saying, "I thought I'd buy a ticket to see just once what it's like—but it sure is boring." Here, the view does not seem to have been worth the price of the ticket; it should be noted that the previously cited quote describes the shogunal officials as *only* one-*mon* dolls, a very cheap price. Or another: "This noh—it looks above all like something created a long time ago."[36] Statements such as these indicate not only that the commoners no longer would provide the high evaluation of the shogun that they once had in earlier, machi-iri negotiations of value, but in addition, they no longer felt part of that time at all. If this was in any way their canonical tradition, they felt increasingly distanced from it in ways which for them were uninteresting; there was no nostalgic longing in this distance. And it was the very fact that they were present at this performance, as the shogun wanted them to be, that brought about that realization.

Finally, in the Kōka production, the image and conditions of consumer capitalism became more integrally and fundamentally part of the enclosed space of officialdom.[37] On the one hand, as noted above, the machi-iri-style differentiation of consumerism and consumer-oriented groups from noncapitalist aristocratic classes was streamlined, and attempts were made to close the kabuki theaters as well as misemono market fairs. On the other hand, commodities of all sorts were sold *within* the Kōka compound walls, and to everybody, rather than being given out freely to just the townspeople. The official scroll and shogunal records went to some length to record and

---

35. The noh actors themselves seem to have understood the general situation quite well, and, also for the first time, the top actors did not play the roles in the "best" and most famous classic plays. They opted instead to take the lead roles in the more irregular, kabuki-like plays. See Yokoi, *Nihon engeki shi*, 1089.
36. Both citations in Ejima, *Kōka kanjin nō to Hōshō Yūkan*, 55–56.
37. In the same way, perhaps, as the shogun was then increasingly utilizing the infrastructure of mercantile capitalism in an attempt to reclaim centralized power.

290 / Visioning Eternity

depict these goods (Figures 7 and 8; these included tea, cakes, fruit, sushi, cushions, sake, bags for sandals; even labor contractors).[38] Consequently, the temporality of capitalism was no longer being used in the same way—there no longer was a deferral of capitalist desire to a place and time beyond the performance grounds, keeping it bounded off from those grounds in the way that had been done at the machi-iri noh. Now capitalist consumerism was itself, like the aesthetic style of kabuki, part of the enclosed and increasingly homogenized official center.[39]

In all of these ways, within the generally traditional format of the Kōka noh, a very different interposing of time and value also appeared. The confluence between two very different economies, discussed in the previous chapter as an "instant" moment when both come together, now seem to actually merge, to form a new, more unilayered center or capital.

Merchant capitalism now became wholly part of the same space and time that included the noh's "ritual" performance. The aesthetics of kabuki, while by legal edict banned from the pleasure quarters' kabuki theaters during the Kōka noh, now also became integrated into this official space. Further, if the commoners were increasingly seeing the shogun's eternal order of the noh as outmoded and of a time no longer related to their own, the shogun was himself similarly distanced: not only was the shogun watching increasingly kabuki-like performance modes, but—despite the transparent mirroring relation of past, stage world and current world of the shogun implied by the presence of the eternal pines on stage and in the shogun's box—it was reported that the shogunal officials in the Kōka noh began watching the actors through "field glasses" (*tōmegane*, 遠眼鏡).[40] These glasses, as technologies of vision that mediate between the eye and what the

---

38. See *Kōka kanjin nō*, 52.
39. Although a few of these practices may have been present in earlier once-in-a-generation performances, they are systematized here along with other gestures such as the closure of the kabuki theater and misemono marketplace. The central point is that this model of things was what the shogun chose to highlight and emphasize at this point in history.
40. Ikeuchi, NS I, 272. New modes of visuality more associated with the world of spectacle and consumerism began appearing in association with samurai classes elsewhere too. For example, in one remarkable scroll produced around 1840, scenes looking out on the world from within the residence of a domainal official were produced in a "peeping" format. Pictures in the scroll utilized different forms of flaps which, when lifted by the reader, revealed a greater view or "peep" behind a wall, window, or other object otherwise blocking one's view. On this scroll (the *Kurume hanshi Edo kinban nagaya emaki*), see Hara Fumihiko, "Kurume Hanshi Edo Kinban Nagaya Emaki," in *Tōkyōjin* 88 (January, 1995), 26–33; and Constantine N. Vaporis, "A Tour of Duty *Kurume Hanshi Edo Kinban Nagaya Emaki*," in *Monumenta Nipponica*, 51:3, 279–307.

Figure 7. Goods for Sale at Kōka *Kanjin* Noh

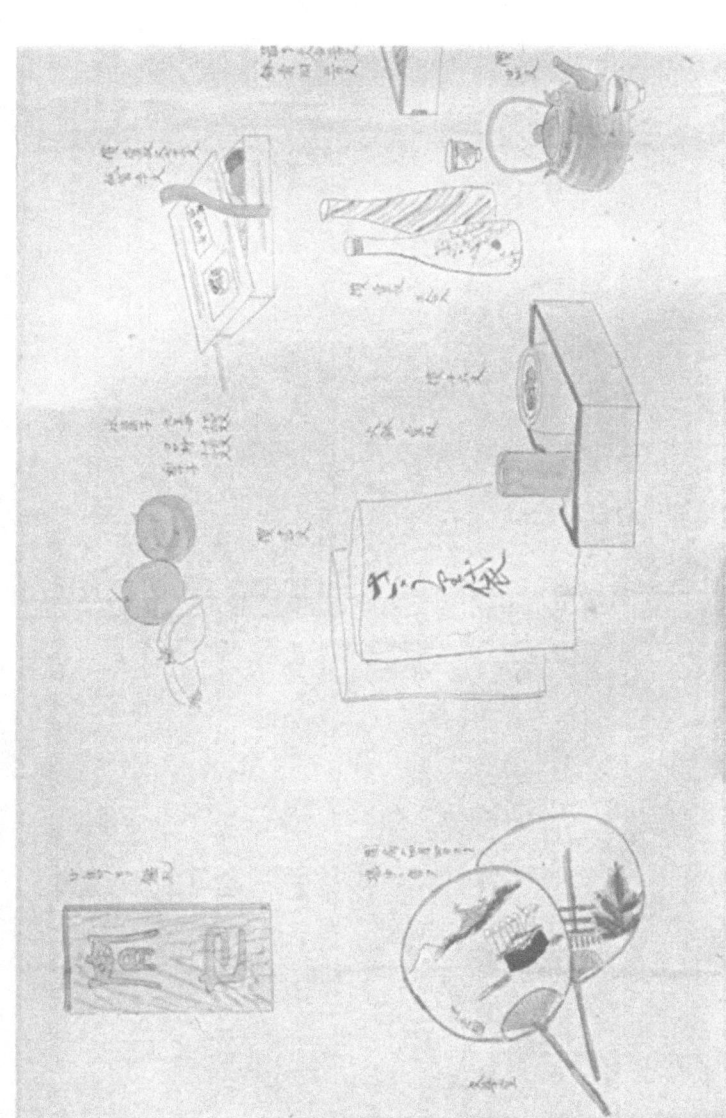

From the *Hōshō tayū kanjin nō no maki*. Courtesy of the Edo Tokyo Museum.

Figure 8. Stalls for Selling Merchandise

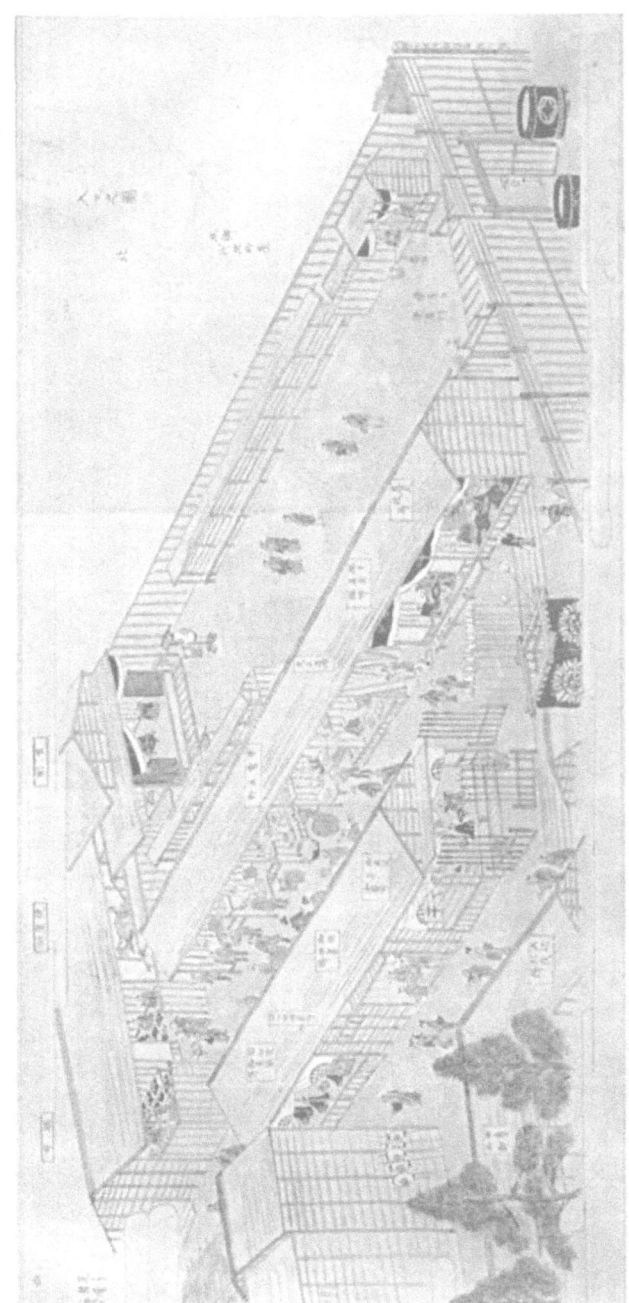

From the *Hōshō tayū kanjin nō no maki*. Courtesy of the Edo Tokyo Museum.

eye sees, can be understood as mediations, creating a separation structurally parallel to the view of a spectacle. This appears to have been the way they were experienced in nineteenth-century Japan (and these fieldglasses first appeared in and were sold at the misemono spectacle market fairs). Hence, the shogun's immediate, transparent view connecting him directly with the past was now being seen through the technological mediations of spectacle. The field glasses thus created a distance for the shogun himself from his own traditional past, not unlike the distance the commoners too were seeing, and made of the shogun himself a spectator of the world in ways now identical to the commoners.[41] Arguably, this is a position that was already emergent in the sublime aesthetic of *Sekidera* and its relation to the divine perspective of plays like *Takasago*, but now, in 1848, the tension with the divine has largely evaporated.

So, again, the effect approaches a newly modern capital of time, space, and value—that is, newly valued orders of space and time. The shutting down of the other spaces of economic and aesthetic difference, as in the misemono fairs and the kabuki theaters, and the incorporation of those economic and aesthetic values into the single confined space of the Kōka compound also emphasizes this. This now is more reminiscent of the strategies of centralization seen in Haussmann's Paris: the creation of a new, unilayered center, anchoring a homogenous order of (capitalist) flow and exchange.[42] The militaristically sweeping strategies seen even in the first Tokugawa shogun's uses of the noh, with its ritualistic cycles of time, space, and value, come into a new kind confluence with the flows of consumer cap-

---

41. It is unclear whether these field glasses (*tōmegami*) were in binocular or telescope form. One could push the argument further: as described in the previous chapter in the section on visuality, the shogun's transcendent gaze off into the eternal past could also be considered "telescopic," in the sense of carrying a line of vision off into a direct connection with a distant point (the epic past). The shogun's use in this case of the telescopic field glasses (the Japanese word itself literally means something like "a mirror to see afar") thus would very nicely exemplify the new overlapping of the old lines and flows of value with the new, more mass-cultural flows of spectacle and consumer capitalism: on the one hand the shogun could be understood as looking "telescopically" in the received, traditional way, directly off into the epic past. And yet the actual use of the telescope, while in perfect accord with the old mode of seeing things, carries with it the altered values of spectacular vision that were part of the misemono context from which the telescope itself came.
42. Though no real reconstruction of city space was undertaken for the Kōka performance, it was set up on one of the few great open spaces, just outside a main castle gate, to which both a major highway and the Kanda river flowed.

italism,[43] to create this new kind of capital.[44] All this emerges from within the space of the Tokugawa shoguns, prefiguring the relations more typically first sought for in the relations and conditions of industrial technologies.

In contrast to the mix of visual orders that made up the space of machi-iri performances, in the Kōka *kanjin* noh one can see the emergence of the homogenous space, and single (capitalist) order of value, that characterize a perspectivally organized world. Within this space, shogun, commoner, and daimyo alike were increasingly watching the noh not only through the technical distance of fieldglasses, or with a sense of temporal distance from a past tradition, but also more simply with each as one consumer among many, seeing the noh as a spectacle (although the shogun was still hoping others would come to the noh rather than the kabuki—after all, it was still *his* spectacle). In these distances one can see the estrangement of aesthetics itself, as a category apart from other forms of value, and free of history. This isolation of an aesthetic attitude was already visible earlier in the Tokugawa era—not only in the consumer culture of kabuki or in the shogun's need for commoners to give theatrical approval to the machi-iri ritual, but to an extent in noh plays themselves, at least as expressed in the longing for beauty's lost divinity in plays like *Sekidera Komachi*. But in the Kōka *kanjin* noh, the noh became part of a larger homogeneity in which kabuki and noh were more equally theatrical works of art, and artistic form was more completely free of economic or historical concern. The birth of aesthetics as an ostensibly autonomous category (and of the noh as "just" an aesthetic form), along with the idea of political economy as an independent realm of value, was in these ways tied to the origins of the nation.

Almost immediately after the Tokugawa period ended, and the new Meiji emperor moved to what now was called Tokyo (capital of the modern nation), one of the emperor's very first outings was a visit to the kabuki theater. The kabuki theater had been newly relocated to the city center. According to reports from that time, this performance of kabuki before the emperor was considered to be "the beginning of [Japanese] society's enlightenment."[45] But that process, of placing kabuki's economics and aesthetics at the center of

---

43. This in itself is not all that different from what Schivelbusch shows occurring in Paris, wherein Haussmann's own military strategies accorded well with the developing needs of consumerism.
44. On changing forms of city space in late Edo-era Japan, see Asao Naohiro et al., eds., *Nihon tsūshi*, vols. 14, 15 (Tokyo: Iwanami Koza, 1995).
45. See Kurata Yoshihiro, *Geinō*, 342.

the nation, and those values—here explicitly phrased as part of modern enlightenment—were already visible in the shogun's noh event of 1848.

The problem of the mid-nineteenth century for the shogun can be seen as a question of the relation between sites: as much a relation between the Kōka *kanjin* noh compound and the world of the kabuki theater, for example, and the fundamental orientations of value that these sites implied, as between the shogun and the varied domains and spheres of power splintering off from the shogun's order. But the difficulties of the mid-nineteenth century can also be conceived of as a relation to history—a relation of the Kōka noh, as an event, to history in all its vagaries and materialities.

The Kōka noh, in other words, can be thought of as a heterotopic site of power along the lines of the *machi-iri* noh and the performances at the shrines at Nikkō. In it, one can see incommensurability—now the incommensurability of historical as well as of social difference. Like Foucault's more spatialized formulation of the heterotopia, however, the Kōka noh shows the impossibility of an event being the opening to absolute differentiation. In part, the Kōka noh event entailed the incorporation and encompassment of difference. The shogun's own organization of this event, as a moment that could negotiate a set of social and historical incompatibilities, was *not* an attempt to merely replicate earlier, now traditional values. Using the received practices of official noh, the shogun's resolution of conflict involved a revaluation of existing relations, not just a reassertion of older conditions. Very temporarily he was successful, reuniting in a new way nearly all the social and historical forces around himself as the anchoring center. However, at the same time, the existing relations were revalued in such a way that the very social and political orientations that had positioned the shogun as powerful were now changed. The Kōka noh was therefore a moment that revealed a new totality, and allowed the glimpse of a new imaginary; a potentiality that was perhaps always present in the noh as the shogun's heterotope. The Kōka noh was accordingly also an event in the sense of an incommensurability in the history of the Tokugawa shoguns.

• • •

It may be that time in general cannot for us seem to exist—to "take place"—without some specific kind of space wherein time can be located. One can read, in the various settings of official Tokugawa noh, a particular kind of space within which particular orders of time were situated.[46]

---

46. I would emphasize, once again, though, that these were multiple orders of time.

It was not just orders of time that were located in these spaces. To return to a remark by Cornelius Castoriadis cited more fully in Chapter 1, orders of time are also forms of the social: "The social makes itself as temporality; and it makes itself in every instance as a specific mode of actual temporality, it is instituted implicitly as a singular quality of temporality."[47] This work has provided some specificity to the relations between time and social form, especially in terms of what has been described as varied modes of value orientation. These modes of orientation are expressed and practiced in realms of action that daily life now tends to continue to isolate out in separate categories such as the economic, social, and aesthetic. At least in the case of early modern Japan, these isolations are not entirely valid, or adequate to the conditions being described. Rather, a consideration of the modes of orientation in economic form as much as in aesthetics—in this case heuristically separated—helps to explain the dynamics of performances such as the Kōka *kanjin* noh, and why the shogun would give so much weight to that performance.

Modes of orientation in time, which can also be seen in and as modes of orientation of economic form, which can also be seen in the orientations of aesthetics—all of these are in fact modes of the social, or modes of orienting different kinds of social form. In the broadest of senses, then, this was what might be called the "value" of the noh stage: the institutionalization of specific forms or modes of orienting the social, which also imply specific forms and modes of power. That was what was at stake in the Kōka performance, and what was at risk at the various levels of social practice, aesthetic as well as economic. At the Kōka performance itself, and the new circumstances visible within it, one can therefore see not only a new structure of sociocultural form, but a new mode of producing the social, including conditions we might now call modern—and well before the intrusions of Admiral Perry's black ships which are so often cited as the harbingers and catalysts of the new and the modern in Japan.

---

47. Castoriadis, *The Imaginary Institution of Society*, 215.

References

Addiss, Stephen, ed. *Japanese Ghosts and Demons*. New York: George Braziller, Inc., 1985.
Aizawa Shigeharu. *Mito han nōgaku no rekishi to Komparu ryū*. Hitachi: Tōhō Insatsu, 1986.
Amino Yoshihiko. *Muen, kugai, raku*. Tokyo: Heibonsha, 1978.
Appadurai, Arjun, ed. *The Social Life of Things*. Cambridge: Cambridge University Press, 1986.
———. *Modernity at Large*. Minneapolis: University of Minnesota Press, 1996.
Argan, Guilio Carlo. *The Baroque Age*. Geneva: Skira, 1989.
Aristotle. *The Politics*. Harmondsworth: Penguin Books, 1962.
Asao Naohiro. *Nihon no rekishi 17, Sakoku*. Tokyo: Shōgakukan, 1975.
Bakhtin, Mikhail. *The Dialogic Imagination*. Austin: The University of Texas Press, 1981.
———. *Art and Answerability: Early Philosophical Essays*. Austin: The University of Texas Press, 1990.
Bataille, Georges. *The Accursed Share*, translated by Robert Hurley. New York: Zone Books, 1988.
Bellamy, Elizabeth J. "Discourses of Impossibility: Can Psychoanalysis Be Political?," in *Diacritics* 23, Spring 1993.
Bender, Ross. "Metamorphosis of a Deity," in *Monumenta Nipponica* 33, 1975.
Benjamin, Walter. *Reflections*, translated by Edmund Jephcott. New York: Schocken Books, 1978.
———. *The Origin of German Tragic Drama*, translated by John Osborne. London: NLB, 1977.
Blanchard, Jean-Marc. "The Pleasures of Description," in *Diacritics* 7, 1977.
Bloch, Ernst. "Nonsynchronism and Dialectics," in *New German Critique* 11, Spring 1977.

Bloch, Maurice. "The Symbolism of Money in Imerina," in J. Parry and M. Bloch, eds., *Money and the Morality of Exchange*. Cambridge: Cambridge University Press, 1989.
Botting, Fred. *Gothic*. London: Routledge, 1996.
Bourdieu, Pierre. *Outline of a Theory of Practice*. Cambridge: Cambridge University Press, 1977.
Brandon, James R., trans. *Kabuki Five Classic Plays*. Cambridge, MA: Harvard University Press, 1975.
Brandon, James R., et al. *Studies in Kabuki*. Honolulu: University of Hawaii Press, 1978.
Brazell, Karen, and Monica Bethe. *Nō as Performance: An Analysis of the Kuse Scene of Yamamba*. Ithaca: Cornell University East Asia Series No. 16, 1978.
Brown, Steven T. *Theatricalities of Power*. Stanford: Stanford University Press, 2001.
Buci-Glucksmann, Christine. *La folie du voir: de l'esthétique baroque*. Paris: Éditions Galilée, 1984.
———. *Baroque Reason*, translated by Patrick Camiller. London: Sage Publications, 1994.
Buck-Morss, Susan. *The Dialectics of Seeing*. Cambridge, MA: MIT Press, 1991.
Burke, Edmund. *Sublime and Beautiful*, translated by Abraham Mills. New York: Harper and Brothers, 1859.
———. *Philosophical Enquiry into the Origin of Our Ideas of the Sublime and the Beautiful*. Oxford: Basil Blackwell, 1987.
Buyō Inshi. "Seji kemmonroku," in *Kinsei shakai keizai sōsho* I. Tokyo: Kaizosha, 1926.
Carter, Steven. *Traditional Japanese Poetry*. Stanford: Stanford University Press, 1991.
Castoriadis, Cornelius. *The Imaginary Institution of Society*, translated by Kathleen Blamey. Cambridge, MA: MIT Press, 1987.
Damisch, Hubert. *The Origin of Perspective*, translated by John Goodman. Cambridge, MA: MIT Press, 1994.
de Certeau, Michel. "On the Oppositional Practices of Everyday Life," in *Social Text* No. 3, 1980.
———. *The Practice of Everyday Life*. Berkeley: University of California Press, 1984.
———. *Heterologies*. Minneapolis: The University of Minnesota Press, 1986.
Derrida, Jacques. *Given Time: 1. Counterfeit Money*. Chicago: University of Chicago Press, 1992.
Doane, Mary Ann. "Commentary: Post-Utopian Difference," in Elizabeth Weed, ed., *Coming to Terms: Feminism, Theory, Politics*. New York: Routledge, 1989.

Ejima Ihe, ed. *Kōka kanjin nō to Hōshō Yūkan*. Tokyo: Wanya Shoten, 1943.
Elison, George, and Bardwell Smith, eds. *Warlords, Artists and Commoners*. Honolulu: University Press of Hawaii, 1981.
Focillon, Henri. *The Work of Art in the Middle Ages*, vol. 2. London: Phaidon, 1969.
———. *The Life of Forms in Art*. New York: Zone Books, 1992.
Foster, Hal, ed. *Vision and Visuality*. Seattle: Bay Press, 1988.
Foucault, Michel. *Discipline and Punish*, translated by Alan Sheridan. New York: Pantheon Books, 1977.
———. "Of Other Spaces," in *Diacritics* 16, 1986.
Freud, Sigmund. "Mourning and Melancholia," in *The Standard Edition of the Complete Psychological Works of Sigmund Freud*, translated by J. Strachey. London: Hogarth Press, 1953–74.
Frost, Peter. *The Bakumatsu Currency Crisis*, Harvard East Asian Monographs 36. Cambridge, MA: Harvard University Press, 1970.
Fujiwara Sōtarō. *Kojitsu sōsho*, vol. 10. Tokyo: Meiji Tosho Shuppan, 1953.
Geinōshi Kenkyūkai, ed. *Nihon shomin bunka shiryō shūsei* 3. Tokyo: Sanichi Shobō, 1975.
Gelley, Alexander. "City Texts: Representation, Semiology, and Urbanism," in Mark Poster, ed., *Politics, Theory, and Contemporary Culture*. New York: Columbia University Press, 1993.
Gerhart, Karen. "Visions of the Dead," in *Monumenta Nipponica*, 59:1, 2004.
Gilroy, Paul. *The Black Atlantic*. Cambridge, MA: Harvard University Press, 1993.
Gotō Hajime. *Nōgaku no kigen*. Tokyo: Mokujisha, 1975.
Goux, Jean-Joseph. *Symbolic Economies*, translated by Jennifer Curtiss Gage. Ithaca: Cornell University Press, 1990.
Gregory, Christopher. *Gifts and Commodities*. London: Academic Press, 1982.
Gunji Masakatsu. "Kabuki to nō no henshin, henge," in *Shizen to bunka* No. 19 (Special Issue: *Henshin henge*), 1988.
———. "Edo bunka ni okeru kabuki no ichi," in Oishi Shinzaburō, *Edojidai to kindaika*. Tokyo: Chikuma Shobō, 1986.
———. *Kabuki—yōshiki to denshō*. Tokyo: Nara Shobō, 1955.
Gupta, Akhil, and James Ferguson. "Beyond 'Culture': Space, Identity, and the Politics of Difference," in *Cultural Anthropology* 7:1, 1992.
Halford, Aubrey S. *Kabuki Handbook*. Tokyo: Charles E. Tuttle Co., 1955.
Hall, John Whitney. "The Castle Town and Japan's Modern Urbanization," in John Whitney Hall and Marius Jansen, eds., *Studies in the Institutional History of Early Modern Japan*, Princeton, NJ: Princeton University Press, 1968.
Hansen, Miriam. "Of Mice and Ducks," in *South Atlantic Quarterly* 92, 1993.

Hare, Thomas Blenman. *Zeami's Style.* Stanford: Stanford University Press, 1986.
Harootunian, H. D. *Things Seen and Unseen.* Chicago: University of Chicago Press, 1988.
———. "Late Tokugawa Culture and Thought," in Marius B. Jansen, *The Nineteenth Century, vol. 5 of Cambridge History of Japan.* Cambridge: Cambridge University Press, 1989.
Harris, O. "The Earth and the State," in J. Parry and M. Bloch, eds., *Money and the Morality of Exchange.* Cambridge: Cambridge University Press, 1989.
Harvey, David. *The Condition of Postmodernity.* Cambridge, MA: Blackwell, 1990.
Hayashiya Tatsusaburō. *Nihon geinō no sekai: minshū bunka no ayumi.* Tokyo: Nihon Hōsō Shuppan Kyōkai, 1973.
Heki Ken. *Kaga han shiryō,* vols. 1–10. Kanazawa: Meiji Insatsu, 1922–1958.
Hidenobu Jinnai. *Tokyo: A Spatial Anthropology.* Berkeley: University of California Press, 1995.
Hirono Saburō. *Tokugawa Iemitsu kōden.* Tokyo: Tōshōgū Shamusho, 1963.
Honjō Eijirō. "Bakufu no shihei hakkō," in *Bakumatsu no shinseisaku.* Tokyo: Yūhikaku, 1935.
Ikeuchi Nobuyoshi. *Nōgaku seisuiki.* Tokyo: Nōgakkai, 1925.
Ishikawa Eisuke. *Edo kūkan.* Tokyo: Toppan Insatsu, 1993.
Inoura Yoshinobu. *Nihon engekishi.* Tokyo: Shibundō, 1963.
Jameson, Fredric. *Postmodernism.* Durham: Duke University Press, 1991.
Jay, Martin. *Downcast Eyes.* Berkeley: University of California Press, 1993.
Jippensha Ikku. *Hizakurige (Shank's Mare).* Rutland, VT: Tuttle, 1960.
Kajii Yukiyo and Mitsuda Ryōji, eds. *Kanazawa no nōgaku.* Kanazawa: Hokkoku Shuppansha, 1973.
Kamo no Chomei. *An Account of My Hut: the Hōjōki,* translated by Donald Keene. Pawlet, VT: Banyan Press, 1976.
Kant, Immanuel. *Observations on the Feeling of the Beautiful and the Sublime,* translated by John T. Goldthwait. Berkeley: University of California Press, 1981.
———. *The Critique of Judgement,* translated by James Creed Meredith. Oxford: Clarendon Press, 1980.
Kantorowicz, Ernst H. *The King's Two Bodies.* Princeton, NJ: Princeton University Press, 1957.
Kantorowicz, Ernst. "Mysteries of State," in *Harvard Theological Review* 48, 1955.
Kawamura Hirotada. *Edo bakufu sen kuni ezu no kenkyū.* Tokyo: Kokon Shoin, 1984.

Kawatake Shigetoshi. *Nihon engeki zenshi*. Tokyo: Iwanami Shoten, 1959.
Keene, Donald, ed. *Twenty Plays of the Noh Theatre*. New York: Columbia University Press, 1970.
——. *Nō and Bunraku*. New York: Columbia University Press, 1990.
Kaempfer, Englebert. *A History of Japan, Together With a Description of the Kingdom of Siam*. Glasgow: J. MacLehose and Sons, 1906.
Kempfer, Englebert. "Kempfer's History of Japan," in John Pinkerton, ed., *Voyages and Travels* 7. London: Longman, Hurst, Rees, Orme, and Brown, 1811.
Kern, Stephen. *The Culture of Time and Space*. Cambridge, MA: Harvard University Press, 1983.
Kishi Fumikazu. *Edo no enkinhō: ukie no shikaku*. Tokyo: Keisō Shobō, 1994.
Klein, Susan Blakeley. "Woman as Serpent: The Demonic Feminine in the Noh Play Dōjōji." In Jane Marie Law, ed., *Religious Reflections on the Human Body*. Bloomington: Indiana University Press, 1995.
Kō Masayoshi. "Kō Masayoshi kudensho," in *Nōgaku shiryō shūsei* 13. Tokyo: Wanya Shoten, 1984.
Koh Masuda, ed. *Kenkyusha's New Japanese-English Dictionary*, fourth edition. Tokyo: Kenkyusha, 1974.
Kōjiro Yūichiro. "Edo: The City on the Plain," in *Tokyo: Form and Spirit*. Minneapolis: Walker Art Center, 1986.
Komiya Toyotaka. *Kaikoku hyakunen kinen bunka jigyōkai*, vol. 3. Tokyo: Ōbunsha, 1956.
Kongo Iwao. *The Noh Drama*. Tokyo: Kokusai Bunka Shinkōkai, 1937.
Konparu Anshō. "Konparu Anshō denshoshū," in Omote Akira and Oda Sachiko, eds., *Nōgaku shiryō shūsei*, vol. 9, 1978.
Koyama and Satō, eds. "Yōkyokushū." *Nihon koten bungaku zenshū*, vol. 33. Tokyo: Shinchōsha, 1983.
Lefort, Claude. *The Political Forms of Modern Society*. Cambridge, MA: The MIT Press, 1986.
Leiter, Samuel L., trans. *Kabuki Encyclopedia*. Westport, CT: Greenwood Press, 1979.
Leutner, Robert W. *Shikitei Sanba and the Comic Tradition*. Cambridge, MA: Harvard-Yenching Institute, 1985.
Looser, Tom. "Superflat and the Layers of Image and History in the 21st Century," in *Mechademia* 1:1, Fall 2006.
Lyotard, Jean-Francois. *Postmodern Condition*. Minneapolis: University of Minnesota Press, 1984.
Marra, Michael, ed. and trans. *A History of Modern Japanese Aesthetics*. Honolulu: University of Hawaii Press, 2001.

Marin, Louis. "Classical, Baroque: Versailles, or the Architecture of the Prince," in Timothy Hampton, ed., *Baroque Topographies, Yale French Studies* 80, 1991.
———. *Utopics: Spatial Play*, translated by Robert A. Vollrath. Atlantic Highlands, NJ: Humanities Press, 1984.
———. *La Critique du discours.* Paris: Les Éditions de minuit, 1975.
Markus, Andrew L. "The Carnival of Edo: Misemono Spectacles from Contemporary Accounts," in *Harvard Journal of Asiatic Studies* 45, no. 2, 1985.
Martin, Jo Nobuko. *Santo Kyōden and His Sharebon.* PhD Dissertation: University of Michigan, 1979.
Maruyama Masao. "The Structure of Matusrigoto: the Basso Ostinato of Japanese Political Life," in Sue Henny and Jean-Pierre Lehmann, eds., *Themes and Theories in Modern Japanese History.* London: Athlone Press, 1988.
Marx, Karl. *Contribution à la critique de l'économie politique.* Paris: Sociales, 1957.
———. *The Eighteenth Brumaire of Louis Bonaparte.* New York: International Publishers, 1963.
———. *Capital, A Critique of Political Economy,* vol. 1. New York: International Publishers, 1967.
Massey, Doreen. *Space, Place, and Gender.* Minneapolis: University of Minnesota Press, 1994.
Mauss, Marcel. *The Gift: The Form and Reason for Exchange in Archaic Societies.* New York: W. W. Norton, 1990.
McClain, James L. *Kanazawa.* New Haven: Yale University Press, 1982.
Milbank, Alison. "The Sublime," in Marie Roberts, ed., *A Handbook to Gothic Literature.* New York: New York University Press, 1998.
Miller, Daniel. "Anthropology, Modernity and Consumption," in *Worlds Apart,* Daniel Miller, ed. London: Routledge, 1991.
Minami Kazuo. *Bakumatsu Edo no bunka.* Tokyo: Hanawa Shobō, 1998.
Mishra,Vijay. *The Gothic Sublime.* New York: State University of New York Press, 1994.
Mitamura Engyo. *Mitamura Engyo Edo seikatsu jiten.* Tokyo: Seiabō, 1959.
Miura Hiroyuki. *Hōseishi no kenkyū.* Tokyo: Iwanami Shoten, 1919.
Miyamoto Mataji. "Daimyōgashi no rishiritsu ni tsuite—Kōnoike ryōgaeshō shihon no kenkyū," in *Osaka Daigaku keizaigaku* 10, No. 2, Nov. 1960.
Miyake Noboru. *Nōgaku hanashi.* Tokyo: Hishoten, 1942.
Moriya Katsuhisa. "Urban Newtorks and Information Networks," in *Tokugawa Japan.* Tokyo: University of Tokyo Press, 1990.

Morris-Suzuki, Tessa. *A History of Japanese Economic Thought*. London: Routledge, 1989.
———. *The Technological Transformation of Japan*. Cambridge: Cambridge University Press, 1994.
Mumford, Lewis. *The City in History*. New York: Harcourt, Brace and World, Inc., 1961.
Munn, Nancy. *The Fame of Gawa*. Cambridge: Cambridge University Press, 1986.
———. "The Cultural Anthropology of Time: A Critical Essay," in *Annual Review of Anthropology* 1992, 21: 93-123.
Murakami Takashi. "Super Flat Manifesto," and "A Theory of Super Flat Japanese Art," in Murakami, ed., *Superflat*. Tokyo: Madras, 2000.
Murray, Timothy. "Translating Montaigne's Crypts: Melancholic Relations and the Sites of Altarbiography," in *Bucknell Review* 35, no. 2, 1992.
Naitō Akira. "Planning and Development of Early Edo," in *Japan Echo*, vol. XIV (Special Issue), 1987.
———. *Edo the City that Became Tokyo*. Tokyo: Kodansha, 2003.
Najita, Tetsuo. *Japan*. Englewood Cliffs, NJ: Prentice-Hall, 1974.
———. "Political Economy in Thought and Practice Among Commoners in Nineteenth-Century Japan: Some Preliminary Comments," in *The Japan Foundation Newsletter* XVI, No. 3.
———. *Visions of Virtue in Tokugawa Japan*. Chicago: University of Chicago Press, 1987.
———. "Keizai roku shūi," in *Readings in Tokugawa Thought*, Select Papers 9. Chicago: Center for East Asian Studies, 1993.
Nakamura Yasuo. *Noh*. New York: Walker/Weatherhill, 1971.
Narita Ryūichi. *Toshi to minshū*. Tokyo: Yoshikawa Kōbunkan, 1993.
Nishiyama Matsunosuke. *Edo Culture*. Honolulu: University of Hawaii Press, 1997.
Nishiyama Matsunosuke. *Nishiyama Matsunosuke chosakushū*, vol. 1. Tokyo: Yoshikawa Kōbunkan, 1982.
Nogami Toyoichirō. *Nōgaku saisei*. Tokyo: Iwanami Shoten, 1935.
Nonomura Kaizō. *Nōen nisshō*. Tokyo: Hinoki Shoten, 1938.
Norman, E. H. "Andō Shōeki and the Anatomy of Japanese Feudalism," in *Transactions of the Asiatic Society of Japan* 2, 1949.
Oda Sachiko. "Nō no engi to enshutsu: shōzokuzuke, katazuke o meguru shomondai," in *Nōgaku kenkyū* 10, 1984.
Ogyū Sorai, *The Political Writings of Ogyū Sorai*, translated by J. R. McEwan. Cambridge: Cambridge University Press, 1962.
Ohnuki-Tierney, Emiko. *Rice as Self*. Princeton, NJ: Princeton University Press, 1993.

Oka Yasumasa. *Megane-e shinkō: ukiyoeshitachi go nozoita Seiyo*. Tokyo: Chikuma Shobō, 1992.
Okawa Naomi. *Edo Architecture*. New York: Weatherhill, 1975.
Okada Jō et al., eds. *Nikkō sono bijutsu to rekishi*. Kyoto: Tankō Shinsha, 1961.
Omote Akira. *Kōzan bunkobon no kenkyū*. Tokyo: Wanya Shoten, 1965.
———. *Nōgakushi shinkō*, vol. 2. Tokyo: Wanya Shoten, 1987.
Omote Akira and Amano Fumio, eds. *Nōgaku no rekishi nō kyōgen* I. Tokyo: Iwanami Kōza, 1987.
Omote Akira, and Amano Fumio, eds. *Nōgaku no rekishi nō kyōgen* II. Tokyo: Iwanami Kōza, 1988.
Omote Akira, and Yokomichi Mario, eds. *Yōkyokushū*. Tokyo: Iwanami Shoten, 1960–1963.
Ono Kiyoshi, ed. "Yanagiei gyōji," in *Tokugawa seido shiryō*. Tokyo: Rokugokan, 1927.
Ooms, Herman. *Tokugawa Ideology*. Princeton: Princeton University Press, 1985.
Orgel, Stephen. *The Illusion of Power*. Berkeley: University of California Press, 1975.
Osborne, Peter. *The Politics of Time*. New York: Verso, 1995.
Panofsky, Erwin. *Perspective as Symbolic Form*. New York: Zone Books, 1991.
Pinnington, Noel. "Invented Origins: Muromachi Interpretations of Okina Sarugaku," in *Bulletin of the School of Oriental and African Studies*, vol. 61, Part 3. London: Oxford University Press, 1998.
Rimer, J. Thomas, and Yamazaki Masakazu, trans. *On the Art of the Nō Drama*. Princeton: Princeton University Press, 1984.
Rodd, Laurel Rasplica, trans. *Kokinshū*. Princeton: Princeton University Press, 1984.
Rosenblatt, Daniel. "The Antisocial Skin: Structure, Resistance, and 'Modern Primitive' Adornment in the United States," in *Cultural Anthropology* 12:3, 1997.
Ross, Kristin. *The Emergence of Social Space*. Minneapolis: University of Minnesota Press, 1988.
Russo, Mary J. *The Female Grotesque: Risk, Excess, and Modernity*. New York: Routledge, 1995.
Sahlins, Marshall. *Culture and Practical Reason*. Chicago: University of Chicago Press, 1976.
Saikaku Ihara. *Teihon Saikaku zenshu*, vol. 7. Tokyo: Chūō Kōronsha, 1951.
———. *The Japanese Family Storehouse*, translated by G. W. Sargent. Cambridge: Cambridge University Press, 1959.
———. *The Life of an Amorous Woman*, translated by Ivan Morris. New York: New Directions Publishing, 1963.

Saitō Gesshin et al. *Bukō nenpyō*. Tokyo: Heibonsha, 1968.
Sakai, Naoki. *Voices of the Past*. Ithaca: Cornell University Press, 1992.
Sansom, George. *A History of Japan 1615-1867*. Stanford: Stanford University Press, 1963.
Sasaki, Junnosuke, and Ronald P. Toby. "The Changing Rationale of Daimyo Control in the Emergence of the Bakuhan State," in John Whitney Hall et al., eds., *Japan Before Tokugawa*. Princeton: Princeton University Press, 1981.
Schivelbusch, Wolfgang. *The Railway Journey*. Berkeley: The University of California Press, 1977.
Screech, Timon. *The Western Scientific Gaze and Popular Culture in Late Edo Japan*. New York: Cambridge University Press, 1996.
Shiba Kōkan. "Seiyoga dan," in *Nihon no meicho* 22. Tokyo: Chūō Kōron, 1971.
———. "Seiyōga dan," translated by T. Looser, in *Readings in Tokugawa Thought*, vol. 9. Chicago: University of Chicago Center for East Asian Studies.
Shimazaki Chifumi. *The Noh*, vol. 3, Ithaca: Cornell University East Asia Program, 1998.
Shively, Donald. "Bakufu vs. Kabuki" in *Harvard Journal of Asiatic Studies*, 18, nos. 3–4, 1955.
———. "Chikamatsu's Satire on the Dog Shogun," in *Harvard Journal of Asiatic Studies* 18, 1955.
———. "Sumptuary Regulation and Status in Early Tokugawa Japan," in *Harvard Journal of Asiatic Studies* 25, 1964–1965.
Smith, Henry D. "World Without Walls: Kuwagata Keisai's Panoramic Vision of Japan," in Gail Lee Bernstein and Haruhiro Fukui, eds., *Japan and the World*. Basingstoke: Macmillan Press, 1988.
Smith, Thomas C. *Political Change and Industrial Development in Japan*. Stanford: Stanford University Press, 1955.
———. *The Agrarian Origins of Modern Japan*. Stanford: Stanford University Press, 1959.
Spivak, Gayatri Chakravorty. "Scattered Speculations on the Question of Value," in *In Other Worlds: Essays in Cultural Politics*. New York: Methuen, 1987.
Stewart, Susan. *On Longing*. Baltimore: Johns Hopkins University Press, 1984.
Suzuki, B. L. *Nōgaku*. London: John Murray, 1932.
Takano Tatsuyuki. *Nihon engekishi*, vol. 1. Tokyo: Tōkyōdō, 1947.
Takayanagi Shinzō and Ishii Ryōsuke, eds. *Ofuregaki kampō shūsei*. Tokyo: Iwanami Shoten, 1959.

Takenobu Ishitaro, ed. *New Japanese-English Dictionary.* Tokyo: Kenkyusha, 1954.
Taki Kōji. *Tennō no shōzō.* Tokyo: Iwanami Shinsho, 1988.
Tanaka Shin. *Shomin no bunka.* Tokyo: Fuji Shoin, 1967.
Tanaka Yūko. *Edo no sōzōryoku.* Tokyo: Chikuma Shobō, 1986.
Taussig, Michael. *The Magic of the State.* New York: Routledge, 1997.
Terasaki, Etsuko. *Figures of Desire: Wordplay, Spirit Possession, Fantasy, Madness, and Mourning in Japanese Noh Plays.* Ann Arbor: Center for Japanese Studies, University of Michigan, 2002.
Thornbury, Barbara E. *Sukeroku's Double Identity.* Ann Arbor: Center for Japanese Studies, University of Michigan, 1982.
Tiedemann, Rolf and Hermann Schweppenhauser, eds. *Gesammelte Schriften* II, 1. Frankfurt/Main: Suhrkamp Verlag, 1972.
Tsuji Tatsuya. *Kyōhō kaikaku no kenkyū.* Tokyo: Sōbunsha, 1963.
Tyler, Royall. *Japanese Nō Dramas.* London: Penguin Books, 1992.
Ueda Akinari. "*Himpukuron*" (On Wealth and Poverty), in *Ugetsu Monogatari,* translated by Leon M. Zolbrod. Vancouver: University of British Columbia Press, 1974.
Ukō Infumi. *Tokugawa ōoku.* Tokyo: Sūzanbō, 1915.
Walker, Brett. *The Conquest of Ainu Lands.* Berkeley: University of California Press, 2001.
Weber, Samuel. "Taking Exception to Decision: Walter Benjamin and Carl Schmitt," in *Diacritics* 22, 1992.
Weiss, Brad. "A Shilling and Embodiment," in *Cultural Anthropology* 12:3, 1997.
Yajima Kiyofumi. *Nikkō tōshōgu.* Tokyo: Shakai shisō kenkyūkai, 1962.
Yanagida Kunio. "Nō to rikisha," in Nogami Toyoichirō, ed., *Nōgaku zensho,* vol. 5. Tokyo: Sōgensha, 1944.
Yokoi Haruno. *Nōgaku zenshi.* Tokyo: Wanya Shoten, 1938.
Yokoi Haruno. "Zeami no gei wa shimpiteki nari," in Yokoi, *Nōgaku hyakumonogatari.* Tokyo: Hakushindō, 1917.
Yokomichi Mario and Omote Akira, eds. *Yōkyokushū. Nihon koten bungaku taikei,* vol. 40. Tokyo: Iwanami Shoten, 1960.
Yokomichi Mario et al., eds. *Nō kyōgen,* vol. 8 (*Nōgaku zusetsu*). Tokyo: Iwanami Kōza, 1992.
Yokota, Gerry. *The Nō Drama of Japan.* PhD Dissertation. Princeton, 1992.
———. *The Formation of the Canon of Noh: The Literary Tradition of Divine Authority.* Osaka: Osaka University Press, 1997.
Zeami Motokiyo. *Zeami Zenchiku, Nihon Shiso Taikei* 24. Tokyo: Iwanami Shoten, 1974.

Index

Ainu people, 9, 10
Aesthetics
 aesthetics as basis of the nation, 294
 aesthetic form, relation to social and historical form, 122n.4, 123, 123nn.5, 7, 124
 aesthetic value, autonomy of, 3–4, 5, 11, 12, 122–123, 165
 affect, desire and, 123–124, 191
 "art" (*bigaku*) as 123, "art" (*geijutsu*) versus "skill" (*gijutsu*) as, 167
 beauty, perfection, and utopia, 21, 29, 168
 beauty, ugliness, and shogunal power, 124, 152, 154, 168, 190–191, 259
 and city form, 253–256
 and Kōka performance, 269–279, 287, 288, 290
 sublime, aesthetic of. See Sublime
 yūgen, aesthetic of. See *Yūgen*
Ashikaga shoguns and noh, 25n.12, 42, 57
Ashikaga Yoshimitsu, 17–18
Ashikari (noh play). See *Reed Cutter*
Azuchi castle, 61, 62nn.101–102, 281nn.21

Bakhtin, Mikhail, 5, 13–14, 15, 133, 134, 135, 137, 140n.38, 143
Baroque
 allegory, 158, 161–162
 melancholy, 163n.101
 Nikkō shrine and, 62–63, 153
 space, 202n.61, 251
 vision, 221, 225
Bataille, Georges, 4, 4n.9, 116, 220n.99
Baudrillard, Jean, 88, 88n.43
Baumgarten, Alexander, 154
Benjamin, Walter, 15, 60n.97, 161–162, 188, 212n.87, 261
Biopower and Tokugawa shoguns, 10
Bonfire (*takigi*) noh, 55, 56

Brunelleschi, Filippo, 238–239
Buddhism, 42, 44, 46, 62, 109n.107, 125n.8, 128, 132, 133, 136, 137n.30, 159, 180, 182, 184, 188n.33, 194n.45, 197n.49, 207, 209, 217, 225, 238n.123, 255, 269, 277, 278
Buyō Inshi
 on agrarian natural value and society, 87
 critique of commodity form, 165n.106
 on extravagant expenditure and memory, 117n.129
 on instant time and extravagant expenditure, 116
 mercantilism, critique of, 90, 106,
 mercantilism, women, and desire, 112–113, 182
 rice economy as critique, 119

Capitalism (*See also* Economics, Value), 4, 5–6
 and abstract money form (*See also* Coins, Money), 98, 104–105, 107–108, 109n.107, 111n.109
 agrarian farm unit, relation to, 78, 81, 83–85, 86, 88n.42, 95
 amortization and eternity, 77
 Buddhism, contrast to, 109n.107
 and cenotaph, 109, 126, 126n.10
 and cinema, 203n.63
 commerce, critique of, 87, 88n.42, 90, 91n.54, 104n.92, 112–113, 119, 165n.106
 commodity and, 85n.31, 90, 96, 97, 109n.105, 165, 188, 191n.41, 193, 241
 and *Dōjōji* (noh play), 180
 Edokko versus *tsū* as figures of, 115–118, 173–174, 220n.99, 249
 Eternal Storehouse of Japan on mercantile capitalism, *The*, 199

307

308 / Visioning Eternity

Capitalism (continued)
 expenditure and excess. See Value
 "floating" quality of commercial value,
  104–105, 253, 255
 general versus restricted economy. See
  Economy
 geography of, 81–83, 87, 90, 99–100,
  103–105, 110, 119n.134, 253–254, 256,
  267–268, 278, 287, 289–290, 293–294
 and gothic form, 165–166
 as illegal, 165
 and kabuki, 78, 79, 104–105, 105n.95, 108,
  110–111, 165–167, 174, 178, 183
 and Kōka *kanjin* noh, 266, 270, 283, 286,
  286n.27, 287, 289–290, 289n.37
 merchant, 79, 82, 105, 106, 108, 110, 116,
  153, 268, 290
 misemono (capitalist) markets. See Spectacle
 and primitive accumulation, 107
 production versus consumption, 82–83,
  88n.42, 90, 118n.132
 rice-based economy versus, 7, 11, 12, 17,
  90, 116, 169, 266, 266n.3
 rice-based economy, dependency on,
  119n.134
 and ritual cycles, 119n.134
 and sublime aesthetic, 165–166, 167
 temporality of capital (See also Time),
  77–78, 90, 107, 108, 111, 116, 167, 192,
  193, 200, 214, 216, 290, 293–294
 vision and capitalism. See Value
Castoriadis, Cornelius, 56n.85, 71, 295
Cenotaph, 109, 126, 126n.10
Change (See also History, Time)
 and city form, 255
 and commodity form, 193
 and event. See Event
 history versus, 58, 59
 and kabuki, 183, 191–192, 193, 197, 198,
  202, 207; (*bukkaeri, hayaguke, hengemono, kizewamono*) 183, (*hayagawari,
  hikinuki* quick change) 199
 and noh, 30, 56–60, 72, 183–184, 185–186,
  187, 188, 193, 205, 207
 as revolt, 54
 and rice value, 90
 and social form, 6
 and specular orders of time, rule, 58
 as transformation. See Transformation
 and utopic practice, 21
 and women, 112
Chikamatsu Monzaemon, 12n.21, 172
Choay, Francoise, 29
Chronotopes, 5

epic and kabuki 173, 177, 260
epic and the noh, 91, 133–140, 142–156,
 159, 164–165, 205, 207–208, 213, 243,
 282–283
epic value of rice, 91
epic and vision 233, 237, 293n.41
 and history, 13–14
 and monetary economic value, 5, 14
 and the novel, 14, 109, 133n.20, 140n.38
 Takasago and epic, 148
Closed country, Japan as
 sakoku, 9, 9n.17, 250, 281–282
 kaikin, 9n.17, 250
 tozasu, 282
Commoners
 and gift economy, 94n.70, 95
 at Kōka *kanjin* noh performance, 270, 273,
  282–283, 284–286, 288–290, 293
 orders of vision, 230, 231, 240, 241, 242,
  243–244, 245–246, 247–248, 249–250
 practicing noh, 18, 182n.18, 256
 and production, 88n.42
 and souvenirs, 243
 subject positions in machi-iri noh, 67,
  69–70, 190, 233, 240–244
Country-entering noh (*nyūkoku shukuga no
 gishiki nō*), 39

Daimyo
 fudai, 9, 33–34, 40, 41n.44, 55, 84, 228,
  279n.19
 Gosanke (Tokugawa family daimyo). See
  Tokugawa branch houses
 and machi-iri noh, 228, 240n.129
 mansions (*yashiki*) of, 253, 277–278, 280
 noh, use of, 33–40, 41, 51, 55–57, 67n.109,
  124, 259n.149
 and participation in commerce, 81,
  91n.54, 97n.72, 101n.85, 105n.94
 and *sankinkōtai* system. See Sankinkōtai
 state power, relation to, 9, 31, 32, 40–41,
  45, 47, 49, 53, 81, 153, 254
 sumptuary expenditure and consumption,
  79
 tozama, 9, 35, 37, 38, 40–41, 49, 41,
  41n.44, 56n.84, 228n.112, 269,
  279n.19
Damisch, Hubert, 238n.125, 239n.127
de Certeau, Michel, 30, 31n.25, 54n.78, 61,
 148, 149
Death portraits (*shini-e*), 197n.49, 217,
 217n.95, 218, 220, 220n.98, 258
Dōjōji (noh play),143, 143n.48, 179–182,
 179n.14, 182n.17, 259n.149, 289
Double consciousness, 171, 173, 260

"Economics," 5, 11–12, 77, 78, 81, 84, 86, 95, 96n.72, 111n.109, 266–268
general and restricted economy, 4, 4n.9
morality versus economy, 5, 111n.109
ritual (*oshūgi, matsurigoto*) as, 91, 92–94, 94n.67
"wealth" (*fuku, fukuri, kanemochi*), 95
Eternity
and chronotope (*See also* Chronotope), 5
and dream image and utopia, 22, 54, 67, 67n.109, 72n.115, 73
and economic value, 77, 90, 98, 107, 110, 111, 118, 286n.30
"*eitai*" as, 77
"*jōjūfumetsu*" as, 184
kabuki and, 192, 197, 216n.93
"*kaei*" as 2, 287n.31
and *Kantan* (noh play), 205–207
and Kōka *kanjin* noh, 20, 269, 284, 288, 290
"*mannen*" as, 204
"*miyo*" as, 184
noh, eternity in, 117, 145, 146–147, 159, 183–184, 186, 189, 197, 209–214
and portrait of Tokugawa Ieyasu, 258
and shogunal gaze. *See* Vision
and *Takasago* (noh play), 208
and Tokugawa noh, 57, 58, 59, 59n.94, 126
Tokugawa order, origins of, and eternity, 43, 58, 71, 91n.53, 190, 258
and utopia (*See also* Utopia), 20, 29, 54, 168
and *utsuri-mai* ("change-dance"), 187
and vision. *See* Vision
Event
catastrophe as, 265–266
and economic value of gift, 114–115, 117, 119n.135
and economic value of rice, 89
and epic time, 134n.22
and eternity, 20, 276, 282. *See also* Utopia
and fashion, temporality of, 192
and fragment or monad. *See* History.
and Hideyoshi as origin, 28n.17
and incommensurability, 294
and instant (*See also* Time), 205, 213, 261, 288, 290
and kabuki, 173, 191
Kōka event in relation to history, 8, 16, 295–296
Kōka performance formalized as, 2
and noh, 182n.18
Perry's arrival in Japan as, 1
and power, 266n.2

and repetition, 8, 57, 60, 182, 216, 216n.92, 263, 265, 268, 284–295
and ritual, 14, 55, 94, 273n.12
Tokugawa temporality of, 56–57, 61, 172
and tournaments of value, 284n.24
and urban form, 117

Foucault, Michel, 10, 63, 69, 70, 294

Genzai (contemporary) noh, 101n.86, 130
Gilroy, Paul, 260
Giri (duty) versus *ninjō* (love), emergence of, 111
Gosanke. *See* Tokugawa branch houses
Goux, Jean-Joseph, 76, 78, 85n.31, 96, 99

Haikai poetry, 199n.52, 222–223, 226
Harootunian, Harry, 7n.14, 16n.26, 80n.15, 87n.39, 89, 90n.47
Haussmann, Baron Georges-Eugène, 251, 253, 254, 293, 293n.43
Hayashi Shihei, 60, 60n.96, 152
Heterotopia, 22, 63, 68–70, 72, 294, 295
Hideyoshi, Toyotomi 23–29
acting as himself in plays, 27–28
as a god, 27, 28
and Komparu school of noh, 24
and modes of power, 24, 26–28, 61
noh and political allegiance, 24, 31
as object of representation, 28
performance in noh plays, 25, 26, 27
and political space, 24–26, 29
tea hut, portable, 278
tea utensils, 278
use of noh for self-deification, 167
war and use of the noh, 25
History
autonomy of theater history, 3
and body. *See* Time
and chronotope, 13–14
commoners' relation to, 69
and Edo era, 8, 13, 14
and event. *See* Event
and fragment or atom, 15–16
Hideyoshi Toyotomi, relation to, 28n.17
and Ise shrine, 58
in kabuki, 172, 176–177, 191–194, 257, 263
in noh, 6–7, 77, 182, 208, 209, 257, 259–260, 263, 273, 288
and rice as value form, 89, 90
and ritual. *See* Time
social form as, 6, 16, 71–72, 295
and social space, 30, 251

310 / Visioning Eternity

History (*continued*)
spectacle and capital, relation to, 107–108, 227
utopia, relation to, 21, 29, 29n.19, 59, 71, 250, 276
and value. *See* Value
Hoide (longevity) noh, 56
Hōshō school of noh, 2n.5, 36, 37, 130n.13, 210n.78, 269n.6, 270, 284n.25
Hōshō Yagorō Yūkan, 75

Ikki protests and rebellions, 1
Izayoi Seishin (kabuki play), 110
Izutsu (noh play), 141, 185–189, 188n.33

jo-ha-kyū aesthetic temporal cycle, 59, 129, 130, 140, 142, 153–154, 155–156, 161, 164, 184, 202, 207, 210, 287

Kaga domain, 36, 37–39, 43n.51, 51, 56n.84, 57n.87, 60, 269 (*See also* Maeda family)
Kagemasa Ikazuchi Mondo (kabuki play), 110
Kagura 148, 174
versus noh, 14, 167
Kamigakari style of noh, 36
Kanjin (subscription) noh, 18, 55, 95n.71, 284n.25
Kant, Immanuel, 122, 154, 160, 161
Kantan (noh play), 204, 205–207, 213, 252
Kantorowicz, Ernst, 46n.54, 154, 155
Kanze school of noh, 17n.30, 32n.29, 36–37, 41, 43, 51, 52n.73, 130n.13, 140n.40, 143–144, 269n.6
Kasuga shrine, 42–43, 56
Kayoi Komachi (noh play), 189n.38, 149n.68
Keizai. See Economy
Kinuta (noh play), 129
Kita school of noh, 33, 36, 51, 130n.13, 143n.47, 144n.50
Kokinshū, 103, 145, 146
Komparu Anshō, 145n.53, 154n.83
Komparu school of noh, 24, 36, 37, 49, 51, 130n.13
Kongō school of noh, 130n.13
Kōya Sankei (noh play), 28n.14
Kozaru Shichinosuke (kabuki play), 110

Lefort, Claude, 27n.16
Love suicide, 174, 175n.9
excess, exchange and, 111, 193n.44
suicide and exchange, 91n.55
and time, 178

Machi-iri noh, 55, 68–72, 94–95, 118n.132, 154n.83, 190, 221, 258, 259, 260–263, 270, 276, 284, 287n.27, 287

as heterotope, 70, 294
and Nikkō, 63–64, 67–68
and time, 71
vision in, 228–250
Maeda family of Kaga domain, 24, 34–35, 37–38, 40–41, 43n.51, 56n.84, 60
and Kōka performance, 269
Maeda Tsunanori, 34–35, 37
Mapping
city form and, 254–255
descriptivist mode of vision and surface mapping, 221n.102
noh and mapping time, 56
Takasago and, 252
Tokugawa Ieyasu and, 45, 52–53, 53n.76
Marin, Louis
on baroque space, 30n.22
on monumental time, 58
on space of power, 46
on utopic architecture, 20, 21, 61n.100
on utopic time, 54
on vision and eternity, 239n.127
Marx, Karl
on absolute monarchy and the general equivalent, 100
on capital and monstrous materiality, 165–166
on fetishism and gold, 107n.100
on money and exchange value, 107
on value, 6, 6n.12, 85n.31, 88n.43
Matsubayashi noh. *See* Pine Singing
Matsudaira Sadanobu, 86, 266–267
Matsukaze (noh play), 137–138, 140–143, 143n.47, 145, 147n.58, 185, 289
Matsumae domain, 9
Mauss, Marcel, 4, 4n.8, 89
Michiyuki (travel scene)
as Edo-era narrative form, 256
and kabuki, 174, 178
and noh, 128, 131n.16, 171
Mirrors and specular relations
anamorphosis, 189, 189n.36, 190, 191n.40
economic value form, as, 96, 97, 99
and heterotopia and utopia, 63
and history, Ise shrine, 58
mirror board (*kagami ita*) in noh, 235, 238, 246, 279, 284, 285
mirror room (*kagami no ma*) in noh, 237, 279
and noh temporality, 188, 189, 195, 290
and perspectival space, 224, 238–239
and rulership, 58, 64, 73n.16, 100n.83
and specular gaze, 64, 226, 233, 235, 237–238, 240, 241, 242, 246, 246n.138, 247, 248, 283, 290, 293n.41

Index / 311

Misemono markets. *See* Spectacle
Monumentalism
  architectural, 21
  and Azuchi castle, 62
  monumental time, 162
  and Nikkō, 45, 47, 58, 62
  noh, political space, and, 6, 21
  and Tokugawa political space, 20, 152
Motomezuka (noh play), 122, 125, 126, 164, 186
Motoori Norinaga, 92, 94n.67
Mūgen (phantasmal) noh, 101n.86
Munn, Nancy, 5n.11, 30n.21, 220n.100

Nara, 24–25, 36, 42–43, 56
  Nikkō versus, 48
Nation and nationalism
  and aesthetics. *See* Aesthetics
  and chronotope of the novel, 14
  and epic past, 134
  geography of, 9, 10, 16n.27, 19, 40, 52n.75, 73, 80n.14, 252
  and invented tradition, 15
  and kabuki, 166n.108, 294
  and Kōka *kanjin* noh, 16
  and modern noh, 18
  national rule, 31
  national time, 57, 118
  nationalism and time, 201–202
  and political economy. *See* Political economy
New Year's ceremonial noh. *See* Utaizome noh
Nogami Toyoichirō, 19, 25n.12

Ogyū Sorai, 92, 93, 94n.66, 104n.93, 201
Okina (noh play), 48n.65, 137, 137n.31, 139, 234, 237, 259n.149
Once-in-a-generation noh, 2, 14, 55, 259, 284n.25
Osome Nanayaku (kabuki play), 192

Panofsky, Irwin, 12
Perry, Commodore, 1, 296
Perspectival space, 10–11, 12–13, 99, 222, 223–225, 227, 233, 233n.115, 238–239
  perspectival differentiation in relation to eternity, 210, 211
  and renga fragmentary perspective, 133, 140
  uki-e perspectival prints, 223n.103, 227
Pine singing/dancing (*matsubayashi*) noh, 56, 56n.83
Political economy (*See also* Economy) 3–4, 80–81, 82, 85, 88, 95, 100, 110–111, 201, 220n.100, 295

  and domains (*han*), 39–40, 42
  and origin of the nation, 294

Reed Cutter, The (noh play Ashikari), 101–103, 150n.72
Religion
  and death, 125n.8
  and ethics, 111n.109
  and Kantan, 205–207
  and Nikkō, 43–48
  place of, 5, 14, 17, 18, 6n.13, 23–24, 42–48, 55, 61, 62n.102, 63, 69, 71, 112, 148, 151–152, 161, 248n.140
  and serial time, 204
  and Takasago, 148
  and tea ceremony, 278
Renga poetry, 67n.109, 133, 140, 142, 222, 269
Repetition and event. *See* Event
Rice economy
  and chronotope (*See also* Chronotope), 5, 91
  commodity, as, 97
  critique of capital, as, 119
  economic value form, 83, 84–85, 90, 91, 97, 99, 100, 105, 118, 165, 258
  geography of, 82–86, (*honsho* "real place") 90–91, 95, 99, 100, 103, 253–254, 287
  gift economy and, 89–90, 91–92, 95, 119n.135
  mercantile capitalism, dependency on, 100, 109, 109n.105, 168, 191, 242, 266n.3, 267
  money versus, 83, 97, 106, 108, 118
  and noh actors, 49, 92, 105
  and noh plays, 101–103, 147
  re-creation of, 77, 82, 83
  and ritual governance, 92–93
  and shogunal order of vision, 246
  and social status, 49, 82
  and taxation, 83, 90–91
  temporality of, 89–90, 91–92
  and use value, 97
  and utopia (*See also* Utopia), 91

Sagami nyūdō sembiki inu (kabuki play), 172
Sahlins, Marshall, 8n.15
Sakai, Naoki, 10n.18, 93
Saikaku, Ihara, 75, 75n.1, 77, 106–109, 109n.107, 117, 126–127, 167, 192, 193, 199, 199n.52, 200, 200n.54, 202–203, 226–227
Sakoku. *See* closed country
Sankinkōtai system, 64, 65, 81
  and shogunal noh, 32, 38, 81

312 / Visioning Eternity

Sekidera Komachi (noh play), 121, 124–125, 126, 127, 139, 142, 144, 144n.50, 149–152, 155, 156, 160, 161, 164, 165, 168, 192n.43, 202, 207, 212, 213, 259, 259n.149, 286, 289, 293
Shiba Kōkan, 99, 123n.5, 223–225
Shibaraku (kabuki play), 110
Shikigaku (ritual of state), 2, 2n.1, 3, 6n.13, 19, 32, 37, 69
Shikitei Sanba, 159
Shimogakari style of noh, 36
Shini-e. See Death portraits
Shogun senge iwai (shogunal proclamation) noh, 55
Shonai affair (1840), 1
Shūgen plays, 58
Shūishū, 101
Social space (*See also* History), 6, 21, 23, 30, 30n.24, 70–71, 221, 261
Soga, Tales of, 177, 178, 179
Space
  capitalism, geography of. *See* Capitalism
  and chronotope, 5. *See also* Chronotope
  fantasy, space of, 22, 62–63, 72
  gardens, space of, 276n.13, 276–279, 281
  and Hideyoshi, 24, 25, 28, 31n.27
  kabuki, space in, 202
  kabuki, space of 253–254, 289–290, 294
  and Kōka *kanjin* noh, 16, 20, 269, 273–276, 282, 289–290, 294
  Medieval, 99
  national, 16n.27, 52n.75, 73, 80n.14, 118, 121
  noh, space of, 6n.13, 16–17, 20, 21, 23, 24–25, 30, 50, 54, 70, 230, 233–234, 237, 242, 246, 250, 282n.20
  noh space in, 101–102, 128–129, 145–146, 148, 202, 208–209, 211
  panoptic, panoramic (*See also* Vision), 72, 153, 253–254
  perspectival space. *See* Perspectival space
  and place, 30, 30nn.20–22, 31–32, 47, 48, 53–54, 61, 69, 76, 82, 116
  political economic, 80–82
  and religion, 42–48, 62n.102, 66, 69, 70, 111n.109
  rice economy, geography of. *See* Rice economy
  social space. *See* Social Space
  tea houses and gardens, space of, 277–278
  and time. *See* Time
  Tokugawa shoguns, sociopolitical space of, 6, 6n.13, 9, 13, 20, 30, 31n.25, 31n.27, 35, 36–37, 39–40, 42, 44–48, 53, 54, 69, 72, 73, 99, 153, 233, 260 *See also* Time

urban, 79, 83, 104, 104n.93, 112, 117, 118n.32, 153, 254–256, 287, 293
utopic. *See* Utopia
Spectacle, 68–70, 72, 79, 217, 246, 294
  and consumption, 79, 118, 118n.32, 293n.41
  and *Dōjōji*, 143n.48
  and exchange, 247–248
  and kabuki theater, 104
  and merchants, 79
  misemono markets, 2, 79, 226, 227, 287, 288n.34, 290n.40, 293
  and power, 62, 190–191, 249–250, 258, 262, 279, 283
  sightseeing as, 68, 241n.133
  and time, 190, 213, 245, 247, 260
  and vision, 226–233, 240–242, 283, 290n.40, 293
Sublime, 154n.82, 156–158 158n.93, 160–162, 164, 165, 167–169, 188n.34, 293
  and *Dōjōji*, 180
  as early modern aesthetic form, 169
  and Edo-era aesthetics, 25
  and Enlightenment rationality, 153n.81
  and instant time, 208n.69, 288
  and perspectival space/time, 211
  and power, 169, 258–259
  state unification, relation to, 162
Sugawaru Denju Tenarai Kagami (kabuki play), 193n.44
Sukeroku (kabuki play), 105n.95, 114, 114nn.120–121, 173–179, 256, 261
Sumidagawa (noh play), 143–144

Takasago (noh play), 124,144–148, 145n.53, 149, 150, 150n.72, 151, 152, 154, 154n.83, 155, 156, 157, 158, 160, 161, 168, 212, 213, 252–53, 257n.147, 258–259, 293
Tea ceremony, 60n.96, 122, 277–278, 281
Time
  and body, materiality, 94n.66, 99, 101, 108, 109, 118, 126, 144, 147, 151, 157, 159–160, 161, 162, 164, 168, 178n.13, 183, 186–189, 193, 197, 211, 237, 260
  and Buddhism, 175n.8, 184, 194n.45
  and change. *See* Change
  chronotope. *See* Chronotope
  clock time, 198–201, 202, 204
  commodity value and natural time, 77–78, 88, 90, 107–108
  cosmological, 59, 60, 65
  cyclical time and progression, 59
  and death, 126, 163, 164, 193, 207, 213, 217, 220, 286n.30

Index / 313

durational time, 184, 189, 190, 208, 220, 245, 247, 248, 260
eternity. *See* Eternity
gift and time, 89, 90, 91, 91n.55, 92, 107, 115
independent existence of, 7
"instant" (*See also* Event), (*katatoki*) 116, (*ha*) 203, 205, 208; (*shunkan*) 209–210; Zeami and (*itten tsukitaru*) 209, (*hima*) 209, (Peerless Charm) 211, 233–234; (astonishment), 212; (death and) 213n.89; (*mie* as) 214–220, 249; (noh and kabuki) 220
kabuki, excess, and time, 109–110, 111, 116, 117, 173, 183
king's two bodies, temporality of, 154–155
layering of time in kabuki, 177, 177n.12, 178
layering of time in noh, 141–142, 145n.53, 182
machi-iri noh, temporalities of, 261–263
messianic, 204, 205, 207, 213
and mirrors, 58
and nation, 40, 201
noh and temporality of permanence, 49, 54, 57, 59, 71, 135, 148
panoptic rule and, 72
and repetition. *See* Event
and reproduction, 61
rice economy and cyclical time, 85, 89–90
ritual calendar/temporality, 58–59, 89, 92, 93n.64, 98, 124, 126, 143, 162, 168, 182, 183, 243, 273
seriality, 151, 162, 188, 189n.38, 192–193, 204, 208, 213, 214
social form and temporality, 30, 56, 71, 295
social form, time as principal basis of, 7, 171
and souvenir, 186–188, 189, 189n.38, 190n.39, 220, 243
space, relation to, 202, 202n. 61, 209–210, 295
spatial mastery over, 61
speed and production time, 198–204
sublime time, 156, 161, 162, 164, 168
"time" in the noh (*miyo, kaikō, nori, toki*), 184
Tokugawa identity, temporality and extension of, 40, 45, 56, 57, 59, 60, 71, 91n.53. *See also* Event.
and transformation. *See* Transformation
utopic. *See* Utopia
value and temporality, 77–78, 171, 245–247, 249–250, 283

vision and, 171, 221, 226, 227, 230, 233, 234, 243, 244, 245, 247, 261–262
Tokugawa branch houses (*Gosanke*), 33, 34, 230, 238–239, 242, 287
Tokugawa, Iemitsu, 35, 44, 46, 47, 58, 60, 64, 66–67, 83
Tokugawa, Ieyasu, 2n.1, 12, 20, 24, 29–35, 52–54, 57–60, 64–68, 79, 155, 268–269, 278
calendar of time, 57
divine aspects of, 43–48, 54, 58, 64, 66–68, 91, 99
dream portrait of, 47, 64, 66–67, 126–127, 155, 168, 250, 258
space and time, extension of identity in. *See* Space, Time
Tokugawa Yoshimune, 46, memory/presence of Ieyasu and, 47, 58
Tōshōgū, 44, 46, 48, 58n.89, 66–67, 67n.109, 68, 72, 127, 167
Transformation, 189n.35, 194n.46. (*See also* History, Time)
fulfillment versus, 192, 197, 273n.12
and ghostliness, 194, 257
in kabuki, 183, 191, 193
and noh, 187, 192, 273

Ueda Akinari, 104, 111n.109
Uki-e. *See* Perspectival space
Ukiyo
Buddhist, 255
floating world, 255
Ukiyo-e, 11, 201, 216, 217, 220n.98
Utaizome (New Year's) noh, 55–56, 60, 92
and ceremonial language, 93–94, 183
national time in relation to, 57, 71
ritual time in relation to, 58–59, 61, 183–184
and *Takasago*, 145
Utopia, 7n.14, 20–22, 29, 38, 54, 59, 61, 62, 63–64, 66–67, 70, 72n.15, 73, 250, 270, 276, 282, 288
Buddhist, 277
and daimyo mansions, 279–281
and economy, 85, 86n.34, 88n.43, 91
and Edo-era aesthetic form, 168
heterotopia. *See* Heterotopia
portrait of Tokugawa Ieyasu in relation to, 67
and tea ceremony, 277–278

Value 3–6, 6n.12, 11–12, 18n.31, 72–73, 76, 78, 99, 101, 171, 257, 284n.24, 295
and absolute monarchy, 100
aesthetic, 5, 8, 14, 122, 123

Value (continued)
    chronotope (See also Chronotope), 5–6, 12–13, 134, 137, 142
    coins, 83, 98–99, 100, 108, 105
    commercial value, 103–104
    commodity, 77–78, 85n.31, 87, 95, 96, 97, 99, 109n.105, 108, 118–119, 188, 192–193, 241, 254, 278
    Confucian, 92, 93–94
    death, value of, 125, 125n.8, 158n.93, 165–166, 167, 184, 188, 192, 193, 197, 197n.49, 204
    divine, 5, 168, 237
    eternity, value of, 77, 118, 209, 245
    expenditure, surplus, and excess, 80, 85n.31, 86, 91, 94n.70, 96, 106, 108, 109n.105, 110, 111, 112, 113–118,167, 220n.99
    farm unit, value in, 84, 100
    and general equivalent/rulership, 96–101, 206, 237, 250, 258
    gift, value of, 88, 90, 91–92, 94–95, 97, 107, 113–114, 115–116, 119n.135, 247
    and history, 6, 8, 14–15, 109
    kabuki, value in, 110–111, 113, 114, 173–174, 176, 177–178, 183, 192, 197, 198, 202
    money, value of, 98, 105–109, 196, 267
    moral, 5, 95, 111, 112
    natural, 77, 83, 85–86, 87, 90, 98, 99, 100, 107n.100, 159, 161, 202, 267
    noh, value in, 102–103, 147, 152, 156, 157, 173, 188, 197, 202, 209
    poetic language, value of, 101, 103, 151
    rice, 83, 89, 90–91, 97, 99–100, 109n.105, 118–119, 168
    social, 3n.7, 6, 76, 88, 100
    and time. See also Time 173, 177, 197, 198, 202, 205, 220n.100, 290
    use value and exchange value, 85, 88, 88n.43, 90, 92, 97, 100, 108, 167, 188
Vision, orders of
    anamorphosis. See Mirrors and specular relations
    and Azuchi castle noh stage, 62n.102, 281n.20
    Cartesian (See also Perspective), 31n.25, 221, 223, 224, 225, 226, 227
    cinematic, 203, 203n.63
    commoners' viewing position. See Commoners
    descriptivist, 221, 221n.102, 222, 223
    empiricist, 221n.102, 222, 223, 226

    eternity and, 54, 118, 210, 234, 237, 239, 240, 244, 245, 246, 279, 284, 293n.41
    "eyes of kabuki," 286
    eyes of money, 228, 241, 242
    gaze, 148n.62, 221, 233–234, 235, 237, 239, 240–241, 246, 279, 293n.41
    gift-giving and lines of vision, 229, 246–247
    glance, 221, 226, 227, 233, 240, 241, 242, 244, 245
    kaigen ("eye opening" in the noh), 238n.123
    Kōka *kanjin* noh and, 13, 284, 286, 290, 293–294
    mie (kabuki instant look), 214–217, 249
    nirami (kabuki instant look), 217–220, 249
    noh actors and, 231–232, 239
    noh as "stage art of no blinking," 210, 244
    nozoki ("peep"), 227, 247n.139, 249, 290n.40
    panoptic gaze of the shogun, 72n.114, 233
    panoramic (See also Space), 53n.77, 72, 153
    Peerless Charm, 211, 233, 234, 246
    perspective. See Perspectival space
    samurai villas, viewing order within, 279–281
    shasei (sketching observation), 223
    shashin (photographic), 223
    shogun's view, 228, 233, 234, 235, 237, 239, 244, 245–246, 250
    "sightseeing" (*kenbutsu*), 68, 241n.133, 258
    specular visual gaze. See Mirrors and specular relations
    telescopic, 227, 290–293, 293n.41
    and time. See Time
    ugachi (look from awry), 226–227, 241, 244–245, 249
    vision as dominant sense, 171
    vision and power, 228, 233, 233n.115, 237–238, 239, 241, 243, 244, 248, 249, 250, 279
    visual image, relation to verbal in noh, 131n.16, 158, 158n.94
    visual regimes, 13, 221, 225n.107, 248, 262
    and Zeami, 133, 211, 231, 233, 234, 239
    and Zen Buddhism, 133, 222, 225

Women and prostitutes as figures of capitalist desire 86, 112n.114, 112–113, 115n.26, 167, 182

and *Dōjōji*, 180–181, 182
  noh and disciplining of desire, 123–124

Yamamba (noh play), 139, 139n.35
Yamato monogatari, 101
Yamato *sarugaku*, 42, 43
Yamato schools of noh, 31
Yoshino Mode (noh play), 28n.14
Yotsuya Kaidan (kabuki play), 194–196, 197, 197n.50
Yūgen, 139–140, 210n.80
Yumiyawata (noh play), 19, 253

Zeami, 17, 129–130, 131, 133, 135, 136, 139–140, 157, 164, 165, 188n.34, 257n.146
  authority and power in the noh, 136–137
  on eternity, 184
  on instant time, 209–211, 233, 234
  and modes of cosmic change, 29–60, 184n.22
  on *Takasago*, 144
  on tempo of noh, 202n.60, 203
  on visual orders in the noh, 234, 239, 246

CORNELL EAST ASIA SERIES

4 Fredrick Teiwes, *Provincial Leadership in China: The Cultural Revolution and Its Aftermath*
8 Cornelius C. Kubler, *Vocabulary and Notes to Ba Jin's Jia: An Aid for Reading the Novel*
16 Monica Bethe & Karen Brazell, *Nō as Performance: An Analysis of the Kuse Scene of Yamamba*
18 Royall Tyler, tr., *Granny Mountains: A Second Cycle of Nō Plays*
23 Knight Biggerstaff, *Nanking Letters, 1949*
28 Diane E. Perushek, ed., *The Griffis Collection of Japanese Books: An Annotated Bibliography*
37 J. Victor Koschmann, Ōiwa Keibō & Yamashita Shinji, eds., *International Perspectives on Yanagita Kunio and Japanese Folklore Studies*
38 James O'Brien, tr., *Murō Saisei: Three Works*
40 Kubo Sakae, *Land of Volcanic Ash: A Play in Two Parts*, revised edition, tr. David G. Goodman
44 Susan Orpett Long, *Family Change and the Life Course in Japan*
48 Helen Craig McCullough, *Bungo Manual: Selected Reference Materials for Students of Classical Japanese*
49 Susan Blakeley Klein, *Ankoku Butō: The Premodern and Postmodern Influences on the Dance of Utter Darkness*
50 Karen Brazell, ed., *Twelve Plays of the Noh and Kyōgen Theaters*
51 David G. Goodman, ed., *Five Plays by Kishida Kunio*
52 Shirō Hara, *Ode to Stone*, tr. James Morita
53 Peter J. Katzenstein & Yutaka Tsujinaka, *Defending the Japanese State: Structures, Norms and the Political Responses to Terrorism and Violent Social Protest in the 1970s and 1980s*
54 Su Xiaokang & Wang Luxiang, *Deathsong of the River: A Reader's Guide to the Chinese TV Series Heshang*, trs. Richard Bodman & Pin P. Wan
55 Jingyuan Zhang, *Psychoanalysis in China: Literary Transformations, 1919-1949*
56 Jane Kate Leonard & John R. Watt, eds., *To Achieve Security and Wealth: The Qing Imperial State and the Economy, 1644-1911*
57 Andrew F. Jones, *Like a Knife: Ideology and Genre in Contemporary Chinese Popular Music*
58 Peter J. Katzenstein & Nobuo Okawara, *Japan's National Security: Structures, Norms and Policy Responses in a Changing World*
59 Carsten Holz, *The Role of Central Banking in China's Economic Reforms*
60 Chifumi Shimazaki, *Warrior Ghost Plays from the Japanese Noh Theater: Parallel Translations with Running Commentary*
61 Emily Groszos Ooms, *Women and Millenarian Protest in Meiji Japan: Deguchi Nao and Ōmotokyō*

62 Carolyn Anne Morley, *Transformation, Miracles, and Mischief: The Mountain Priest Plays of Kōygen*
63 David R. McCann & Hyunjae Yee Sallee, tr., *Selected Poems of Kim Namjo*, afterword by Kim Yunsik
64 Hua Qingzhao, *From Yalta to Panmunjom: Truman's Diplomacy and the Four Powers, 1945-1953*
65 Margaret Benton Fukasawa, *Kitahara Hakushū: His Life and Poetry*
66 Kam Louie, ed., *Strange Tales from Strange Lands: Stories by Zheng Wanlong*, with introduction
67 Wang Wen-hsing, *Backed Against the Sea*, tr. Edward Gunn
69 Brian Myers, *Han Sōrya and North Korean Literature: The Failure of Socialist Realism in the DPRK*
70 Thomas P. Lyons & Victor Nee, eds., *The Economic Transformation of South China: Reform and Development in the Post-Mao Era*
71 David G. Goodman, tr., *After Apocalypse: Four Japanese Plays of Hiroshima and Nagasaki*, with introduction
72 Thomas Lyons, *Poverty and Growth in a South China County: Anxi, Fujian, 1949-1992*
74 Martyn Atkins, *Informal Empire in Crisis: British Diplomacy and the Chinese Customs Succession, 1927-1929*
76 Chifumi Shimazaki, *Restless Spirits from Japanese Noh Plays of the Fourth Group: Parallel Translations with Running Commentary*
77 Brother Anthony of Taizé & Young-Moo Kim, trs., *Back to Heaven: Selected Poems of Ch'ŏn Sang Pyŏng*
78 Kevin O'Rourke, tr., *Singing Like a Cricket, Hooting Like an Owl: Selected Poems by Yi Kyu-bo*
79 Irit Averbuch, *The Gods Come Dancing: A Study of the Japanese Ritual Dance of Yamabushi Kagura*
80 Mark Peterson, *Korean Adoption and Inheritance: Case Studies in the Creation of a Classic Confucian Society*
81 Yenna Wu, tr., *The Lioness Roars: Shrew Stories from Late Imperial China*
82 Thomas Lyons, *The Economic Geography of Fujian: A Sourcebook*, Vol. 1
83 Pak Wan-so, *The Naked Tree*, tr. Yu Young-nan
84 C.T. Hsia, *The Classic Chinese Novel: A Critical Introduction*
85 Cho Chong-Rae, *Playing With Fire*, tr. Chun Kyung-Ja
86 Hayashi Fumiko, *I Saw a Pale Horse and Selections from Diary of a Vagabond*, tr. Janice Brown
87 Motoori Norinaga, *Kojiki-den, Book 1*, tr. Ann Wehmeyer
88 Chang Soo Ko, tr., *Sending the Ship Out to the Stars: Poems of Park Je-chun*
89 Thomas Lyons, *The Economic Geography of Fujian: A Sourcebook*, Vol. 2
90 Brother Anthony of Taizé, tr., *Midang: Early Lyrics of So Chong-Ju*
92 Janice Matsumura, *More Than a Momentary Nightmare: The Yokohama Incident and Wartime Japan*
93 Kim Jong-Gil tr., *The Snow Falling on Chagall's Village: Selected Poems of Kim Ch'un-Su*

94 Wolhee Choe & Peter Fusco, trs., *Day-Shine: Poetry by Hyon-jong Chong*
95 Chifumi Shimazaki, *Troubled Souls from Japanese Noh Plays of the Fourth Group*
96 Hagiwara Sakutarō, *Principles of Poetry (Shi no Genri)*, tr. Chester Wang
97 Mae J. Smethurst, *Dramatic Representations of Filial Piety: Five Noh in Translation*
98 Ross King, ed., *Description and Explanation in Korean Linguistics*
99 William Wilson, *Hōgen Monogatari: Tale of the Disorder in Hōgen*
100 Yasushi Yamanouchi, J. Victor Koschmann and Ryūichi Narita, eds., *Total War and 'Modernization'*
101 Yi Ch'ŏng-jun, *The Prophet and Other Stories*, tr. Julie Pickering
102 S.A. Thornton, *Charisma and Community Formation in Medieval Japan: The Case of the Yugyō-ha (1300-1700)*
103 Sherman Cochran, ed., *Inventing Nanjing Road: Commercial Culture in Shanghai, 1900-1945*
104 Harold M. Tanner, *Strike Hard! Anti-Crime Campaigns and Chinese Criminal Justice, 1979-1985*
105 Brother Anthony of Taizé & Young-Moo Kim, trs., *Farmers' Dance: Poems by Shin Kyŏng-nim*
106 Susan Orpett Long, ed., *Lives in Motion: Composing Circles of Self and Community in Japan*
107 Peter J. Katzenstein, Natasha Hamilton-Hart, Kozo Kato, & Ming Yue, *Asian Regionalism*
108 Kenneth Alan Grossberg, *Japan's Renaissance: The Politics of the Muromachi Bakufu*
109 John W. Hall & Toyoda Takeshi, eds., *Japan in the Muromachi Age*
110 Kim Su-Young, Shin Kyong-Nim, Lee Si-Young; *Variations: Three Korean Poets;* trs. Brother Anthony of Taizé & Young-Moo Kim
111 Samuel Leiter, *Frozen Moments: Writings on* Kabuki, *1966-2001*
112 Pilwun Shih Wang & Sarah Wang, *Early One Spring: A Learning Guide to Accompany the Film Video* February
113 Thomas Conlan, *In Little Need of Divine Intervention: Scrolls of the Mongol Invasions of Japan*
114 Jane Kate Leonard & Robert Antony, eds., *Dragons, Tigers, and Dogs: Qing Crisis Management and the Boundaries of State Power in Late Imperial China*
115 Shu-ning Sciban & Fred Edwards, eds., *Dragonflies: Fiction by Chinese Women in the Twentieth Century*
116 David G. Goodman, ed., *The Return of the Gods: Japanese Drama and Culture in the 1960s*
117 Yang Hi Choe-Wall, *Vision of a Phoenix: The Poems of Hŏ Nansŏrhŏn*
118 Mae J. Smethurst and Christina Laffin, eds., *The Noh* Ominameshi: *A Flower Viewed from Many Directions*
119 Joseph A. Murphy, *Metaphorical Circuit: Negotiations Between Literature and Science in Twentieth-Century Japan*

120 Richard F. Calichman, *Takeuchi Yoshimi: Displacing the West*
121 Fan Pen Li Chen, *Visions for the Masses: Chinese Shadow Plays from Shaanxi and Shanxi*
122 S. Yumiko Hulvey, *Sacred Rites in Moonlight: Ben no Naishi Nikki*
123 Tetsuo Najita and J. Victor Koschmann, *Conflict in Modern Japanese History: The Neglected Tradition*
124 Naoki Sakai, Brett de Bary, & Iyotani Toshio, eds., *Deconstructing Nationality*
125 Judith N. Rabinovitch and Timothy R. Bradstock, *Dance of the Butterflies: Chinese Poetry from the Japanese Court Tradition*
126 Yang Gui-ja, *Contradictions*, trs. Stephen Epstein and Kim Mi-Young
127 Ann Sung-hi Lee, *Yi Kwang-su and Modern Korean Literature:* Mujŏng
128 Pang Kie-chung & Michael D. Shin, eds., *Landlords, Peasants, & Intellectuals in Modern Korea*
129 Joan R. Piggott, ed., *Capital and Countryside in Japan, 300-1180: Japanese Historians Interpreted in English*
130 Kyoko Selden and Jolisa Gracewood, eds., *Annotated Japanese Literary Gems: Stories by Tawada Yōko, Nakagami Kenji, and Hayashi Kyōko* (Vol. 1)
131 Michael G. Murdock, *Disarming the Allies of Imperialism: The State, Agitation, and Manipulation during China's Nationalist Revolution, 1922-1929*
132 Noel J. Pinnington, *Traces in the Way: Michi and the Writings of Komparu Zenchiku*
133 Charlotte von Verschuer, *Across the Perilous Sea: Japanese Trade with China and Korea from the Seventh to the Sixteenth Centuries*, Kristen Lee Hunter, tr.
134 John Timothy Wixted, *A Handbook to Classical Japanese*
135 Kyoko Selden et al, eds., *Annotated Japanese Literary Gems: Stories by Natsume Sōseki, Tomioka Taeko, and Inoue Yasushi* (Vol. 2)
136 Yi Tae-Jin, *The Dynamics of Confucianism and Modernization in Korean History*
137 Jennifer Rudolph, *Negotiated Power in Late Imperial China: The Zongli Yamen and the Politics of Reform*
138 Thomas D. Loooser, *Visioning Eternity: Aesthetics, Politics, and History in the Early Modern Noh Theater*
139 Gustav Heldt, *The Pursuit of Harmony: Poetry and Power in Late Heian Japan*
140 Joan R. Piggott and Yoshida Sanae, eds. *Teishinkōki: The Year 939 in the Journal of Regent Fujiwara no Tadahira*
141 Robert Bagley, *Max Loehr and the Study of Chinese Bronzes: Style and Classification in the History of Art*

Order online: www.einaudi.cornell.edu/eastasia/publications
or contact Cornell University Press Services, P.O. Box 6525, 750 Cascadilla Street,
Ithaca, NY 14851, USA. Tel toll-free: 1-800-666-2211; Fax: 1-800-688-2877;
E-mail: orderbook@cupserv.org or ceas@cornell.edu

www.ingramcontent.com/pod-product-compliance
Lightning Source LLC
Chambersburg PA
CBHW022009300426
44117CB00005B/99